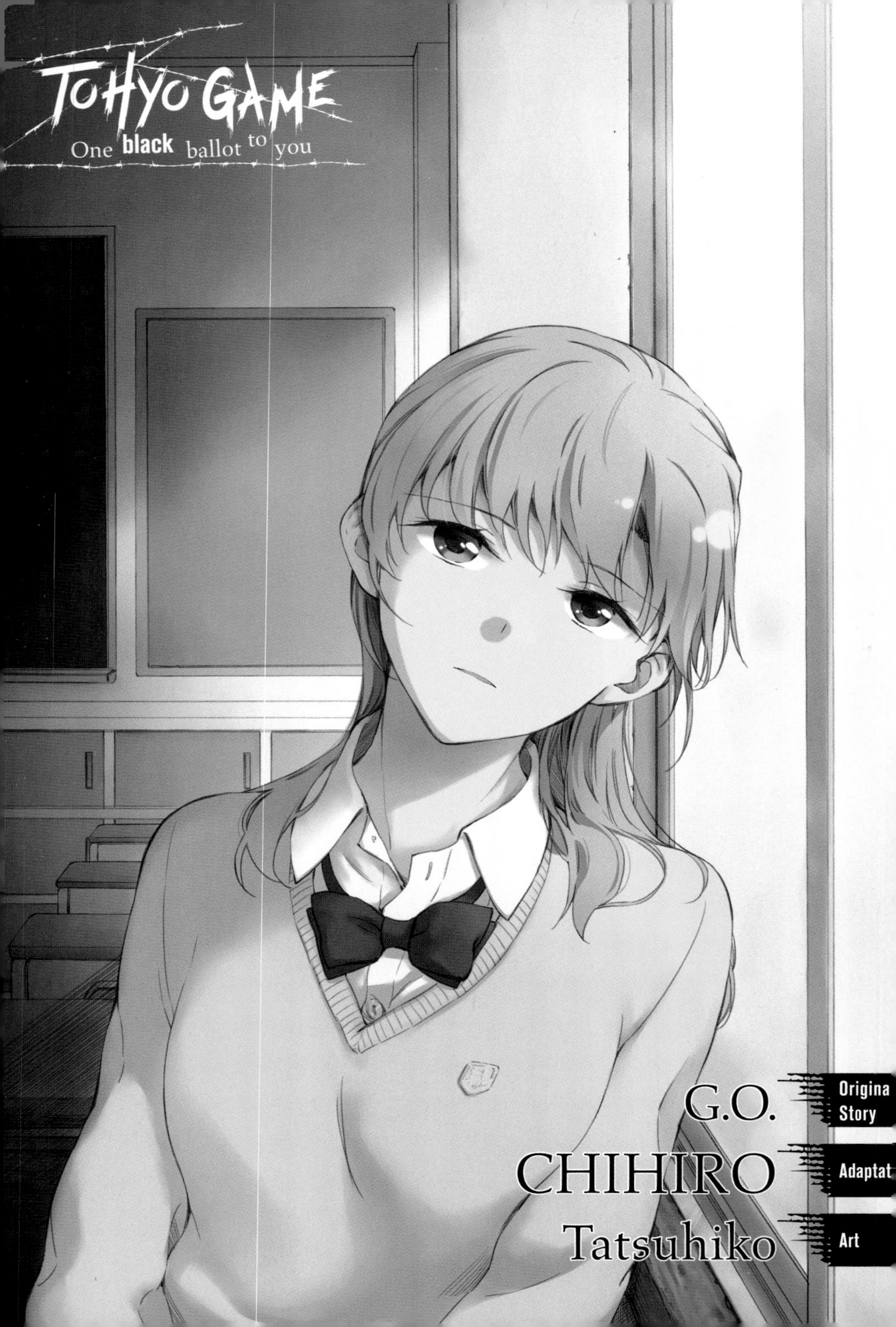
TOHYO GAME
One black ballot to you
G.O.
Origina Story
CHIHIRO
Adaptat
Tatsuhiko
Art

TOHYO GAME

One **black** ballot to you

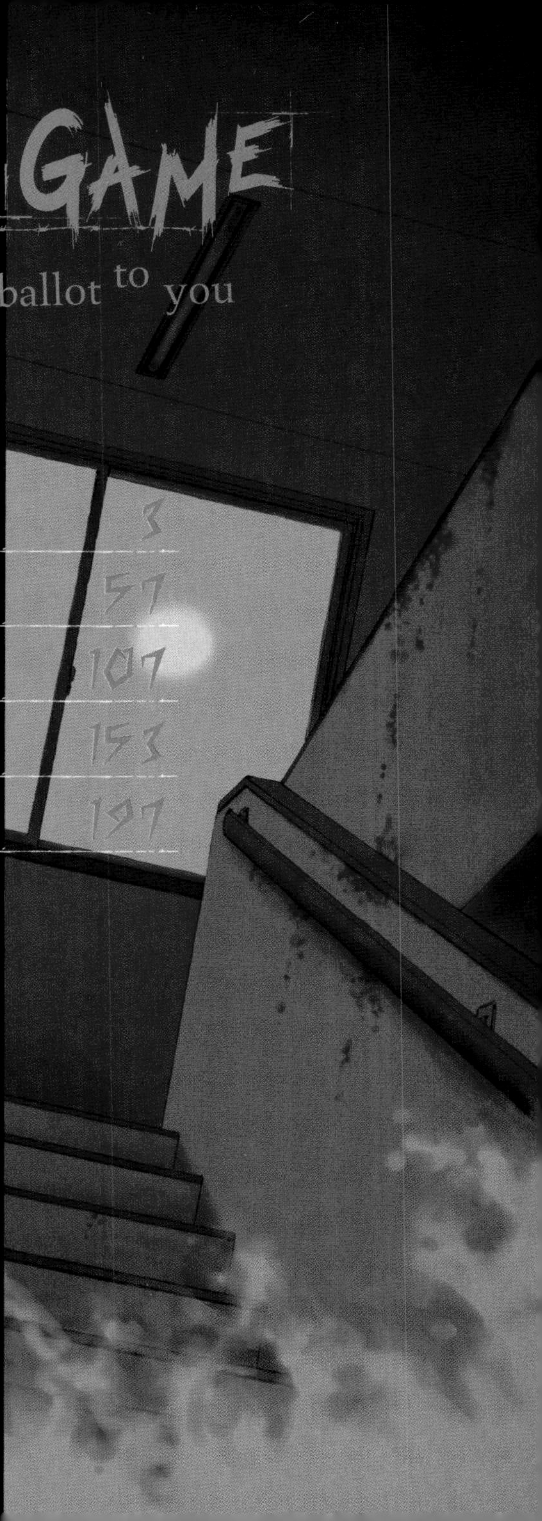

CONTENTS

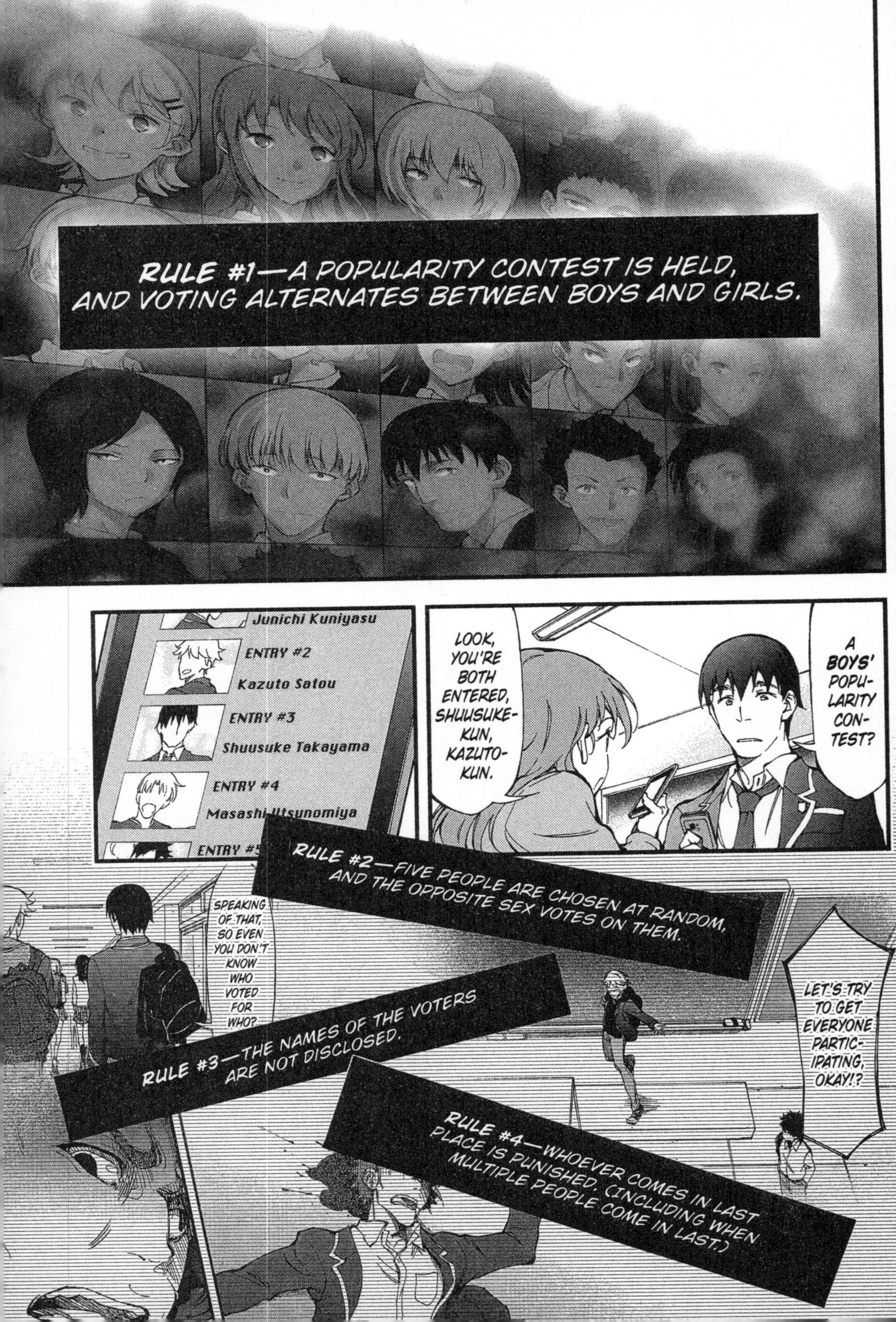
RULE #1—A POPULARITY CONTEST IS HELD, AND VOTING ALTERNATES BETWEEN BOYS AND GIRLS.
A BOYS' POPULARITY CONTEST?
LOOK, YOU'RE BOTH ENTERED, SHUUSUKE-KUN, KAZUTO-KUN.
Junichi Kuniyasu
ENTRY #2
Kazuto Satou
ENTRY #3
Shuusuke Takayama
ENTRY #4
Masashi Utsunomiya
RULE #2—FIVE PEOPLE ARE CHOSEN AT RANDOM, AND THE OPPOSITE SEX VOTES ON THEM.
LET'S TRY TO GET EVERYONE PARTICIPATING, OKAY!?
SPEAKING OF THAT, SO EVEN YOU DON'T KNOW WHO VOTED FOR WHO?
RULE #3—THE NAMES OF THE VOTERS ARE NOT DISCLOSED.
RULE #4—WHOEVER COMES IN LAST PLACE IS PUNISHED. (INCLUDING WHEN MULTIPLE PEOPLE COME IN LAST.)

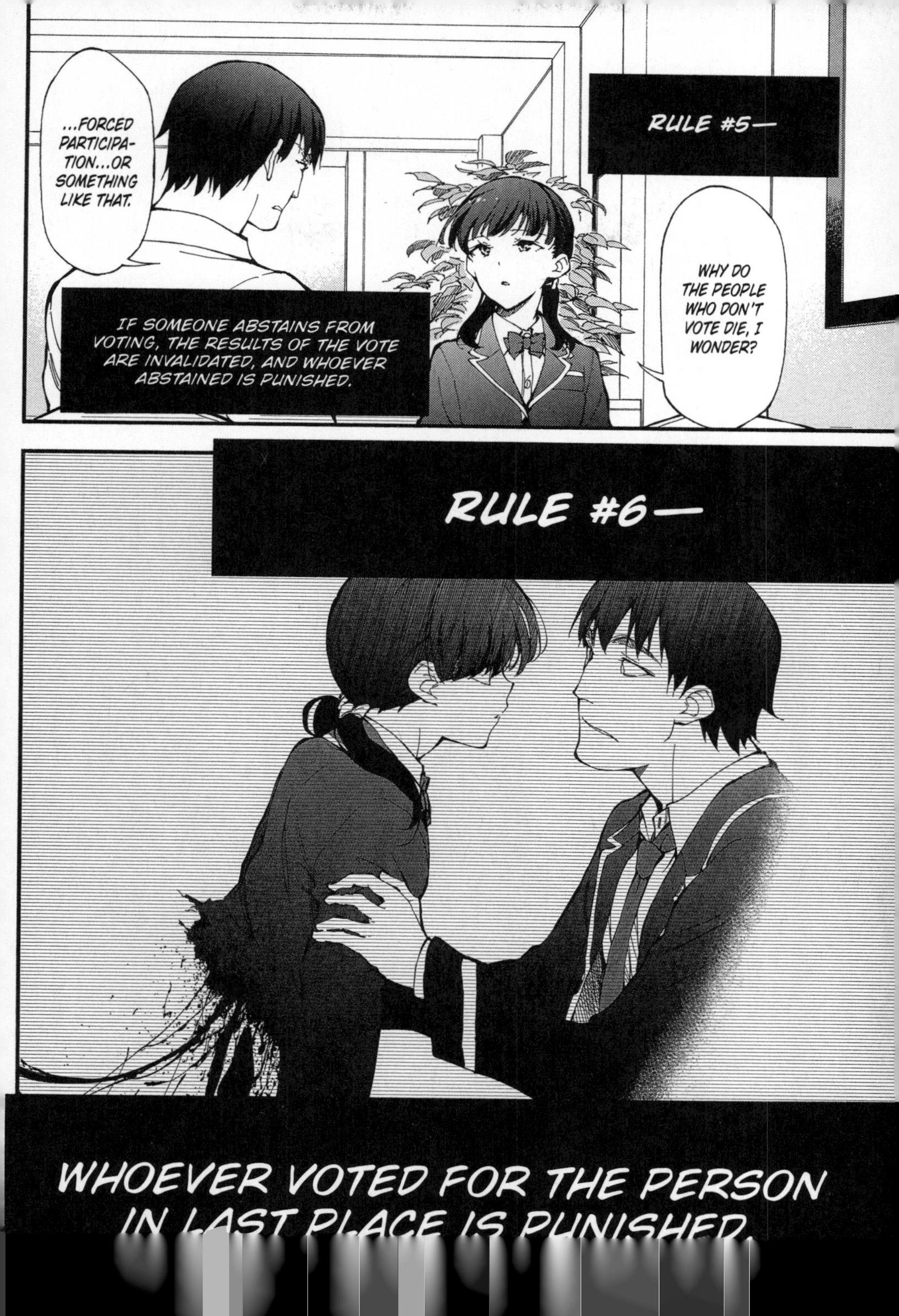
RULE #5—
WHY DO THE PEOPLE WHO DON'T VOTE DIE, I WONDER?
...FORCED PARTICIPA-TION...OR SOMETHING LIKE THAT.
IF SOMEONE ABSTAINS FROM VOTING, THE RESULTS OF THE VOTE ARE INVALIDATED, AND WHOEVER ABSTAINED IS PUNISHED.
RULE #6—
WHOEVER VOTED FOR THE PERSON IN LAST PLACE IS PUNISHED.

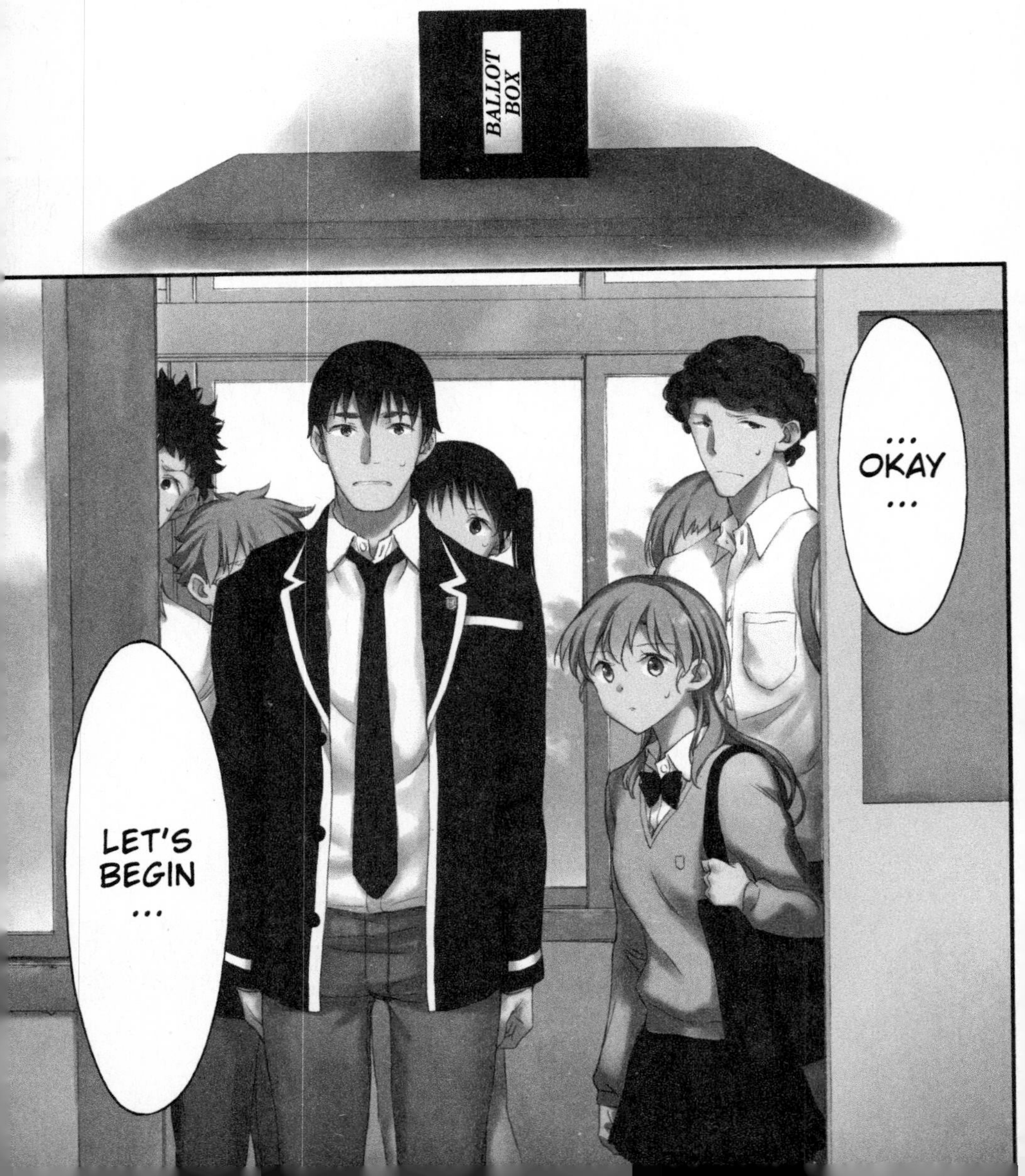
BALLOT BOX
...OKAY...
LET'S BEGIN...

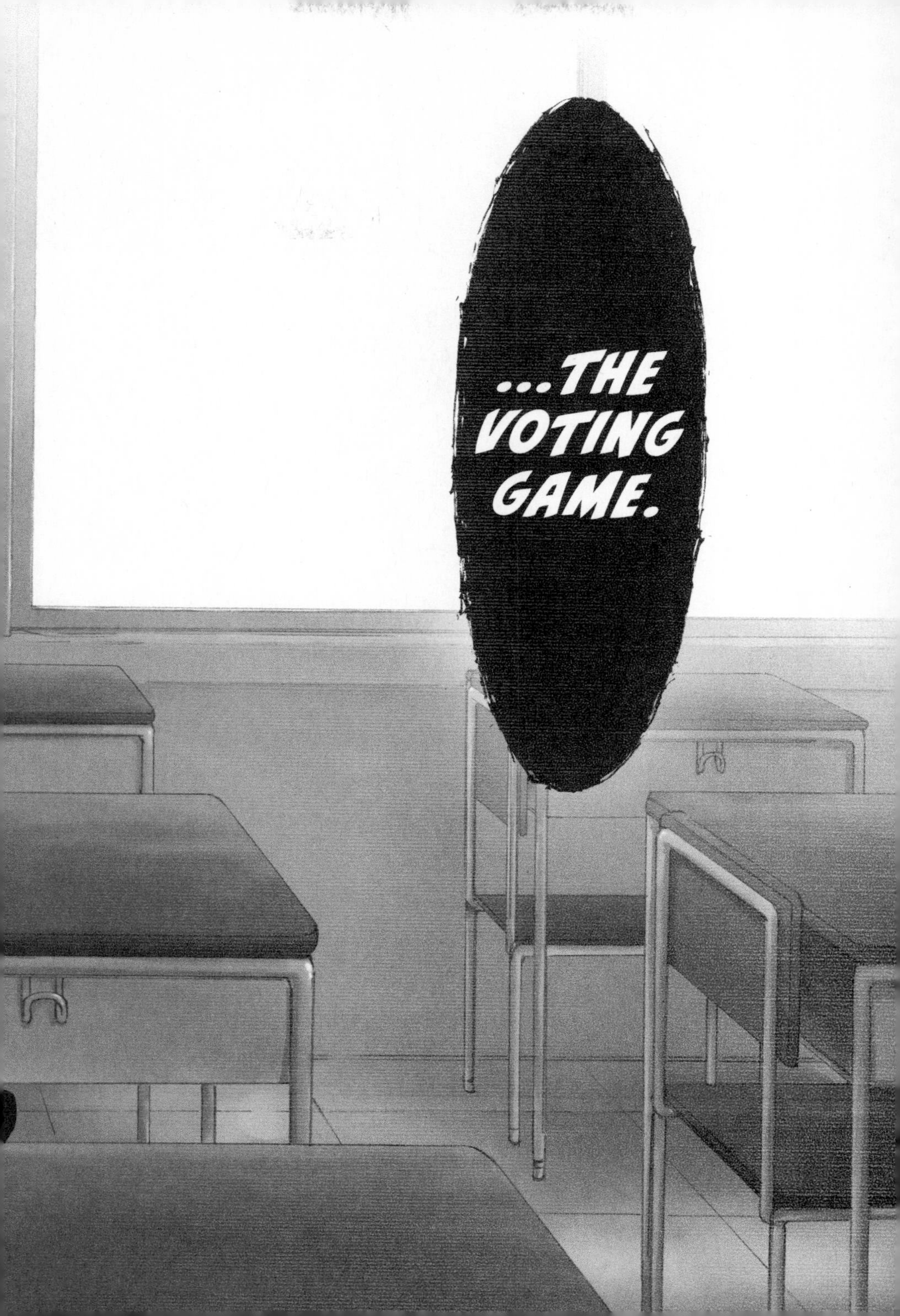
...THE VOTING GAME.

#8

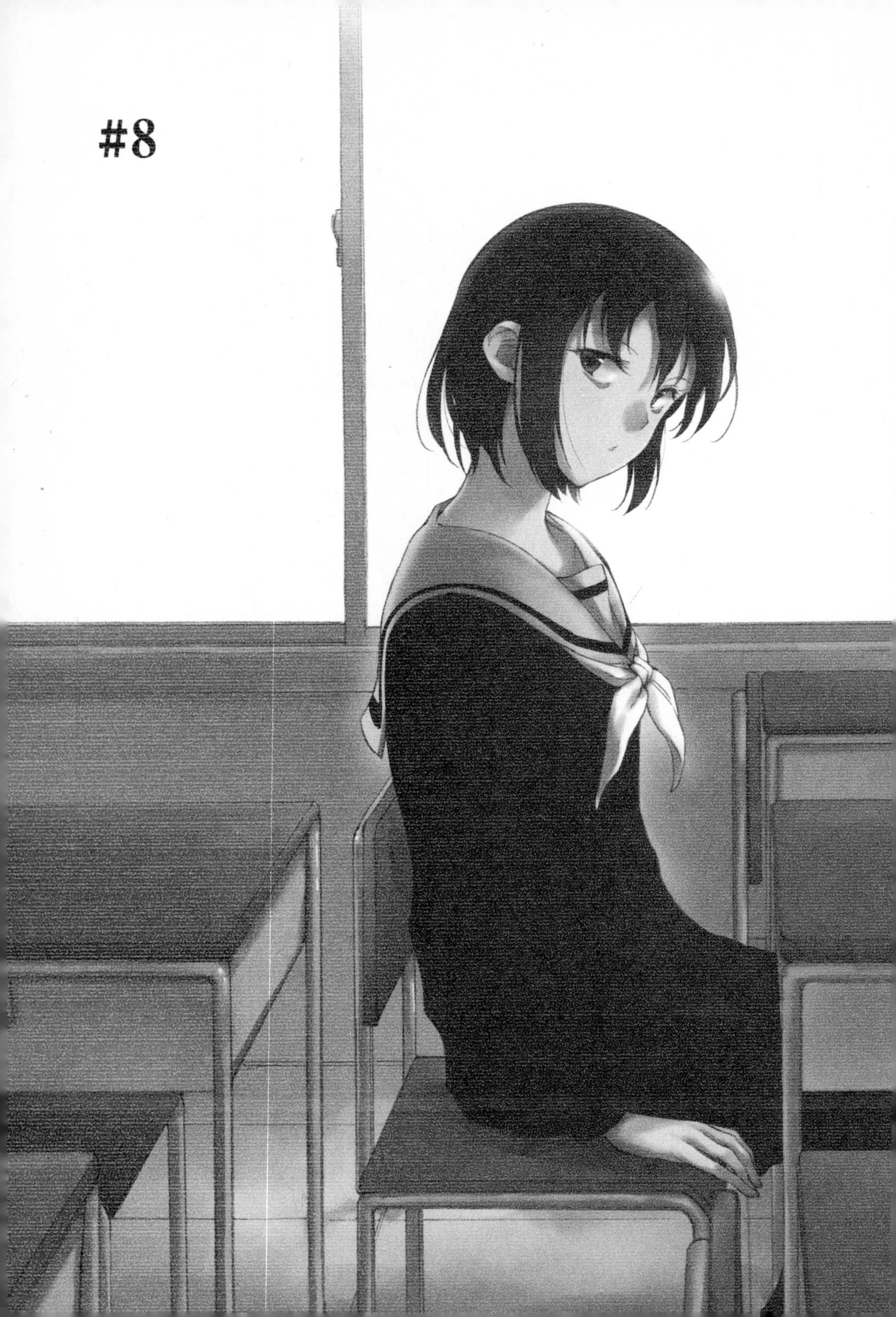

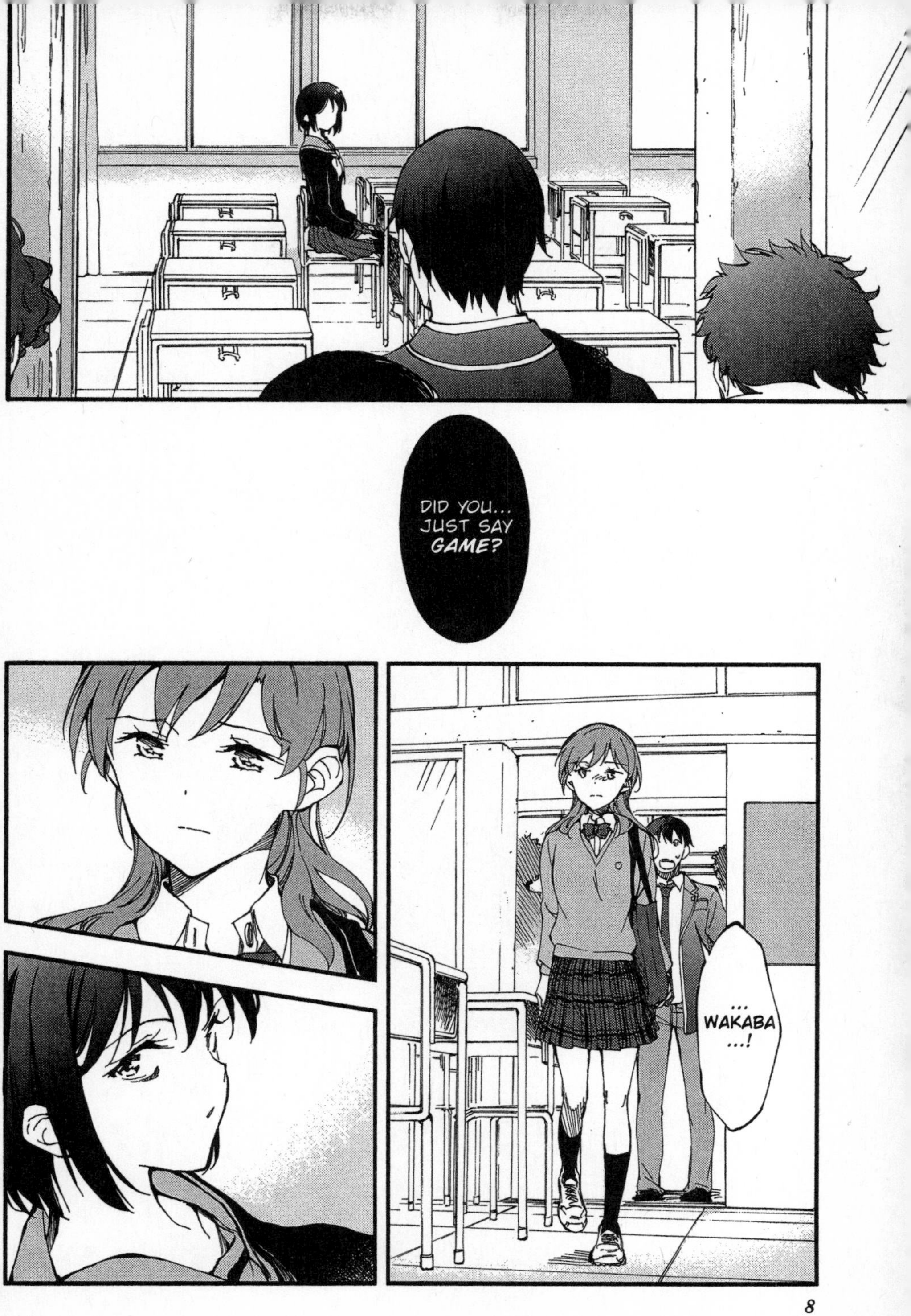
DID YOU... JUST SAY GAME?
...WAKABA ...!

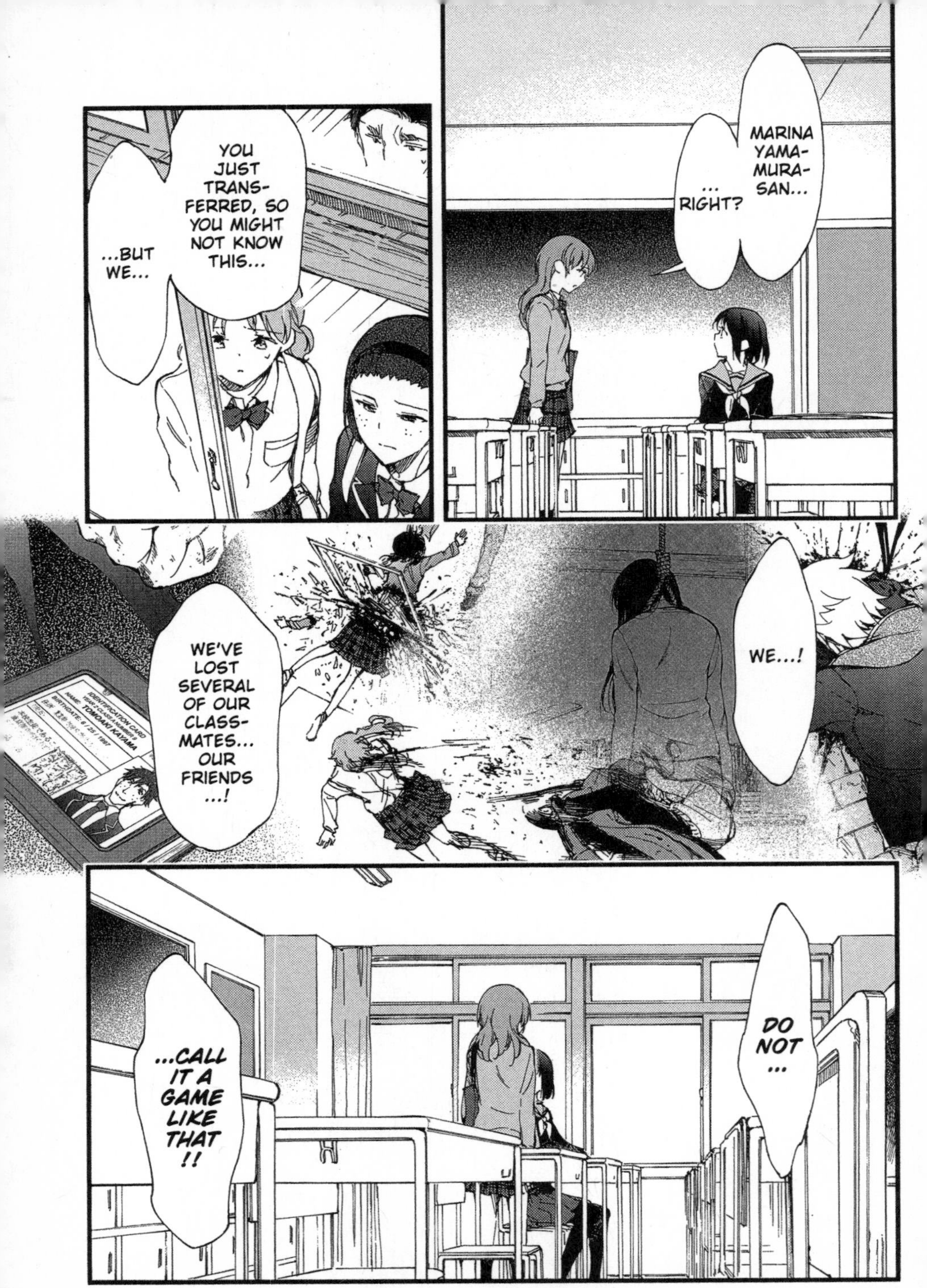
MARINA YAMAMURA-SAN...
...RIGHT?
YOU JUST TRANSFERRED, SO YOU MIGHT NOT KNOW THIS...
...BUT WE...
WE...!
WE'VE LOST SEVERAL OF OUR CLASSMATES... OUR FRIENDS...!
DO NOT...
...CALL IT A GAME LIKE THAT!!

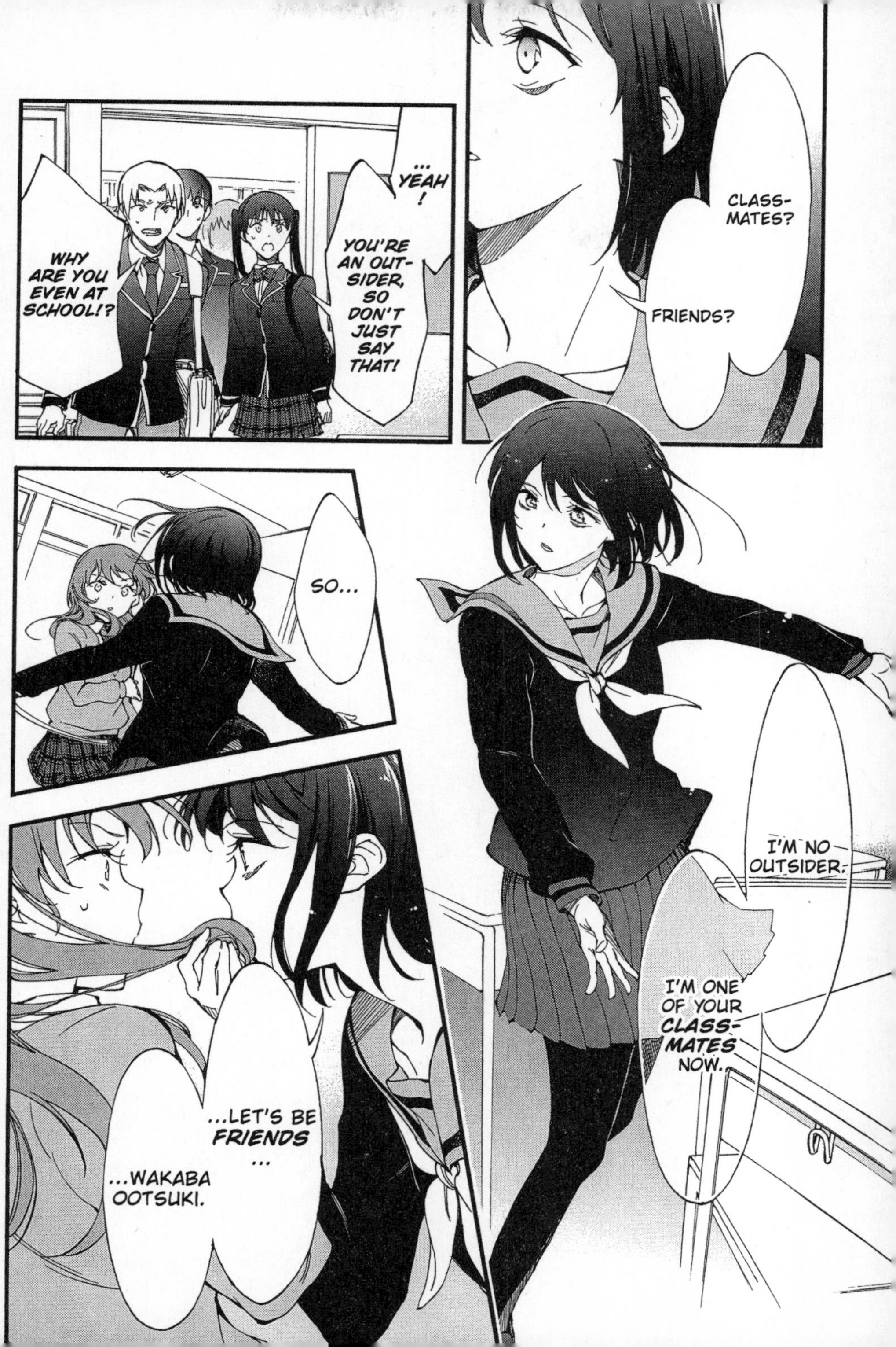
CLASS-MATES?
FRIENDS?
...YEAH!
YOU'RE AN OUT-SIDER, SO DON'T JUST SAY THAT!
WHY ARE YOU EVEN AT SCHOOL!?
I'M NO OUTSIDER.
I'M ONE OF YOUR CLASS-MATES NOW.
SO...
...LET'S BE FRIENDS...
...WAKABA OOTSUKI.

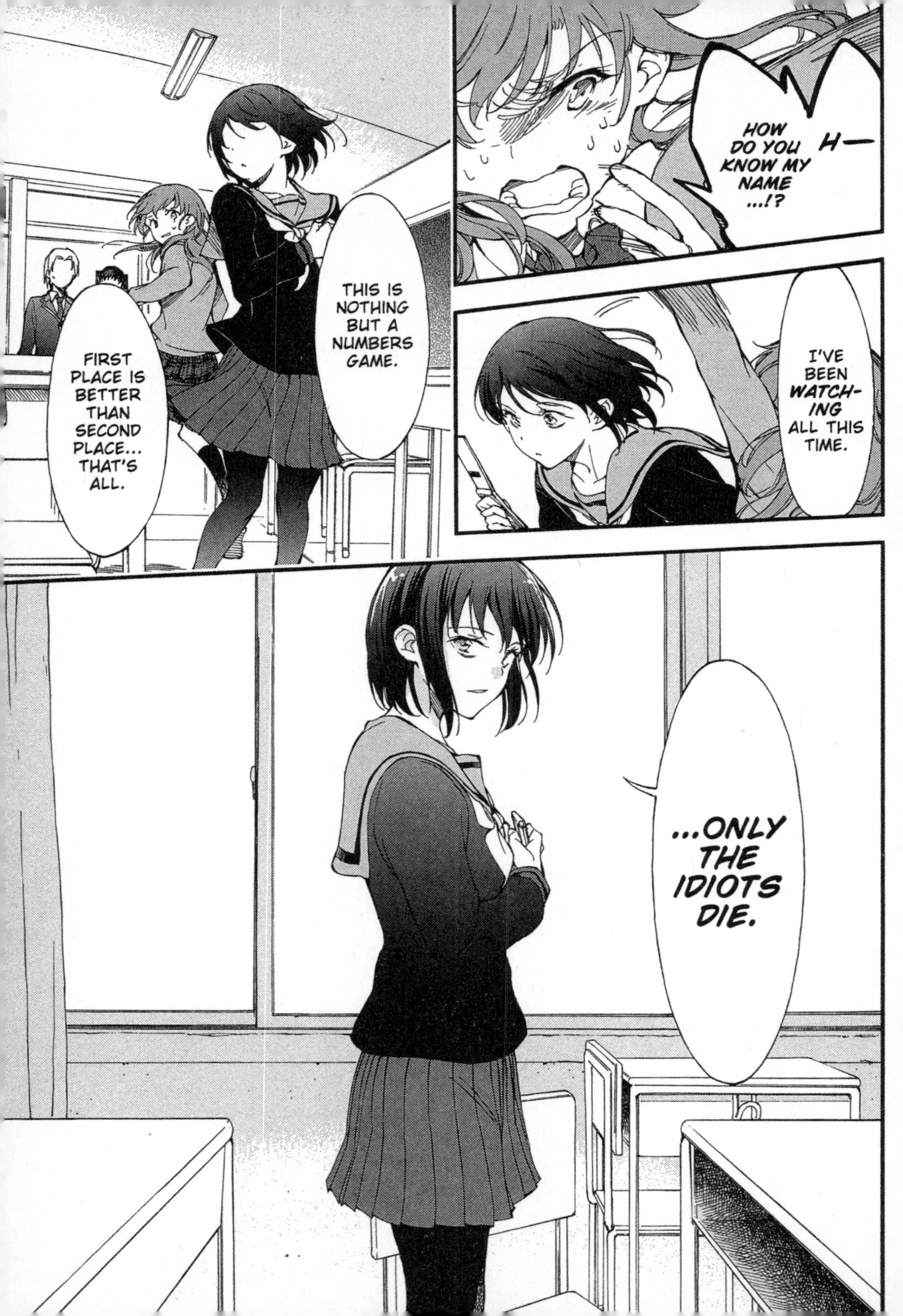
H—
HOW DO YOU KNOW MY NAME ...!?
I'VE BEEN WATCHING ALL THIS TIME.
THIS IS NOTHING BUT A NUMBERS GAME.
FIRST PLACE IS BETTER THAN SECOND PLACE... THAT'S ALL.
...ONLY THE IDIOTS DIE.

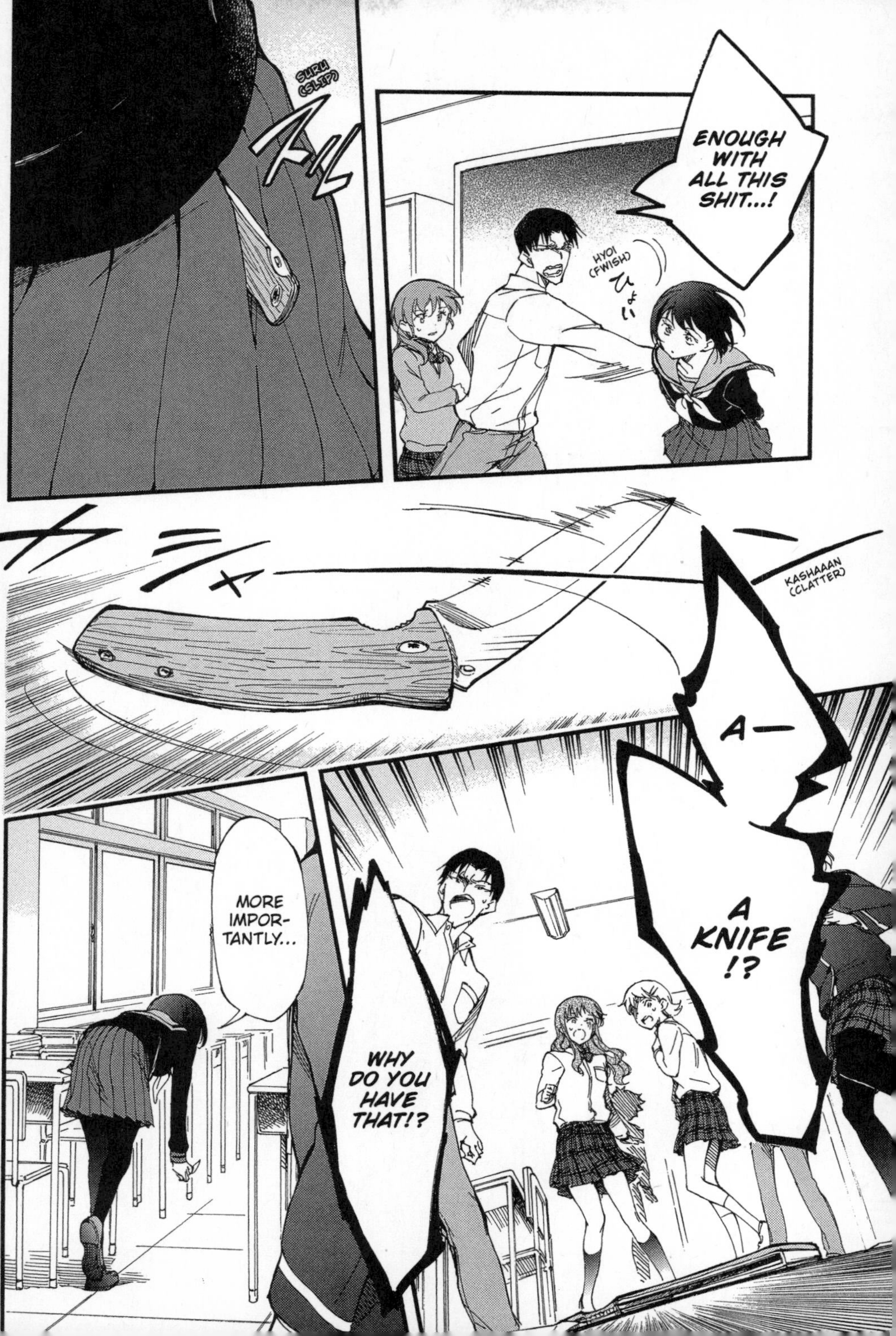
ENOUGH WITH ALL THIS SHIT...!
HYOI (FWISH)
ひょい
SURU (SLIP)
スル
カシャーン
KASHAAAN (CLATTER)
A—
A KNIFE !?
MORE IMPOR-TANTLY...
WHY DO YOU HAVE THAT!?

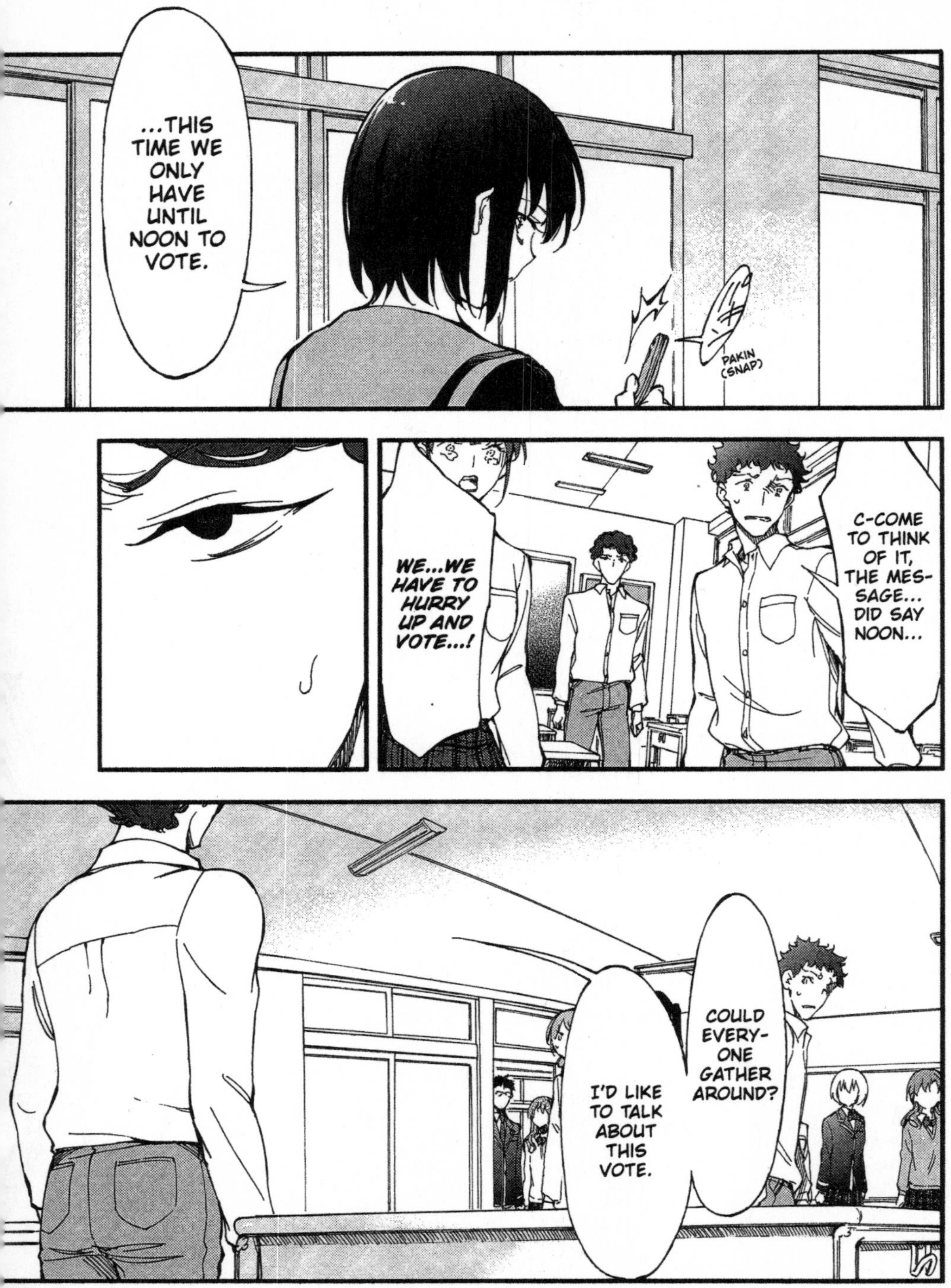
...THIS TIME WE ONLY HAVE UNTIL NOON TO VOTE.
PAKIN (SNAP)
C-COME TO THINK OF IT, THE MESSAGE... DID SAY NOON...
WE...WE HAVE TO HURRY UP AND VOTE...!
COULD EVERYONE GATHER AROUND?
I'D LIKE TO TALK ABOUT THIS VOTE.

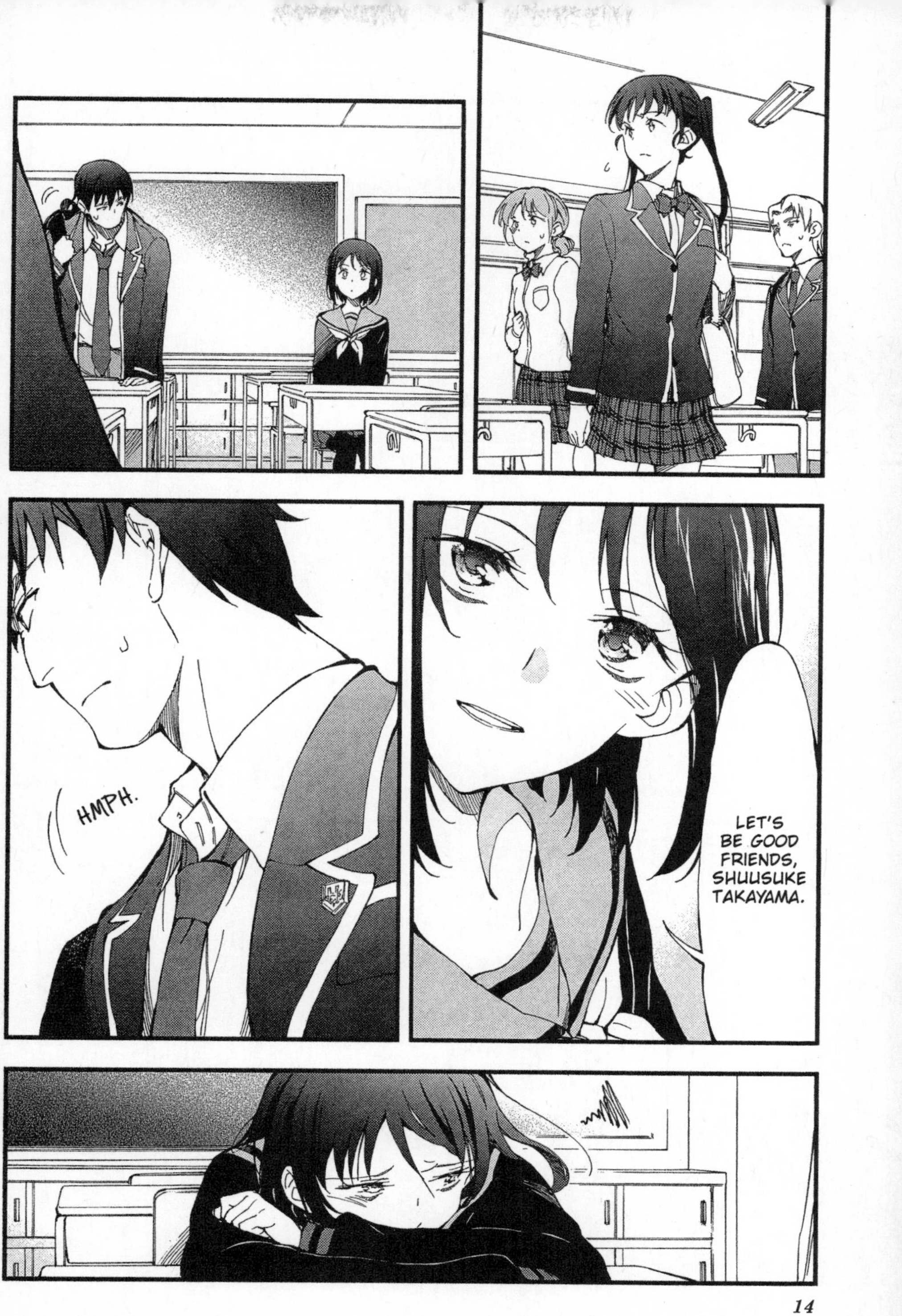
LET'S BE GOOD FRIENDS, SHUUSUKE TAKAYAMA.
HMPH.

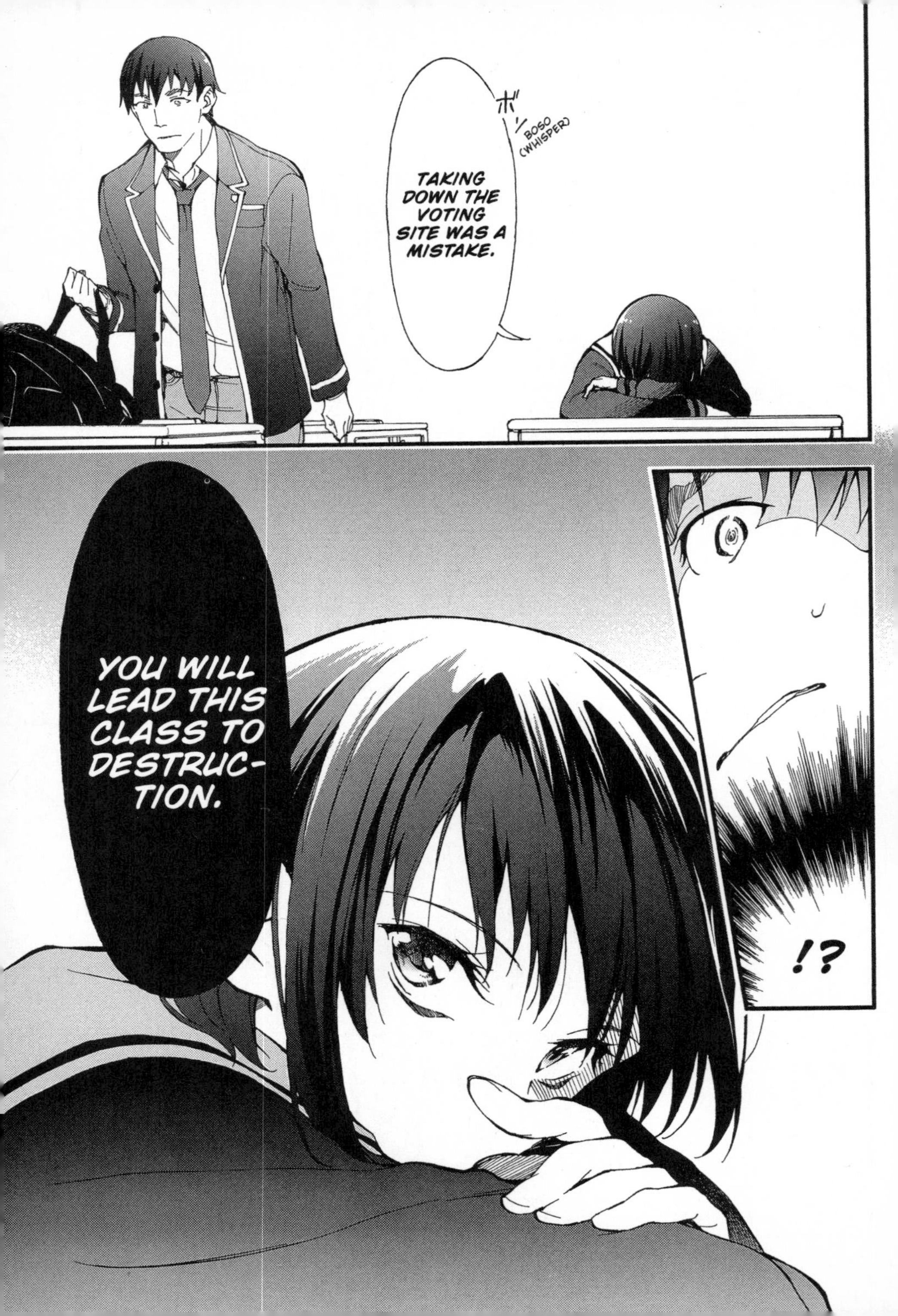
ボソ
BOSO (WHISPER)
TAKING DOWN THE VOTING SITE WAS A MISTAKE.
!?
YOU WILL LEAD THIS CLASS TO DESTRUCTION.

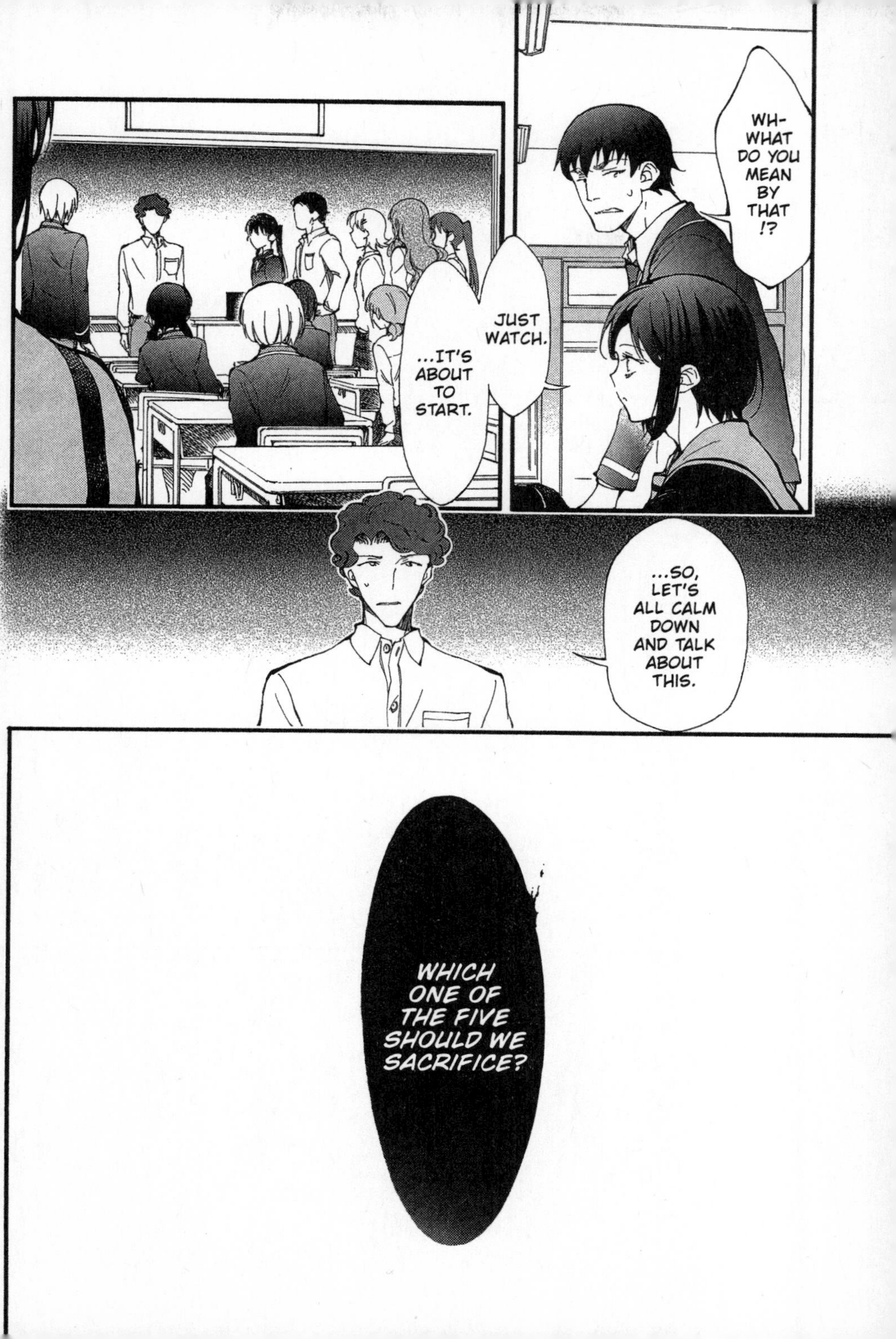
WH- WHAT DO YOU MEAN BY THAT !?
JUST WATCH.
...IT'S ABOUT TO START.
...SO, LET'S ALL CALM DOWN AND TALK ABOUT THIS.
WHICH ONE OF THE FIVE SHOULD WE SACRIFICE?

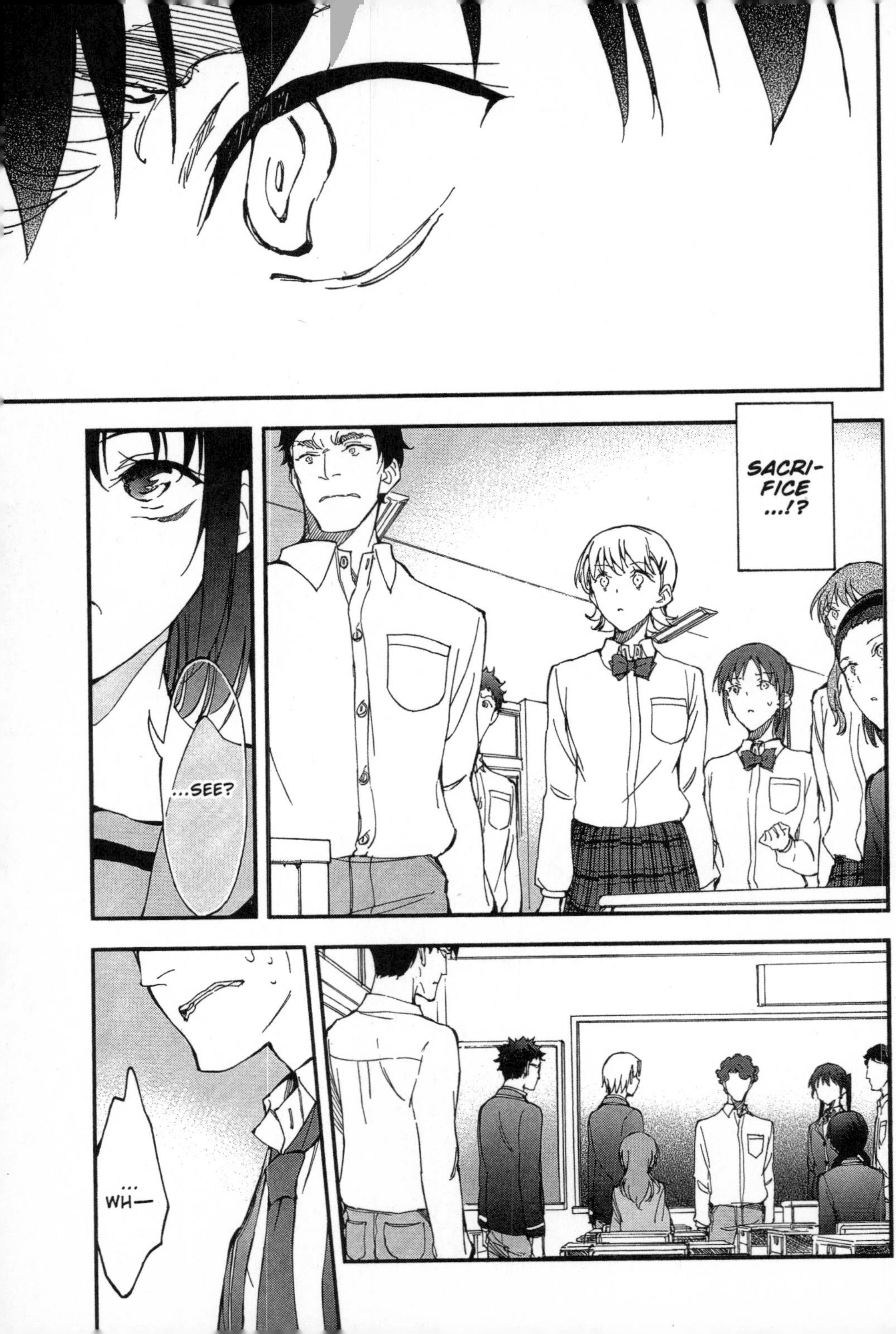
SACRI-FICE ...!?
...SEE?
... WH—

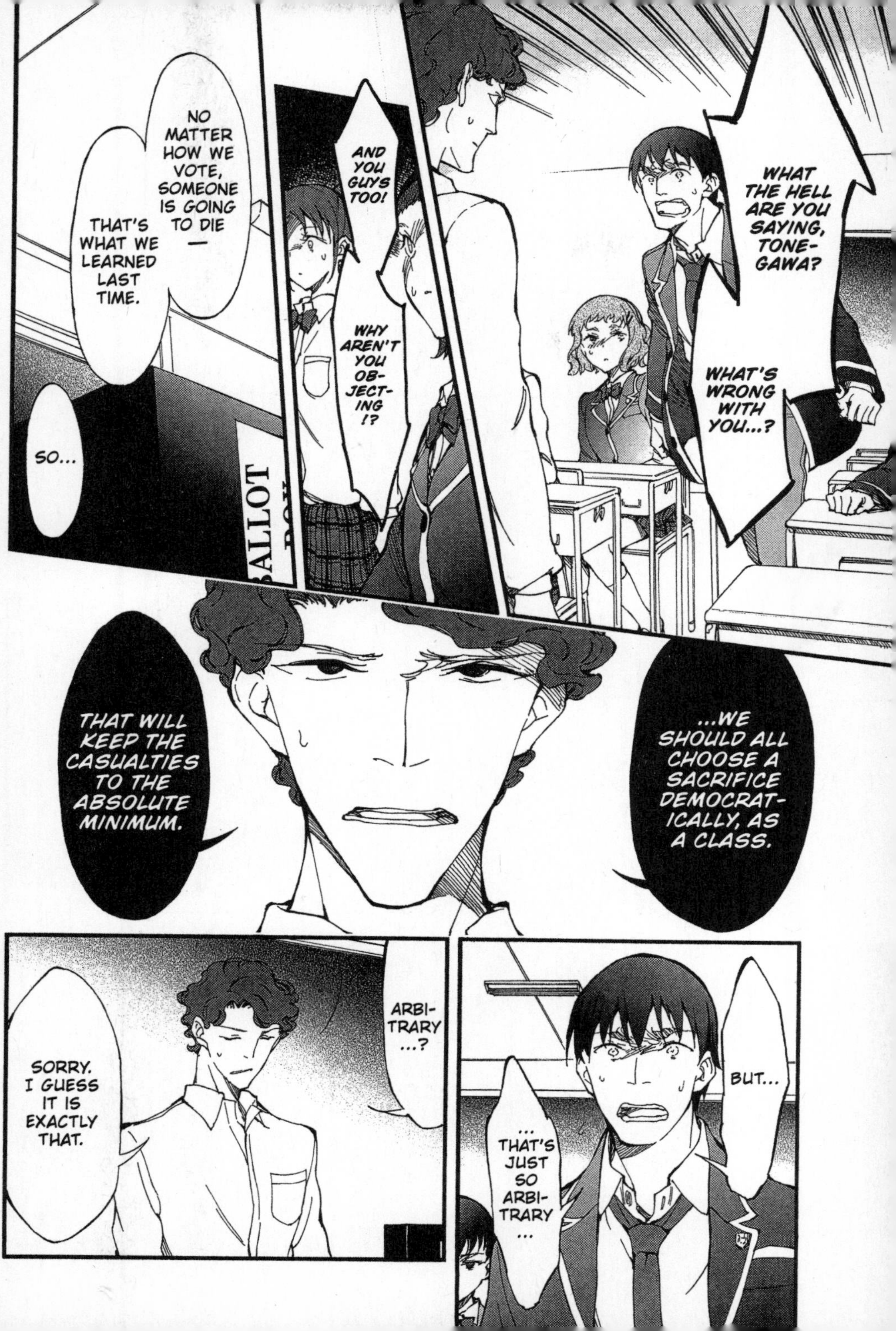
WHAT THE HELL ARE YOU SAYING, TONE-GAWA?
WHAT'S WRONG WITH YOU...?
AND YOU GUYS TOO!
WHY AREN'T YOU OBJECTING!?
NO MATTER HOW WE VOTE, SOMEONE IS GOING TO DIE —
THAT'S WHAT WE LEARNED LAST TIME.
SO...
BALLOT BOX
...WE SHOULD ALL CHOOSE A SACRIFICE DEMOCRATICALLY, AS A CLASS.
THAT WILL KEEP THE CASUALTIES TO THE ABSOLUTE MINIMUM.
BUT...
...THAT'S JUST SO ARBITRARY...
ARBITRARY...?
SORRY. I GUESS IT IS EXACTLY THAT.

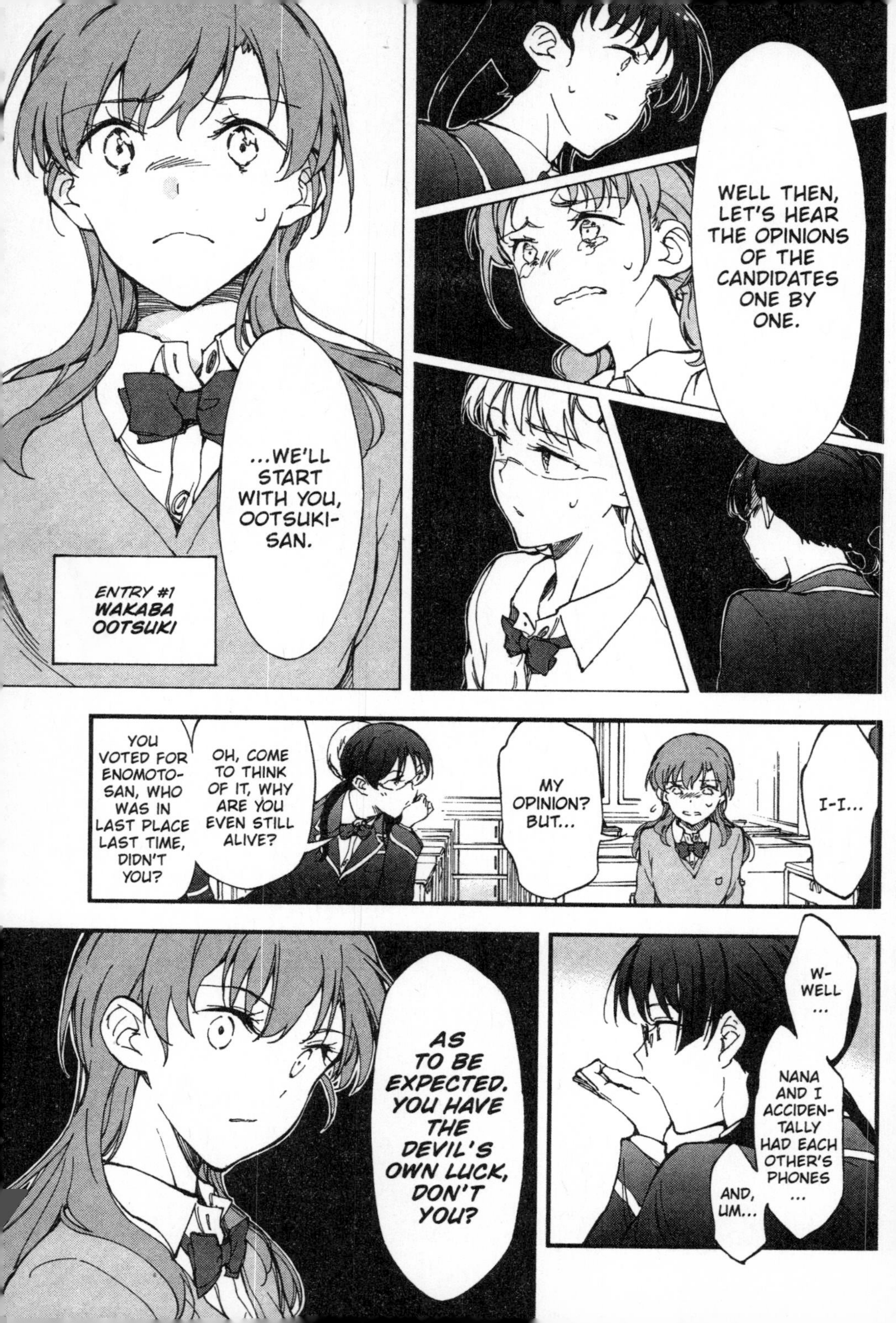
WELL THEN, LET'S HEAR THE OPINIONS OF THE CANDIDATES ONE BY ONE.
...WE'LL START WITH YOU, OOTSUKI-SAN.
ENTRY #1 **WAKABA OOTSUKI**
I-I...
MY OPINION? BUT...
OH, COME TO THINK OF IT, WHY ARE YOU EVEN STILL ALIVE?
YOU VOTED FOR ENOMOTO-SAN, WHO WAS IN LAST PLACE LAST TIME, DIDN'T YOU?
W-WELL...
NANA AND I ACCIDENTALLY HAD EACH OTHER'S PHONES...
AND, UM...
AS TO BE EXPECTED. YOU HAVE THE DEVIL'S OWN LUCK, DON'T YOU?

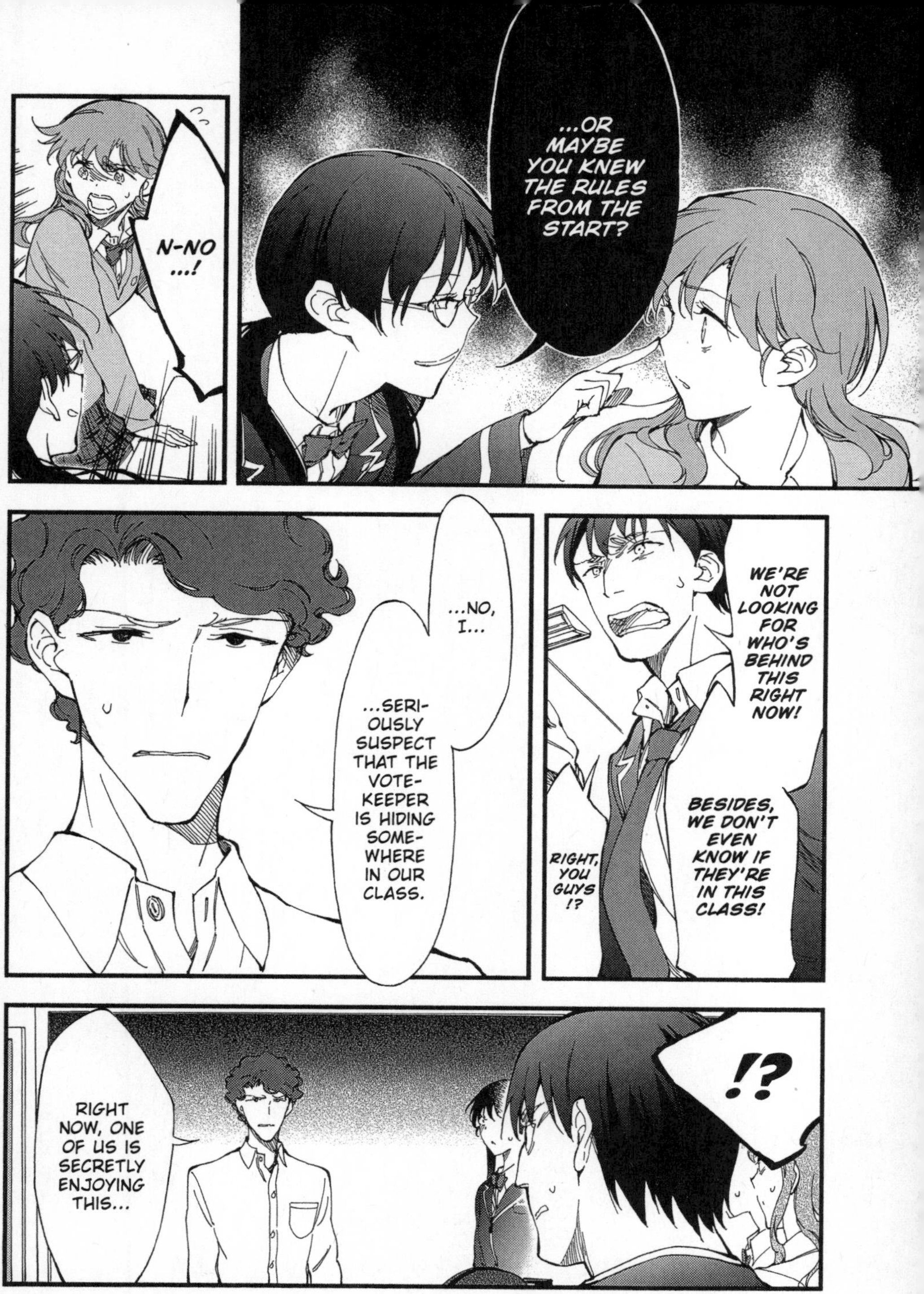
...OR MAYBE YOU KNEW THE RULES FROM THE START?
N-NO ...!
WE'RE NOT LOOKING FOR WHO'S BEHIND THIS RIGHT NOW!
BESIDES, WE DON'T EVEN KNOW IF THEY'RE IN THIS CLASS!
RIGHT, YOU GUYS !?
...NO, I...
...SERI-OUSLY SUSPECT THAT THE VOTE-KEEPER IS HIDING SOME-WHERE IN OUR CLASS.
!?
RIGHT NOW, ONE OF US IS SECRETLY ENJOYING THIS...

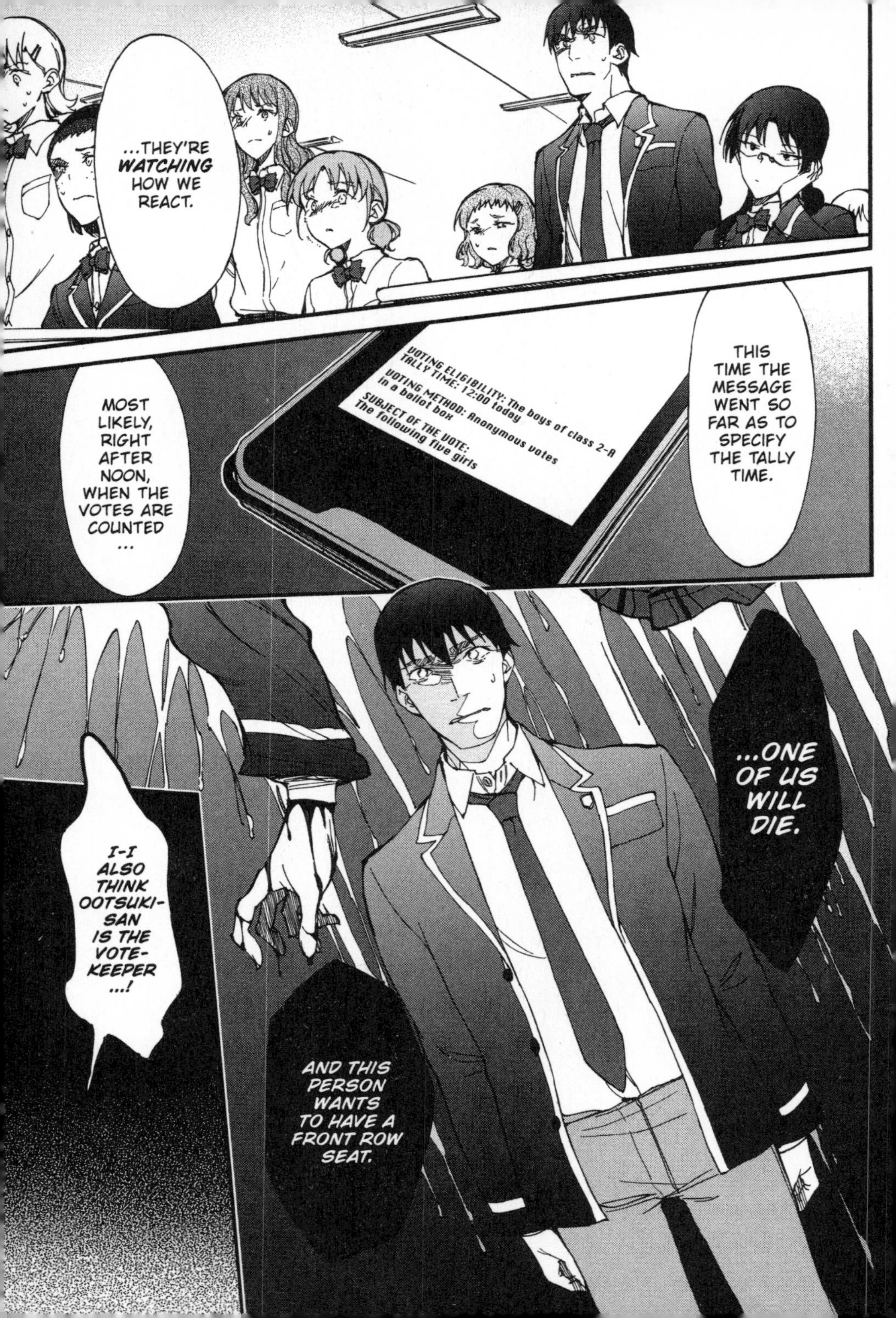
...THEY'RE WATCHING HOW WE REACT.
THIS TIME THE MESSAGE WENT SO FAR AS TO SPECIFY THE TALLY TIME.
VOTING ELIGIBILITY: The boys of class 2-A
TALLY TIME: 12:00 today
VOTING METHOD: Anonymous votes in a ballot box
SUBJECT OF THE VOTE: The following five girls
MOST LIKELY, RIGHT AFTER NOON, WHEN THE VOTES ARE COUNTED...
...ONE OF US WILL DIE.
AND THIS PERSON WANTS TO HAVE A FRONT ROW SEAT.
I-I ALSO THINK OOTSUKI-SAN IS THE VOTE-KEEPER...!

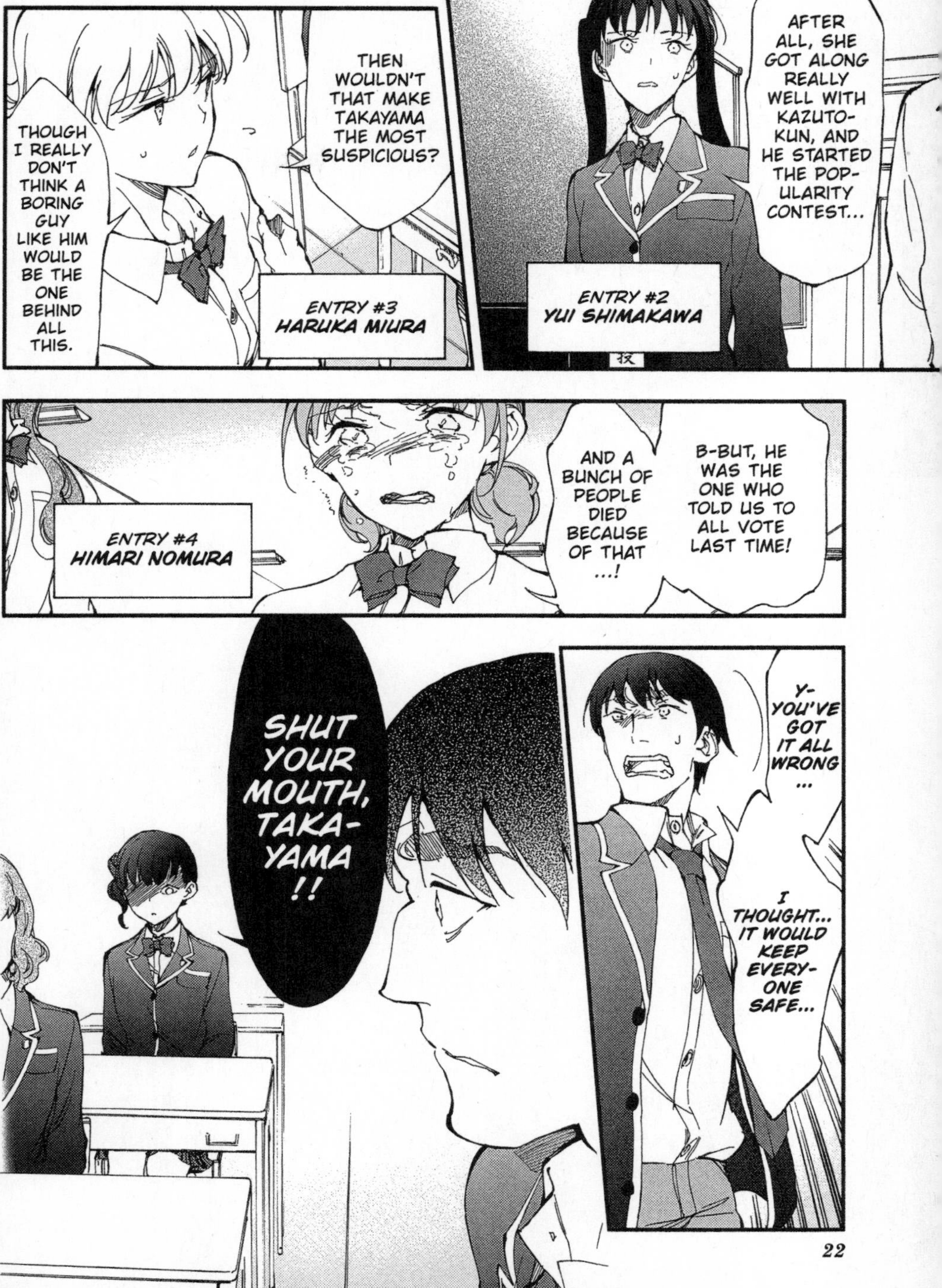
AFTER ALL, SHE GOT ALONG REALLY WELL WITH KAZUTO-KUN, AND HE STARTED THE POPULARITY CONTEST...
ENTRY #2 YUI SHIMAKAWA
THEN WOULDN'T THAT MAKE TAKAYAMA THE MOST SUSPICIOUS?
THOUGH I REALLY DON'T THINK A BORING GUY LIKE HIM WOULD BE THE ONE BEHIND ALL THIS.
ENTRY #3 HARUKA MIURA
B-BUT, HE WAS THE ONE WHO TOLD US TO ALL VOTE LAST TIME!
AND A BUNCH OF PEOPLE DIED BECAUSE OF THAT ...!
ENTRY #4 HIMARI NOMURA
Y-YOU'VE GOT IT ALL WRONG ...
I THOUGHT... IT WOULD KEEP EVERYONE SAFE...
SHUT YOUR MOUTH, TAKAYAMA!!

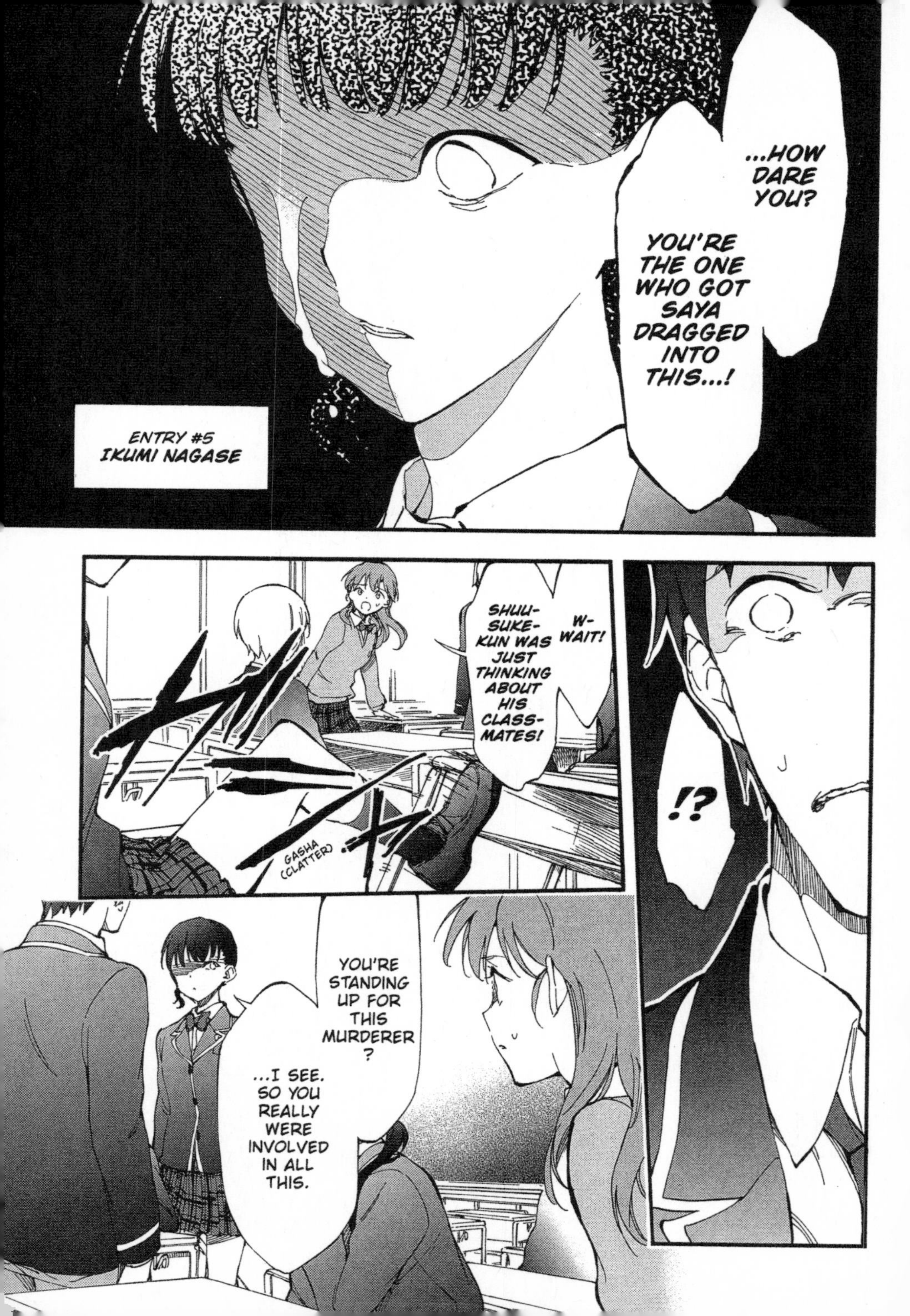
...HOW DARE YOU?
YOU'RE THE ONE WHO GOT SAYA DRAGGED INTO THIS...!
ENTRY #5 IKUMI NAGASE
!?
W-WAIT!
SHUU-SUKE-KUN WAS JUST THINKING ABOUT HIS CLASS-MATES!
GASHA (CLATTER)
YOU'RE STANDING UP FOR THIS MURDERER?
...I SEE. SO YOU REALLY WERE INVOLVED IN ALL THIS.

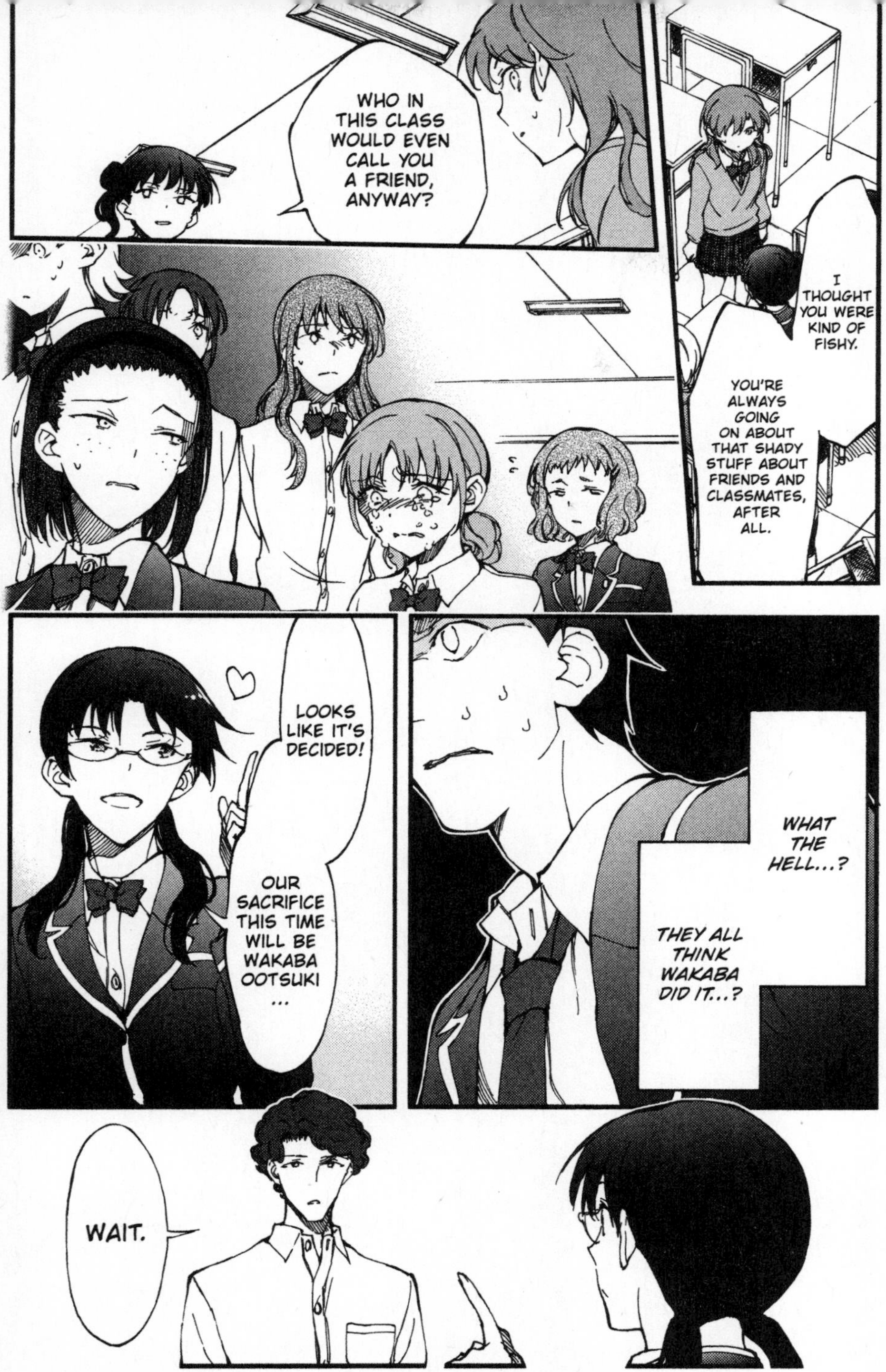
I THOUGHT YOU WERE KIND OF FISHY.
YOU'RE ALWAYS GOING ON ABOUT THAT SHADY STUFF ABOUT FRIENDS AND CLASSMATES, AFTER ALL.
WHO IN THIS CLASS WOULD EVEN CALL YOU A FRIEND, ANYWAY?
WHAT THE HELL...?
THEY ALL THINK WAKABA DID IT...?
LOOKS LIKE IT'S DECIDED!
OUR SACRIFICE THIS TIME WILL BE WAKABA OOTSUKI ...
WAIT.

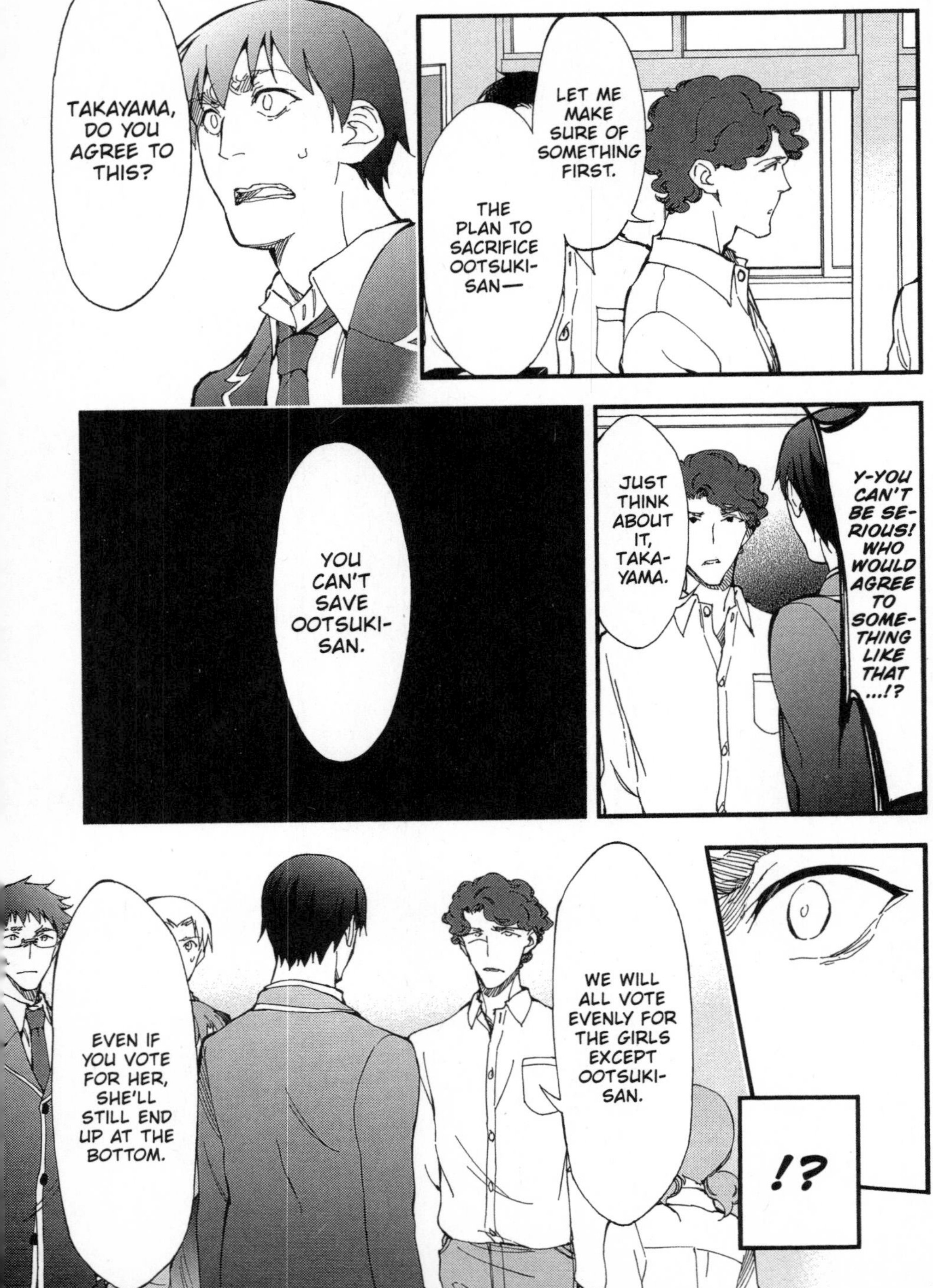
LET ME MAKE SURE OF SOMETHING FIRST.
THE PLAN TO SACRIFICE OOTSUKI-SAN—
TAKAYAMA, DO YOU AGREE TO THIS?
Y-YOU CAN'T BE SERIOUS! WHO WOULD AGREE TO SOMETHING LIKE THAT...!?
JUST THINK ABOUT IT, TAKAYAMA.
YOU CAN'T SAVE OOTSUKI-SAN.
!?
WE WILL ALL VOTE EVENLY FOR THE GIRLS EXCEPT OOTSUKI-SAN.
EVEN IF YOU VOTE FOR HER, SHE'LL STILL END UP AT THE BOTTOM.

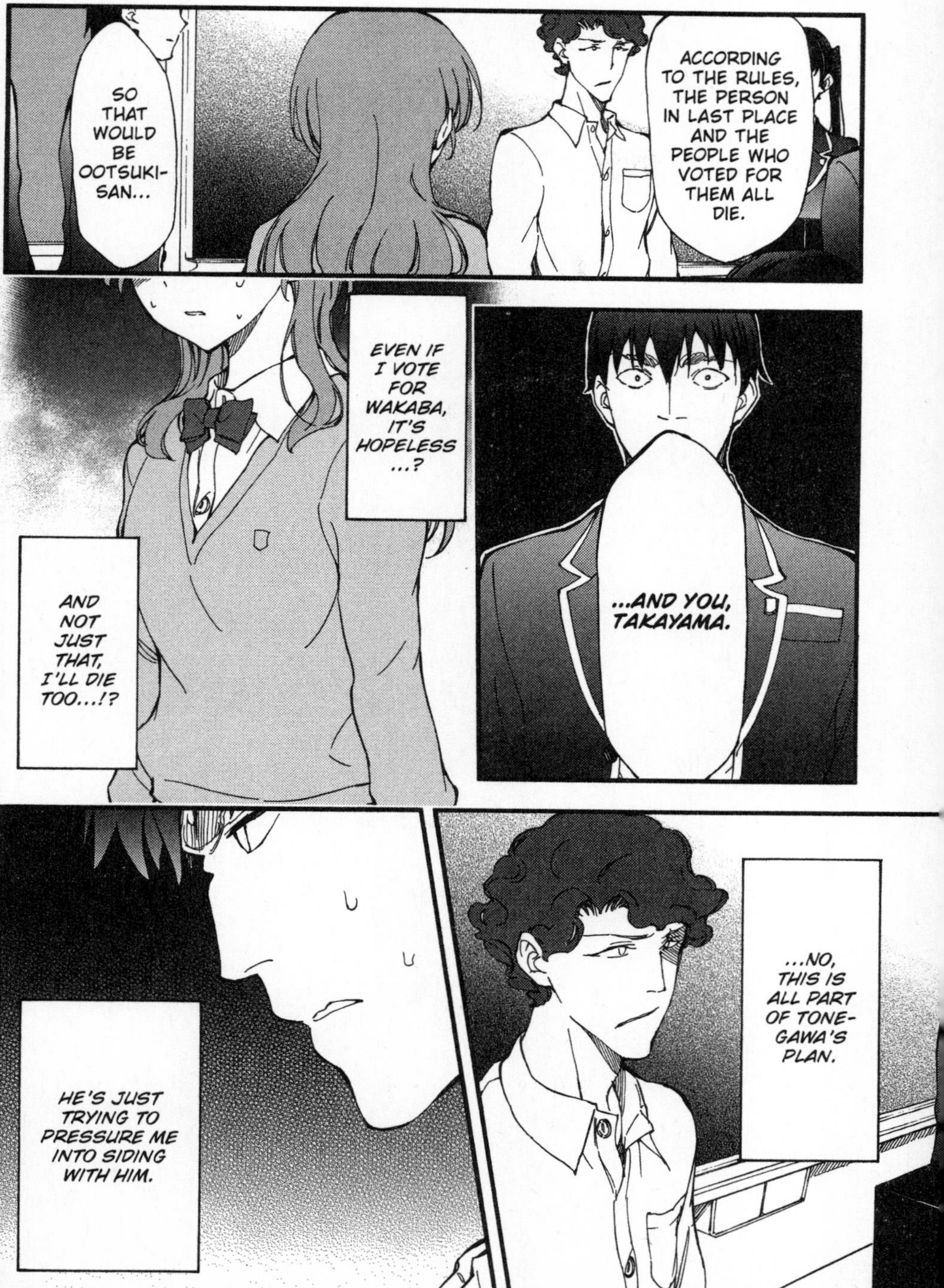
ACCORDING TO THE RULES, THE PERSON IN LAST PLACE AND THE PEOPLE WHO VOTED FOR THEM ALL DIE.
SO THAT WOULD BE OOTSUKI-SAN...
...AND YOU, TAKAYAMA.
EVEN IF I VOTE FOR WAKABA, IT'S HOPELESS...?
AND NOT JUST THAT, I'LL DIE TOO...!?
...NO, THIS IS ALL PART OF TONE-GAWA'S PLAN.
HE'S JUST TRYING TO PRESSURE ME INTO SIDING WITH HIM.

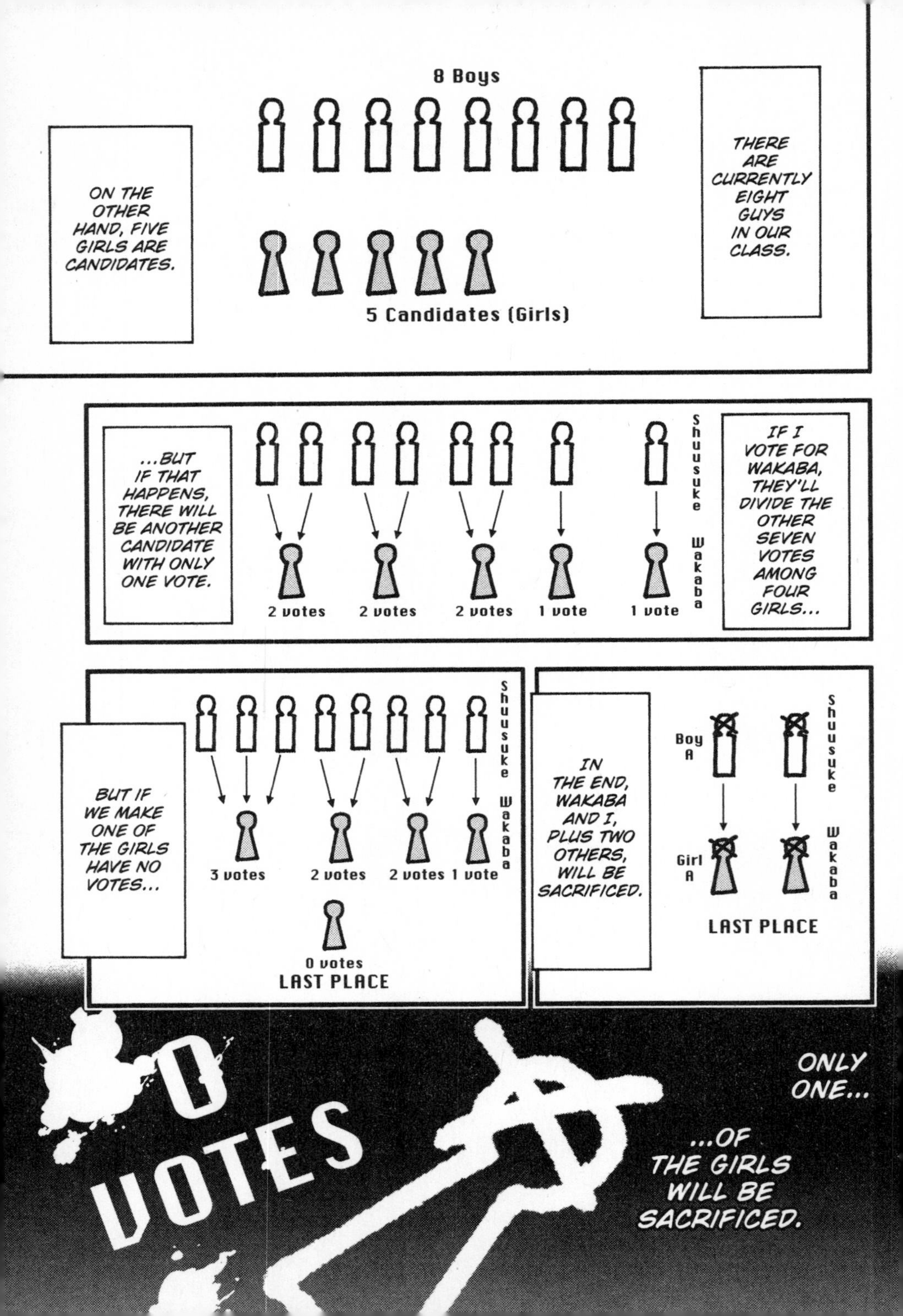

THERE ARE CURRENTLY EIGHT GUYS IN OUR CLASS.
8 Boys
5 Candidates (Girls)
ON THE OTHER HAND, FIVE GIRLS ARE CANDIDATES.
IF I VOTE FOR WAKABA, THEY'LL DIVIDE THE OTHER SEVEN VOTES AMONG FOUR GIRLS...
Shuusuke
Wakaba
1 vote
1 vote
2 votes
2 votes
2 votes
...BUT IF THAT HAPPENS, THERE WILL BE ANOTHER CANDIDATE WITH ONLY ONE VOTE.
Shuusuke
Boy A
Girl A
Wakaba
LAST PLACE
IN THE END, WAKABA AND I, PLUS TWO OTHERS, WILL BE SACRIFICED.
Shuusuke
Wakaba
1 vote
2 votes
2 votes
3 votes
0 votes
LAST PLACE
BUT IF WE MAKE ONE OF THE GIRLS HAVE NO VOTES...
ONLY ONE...
...OF THE GIRLS WILL BE SACRIFICED.
0 VOTES

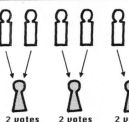

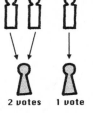

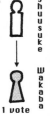

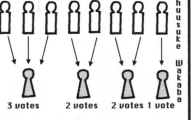

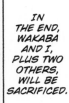

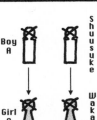

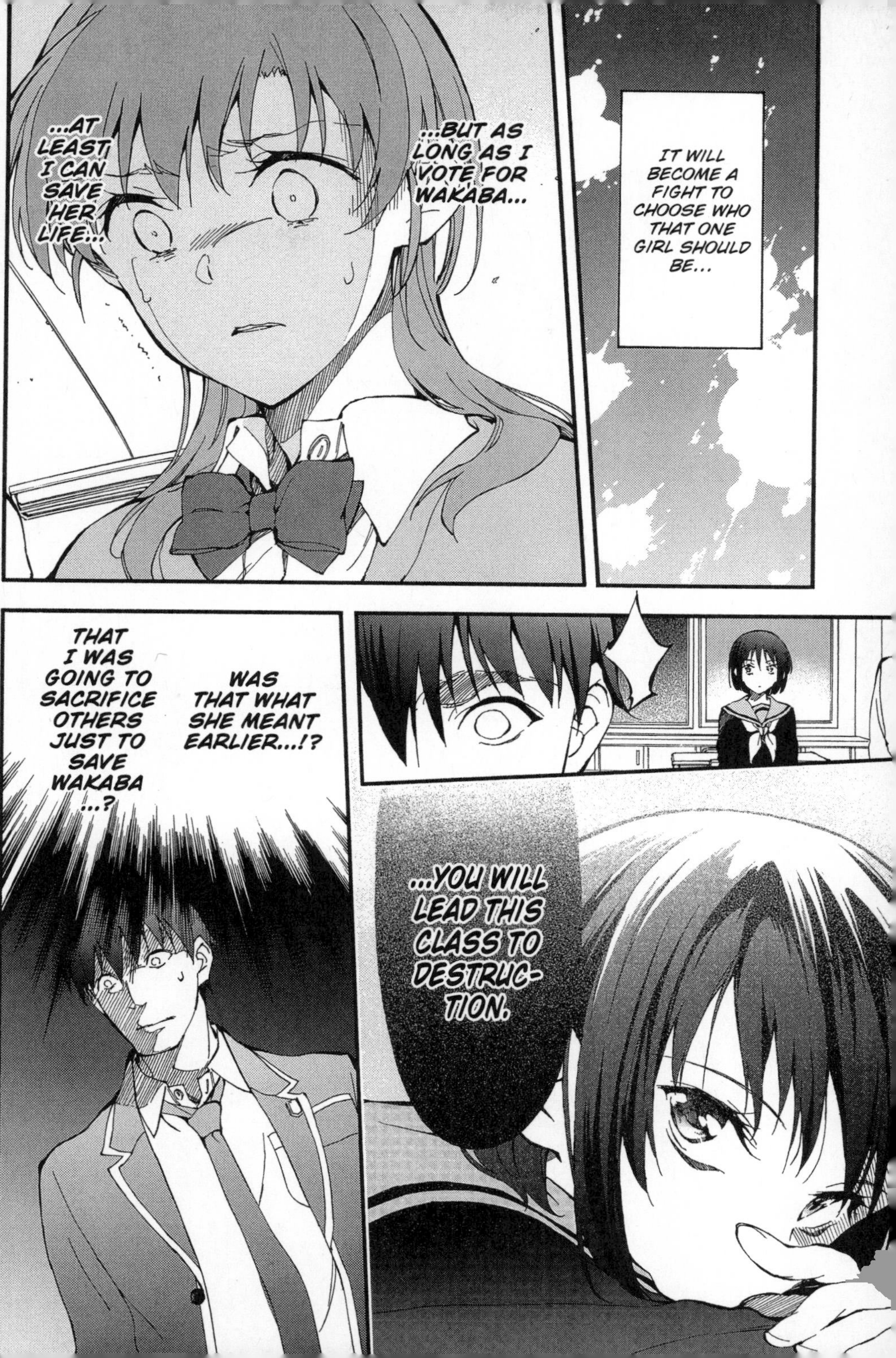
IT WILL BECOME A FIGHT TO CHOOSE WHO THAT ONE GIRL SHOULD BE...
...BUT AS LONG AS I VOTE FOR WAKABA...
...AT LEAST I CAN SAVE HER LIFE...
...YOU WILL LEAD THIS CLASS TO DESTRUCTION.
WAS THAT WHAT SHE MEANT EARLIER...!?
THAT I WAS GOING TO SACRIFICE OTHERS JUST TO SAVE WAKABA...?

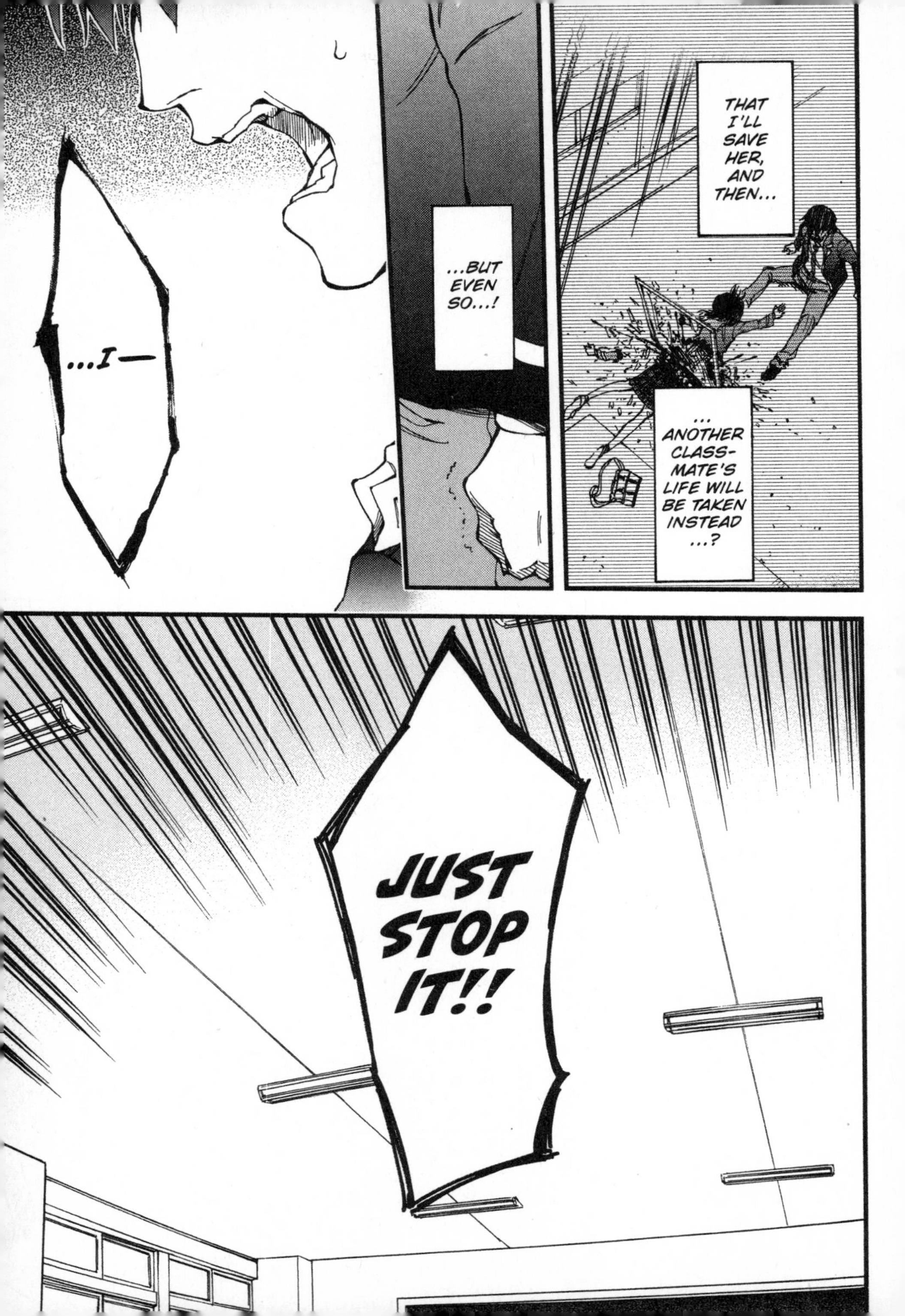
THAT I'LL SAVE HER, AND THEN...
...ANOTHER CLASS-MATE'S LIFE WILL BE TAKEN INSTEAD...?
...BUT EVEN SO...!
...I—
JUST STOP IT!!

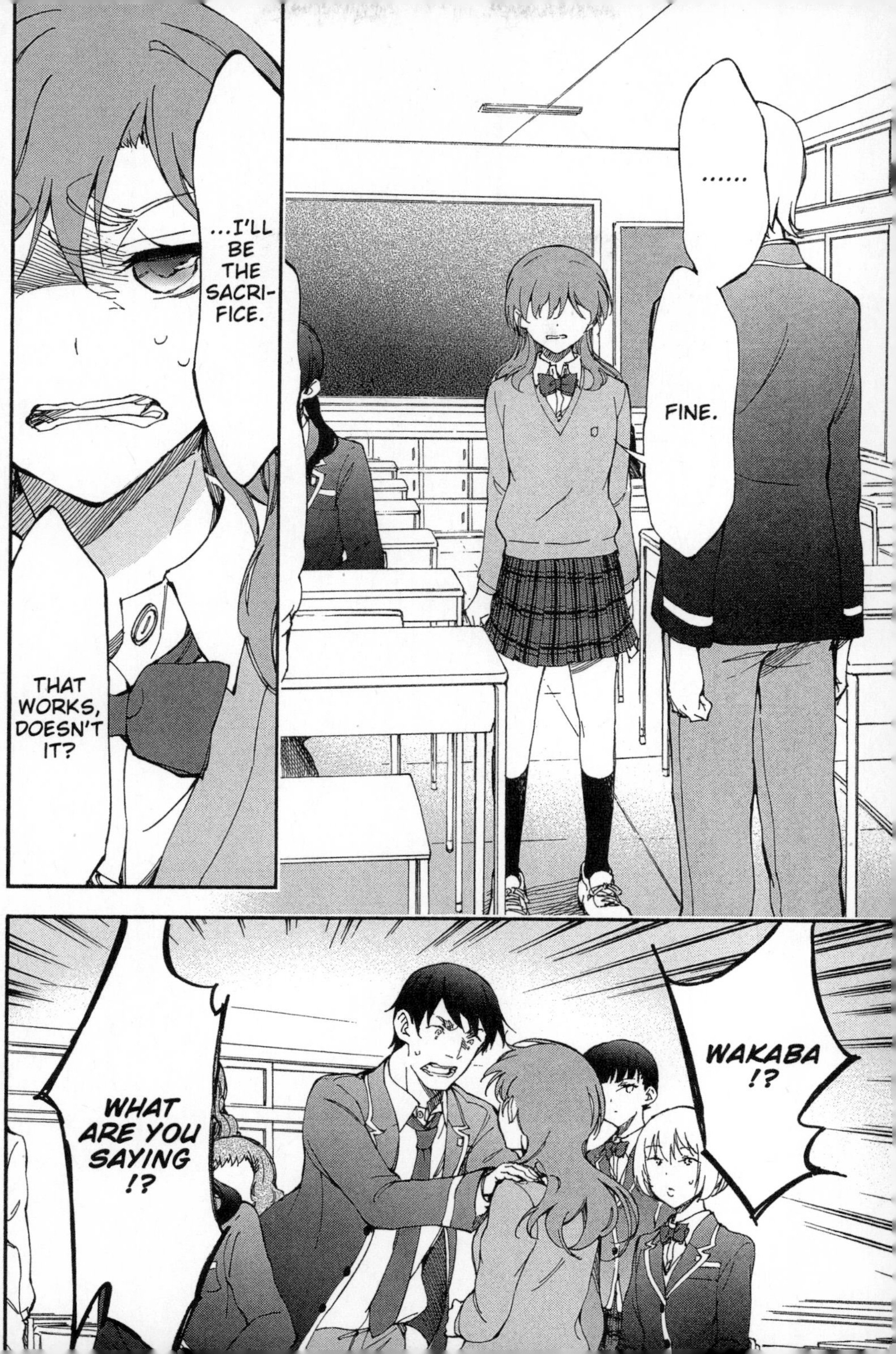
......
FINE.
...I'LL BE THE SACRI-FICE.
THAT WORKS, DOESN'T IT?
WAKABA!?
WHAT ARE YOU SAYING!?

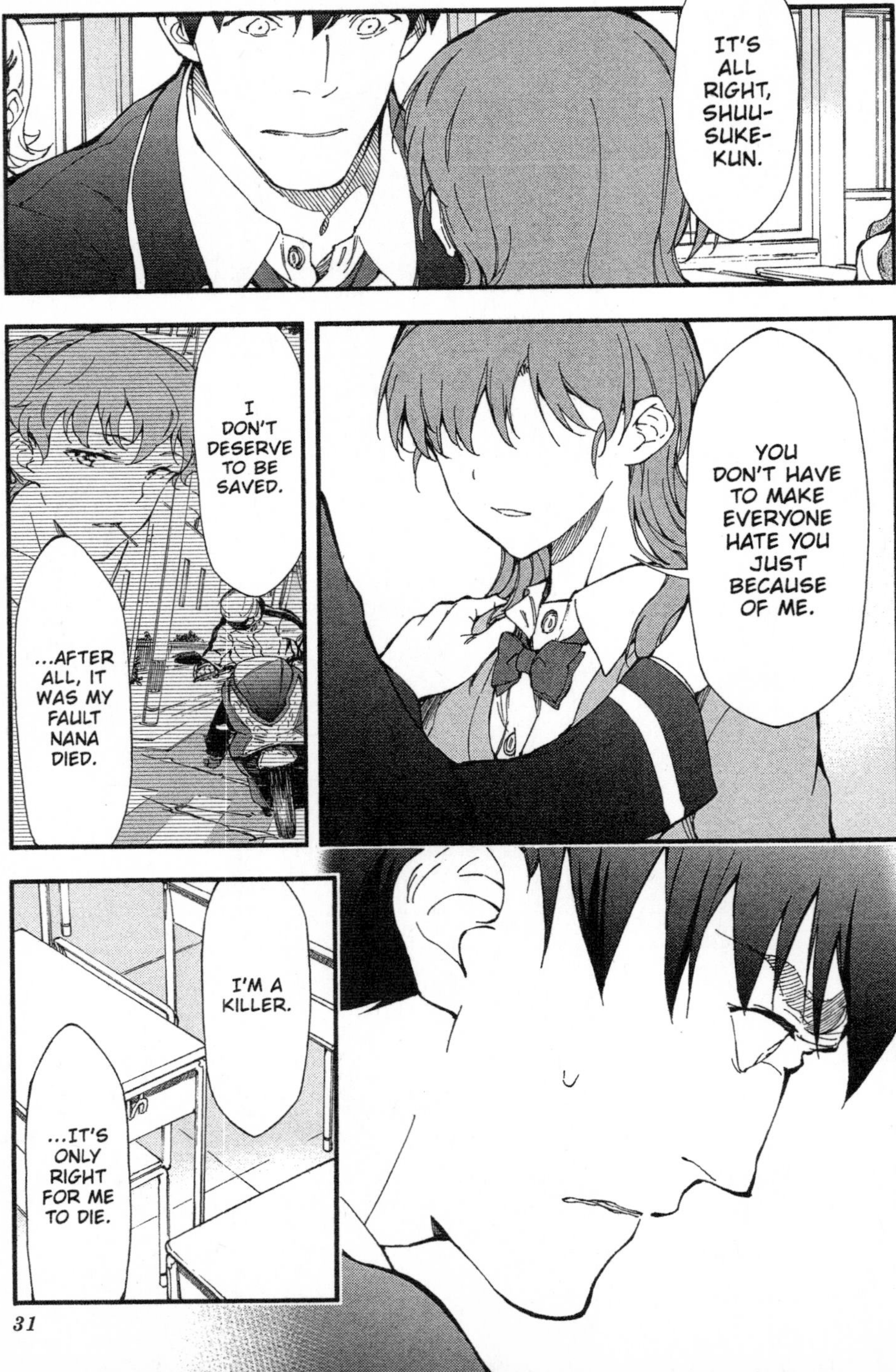
IT'S ALL RIGHT, SHUUSUKE-KUN.
YOU DON'T HAVE TO MAKE EVERYONE HATE YOU JUST BECAUSE OF ME.
I DON'T DESERVE TO BE SAVED.
...AFTER ALL, IT WAS MY FAULT NANA DIED.
I'M A KILLER.
...IT'S ONLY RIGHT FOR ME TO DIE.

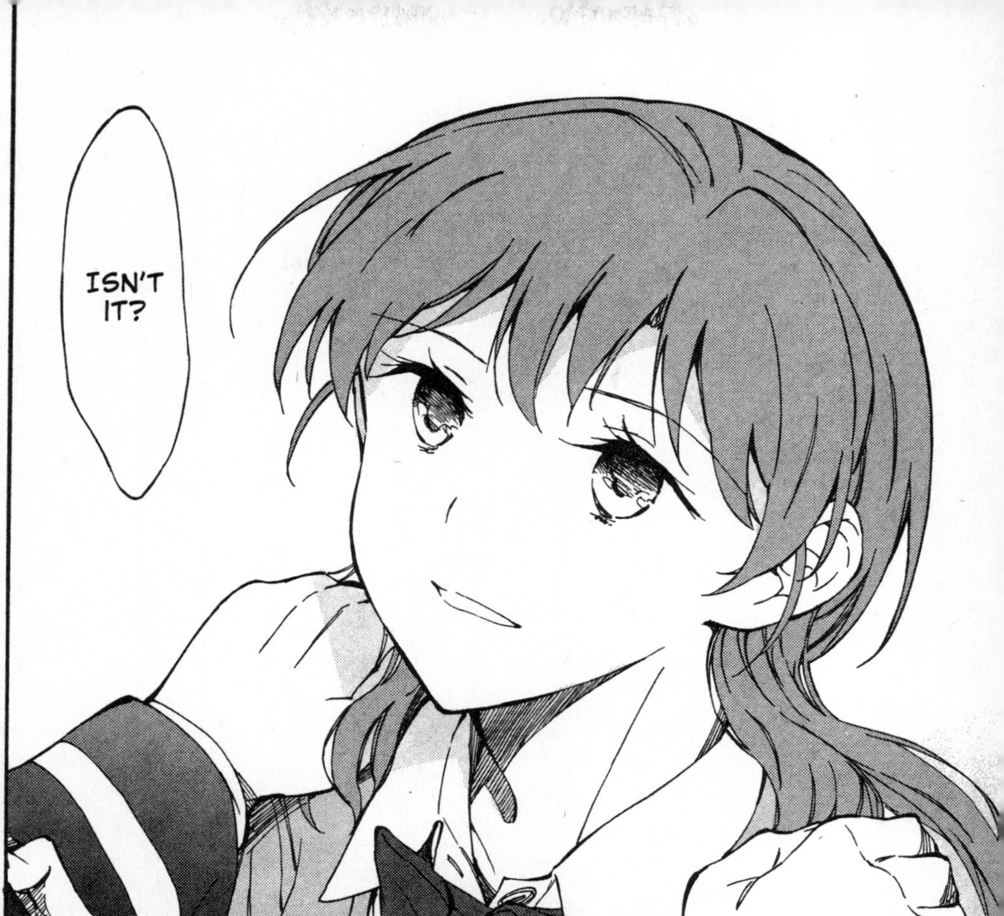
ISN'T IT?
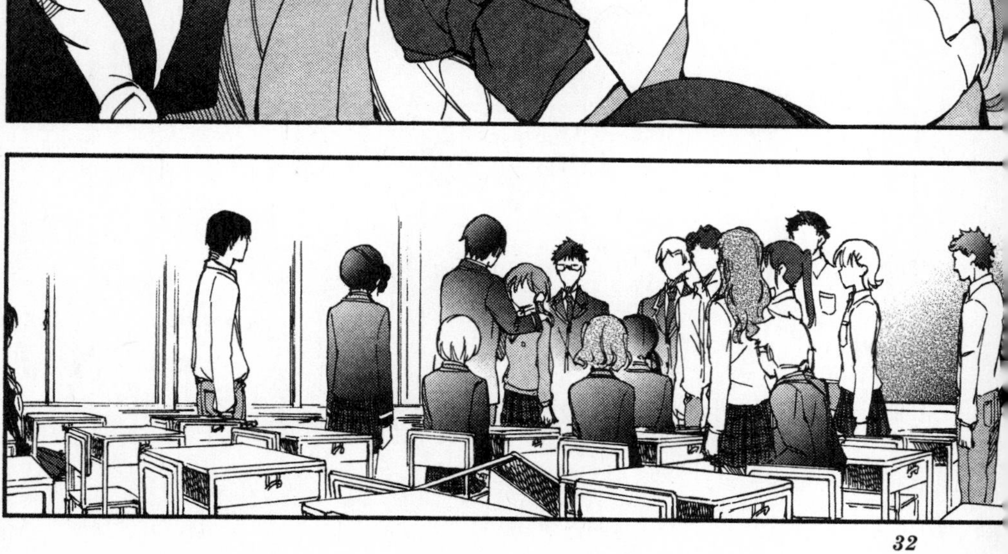

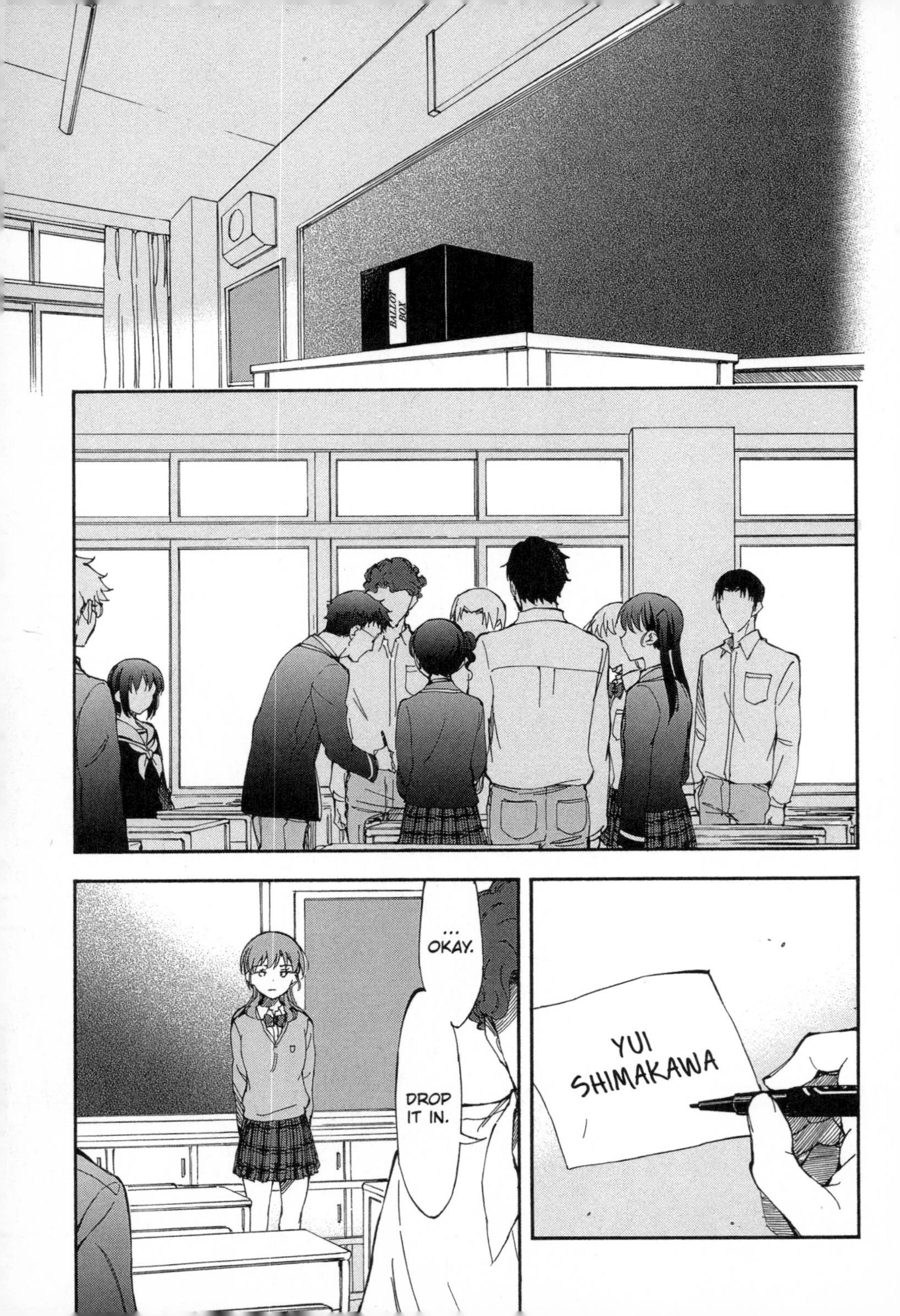
BALLOT BOX
YUI SHIMAKAWA
...OKAY.
DROP IT IN.

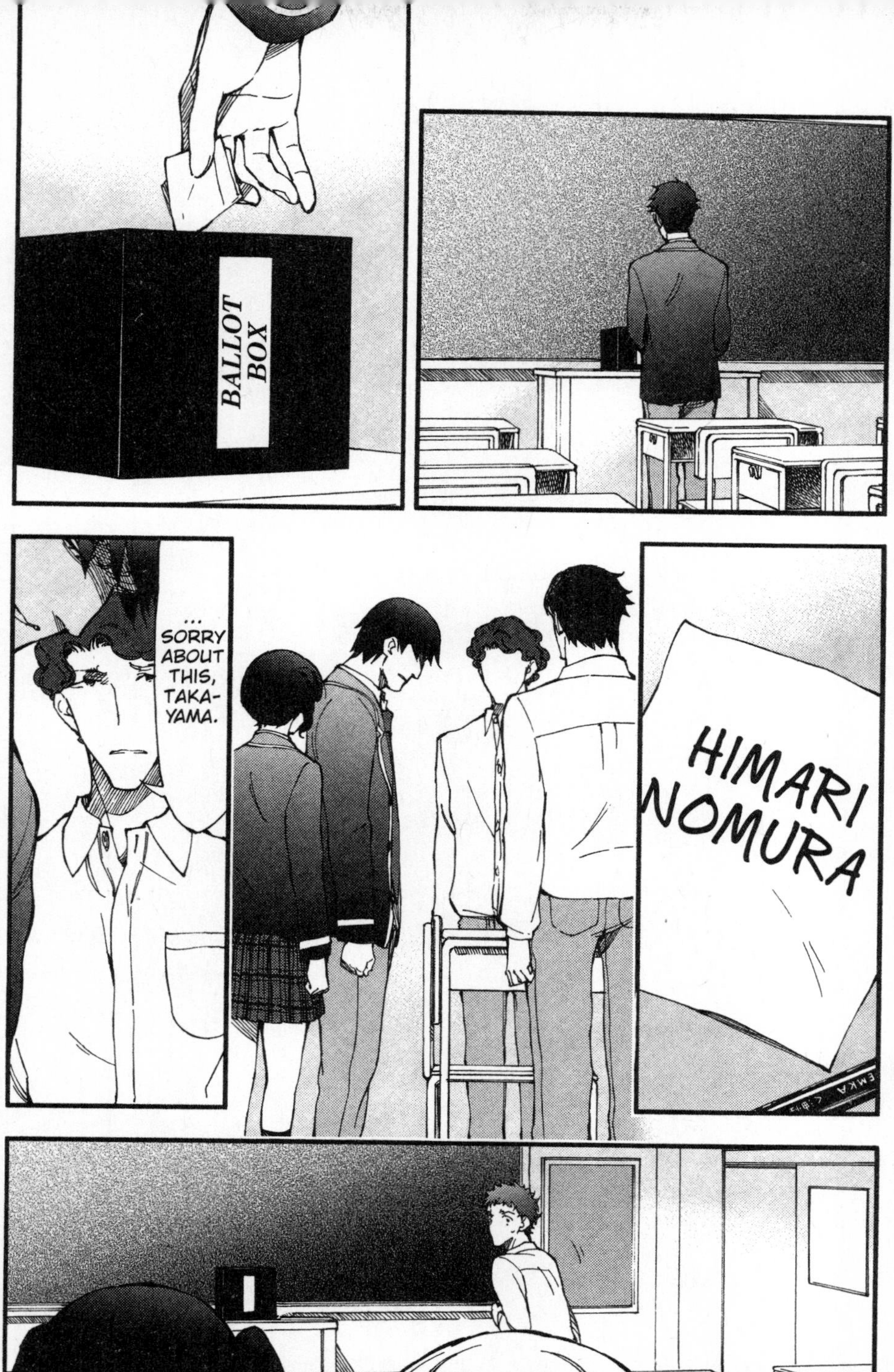
BALLOT BOX
HIMARI NOMURA
... SORRY ABOUT THIS, TAKAYAMA.

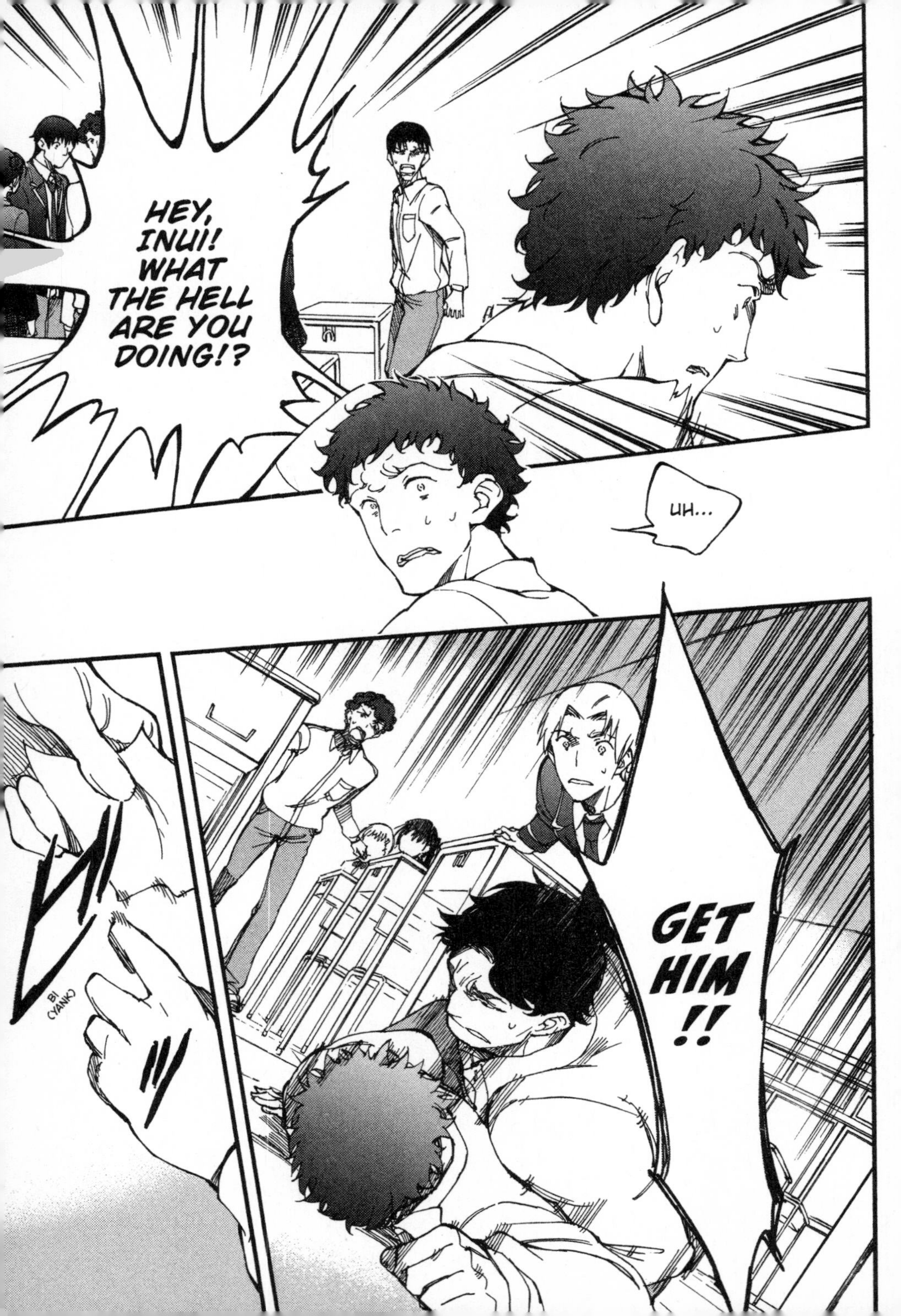
HEY, INUI! WHAT THE HELL ARE YOU DOING!?
UH...
GET HIM!!
BI (YANK)

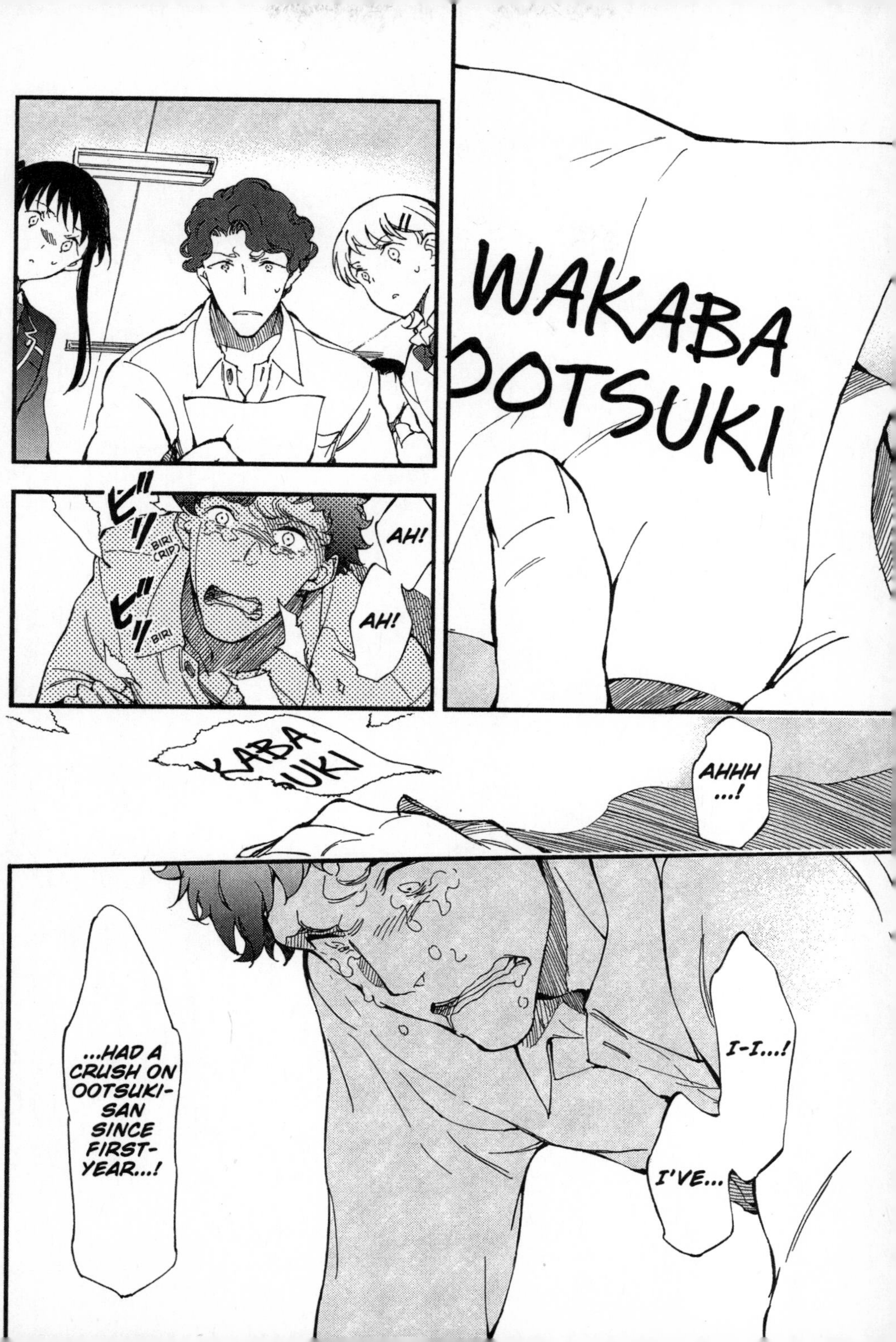
WAKABA OOTSUKI
AH!
ビリ BIRI (RIP)
AH!
ビリ BIRI
AHHH ...!
KABA UKI
I-I...!
I'VE...
...HAD A CRUSH ON OOTSUKI-SAN SINCE FIRST-YEAR...!

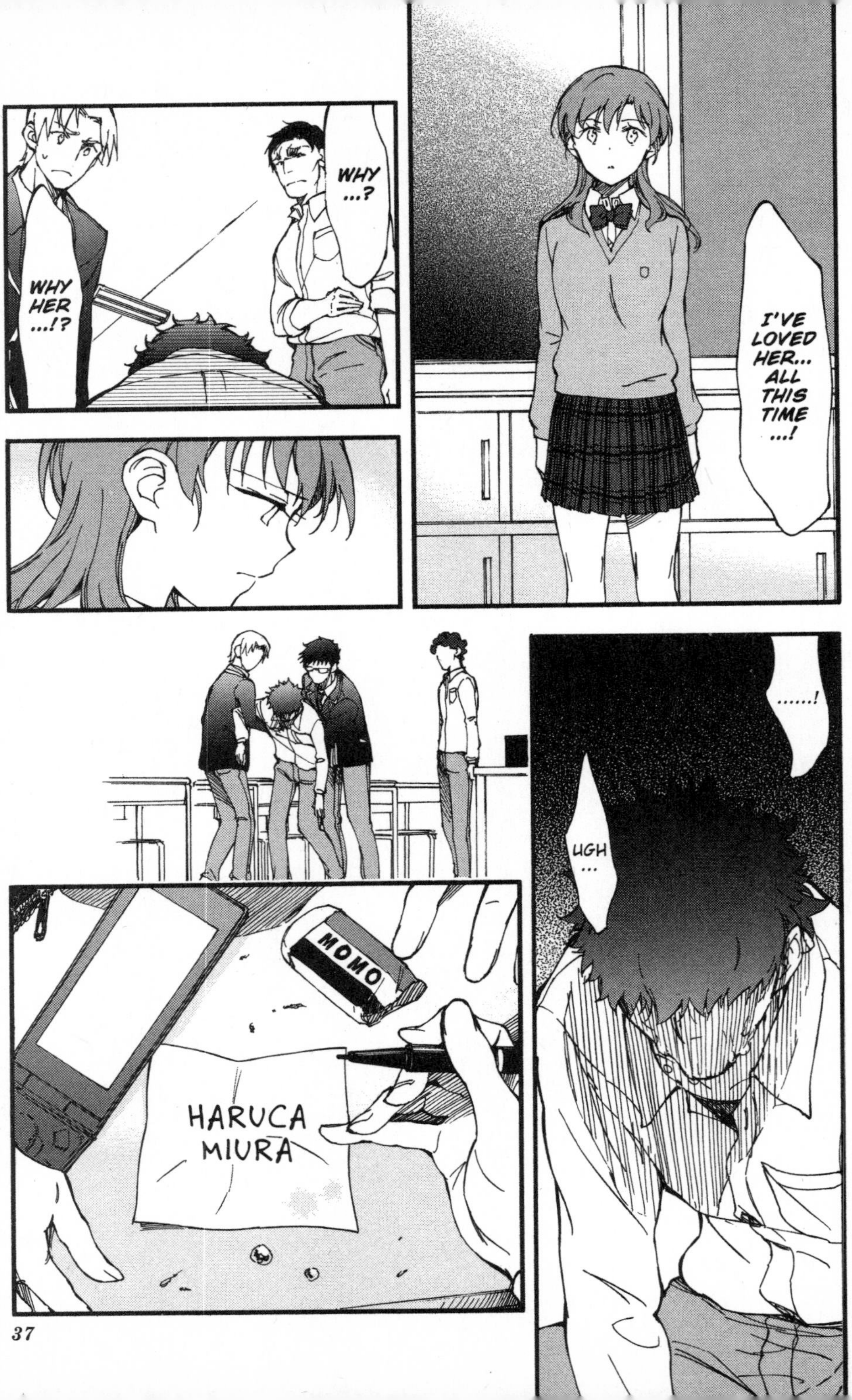
I'VE LOVED HER... ALL THIS TIME ...!
WHY ...?
WHY HER ...!?
......!
UGH ...
MOMO
HARUCA MIURA

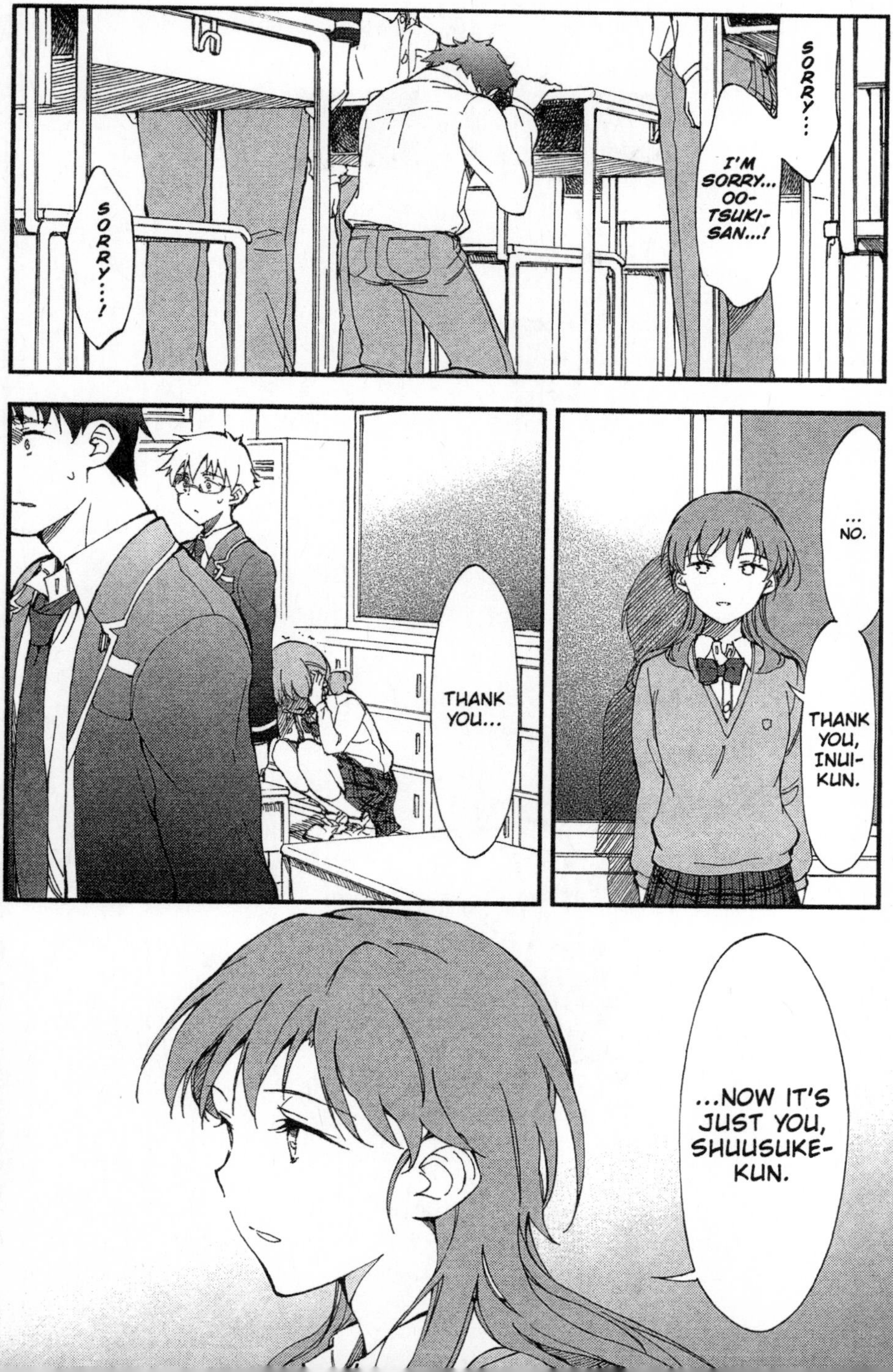
SORRY...
I'M SORRY... OO-TSUKI-SAN...!
SORRY...!
...NO.
THANK YOU, INUI-KUN.
THANK YOU...
...NOW IT'S JUST YOU, SHUUSUKE-KUN.

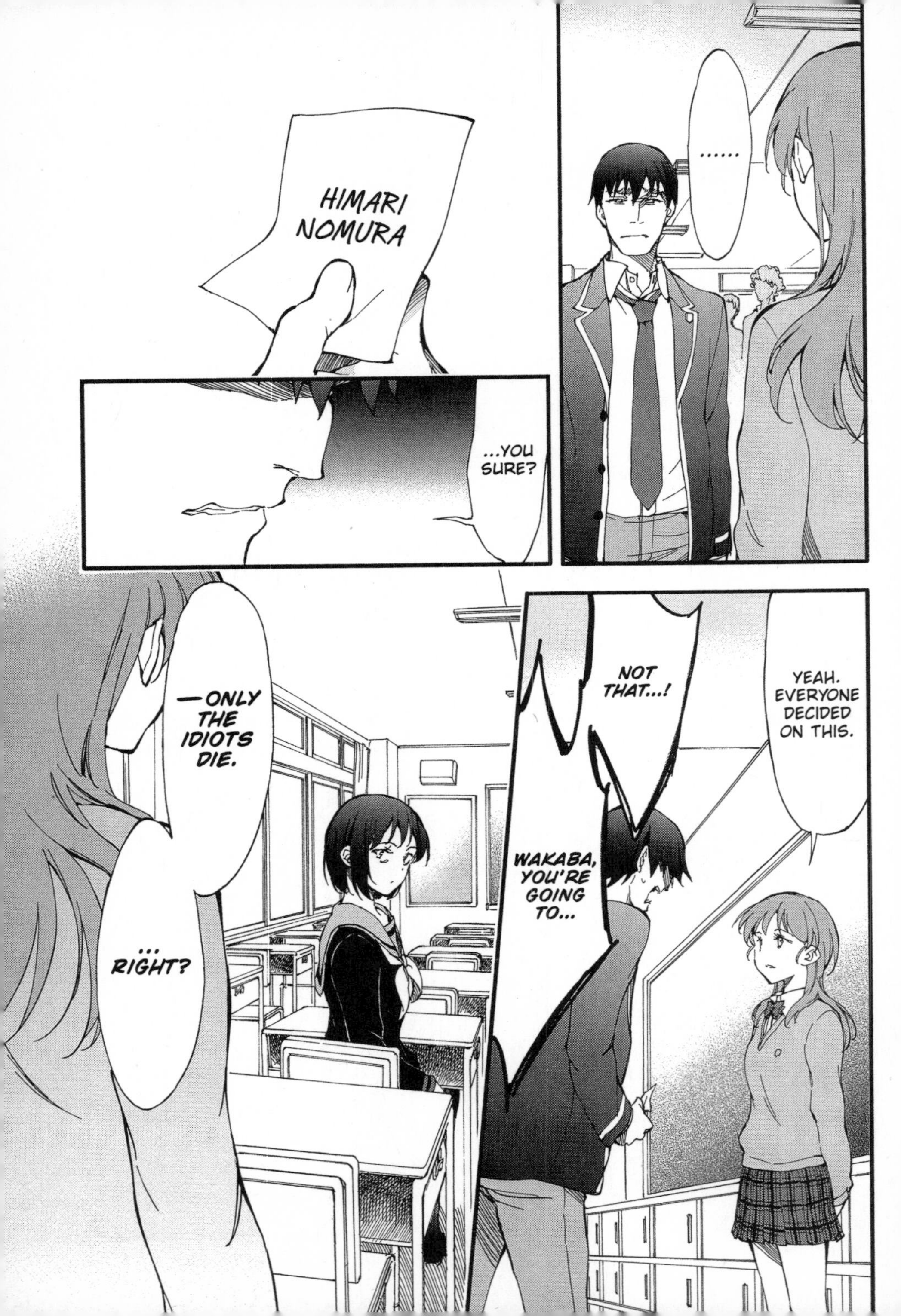
......
HIMARI NOMURA
...YOU SURE?
YEAH. EVERYONE DECIDED ON THIS.
NOT THAT...!
WAKABA, YOU'RE GOING TO...
—ONLY THE IDIOTS DIE.
...RIGHT?

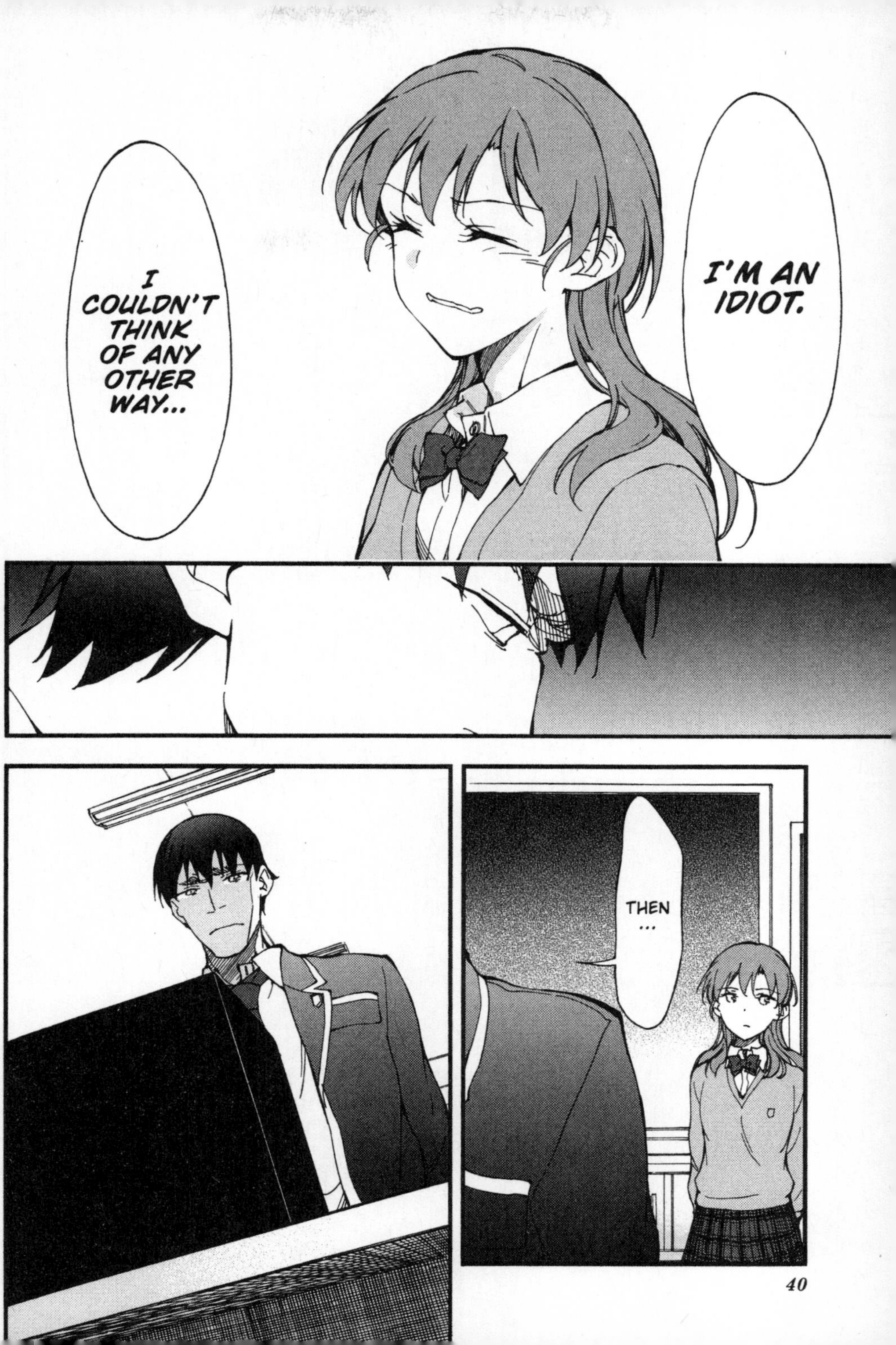
I'M AN IDIOT.
I COULDN'T THINK OF ANY OTHER WAY...
THEN ...

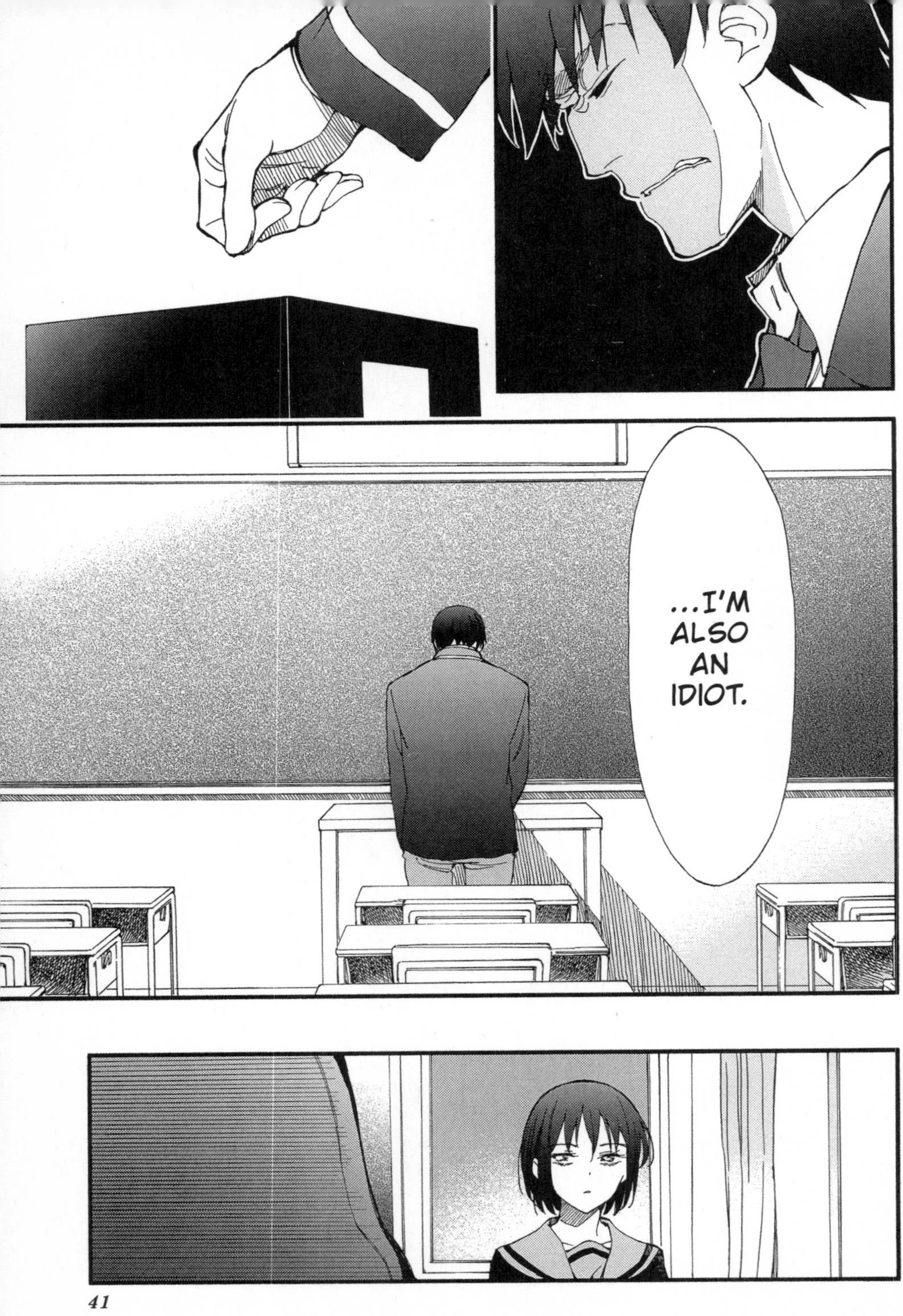
...I'M ALSO AN IDIOT.

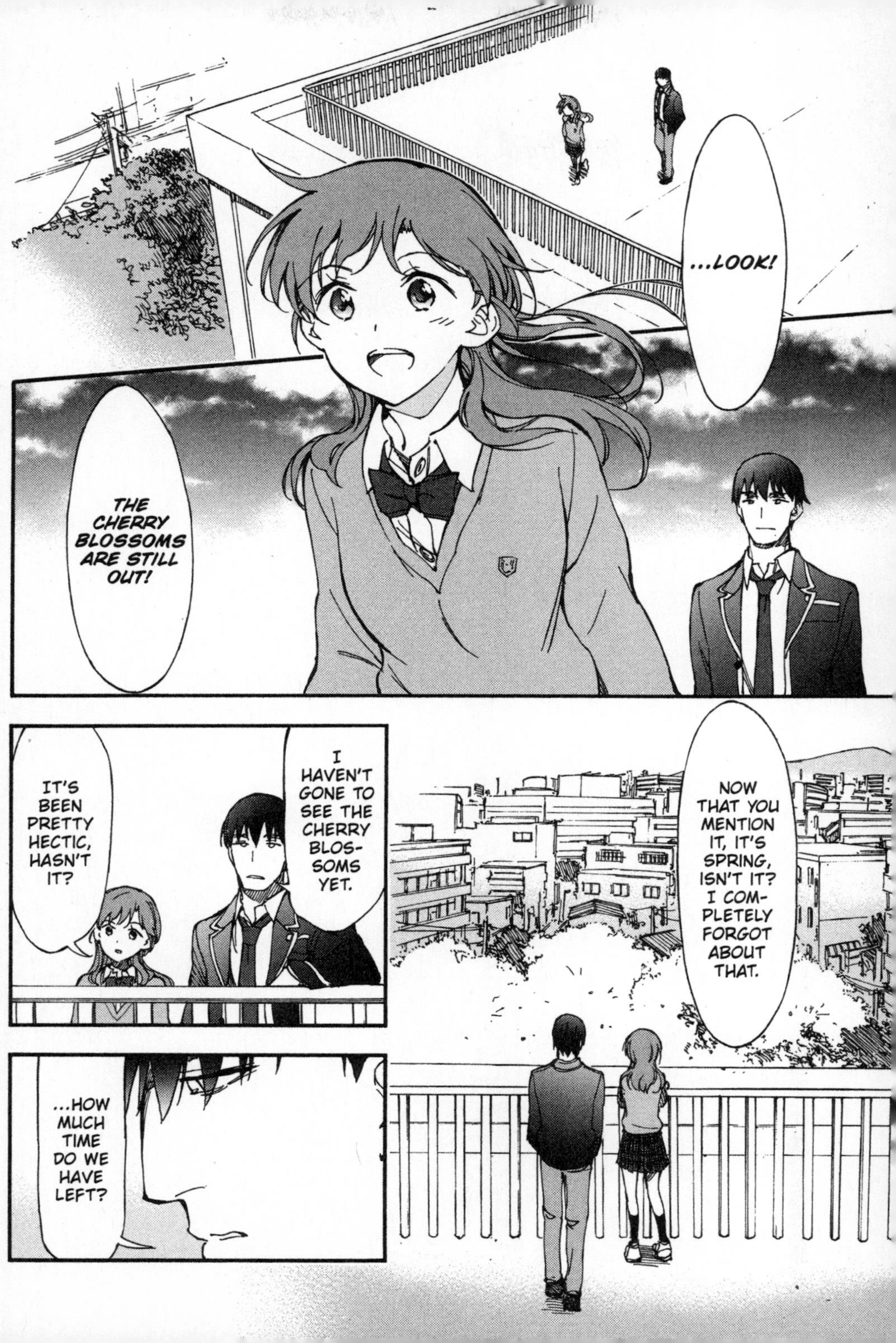
...LOOK!
THE CHERRY BLOSSOMS ARE STILL OUT!
NOW THAT YOU MENTION IT, IT'S SPRING, ISN'T IT? I COMPLETELY FORGOT ABOUT THAT.
I HAVEN'T GONE TO SEE THE CHERRY BLOSSOMS YET.
IT'S BEEN PRETTY HECTIC, HASN'T IT?
...HOW MUCH TIME DO WE HAVE LEFT?

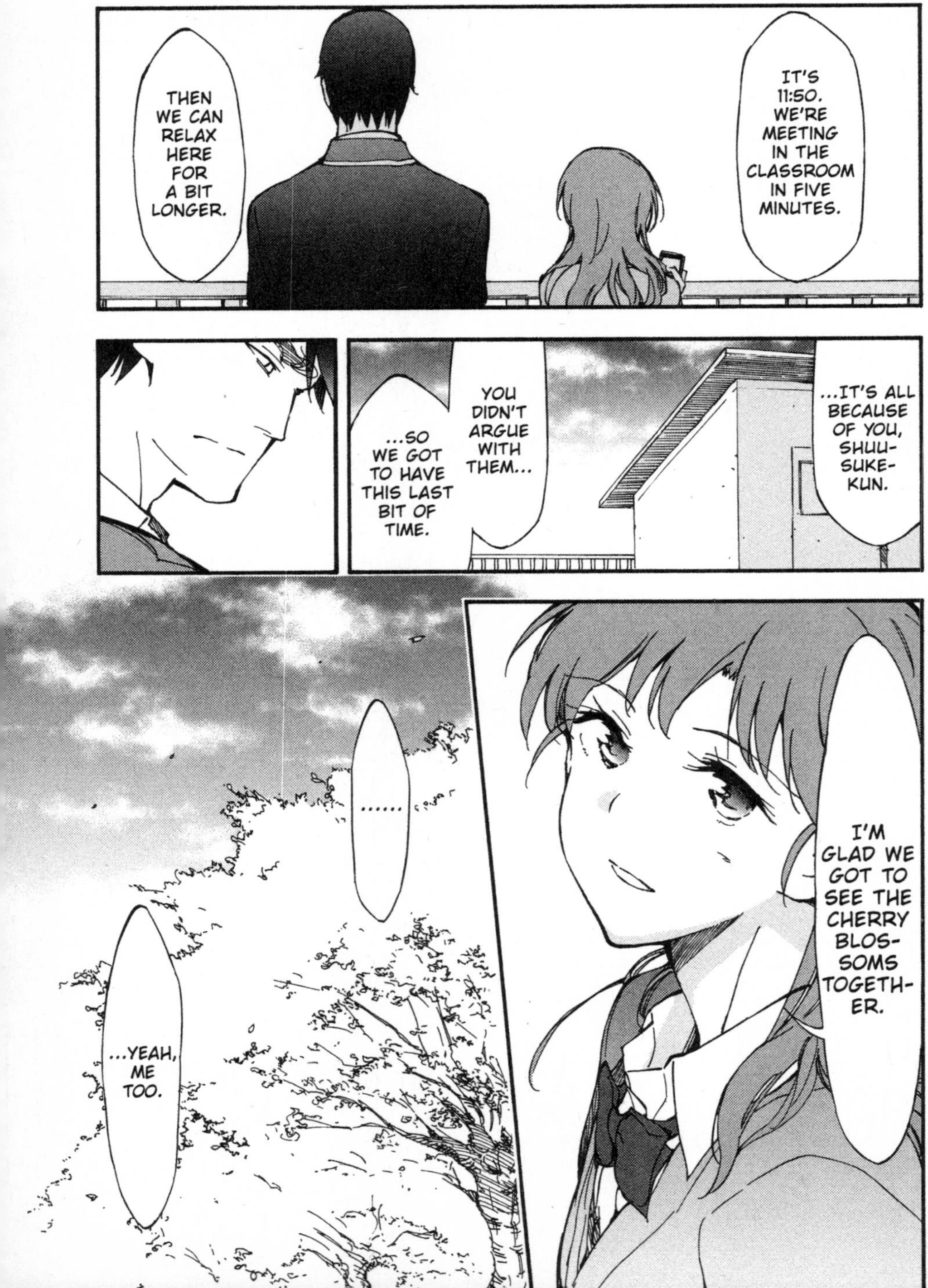
IT'S 11:50. WE'RE MEETING IN THE CLASSROOM IN FIVE MINUTES.
THEN WE CAN RELAX HERE FOR A BIT LONGER.
...IT'S ALL BECAUSE OF YOU, SHUU-SUKE-KUN.
YOU DIDN'T ARGUE WITH THEM...
...SO WE GOT TO HAVE THIS LAST BIT OF TIME.
I'M GLAD WE GOT TO SEE THE CHERRY BLOS-SOMS TOGETH-ER.
......
...YEAH, ME TOO.

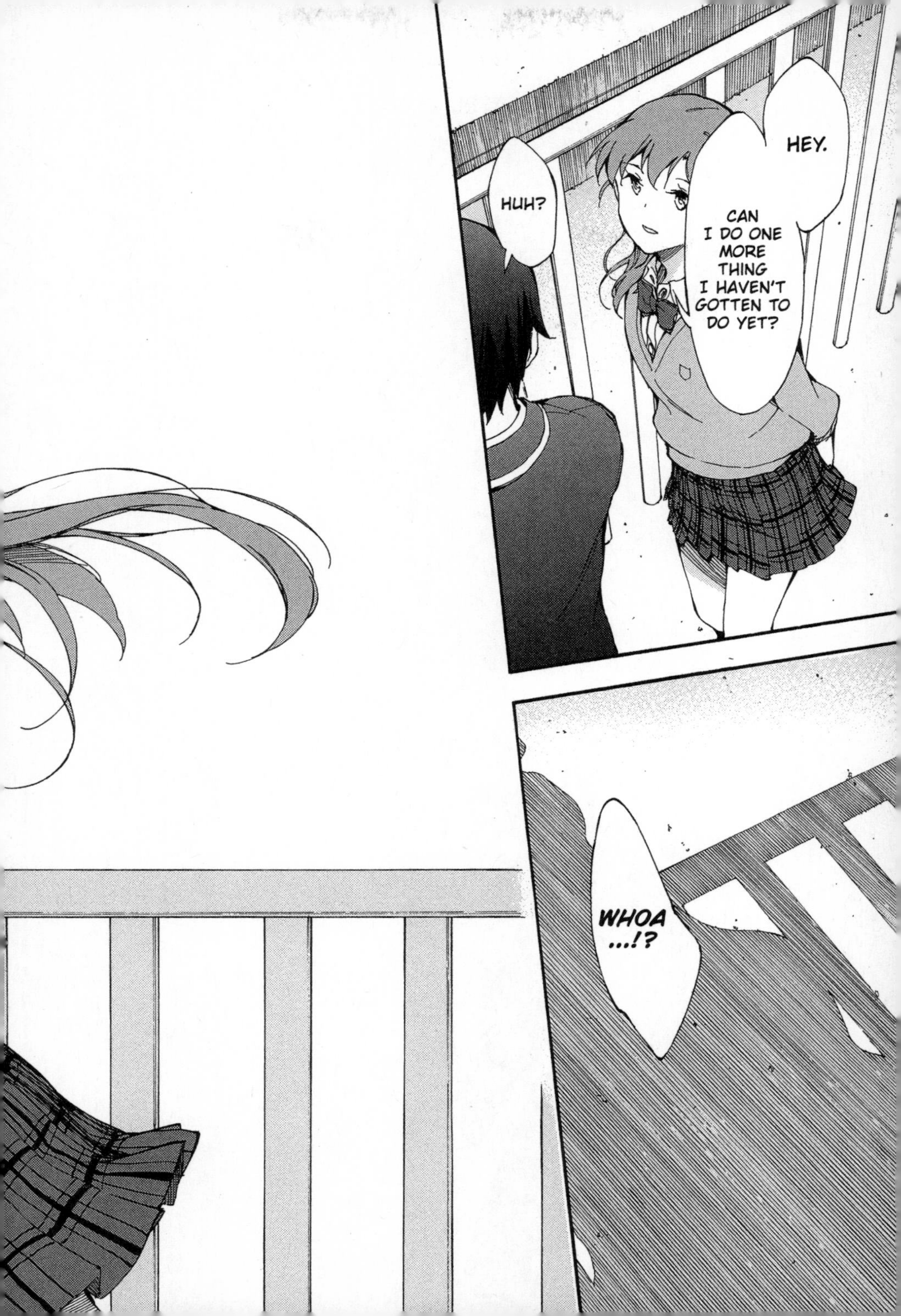
HEY.
CAN I DO ONE MORE THING I HAVEN'T GOTTEN TO DO YET?
HUH?
WHOA ...!?

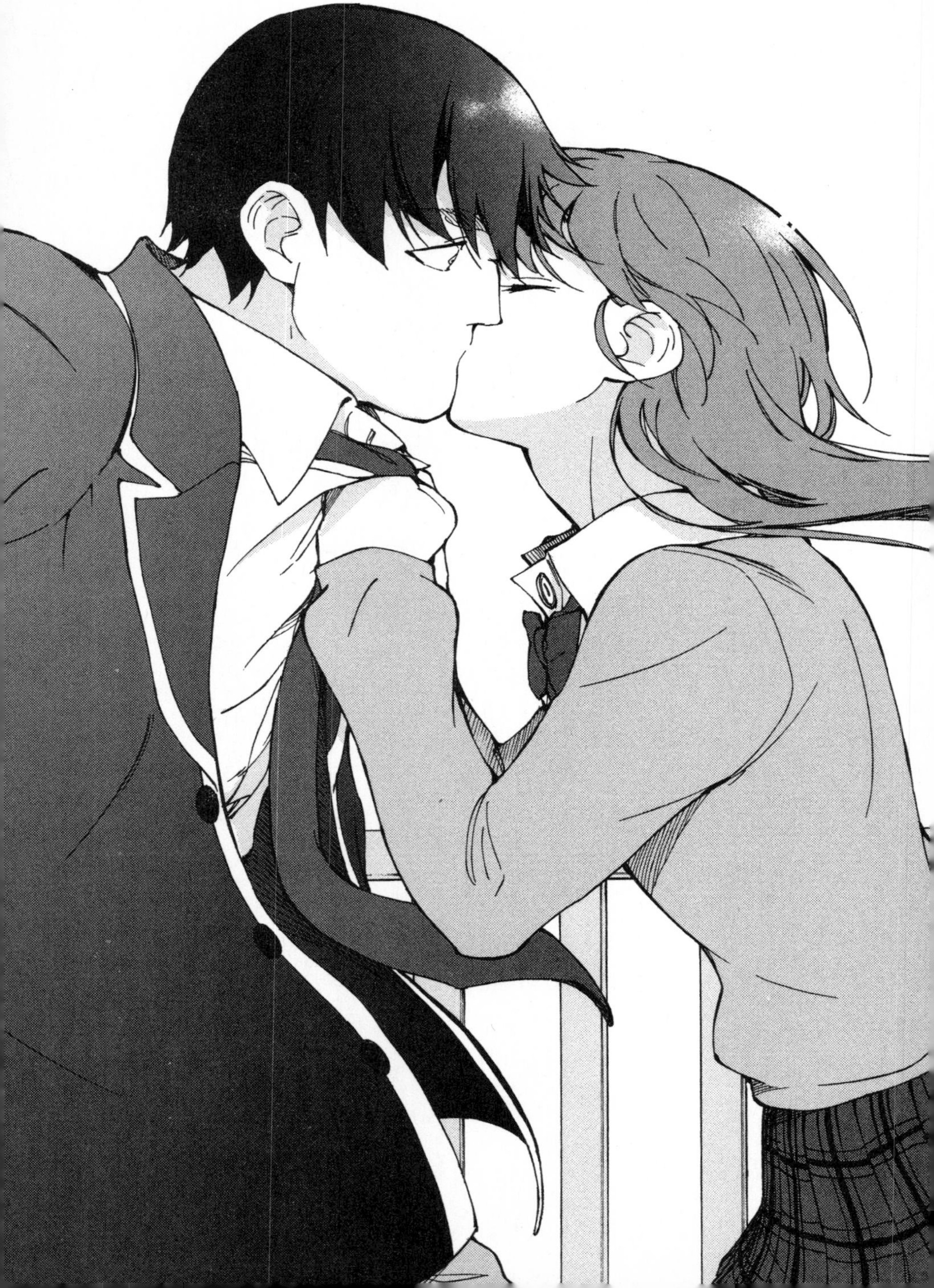

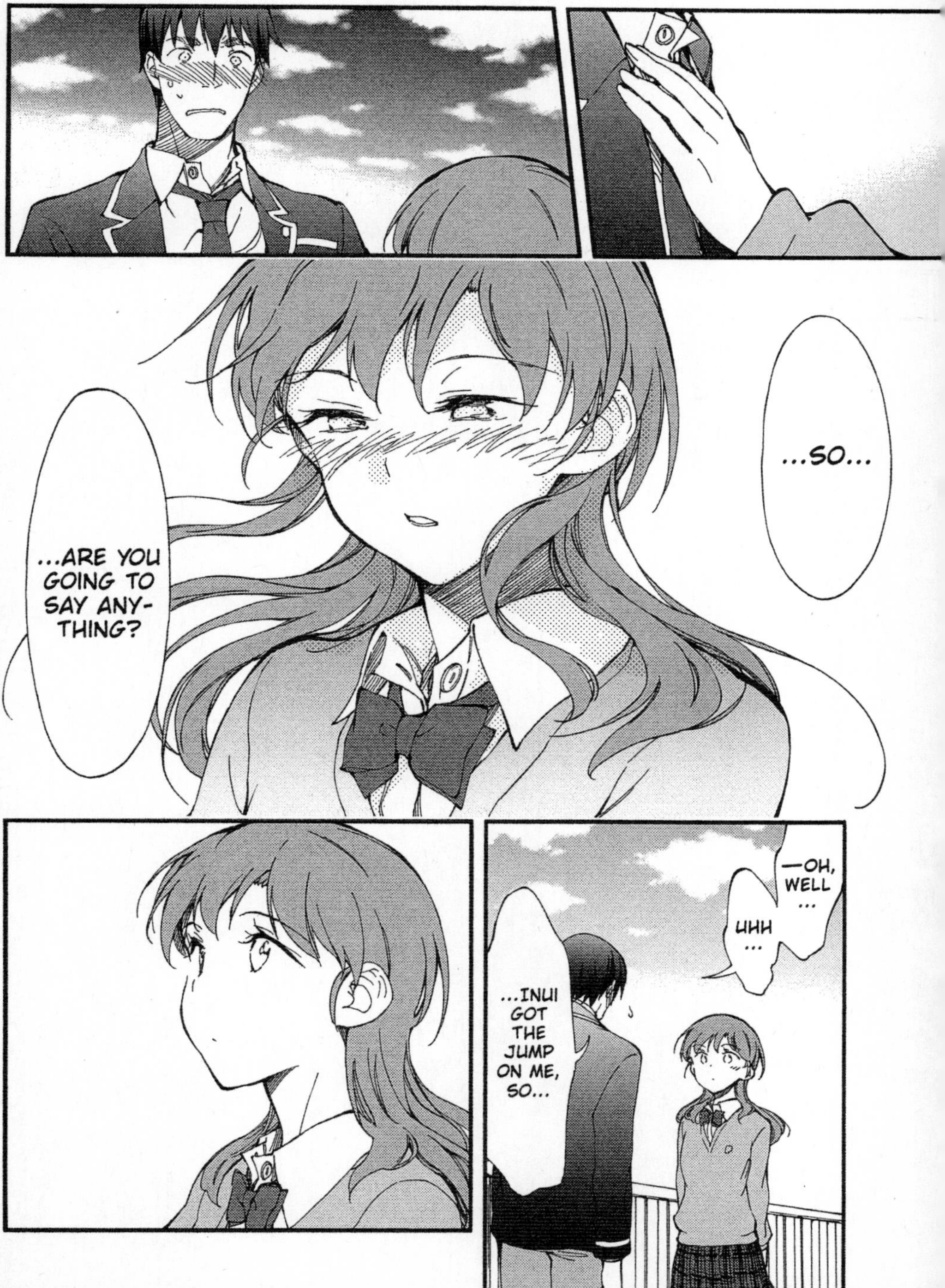
...SO...
...ARE YOU GOING TO SAY ANY-THING?
—OH, WELL ...
UHH ...
...INUI GOT THE JUMP ON ME, SO...

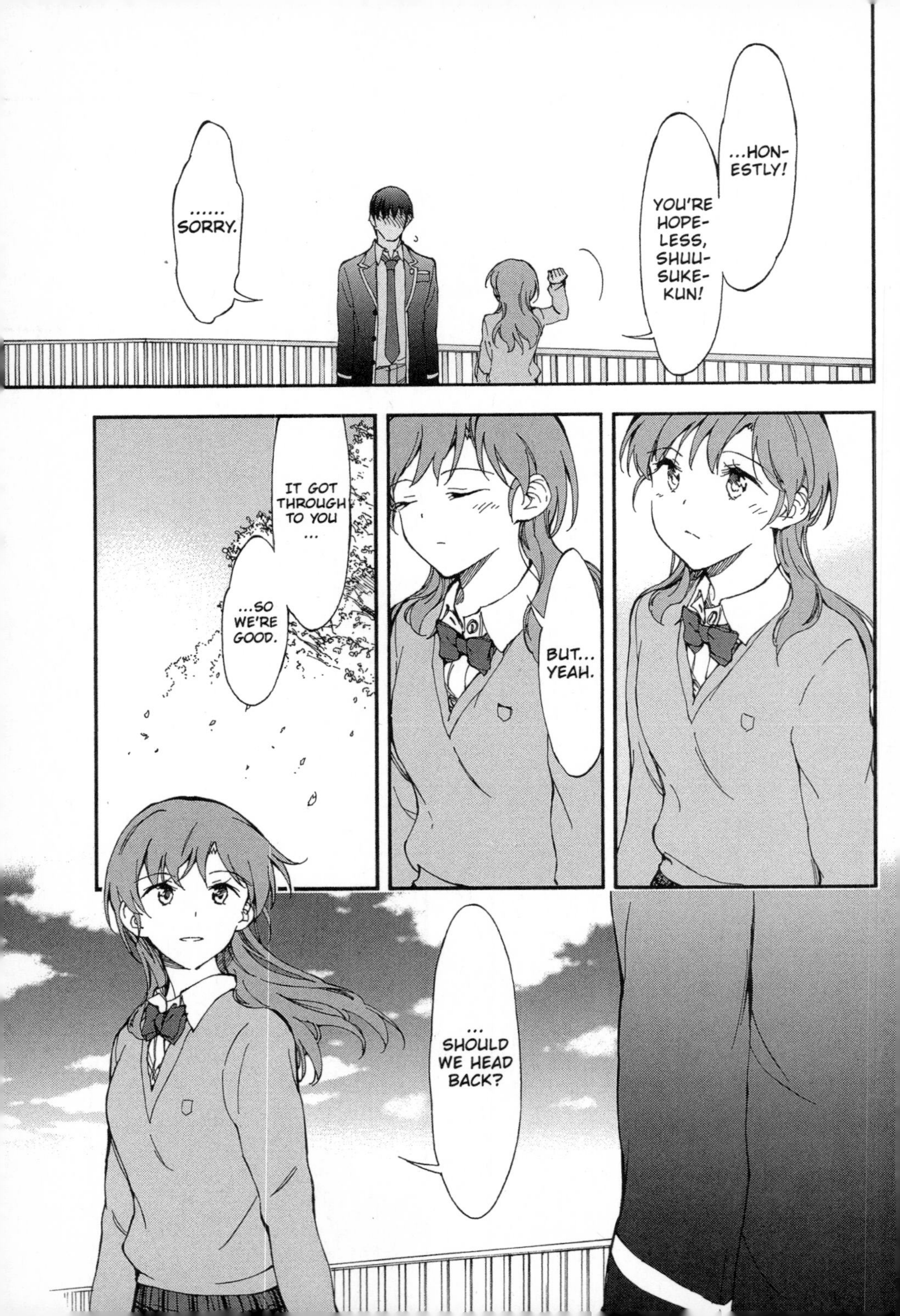
...HON-ESTLY!
YOU'RE HOPE-LESS, SHUU-SUKE-KUN!
...... SORRY.
BUT... YEAH.
IT GOT THROUGH TO YOU ...
...SO WE'RE GOOD.
... SHOULD WE HEAD BACK?

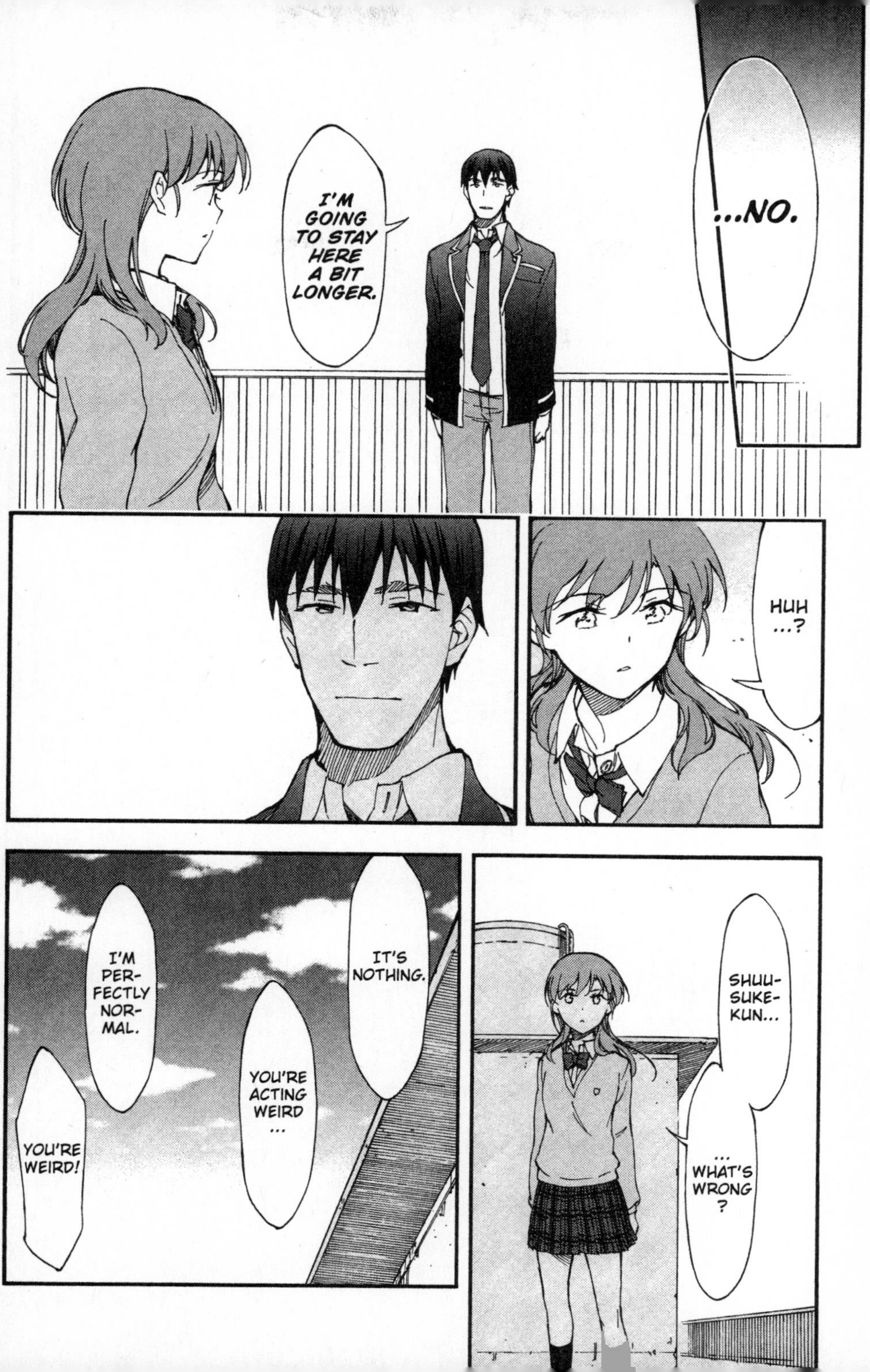
...NO.
I'M GOING TO STAY HERE A BIT LONGER.
HUH ...?
SHUU-SUKE-KUN...
... WHAT'S WRONG ?
IT'S NOTHING.
YOU'RE ACTING WEIRD ...
I'M PER-FECTLY NOR-MAL.
YOU'RE WEIRD!

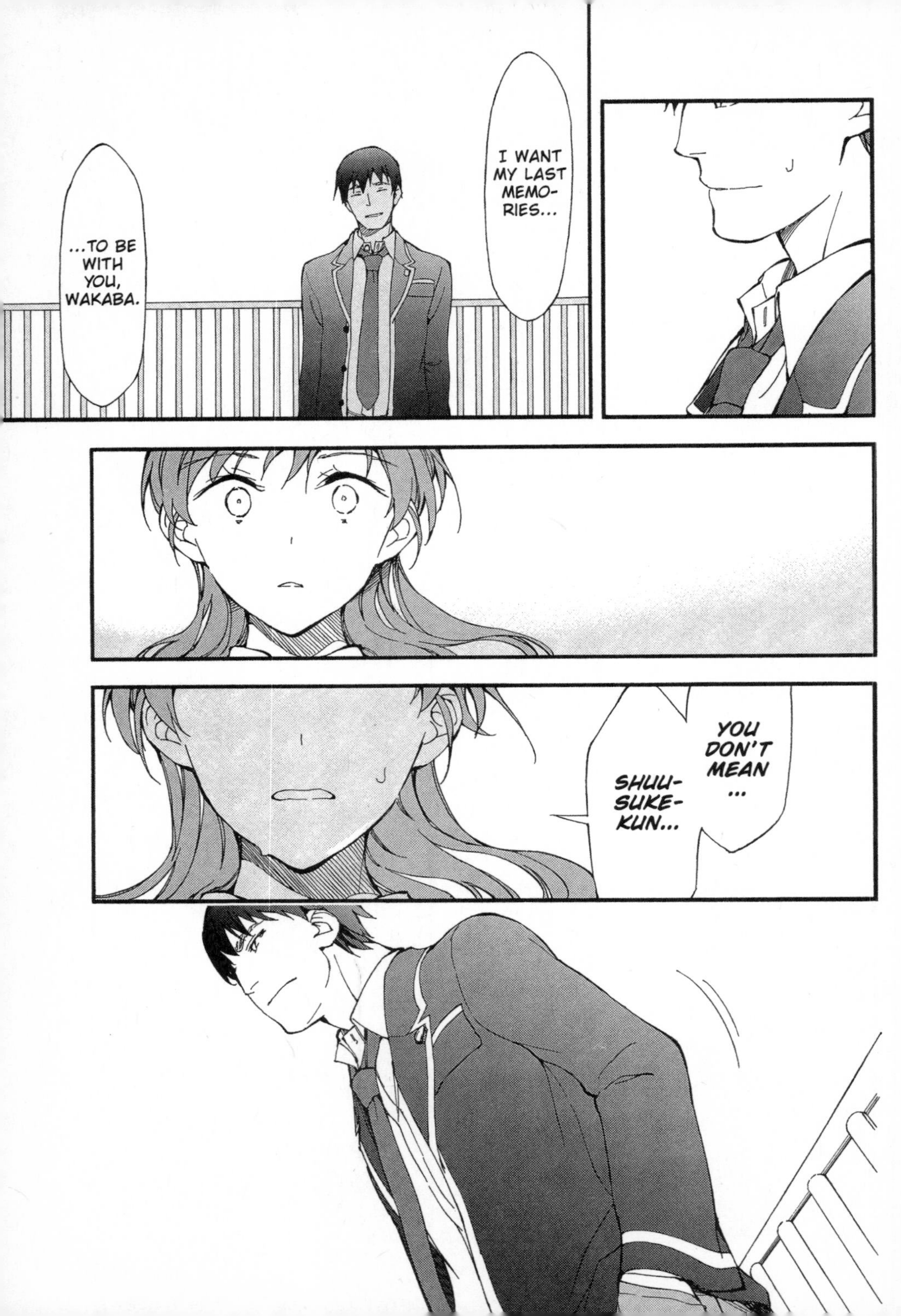
I WANT MY LAST MEMO-RIES...
...TO BE WITH YOU, WAKABA.
YOU DON'T MEAN ...
SHUU-SUKE-KUN...

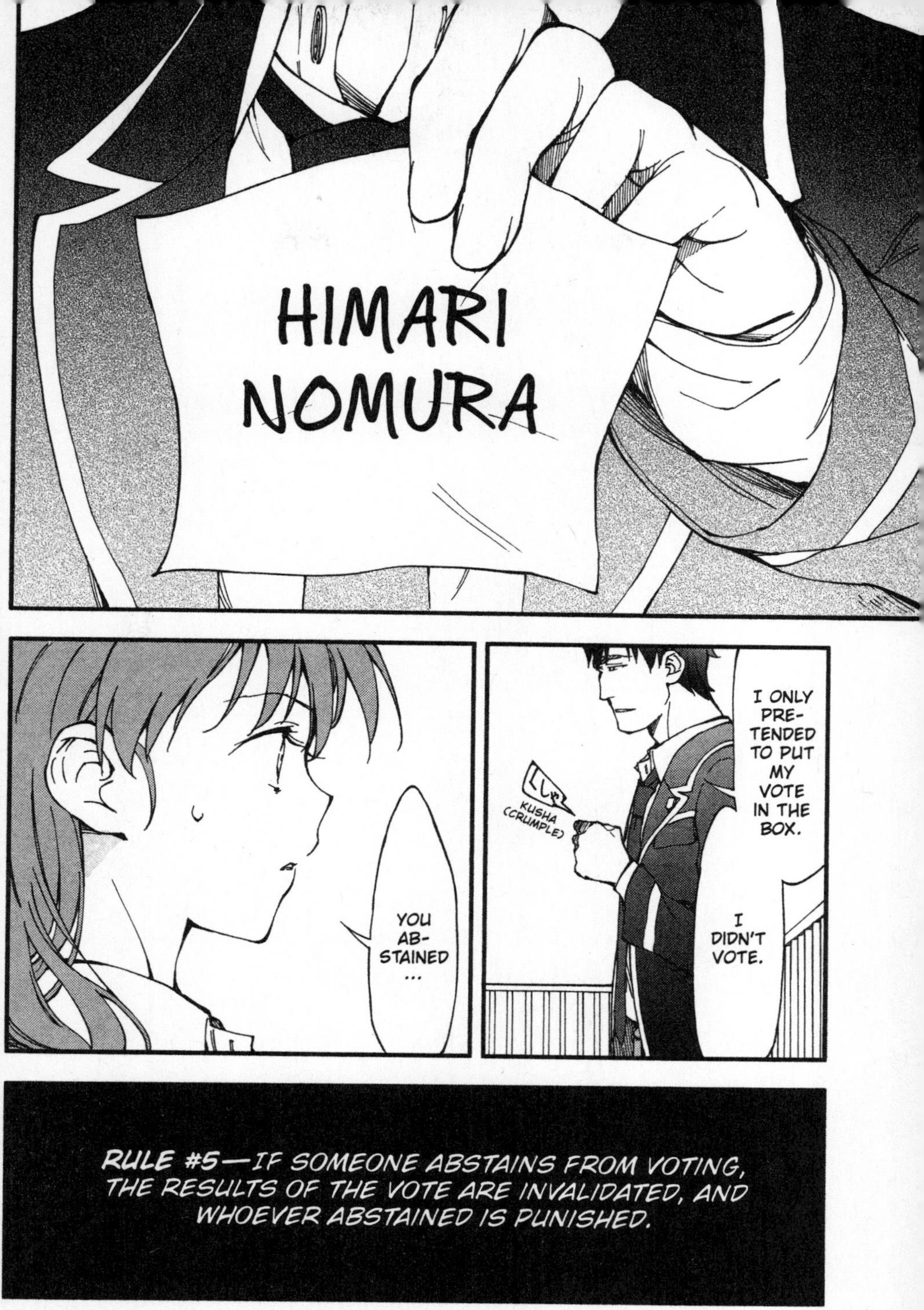
HIMARI NOMURA
I ONLY PRETENDED TO PUT MY VOTE IN THE BOX.
くしゃ
KUSHA (CRUMPLE)
I DIDN'T VOTE.
YOU ABSTAINED...
RULE #5—IF SOMEONE ABSTAINS FROM VOTING, THE RESULTS OF THE VOTE ARE INVALIDATED, AND WHOEVER ABSTAINED IS PUNISHED.

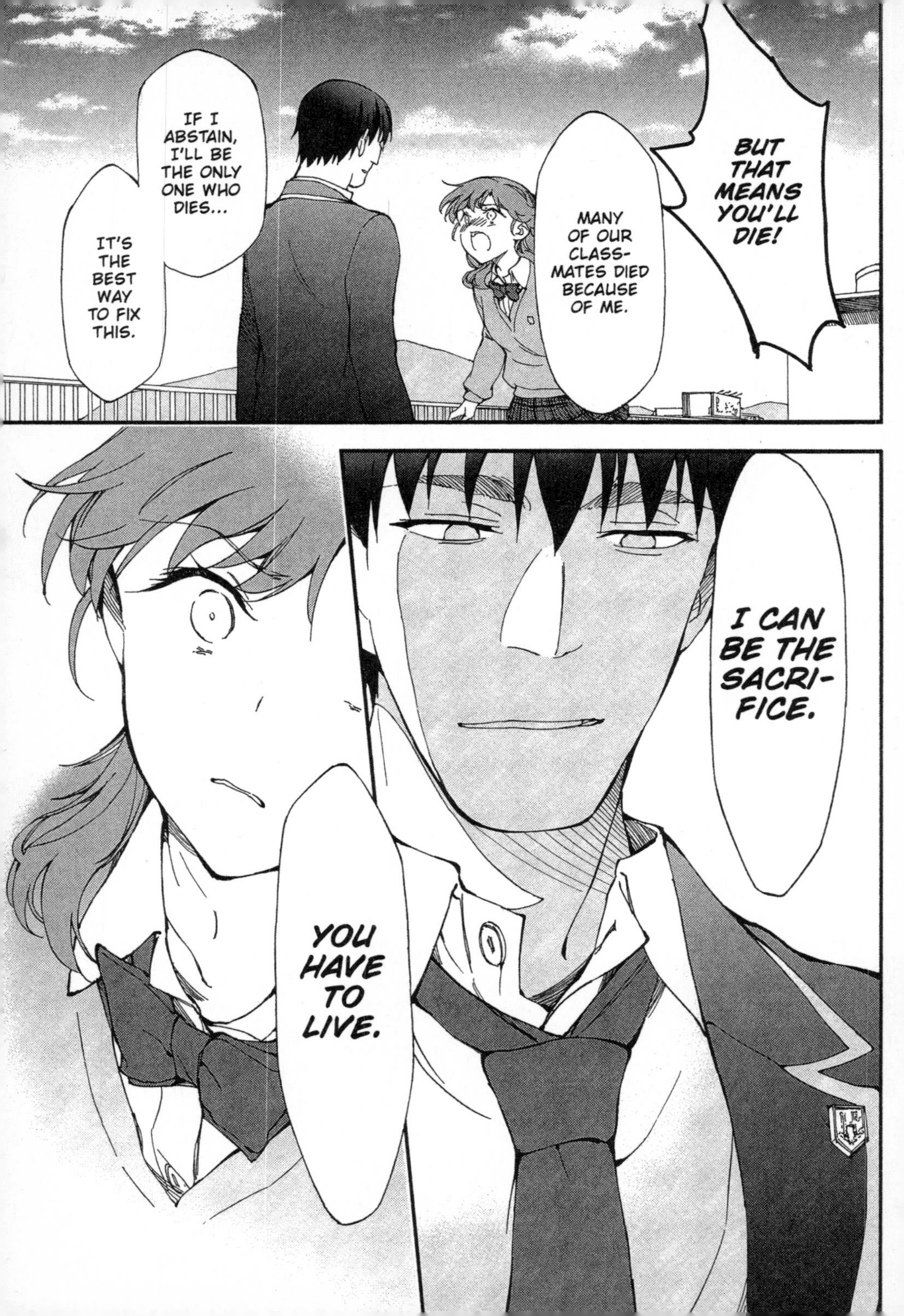
BUT THAT MEANS YOU'LL DIE!
MANY OF OUR CLASS-MATES DIED BECAUSE OF ME.
IF I ABSTAIN, I'LL BE THE ONLY ONE WHO DIES...
IT'S THE BEST WAY TO FIX THIS.
I CAN BE THE SACRI-FICE.
YOU HAVE TO LIVE.

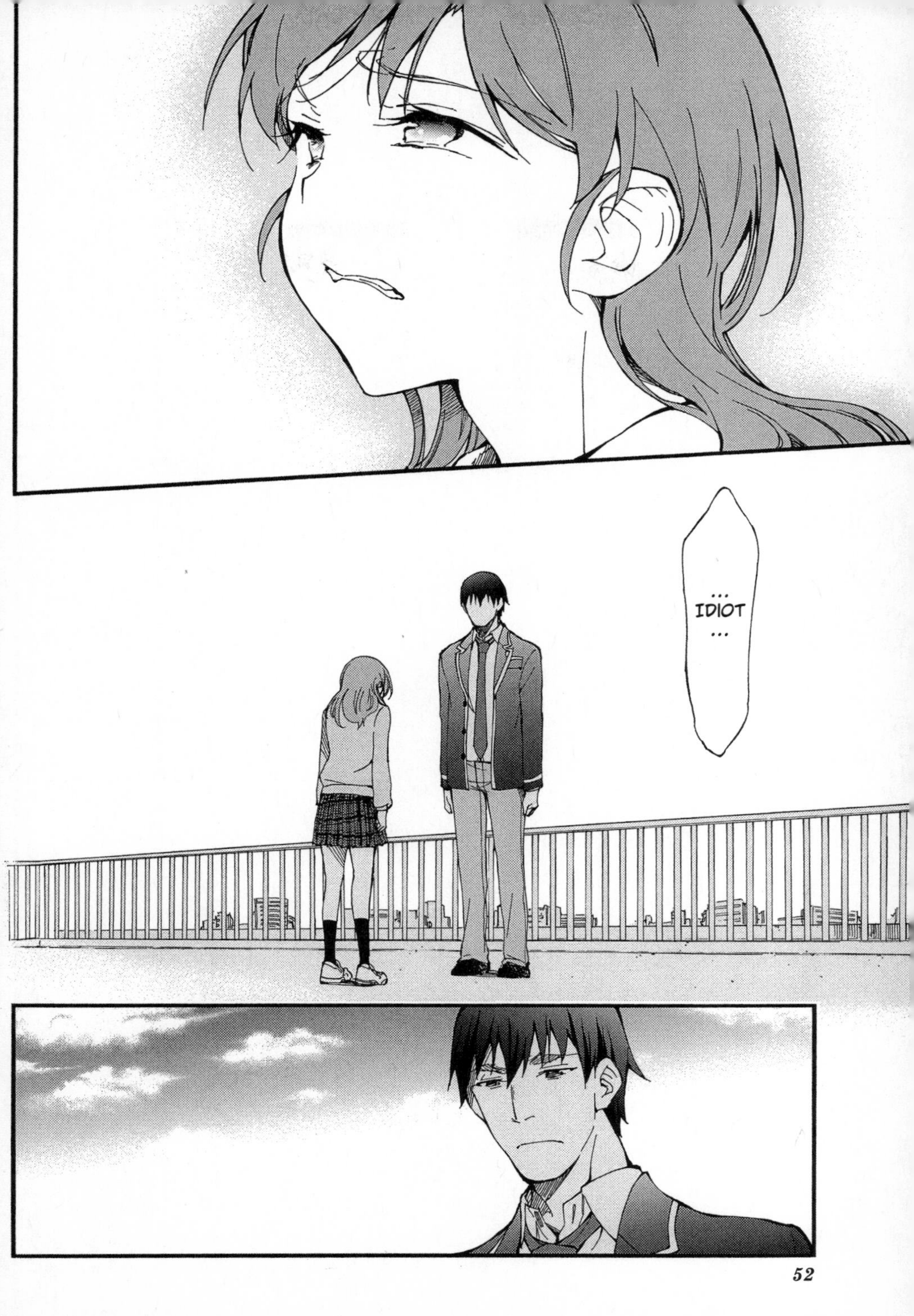
...
IDIOT
...

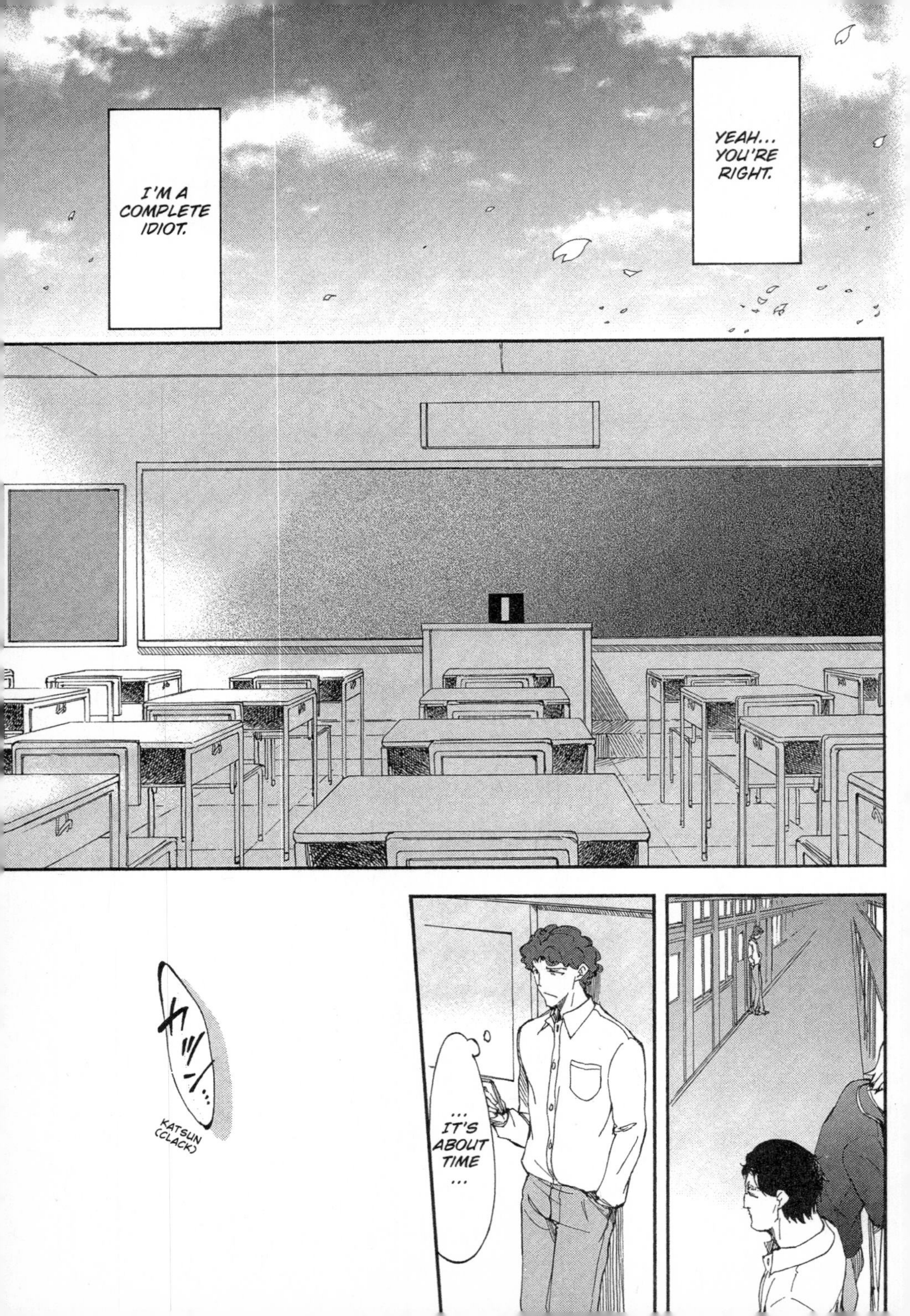
YEAH... YOU'RE RIGHT.
I'M A COMPLETE IDIOT.
... IT'S ABOUT TIME ...
KATSUN (CLACK)

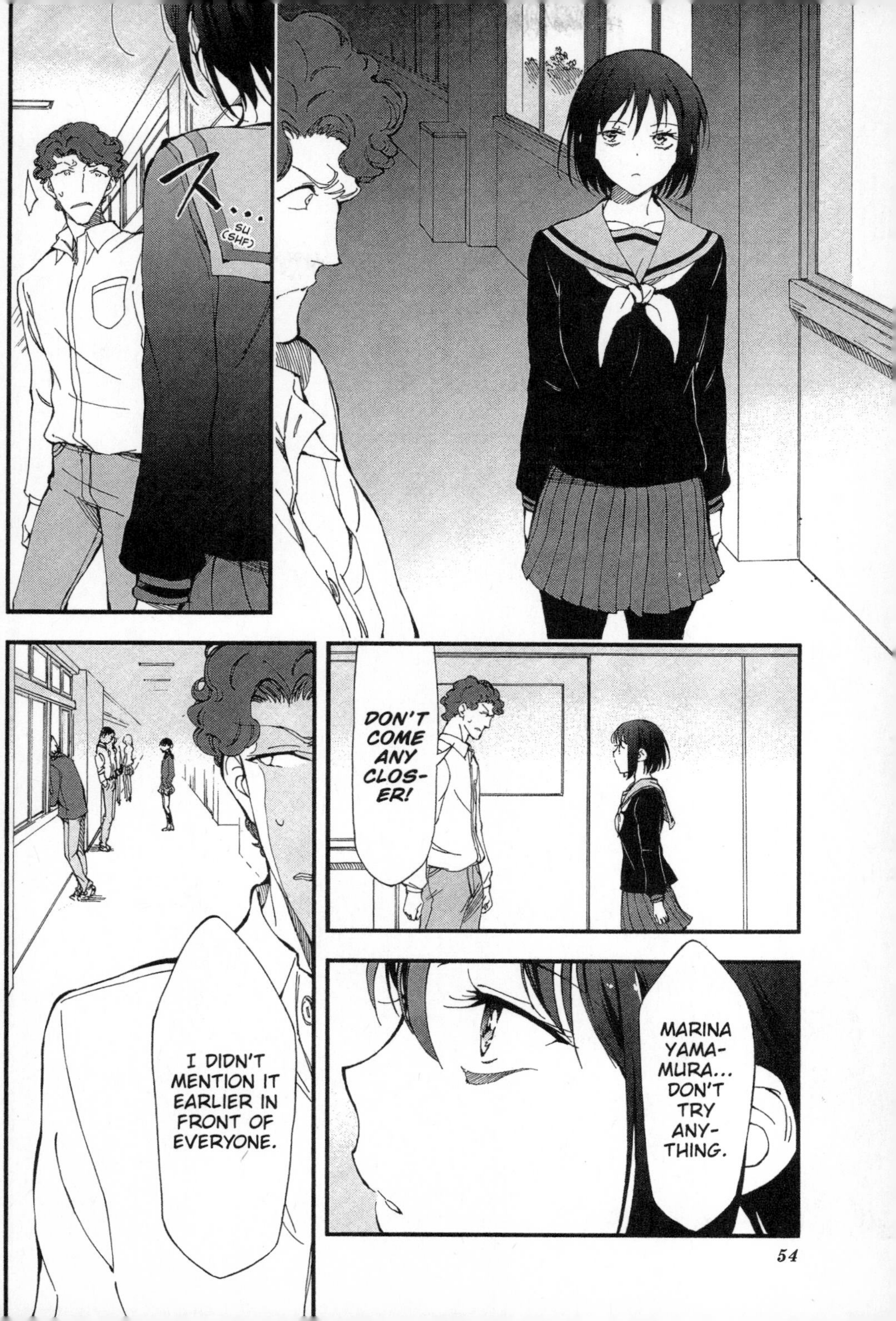
ス...
SU (SHF)
DON'T COME ANY CLOSER!
MARINA YAMAMURA... DON'T TRY ANYTHING.
I DIDN'T MENTION IT EARLIER IN FRONT OF EVERYONE.

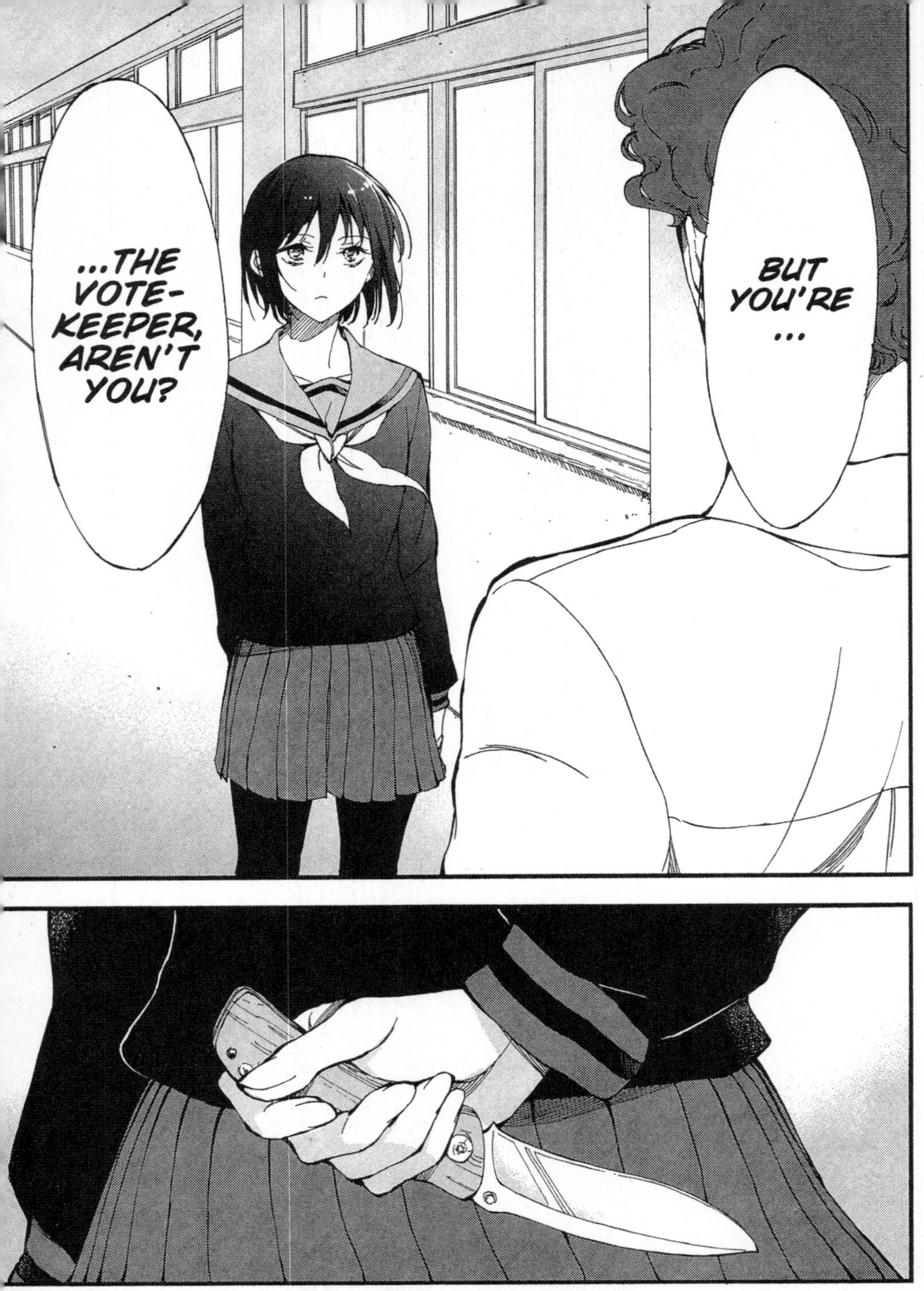
BUT YOU'RE ...
...THE VOTE-KEEPER, AREN'T YOU?

TOHYO GAME

One **black** ballot ^{to} you

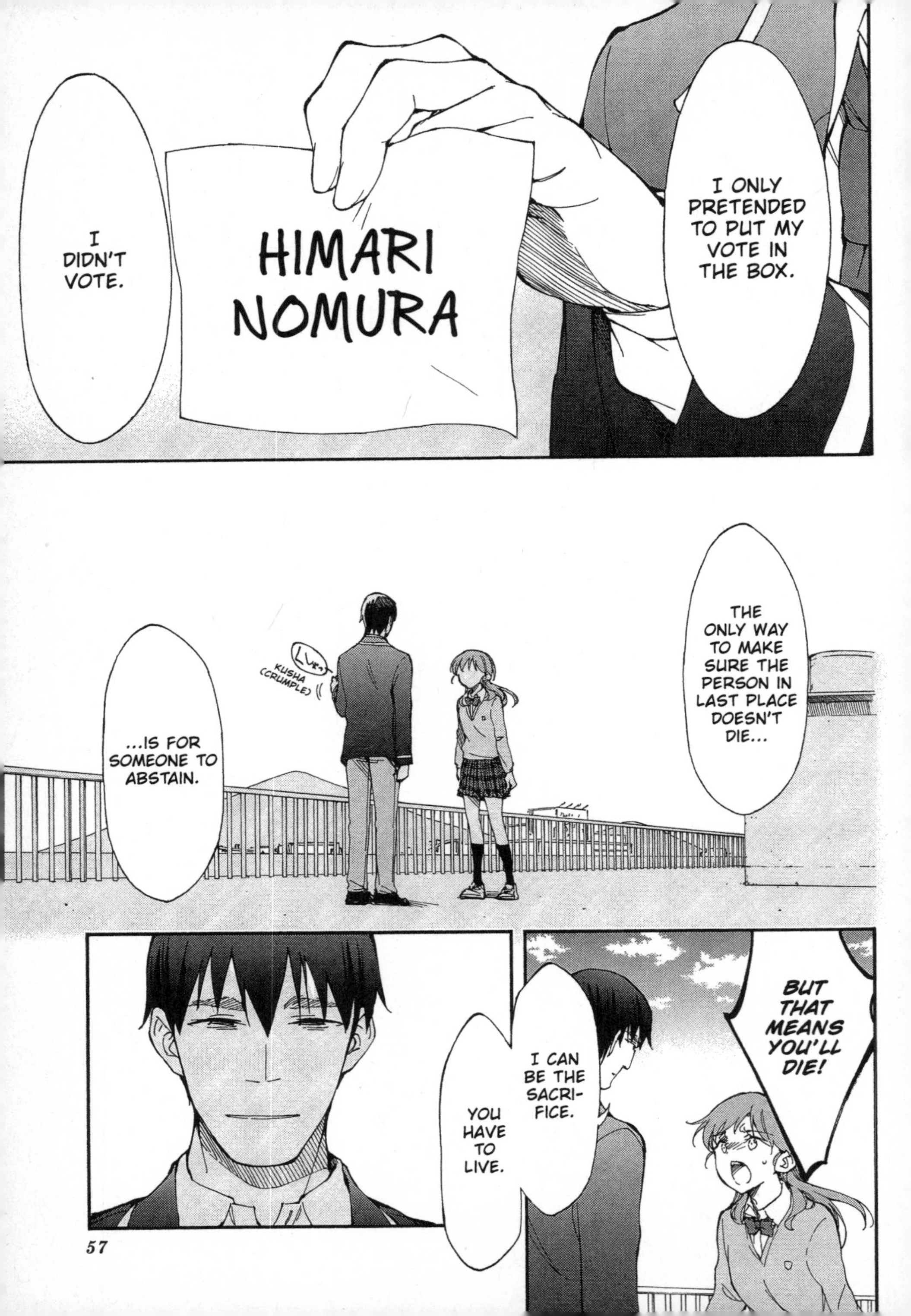
I ONLY PRETENDED TO PUT MY VOTE IN THE BOX.
HIMARI NOMURA
I DIDN'T VOTE.
THE ONLY WAY TO MAKE SURE THE PERSON IN LAST PLACE DOESN'T DIE...
KUSHA (CRUMPLE)
...IS FOR SOMEONE TO ABSTAIN.
BUT THAT MEANS YOU'LL DIE!
I CAN BE THE SACRIFICE.
YOU HAVE TO LIVE.

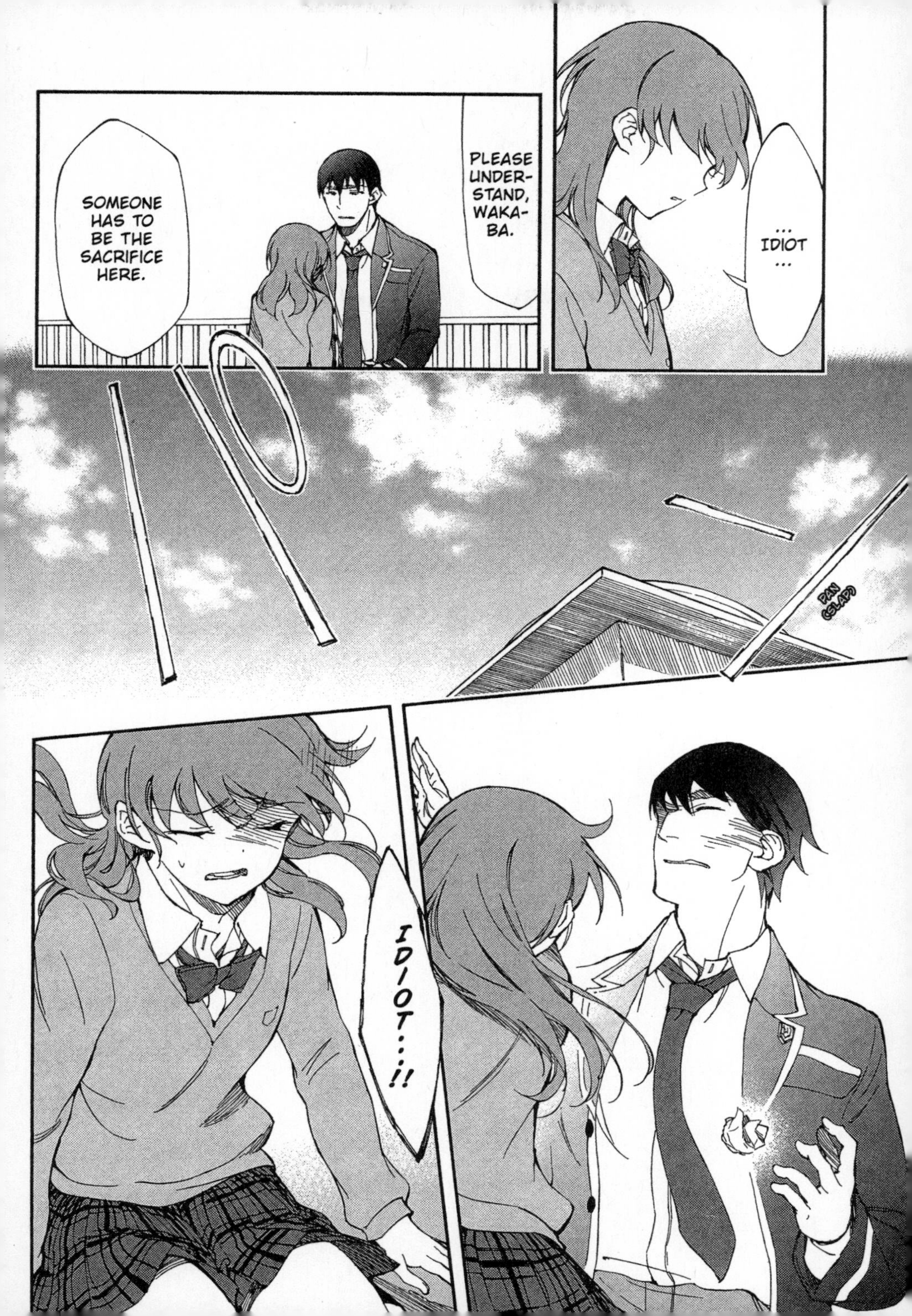
...IDIOT...
PLEASE UNDERSTAND, WAKABA.
SOMEONE HAS TO BE THE SACRIFICE HERE.
PAN (SLAP)
IDIOT...!!

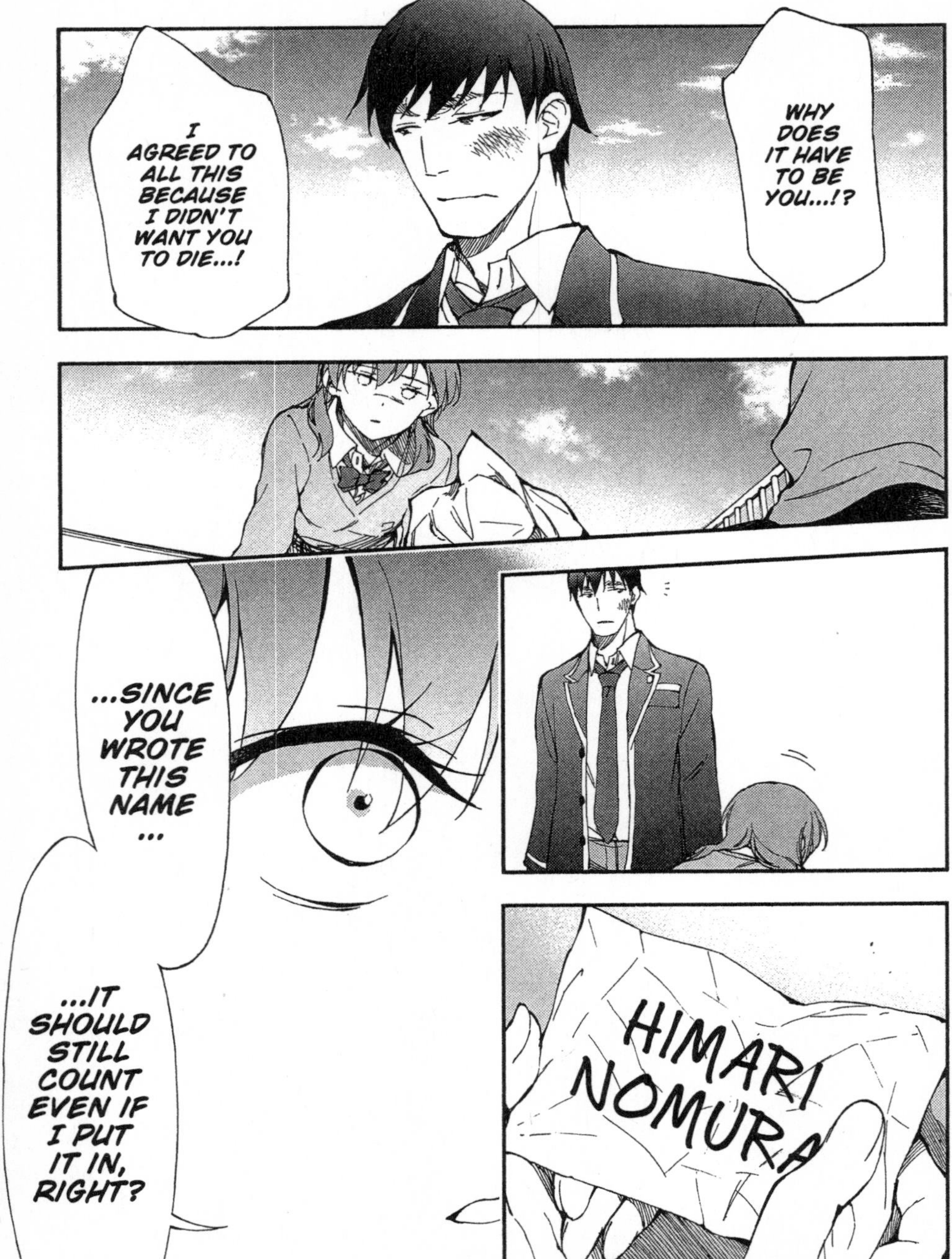
WHY DOES IT HAVE TO BE YOU...!?
I AGREED TO ALL THIS BECAUSE I DIDN'T WANT YOU TO DIE...!
HIMARI NOMURA
...SINCE YOU WROTE THIS NAME ...
...IT SHOULD STILL COUNT EVEN IF I PUT IT IN, RIGHT?

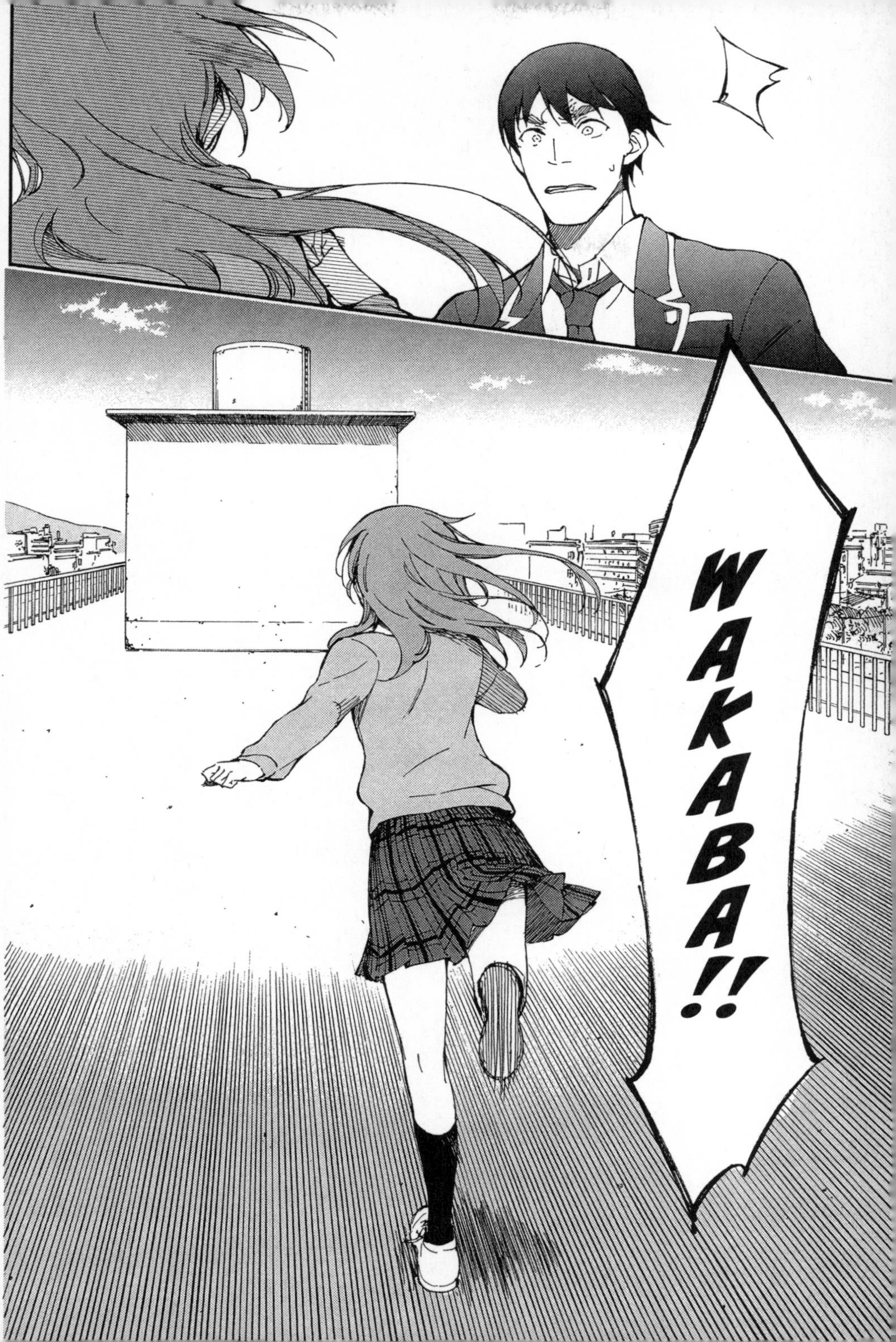
WAKABA!!

Popularity Vote Round 5 Current Results

ENTRY #1
WAKABA OOTSUKI
O VOTES

ENTRY #2
YUI SHIMAKAWA
2 VOTES

ENTRY #3
HARUKA MIURA
2 VOTES

ENTRY #4
HIMARI NOMURA
1 VOTE

ENTRY #5
IKUMI NAGASE
2 VOTES

minutes left until the end of voting

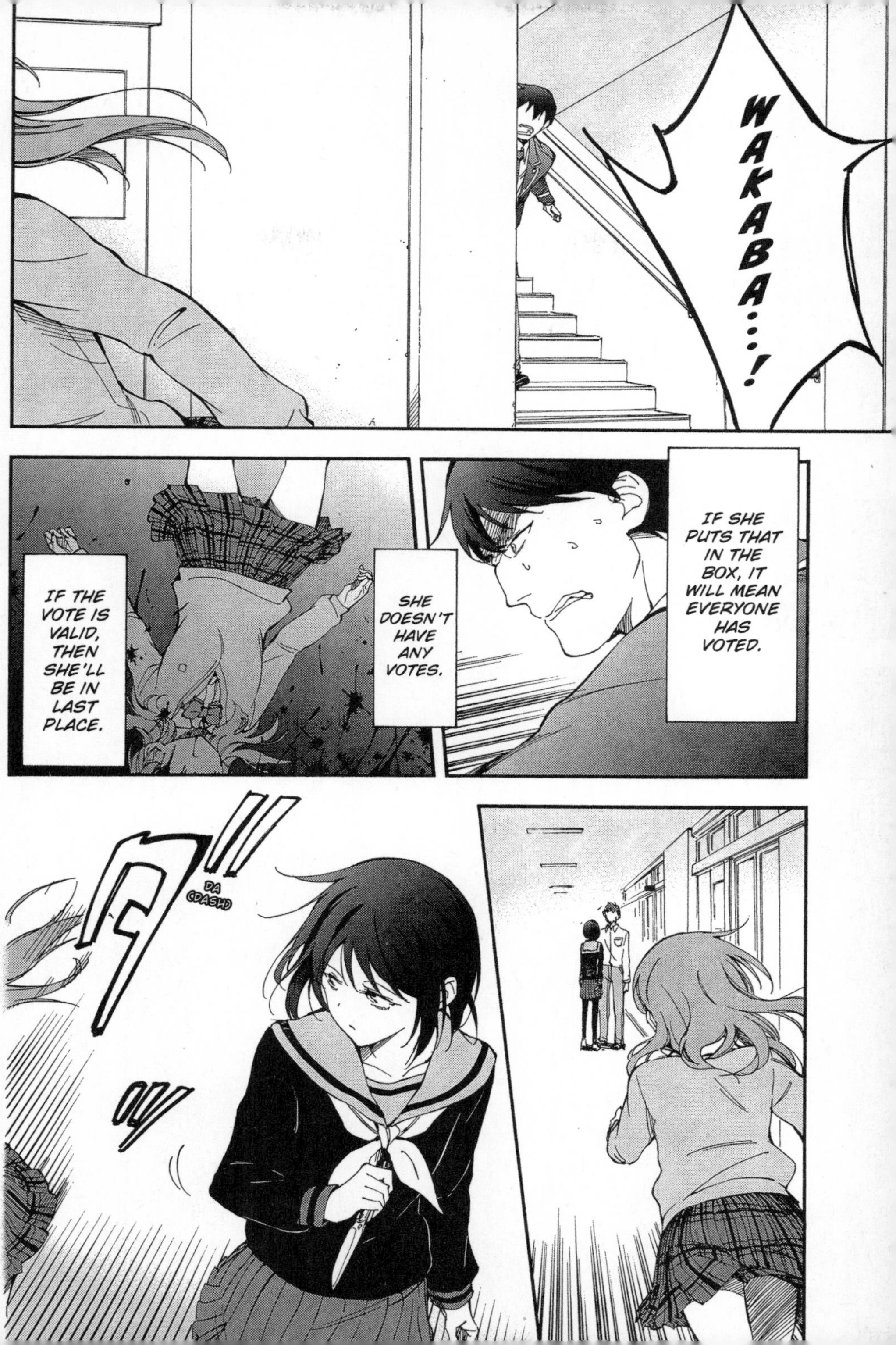
WAKABA...!
IF SHE PUTS THAT IN THE BOX, IT WILL MEAN EVERYONE HAS VOTED.
SHE DOESN'T HAVE ANY VOTES.
IF THE VOTE IS VALID, THEN SHE'LL BE IN LAST PLACE.
DA (DASH)

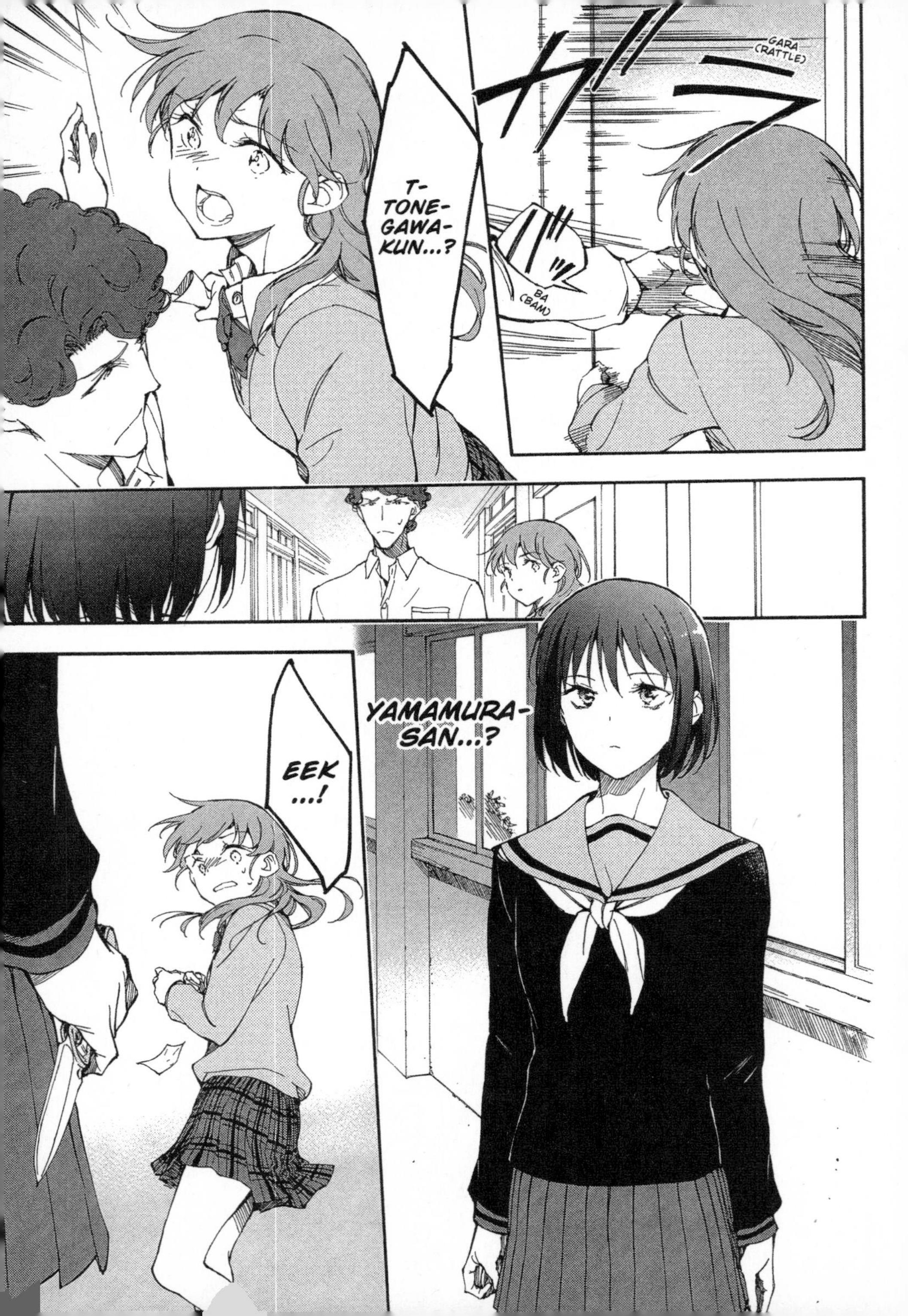
GARA (RATTLE)
BA (BAM)
T-TONE-GAWA-KUN...?
YAMAMURA-SAN...?
EEK ...!

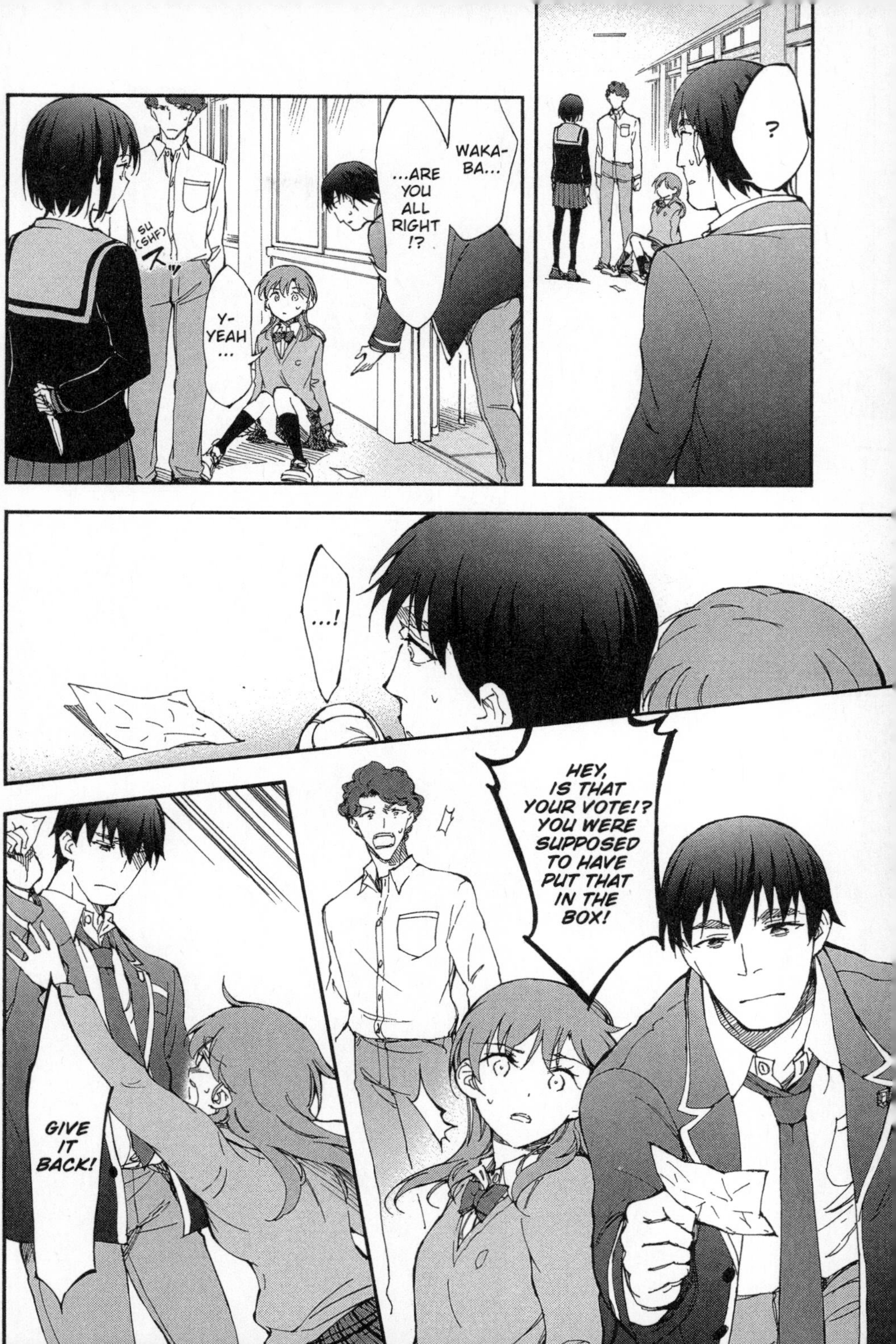
?
WAKA-BA...
...ARE YOU ALL RIGHT!?
Y-YEAH...
SU (SHF)
...!
HEY, IS THAT YOUR VOTE!? YOU WERE SUPPOSED TO HAVE PUT THAT IN THE BOX!
GIVE IT BACK!

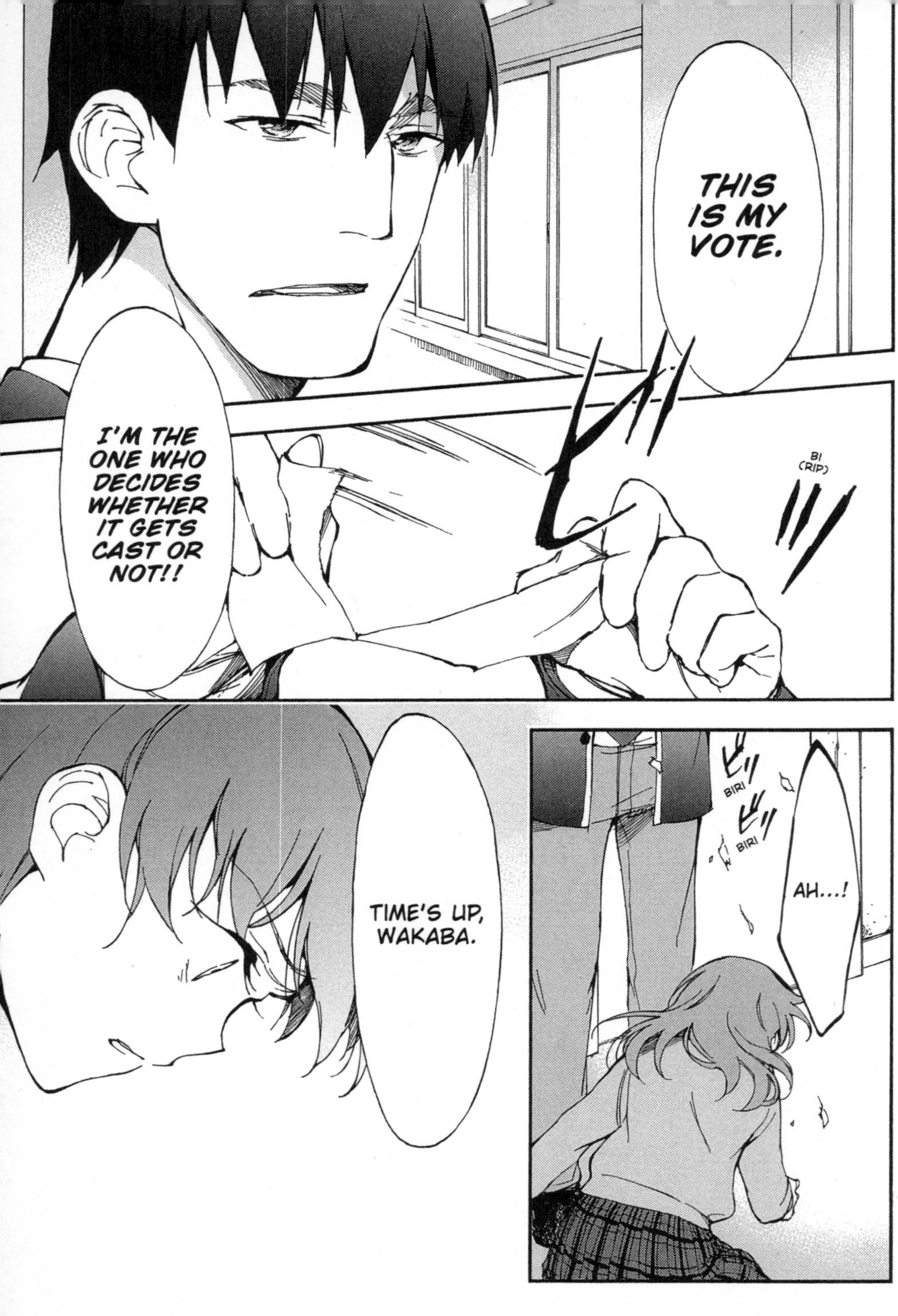
THIS IS MY VOTE.
BI (RIP)
I'M THE ONE WHO DECIDES WHETHER IT GETS CAST OR NOT!!
BIRI
BIRI
AH...!
TIME'S UP, WAKABA.

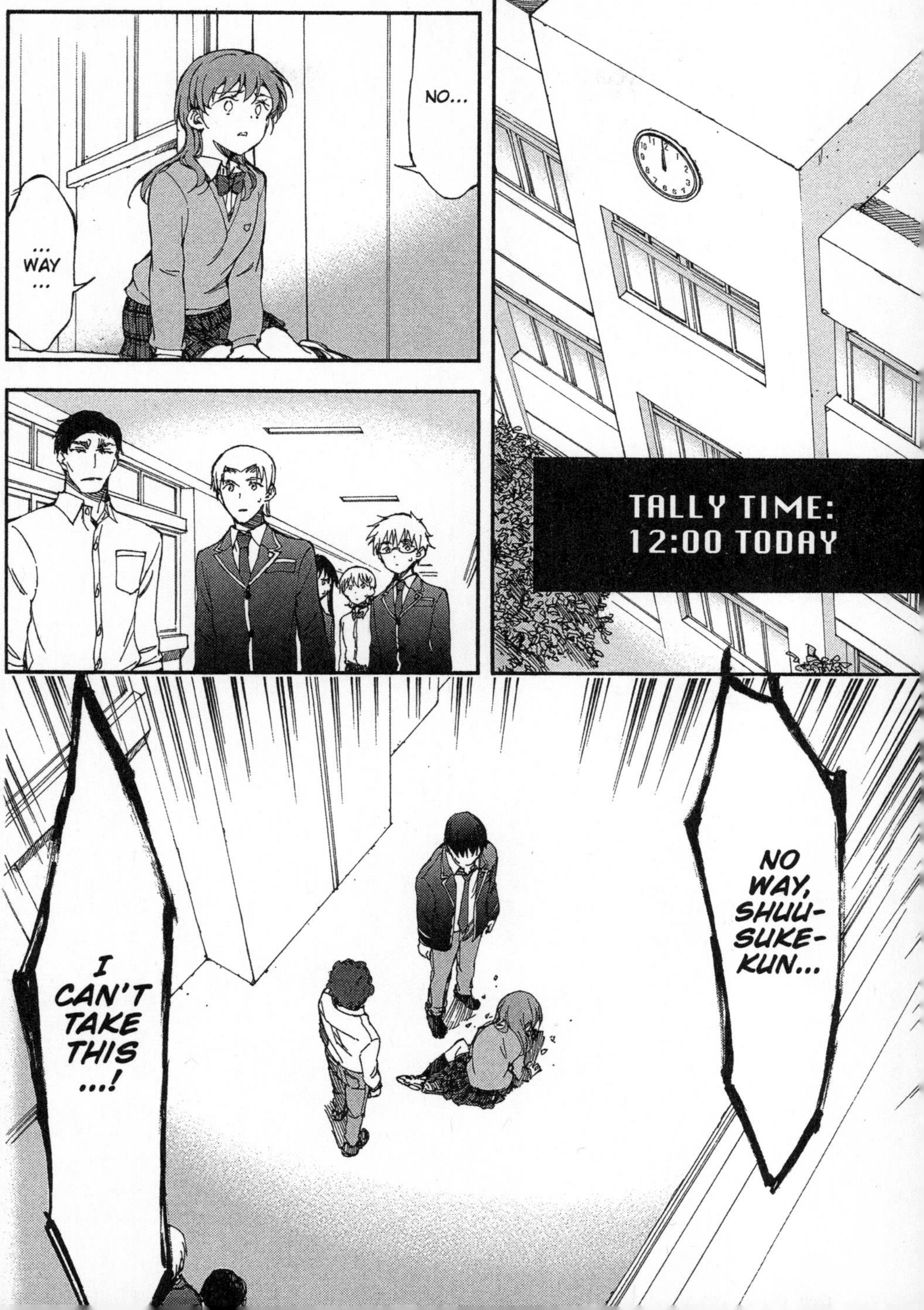
TALLY TIME:
12:00 TODAY
NO...
... WAY ...
NO WAY, SHUU-SUKE-KUN...
I CAN'T TAKE THIS ...!

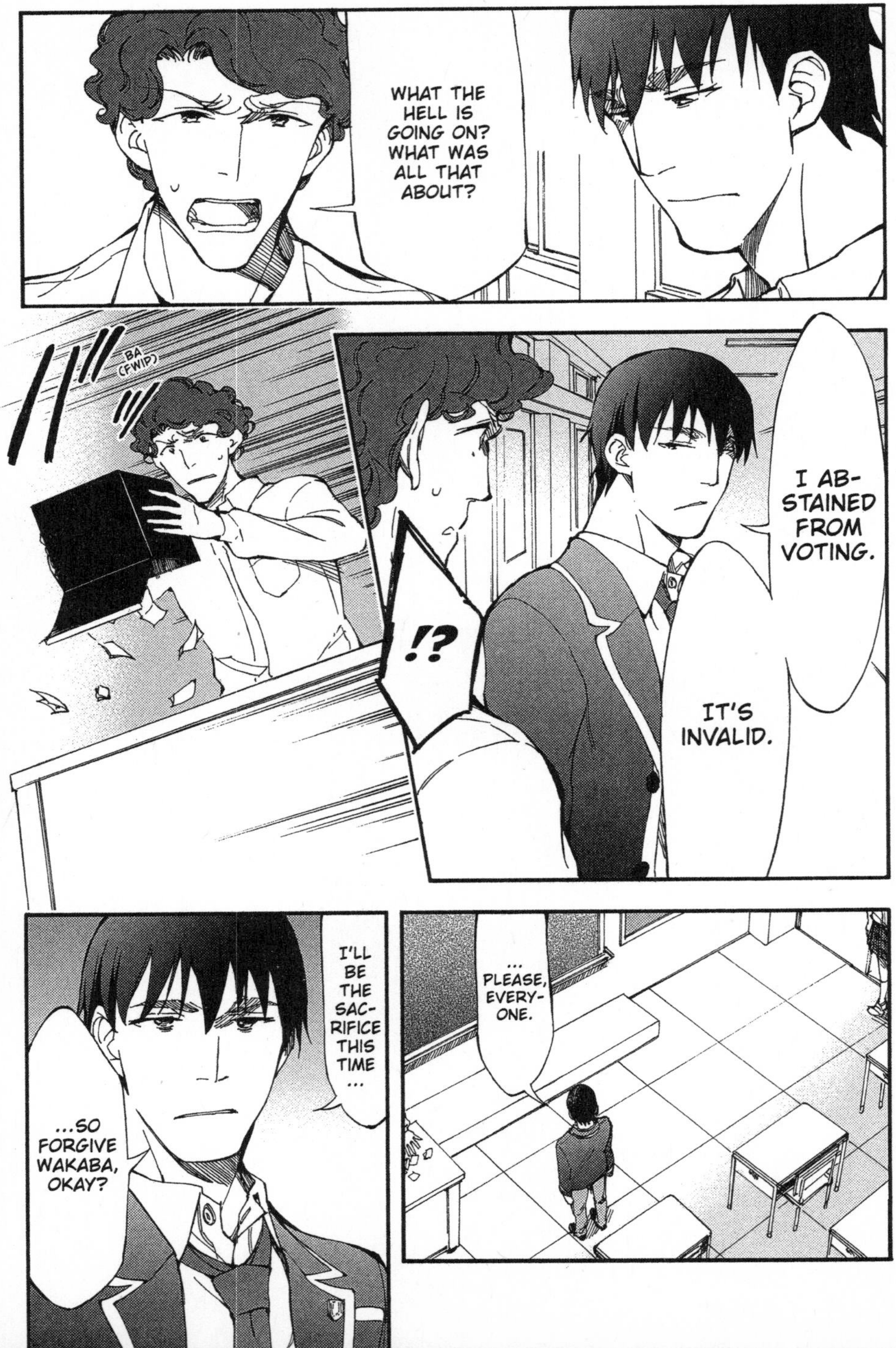
WHAT THE HELL IS GOING ON? WHAT WAS ALL THAT ABOUT?
I AB-STAINED FROM VOTING.
IT'S INVALID.
!?
BA (FWIP)
...PLEASE, EVERY-ONE.
I'LL BE THE SAC-RIFICE THIS TIME...
...SO FORGIVE WAKABA, OKAY?

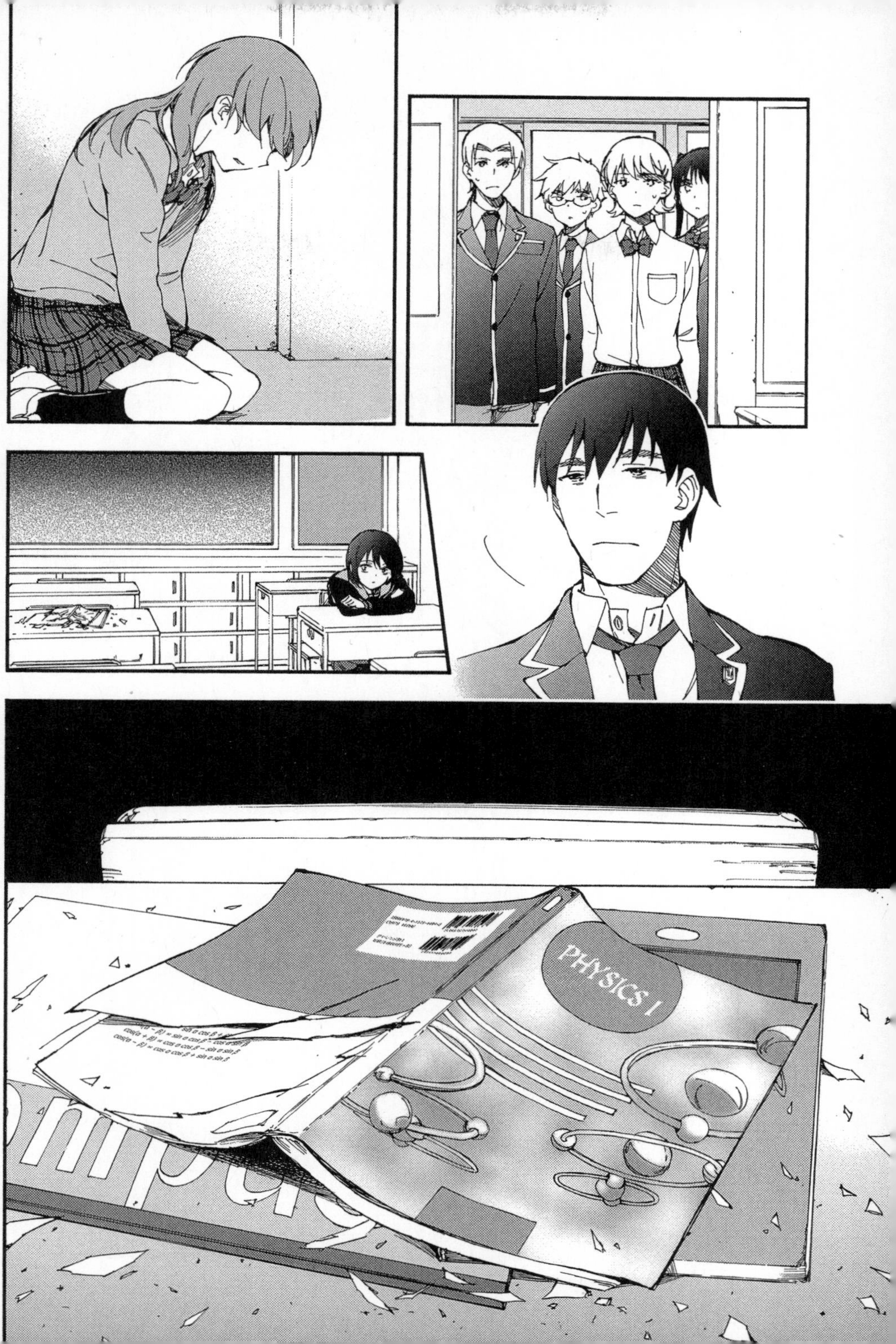
PHYSICS I

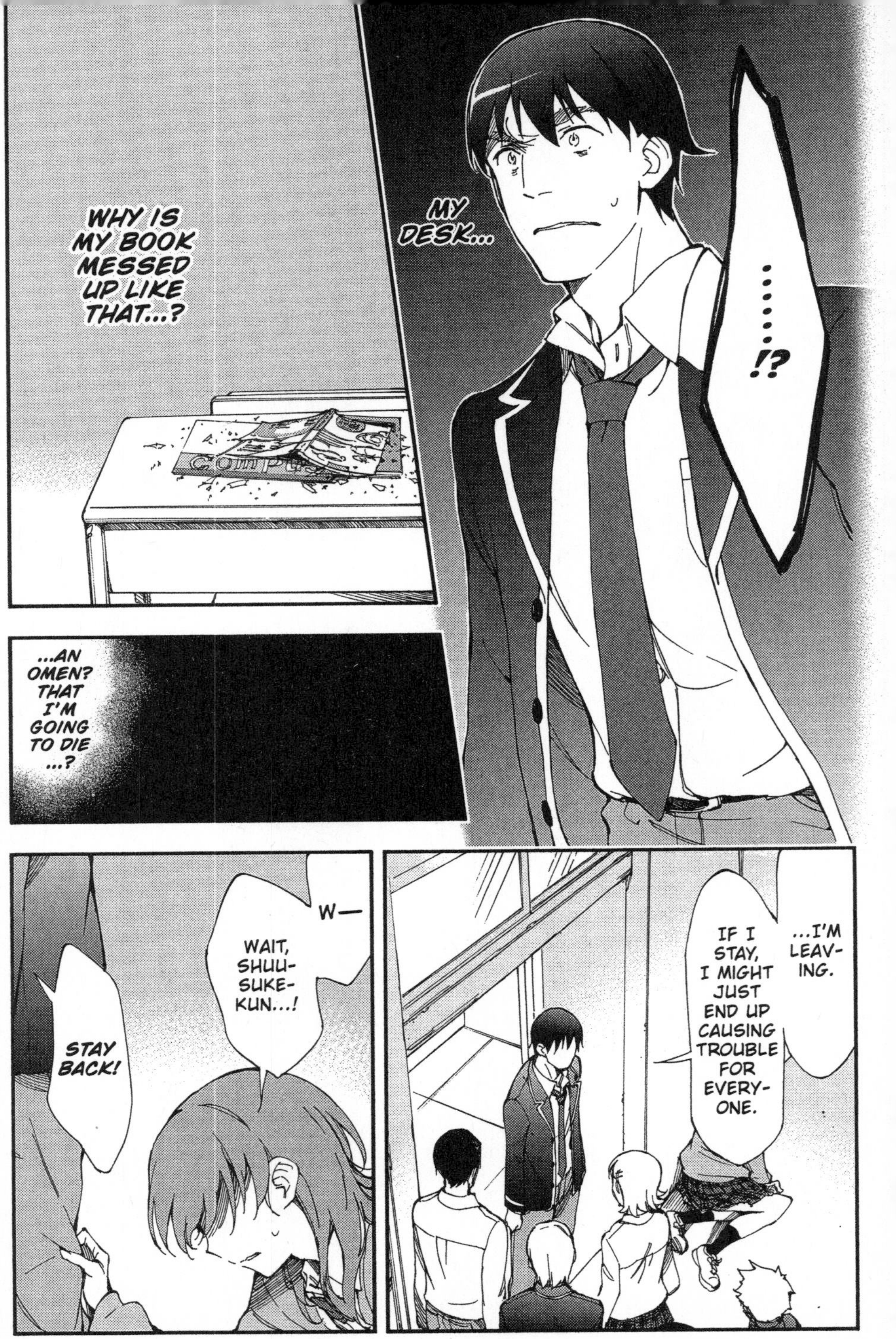
......!?
MY DESK...
WHY IS MY BOOK MESSED UP LIKE THAT...?
...AN OMEN? THAT I'M GOING TO DIE ...?
...I'M LEAVING.
IF I STAY, I MIGHT JUST END UP CAUSING TROUBLE FOR EVERYONE.
W—
WAIT, SHUUSUKE-KUN...!
STAY BACK!

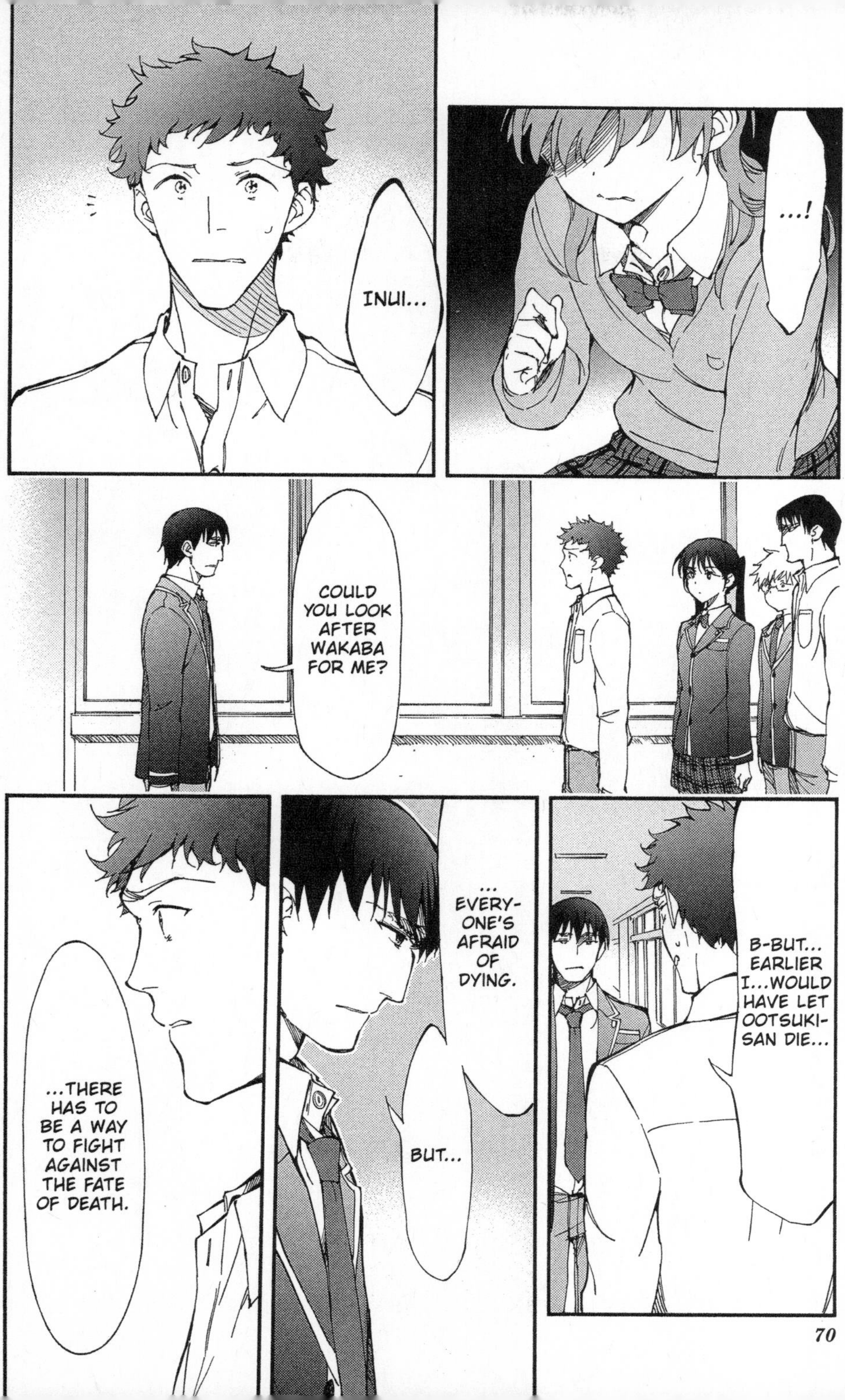
...!
INUI...
COULD YOU LOOK AFTER WAKABA FOR ME?
B-BUT... EARLIER I...WOULD HAVE LET OOTSUKI-SAN DIE...
... EVERYONE'S AFRAID OF DYING.
BUT...
...THERE HAS TO BE A WAY TO FIGHT AGAINST THE FATE OF DEATH.

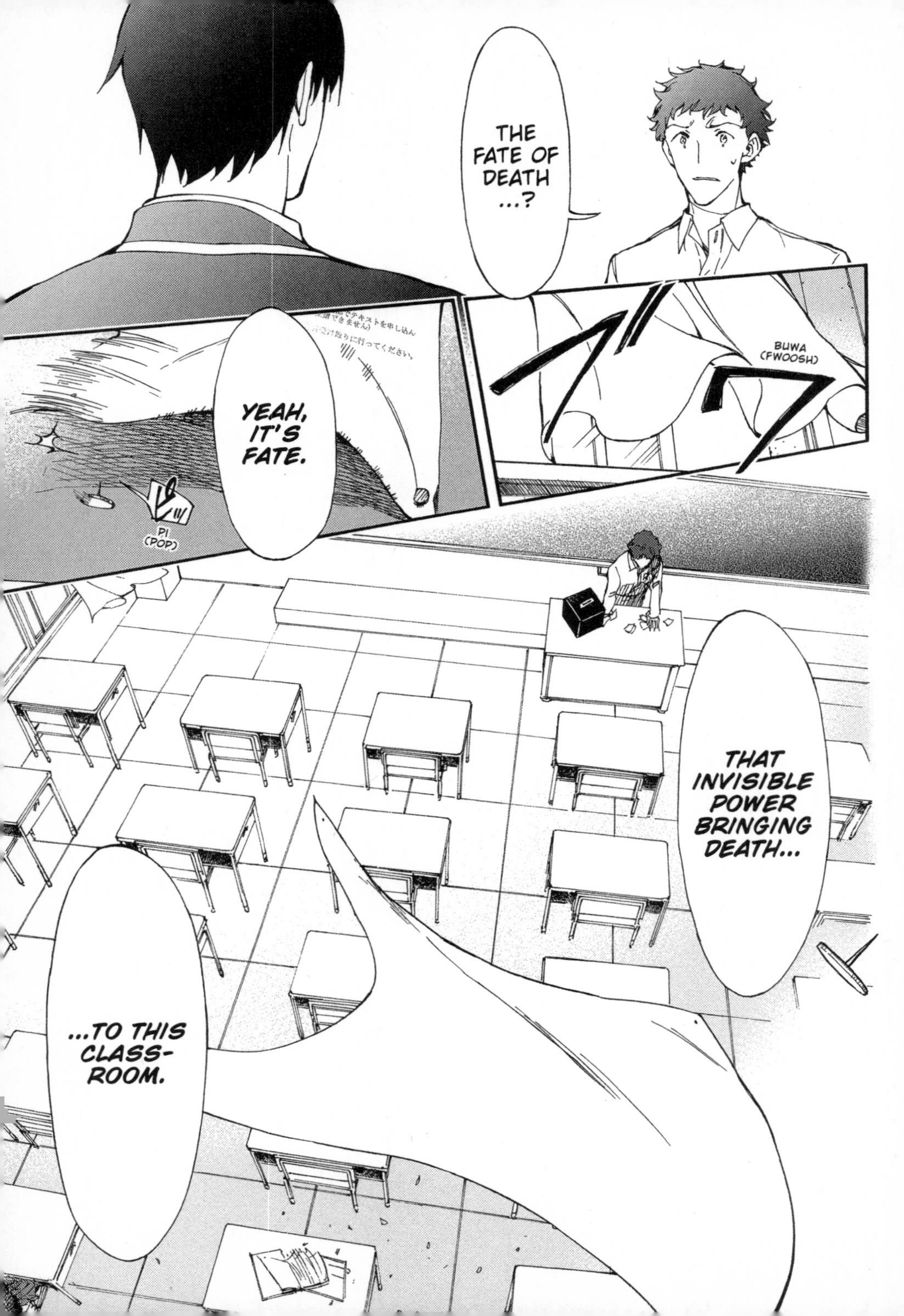
THE FATE OF DEATH ...?
BUWA (FWOOSH)
YEAH, IT'S FATE.
PI (POP)
THAT INVISIBLE POWER BRINGING DEATH...
...TO THIS CLASS-ROOM.

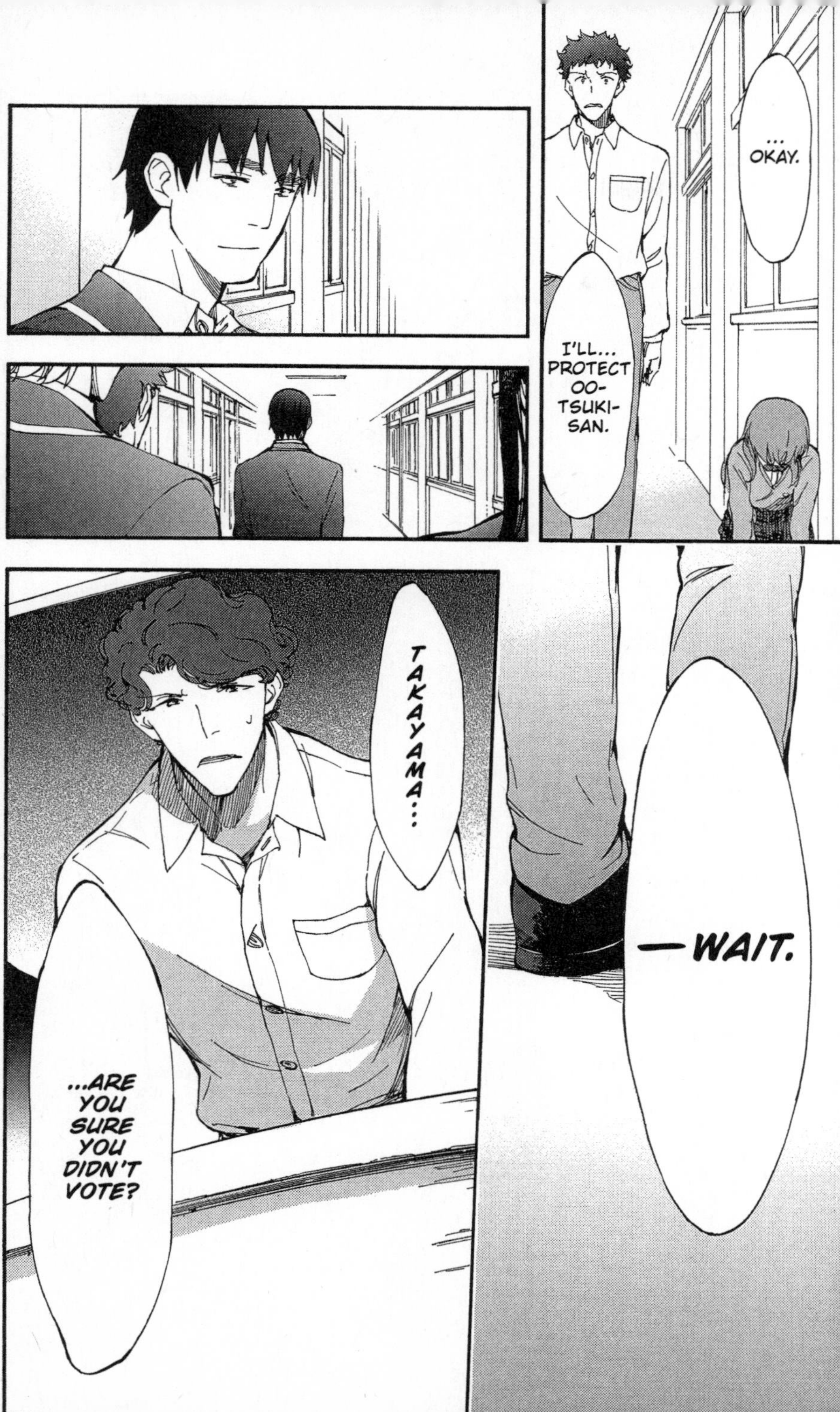
...OKAY.
I'LL... PROTECT OO-TSUKI-SAN.
—WAIT.
TAKAYAMA...
...ARE YOU SURE YOU DIDN'T VOTE?

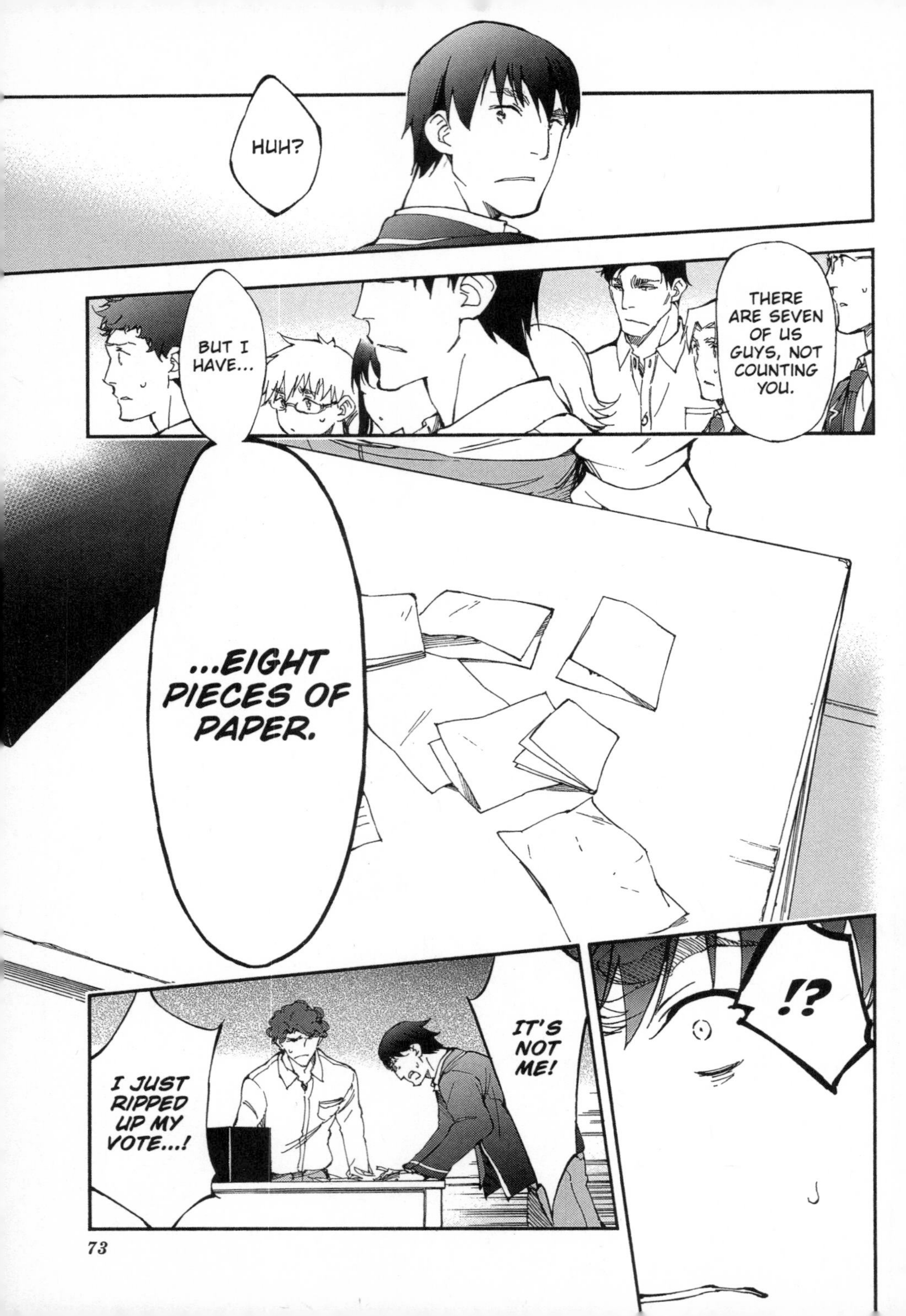
HUH?
THERE ARE SEVEN OF US GUYS, NOT COUNTING YOU.
BUT I HAVE...
...EIGHT PIECES OF PAPER.
!?
IT'S NOT ME!
I JUST RIPPED UP MY VOTE...!

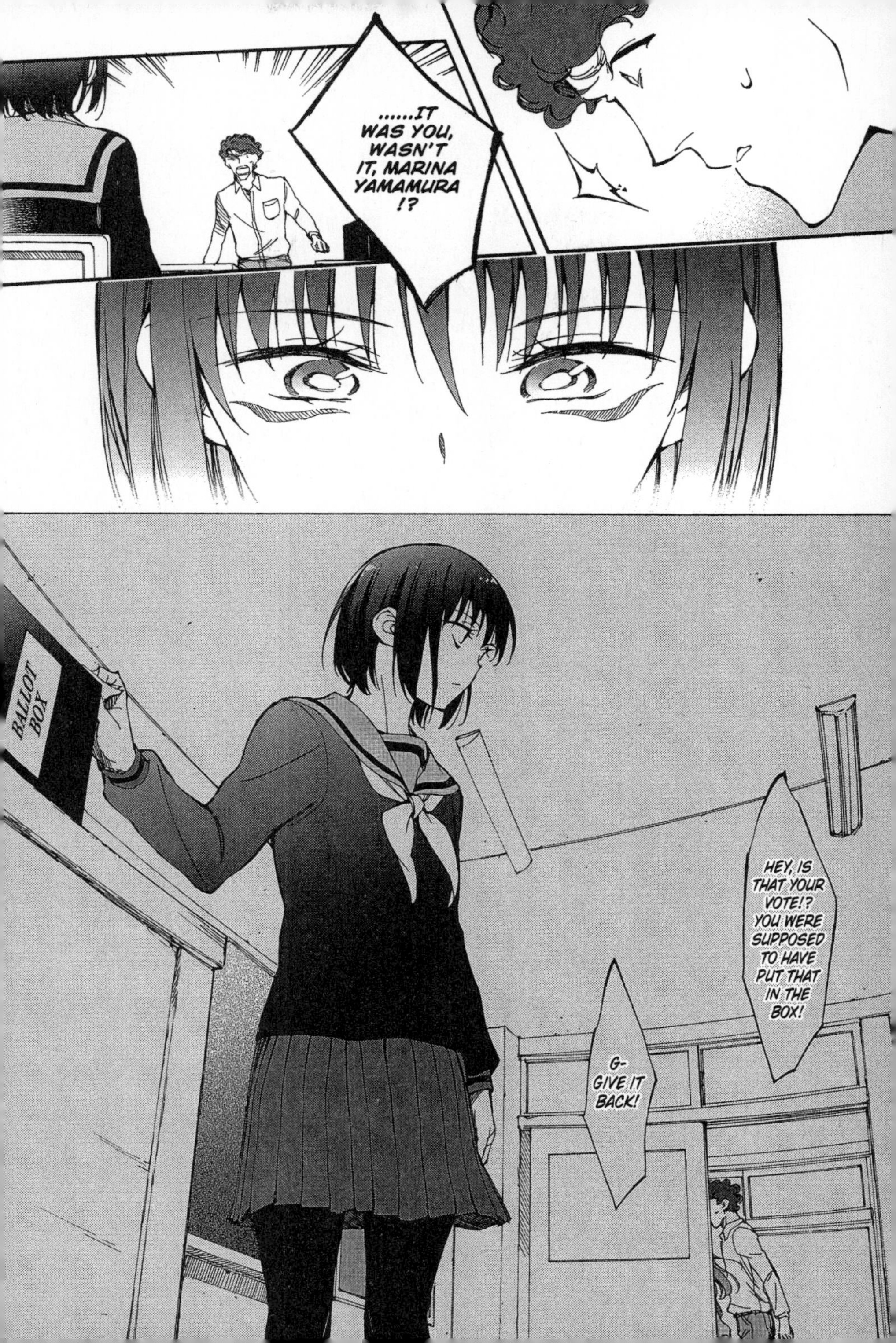
......IT WAS YOU, WASN'T IT, MARINA YAMAMURA !?
BALLOT BOX
HEY, IS THAT YOUR VOTE!? YOU WERE SUPPOSED TO HAVE PUT THAT IN THE BOX!
G- GIVE IT BACK!

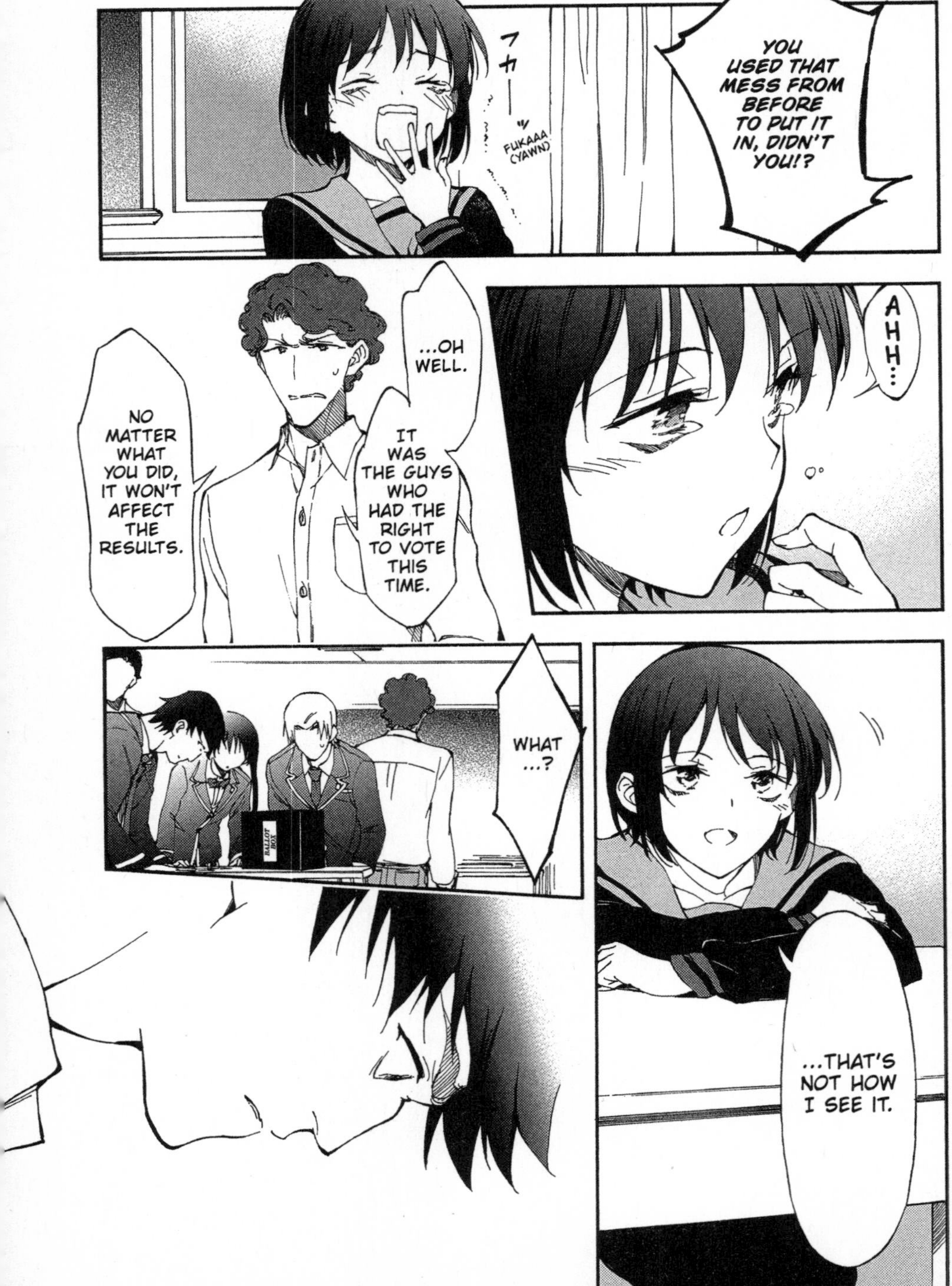
YOU USED THAT MESS FROM BEFORE TO PUT IT IN, DIDN'T YOU!?
フカー
FUKAAA (YAWN)
AHH...
...OH WELL.
IT WAS THE GUYS WHO HAD THE RIGHT TO VOTE THIS TIME.
NO MATTER WHAT YOU DID, IT WON'T AFFECT THE RESULTS.
...THAT'S NOT HOW I SEE IT.
WHAT ...?
BALLOT BOX

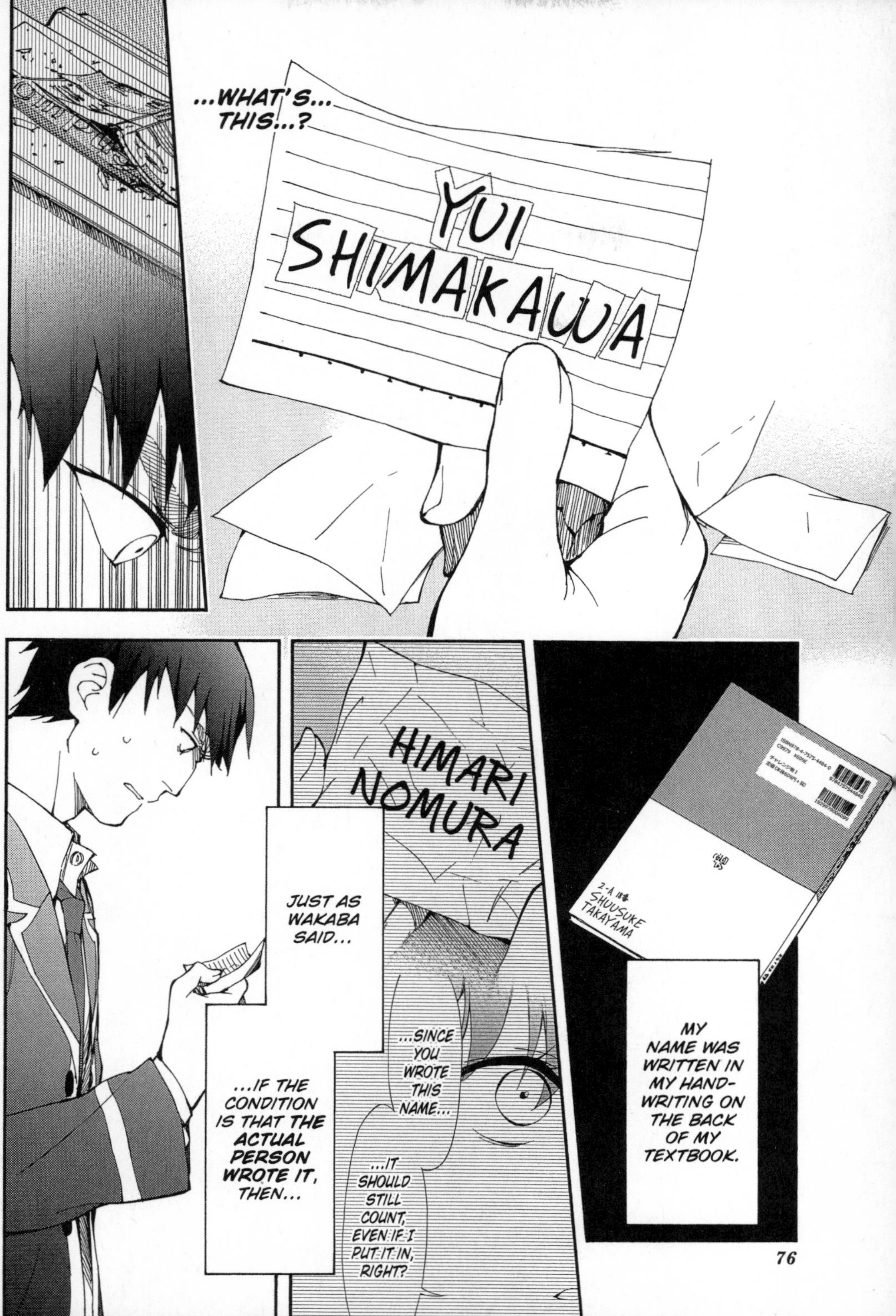
...WHAT'S... THIS...?
YUI SHIMAKAWA
SHUUSUKE TAKAYAMA
MY NAME WAS WRITTEN IN MY HAND-WRITING ON THE BACK OF MY TEXTBOOK.
HIMARI NOMURA
...SINCE YOU WROTE THIS NAME...
...IT SHOULD STILL COUNT, EVEN IF I PUT IT IN, RIGHT?
JUST AS WAKABA SAID...
...IF THE CONDITION IS THAT THE ACTUAL PERSON WROTE IT, THEN...

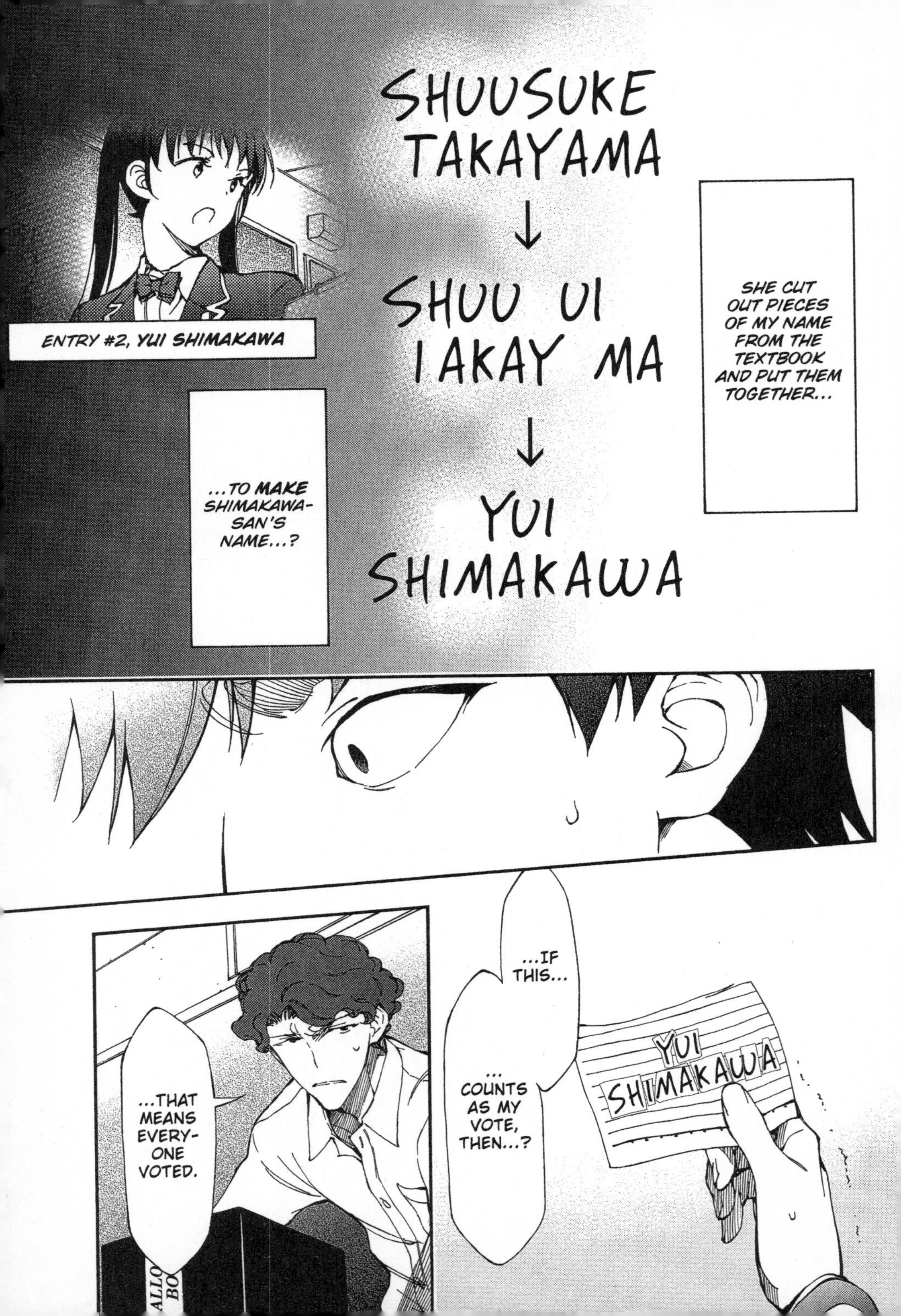
SHE CUT OUT PIECES OF MY NAME FROM THE TEXTBOOK AND PUT THEM TOGETHER...
SHUUSUKE TAKAYAMA
↓
SHUU UI IAKAY MA
↓
YUI SHIMAKAWA
...TO MAKE SHIMAKAWA-SAN'S NAME...?
ENTRY #2, YUI SHIMAKAWA
...IF THIS...
...COUNTS AS MY VOTE, THEN...?
YUI SHIMAKAWA
...THAT MEANS EVERY-ONE VOTED.

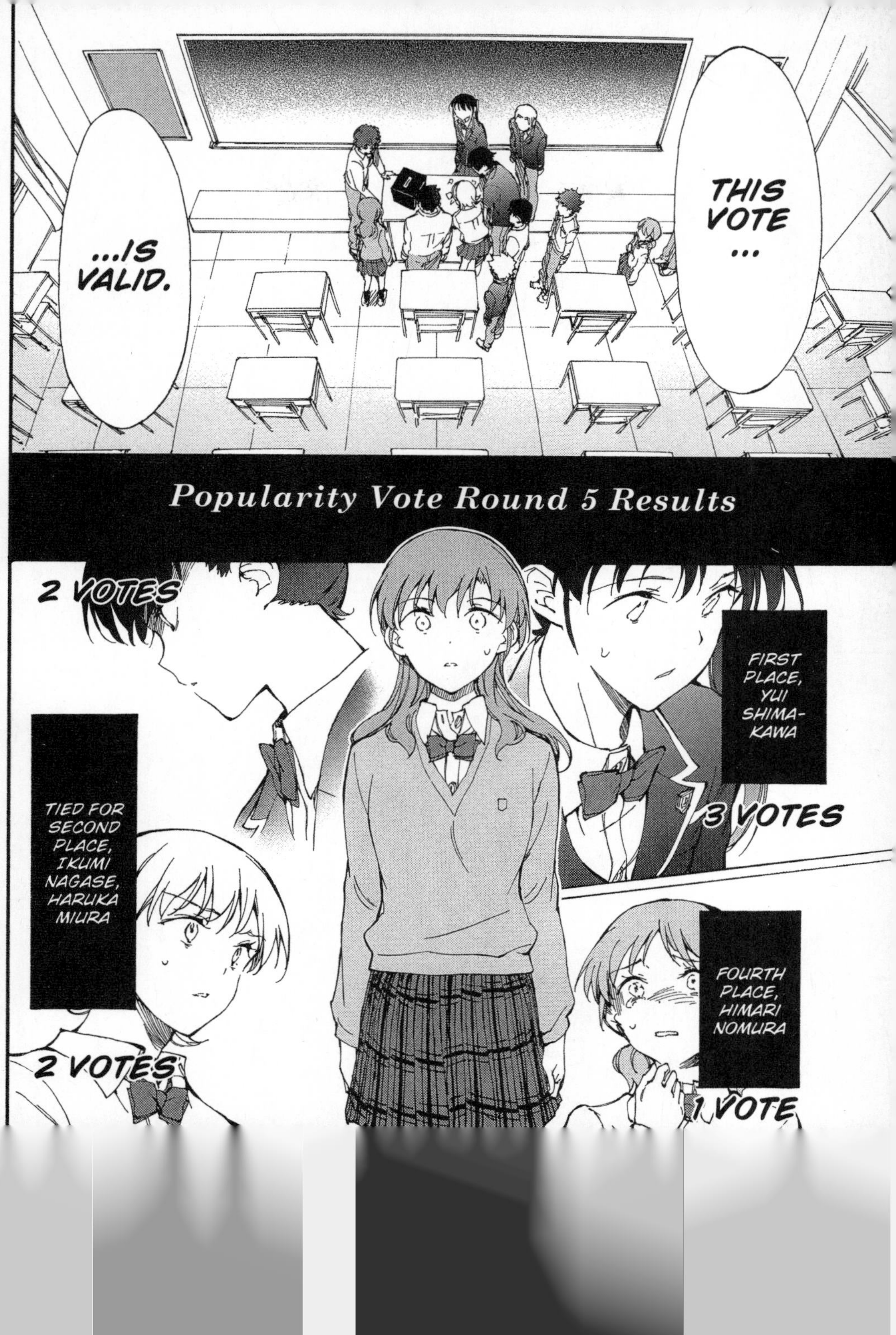
THIS VOTE ...
...IS VALID.
Popularity Vote Round 5 Results
FIRST PLACE, YUI SHIMAKAWA
3 VOTES
2 VOTES
TIED FOR SECOND PLACE, IKUMI NAGASE, HARUKA MIURA
2 VOTES
FOURTH PLACE, HIMARI NOMURA
1 VOTE

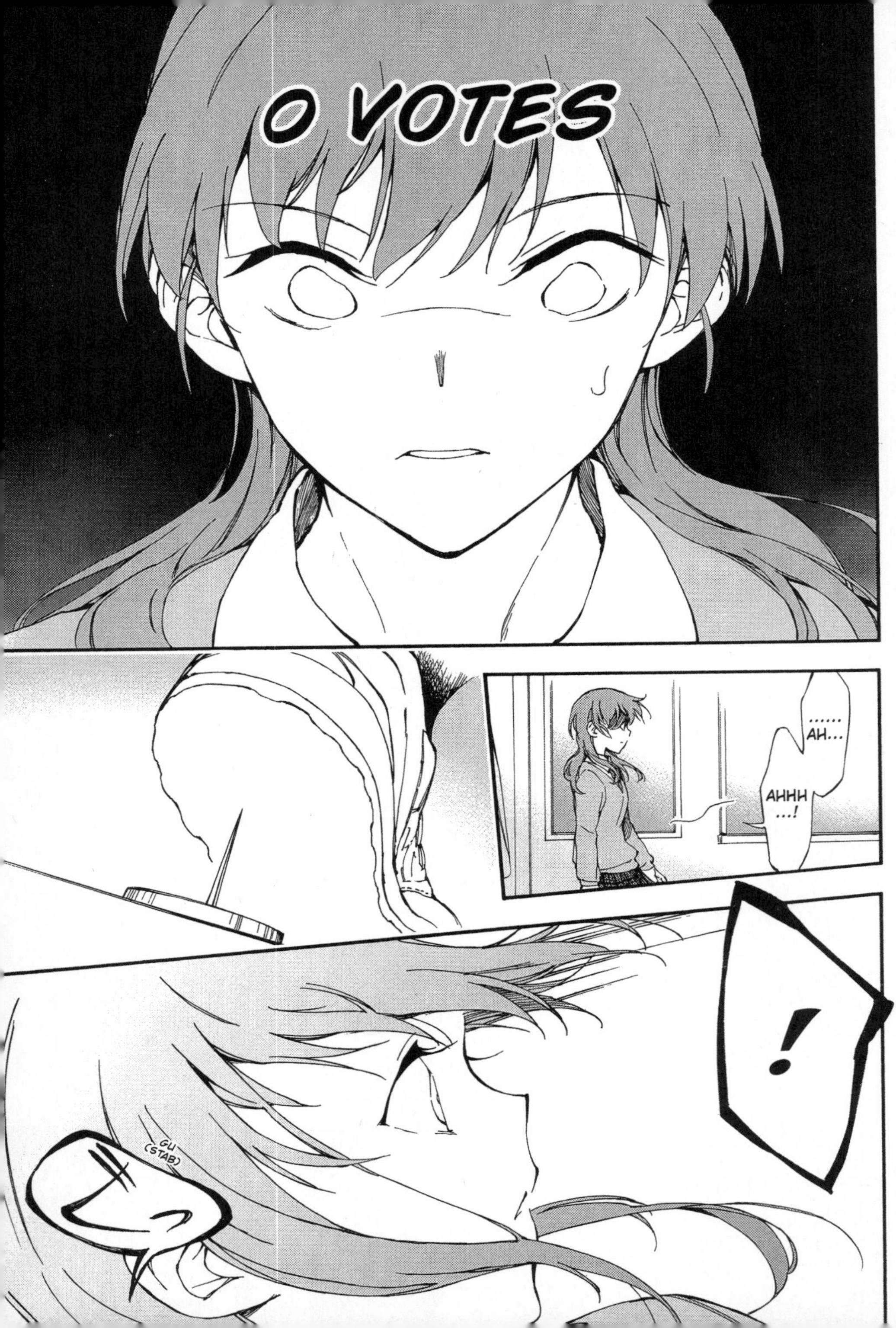
0 VOTES
......AH...
AHHH...!
!
GU (STAB)

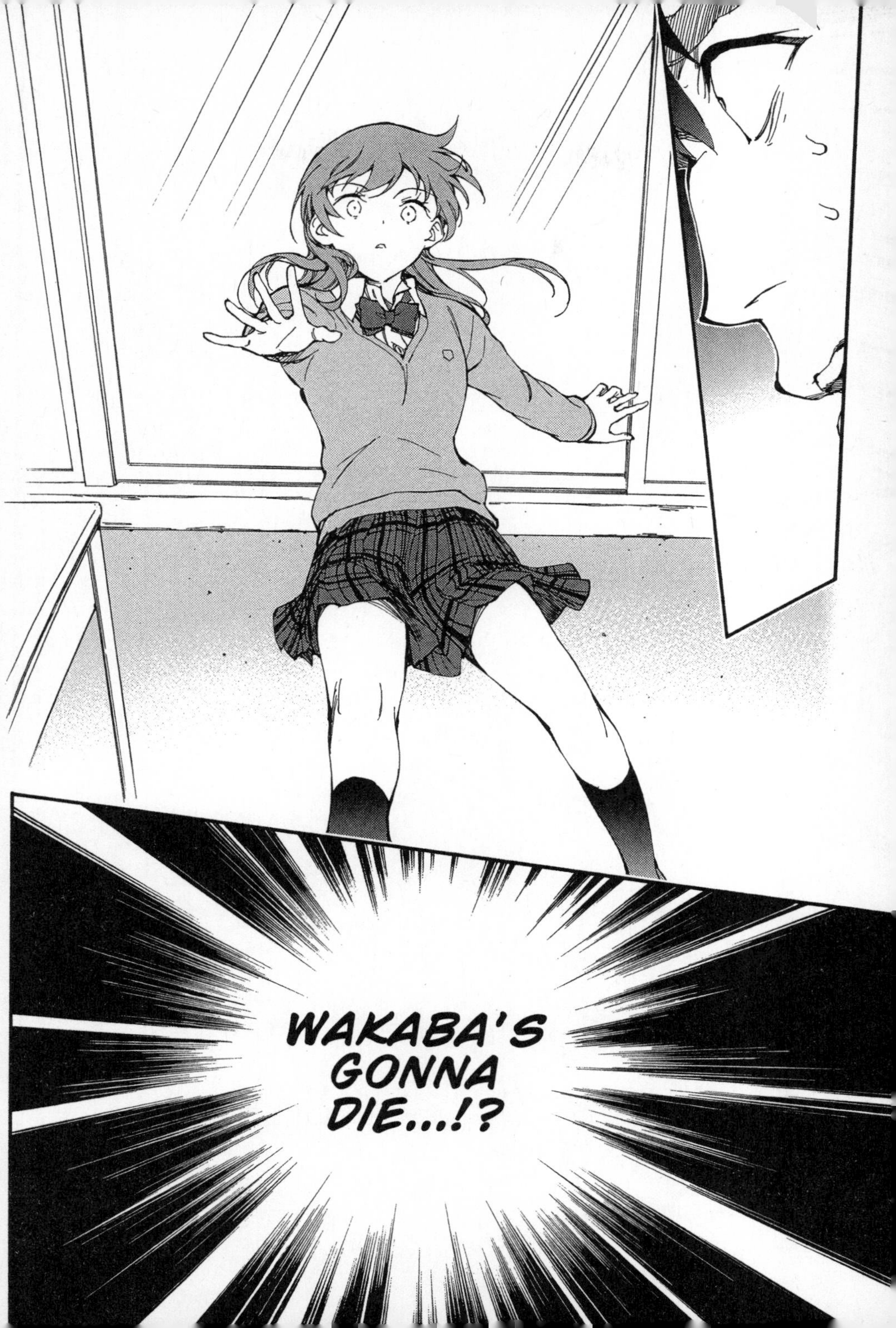
WAKABA'S GONNA DIE...!?

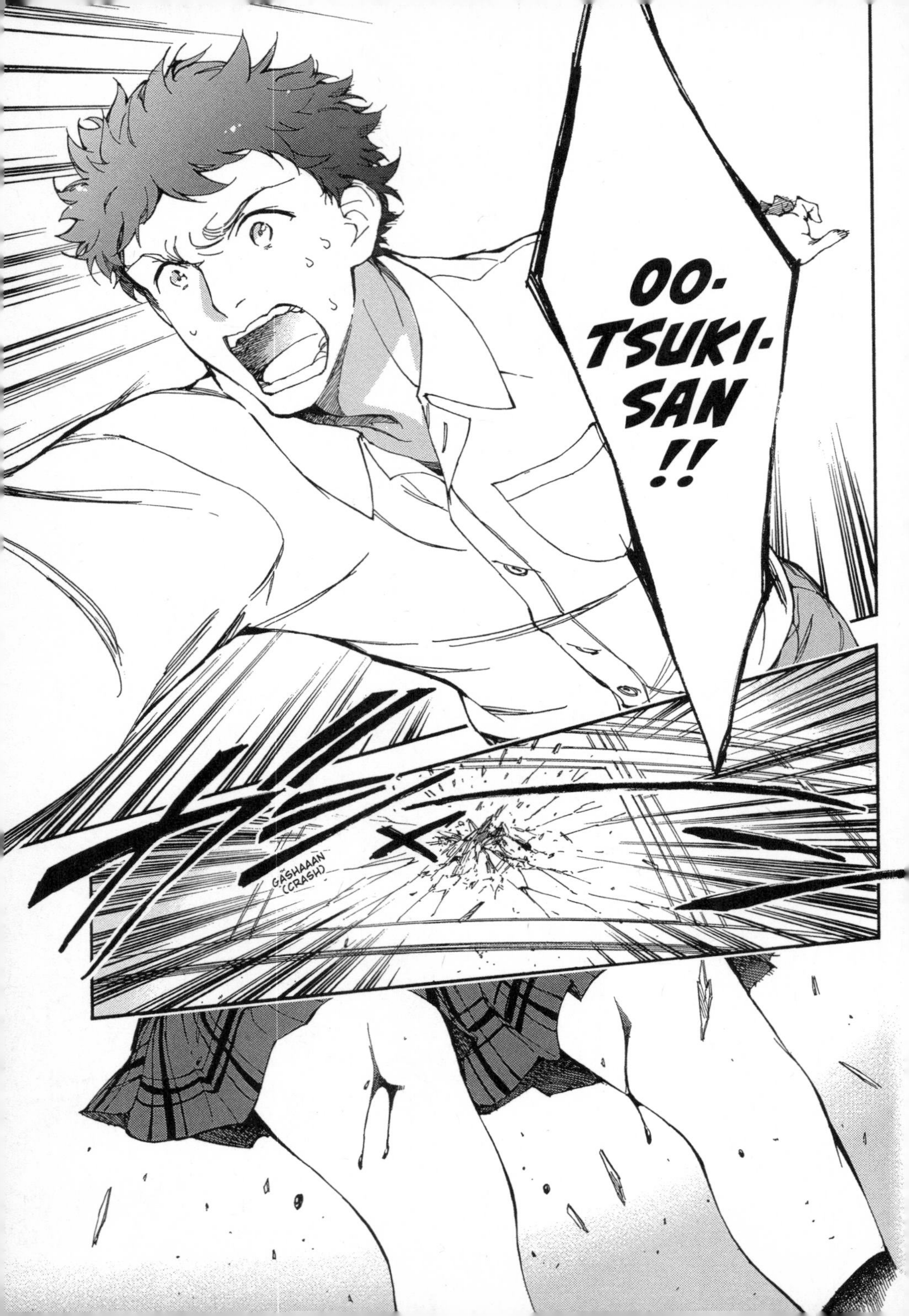
OO-
TSUKI-
SAN
!!
GASHAAAN
(CRASH)

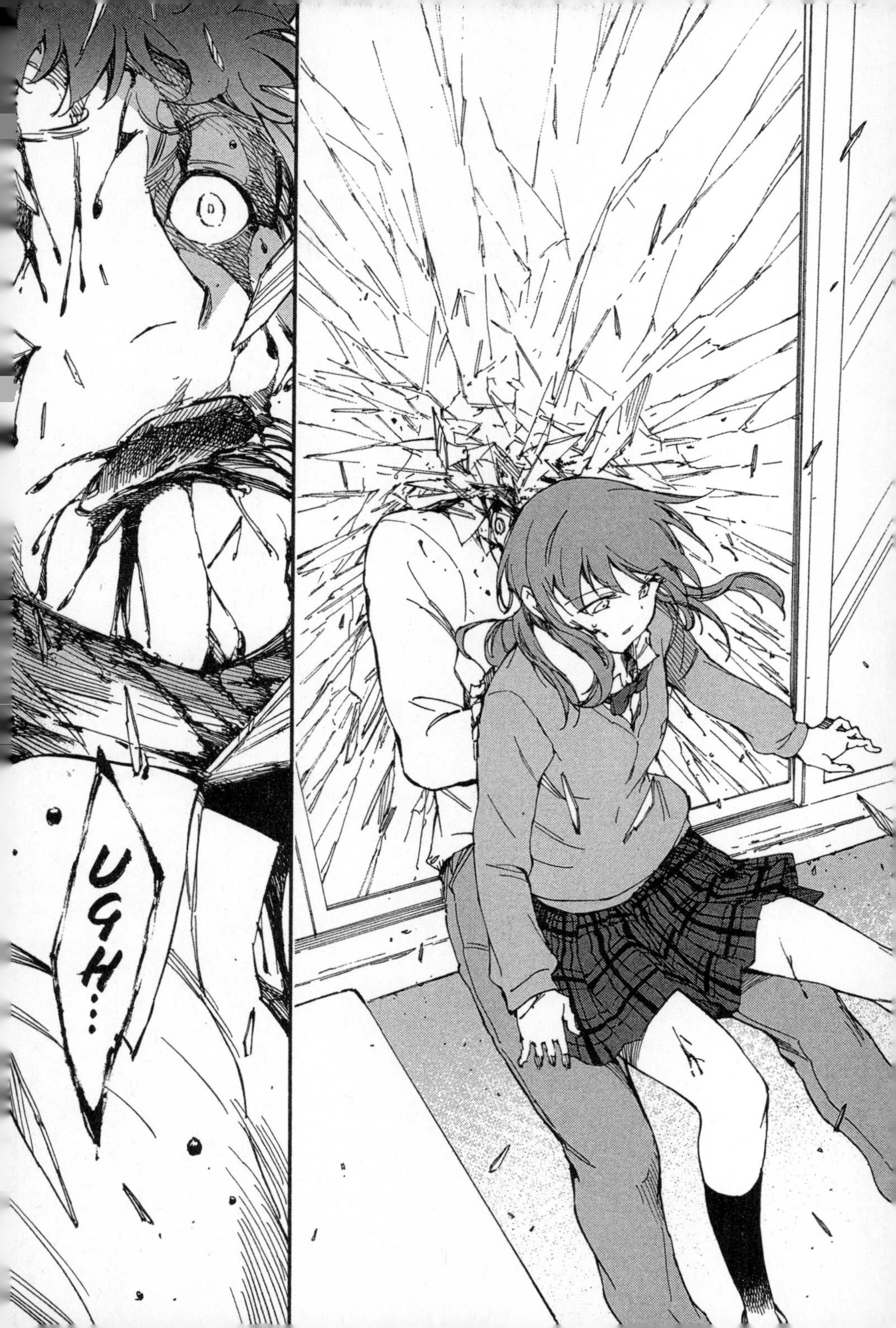
UGH...

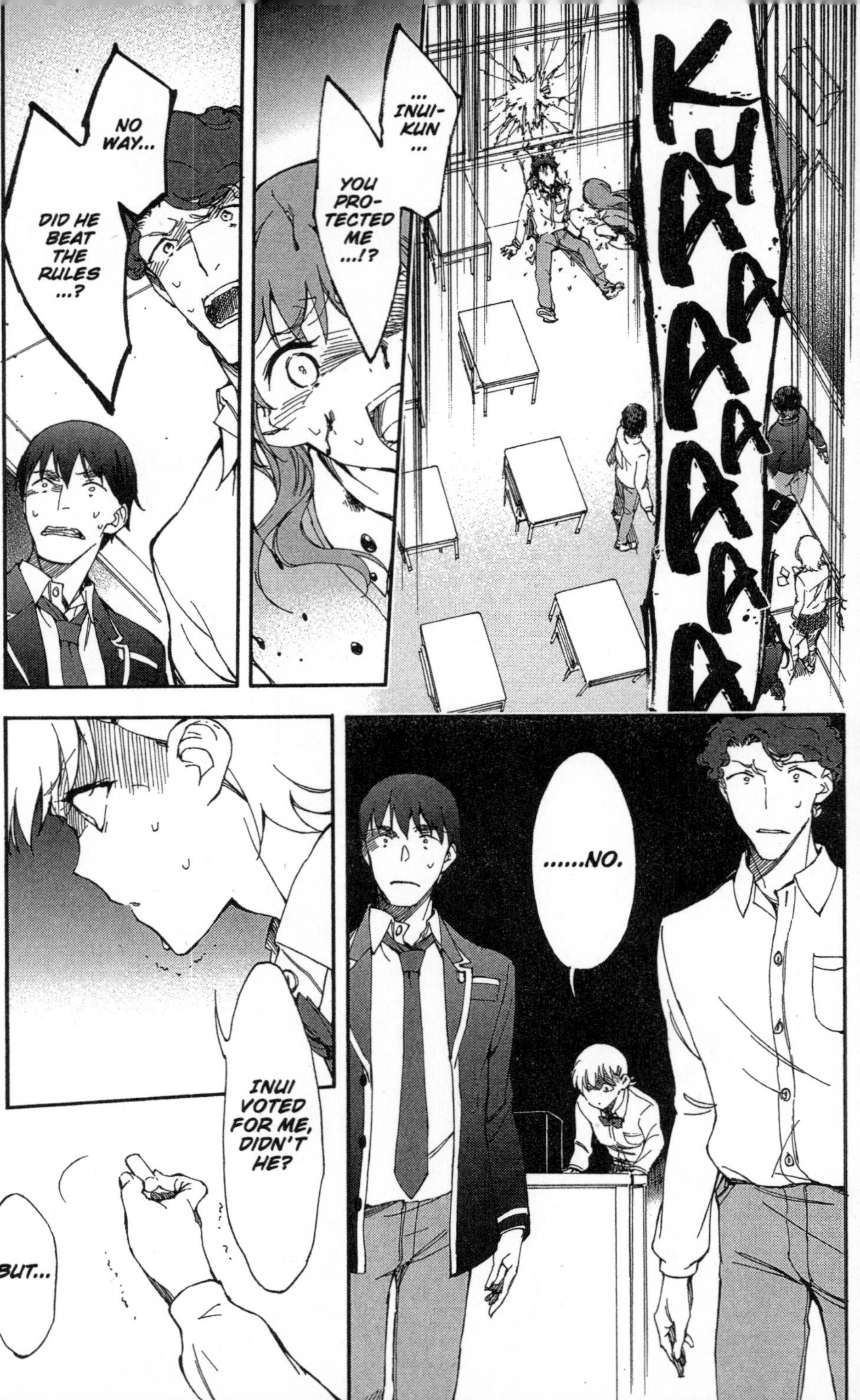
KYAAAAAAA
... INUI-KUN ...
YOU PROTECTED ME ...!?
NO WAY...
DID HE BEAT THE RULES ...?
......NO.
INUI VOTED FOR ME, DIDN'T HE?
BUT...

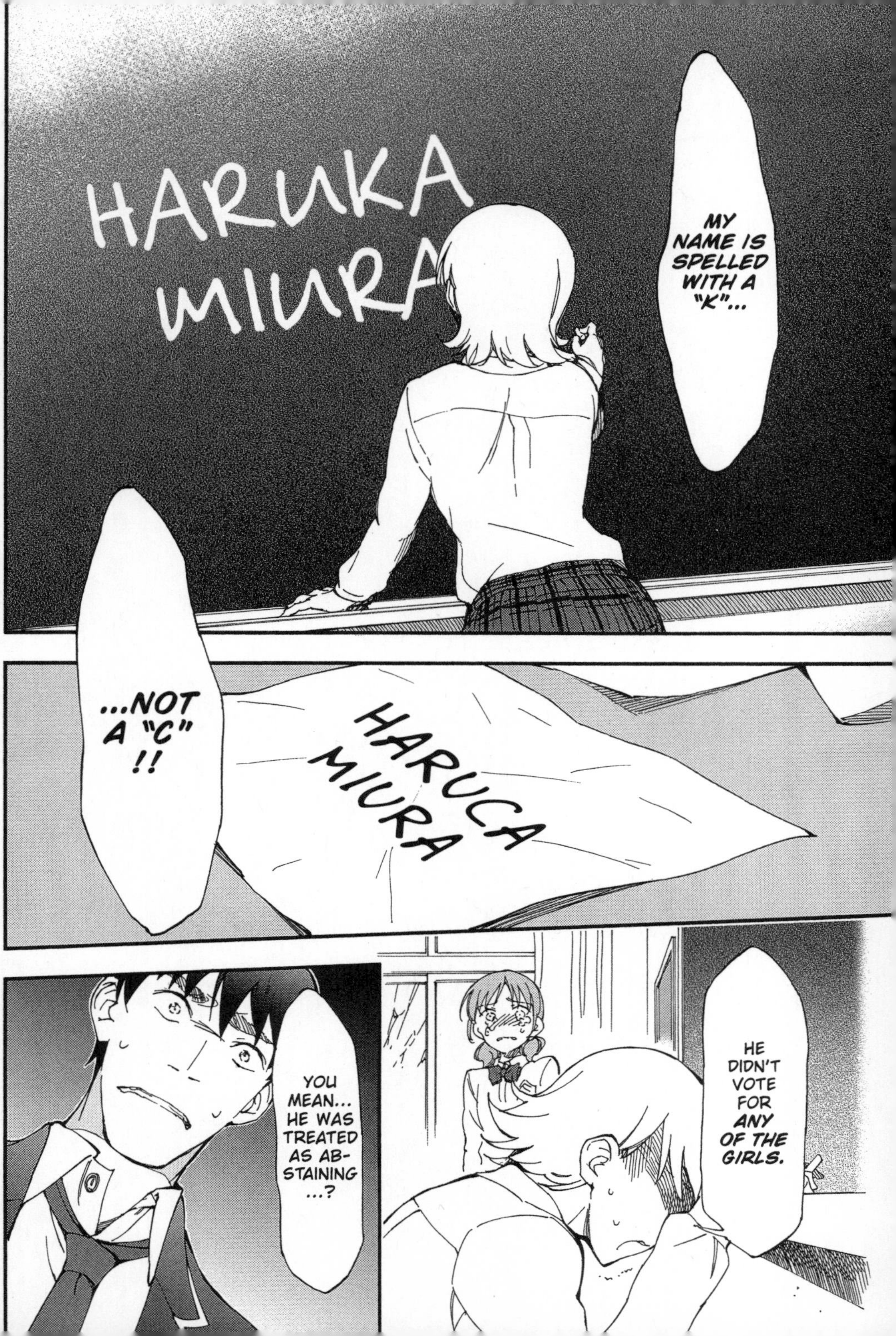
HARUKA MIURA
MY NAME IS SPELLED WITH A "K"...
...NOT A "C" !!
HARUCA MIURA
HE DIDN'T VOTE FOR ANY OF THE GIRLS.
YOU MEAN... HE WAS TREATED AS AB- STAINING ...?

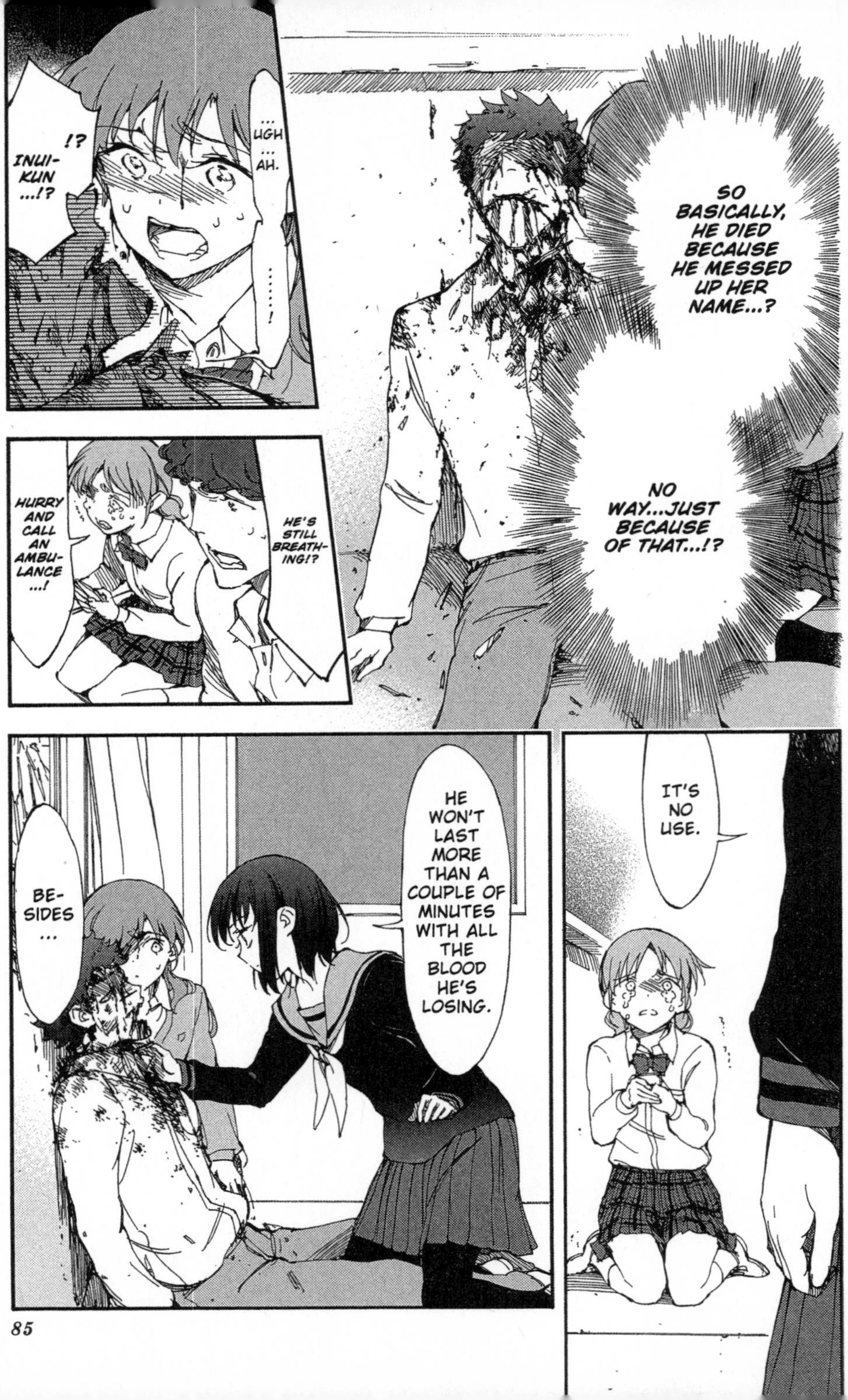
SO BASICALLY, HE DIED BECAUSE HE MESSED UP HER NAME...?
NO WAY...JUST BECAUSE OF THAT...!?
...UGH...AH.
!?
INUI-KUN...!?
......!
HE'S STILL BREATHING!?
HURRY AND CALL AN AMBULANCE...!
IT'S NO USE.
HE WON'T LAST MORE THAN A COUPLE OF MINUTES WITH ALL THE BLOOD HE'S LOSING.
BESIDES...

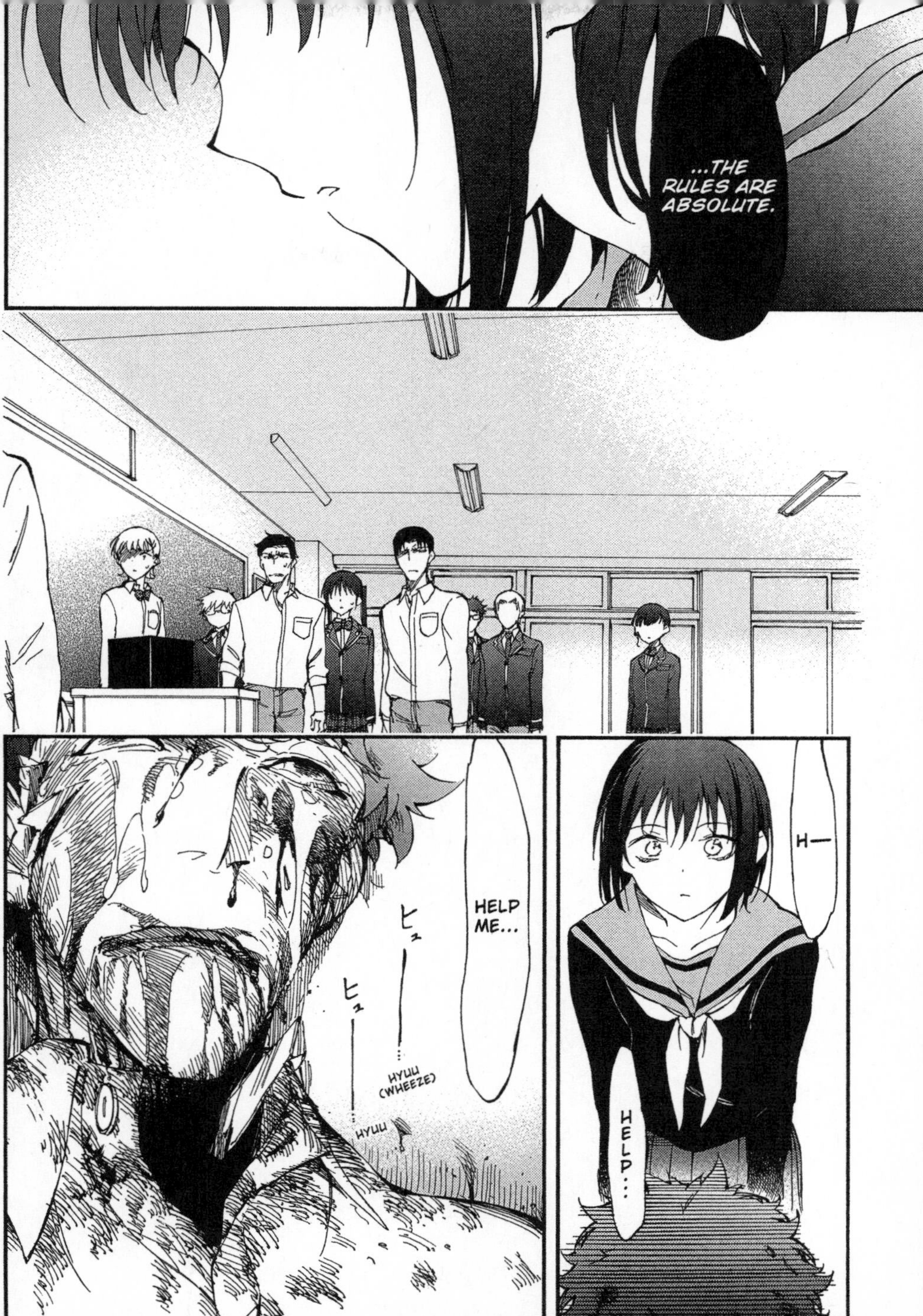
...THE RULES ARE ABSOLUTE.
H—
HELP...
HELP ME...
ヒュー
HYUU (WHEEZE)
ヒュー
HYUU

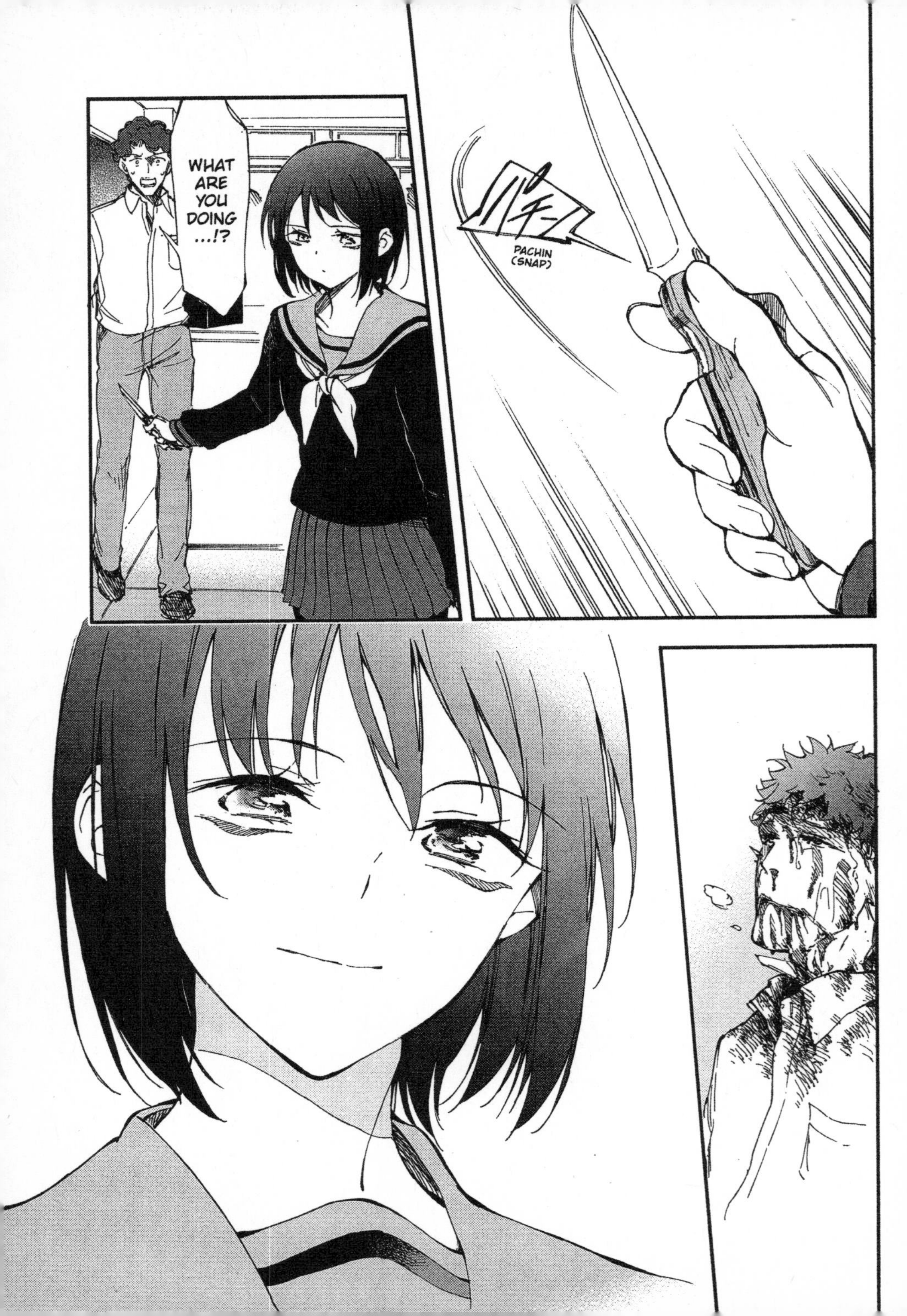
パチーン
PACHIN (SNAP)
WHAT ARE YOU DOING ...!?

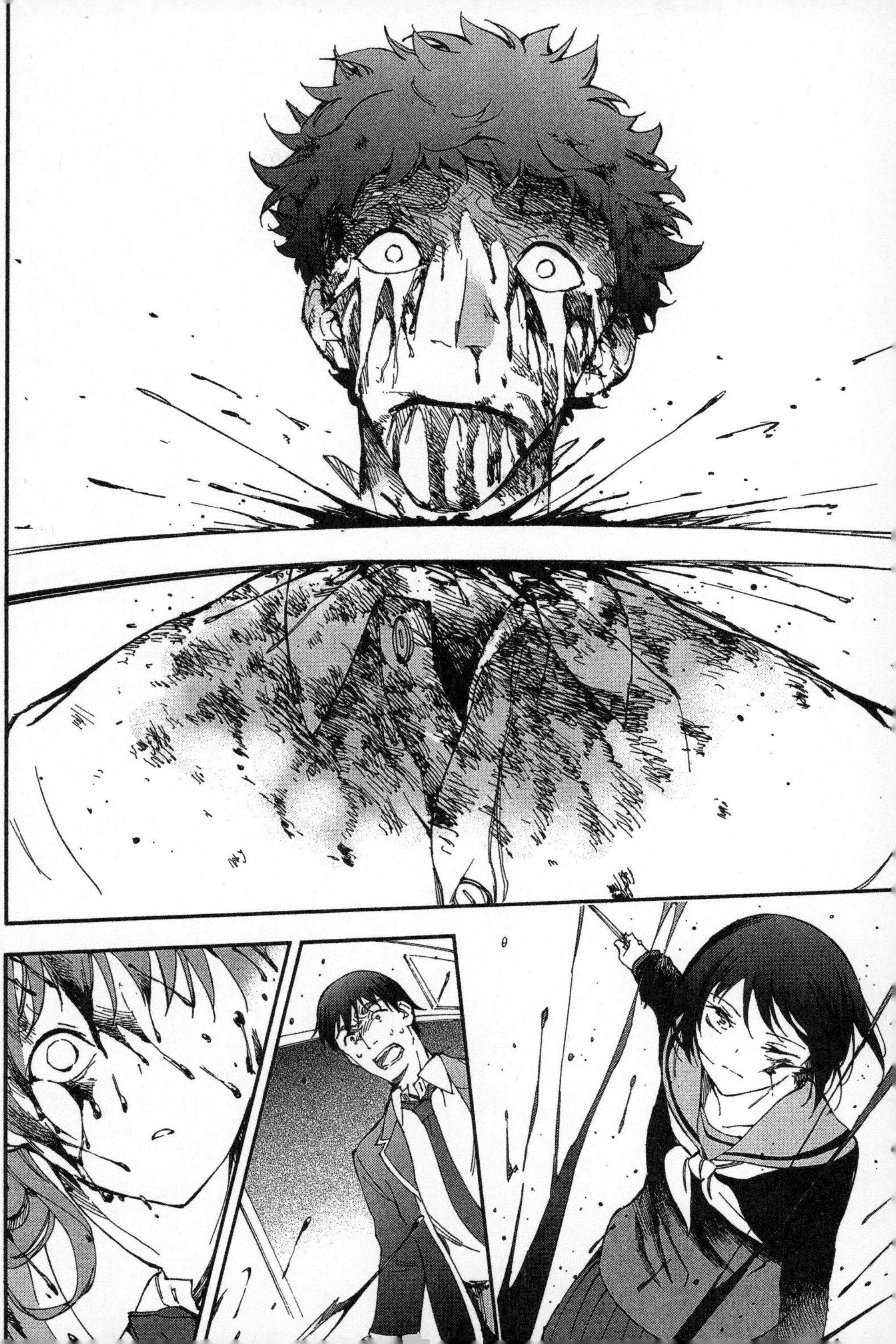

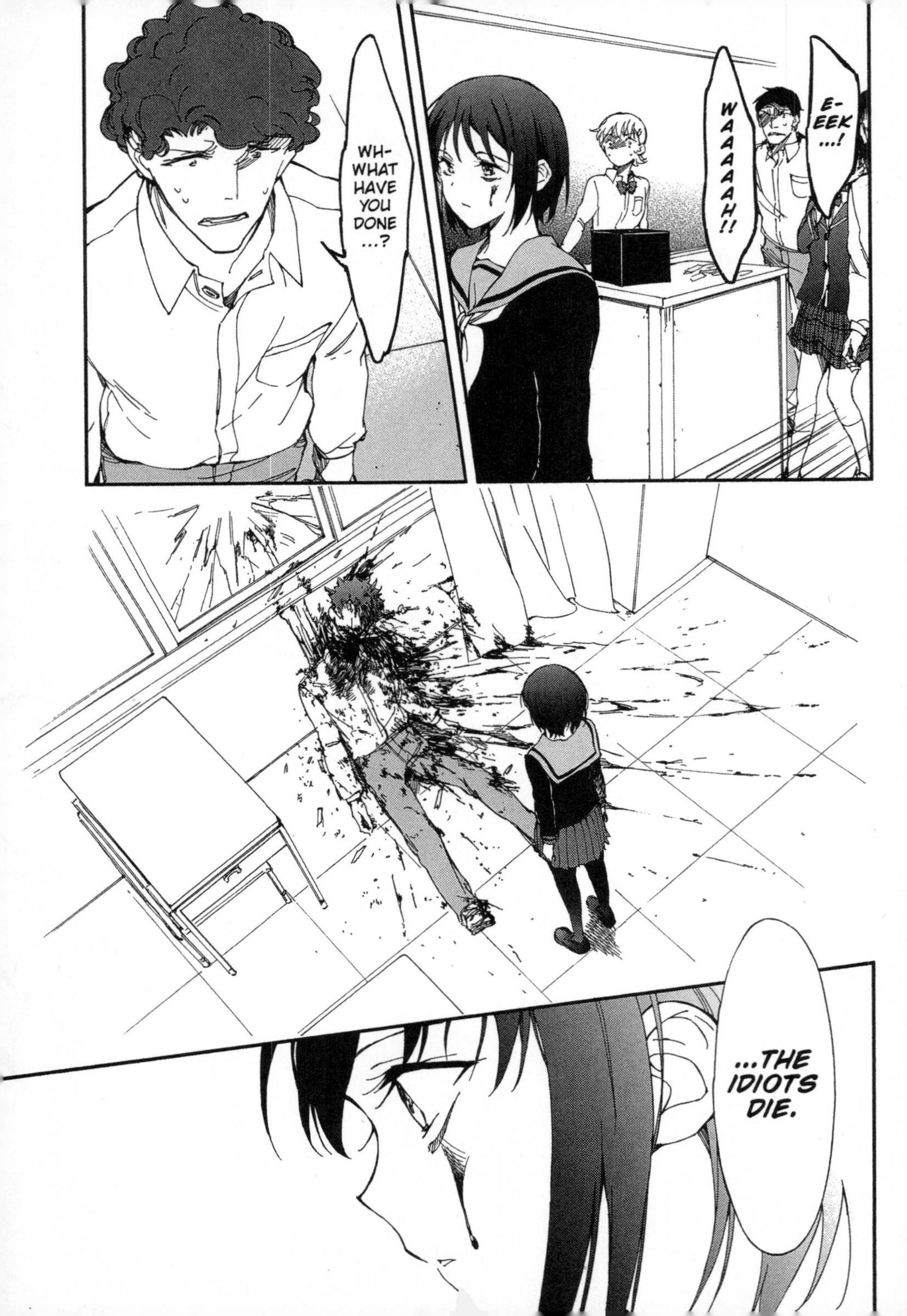
E-EEK...!
WAAAAAAH!!
WH-WHAT HAVE YOU DONE...?
...THE IDIOTS DIE.

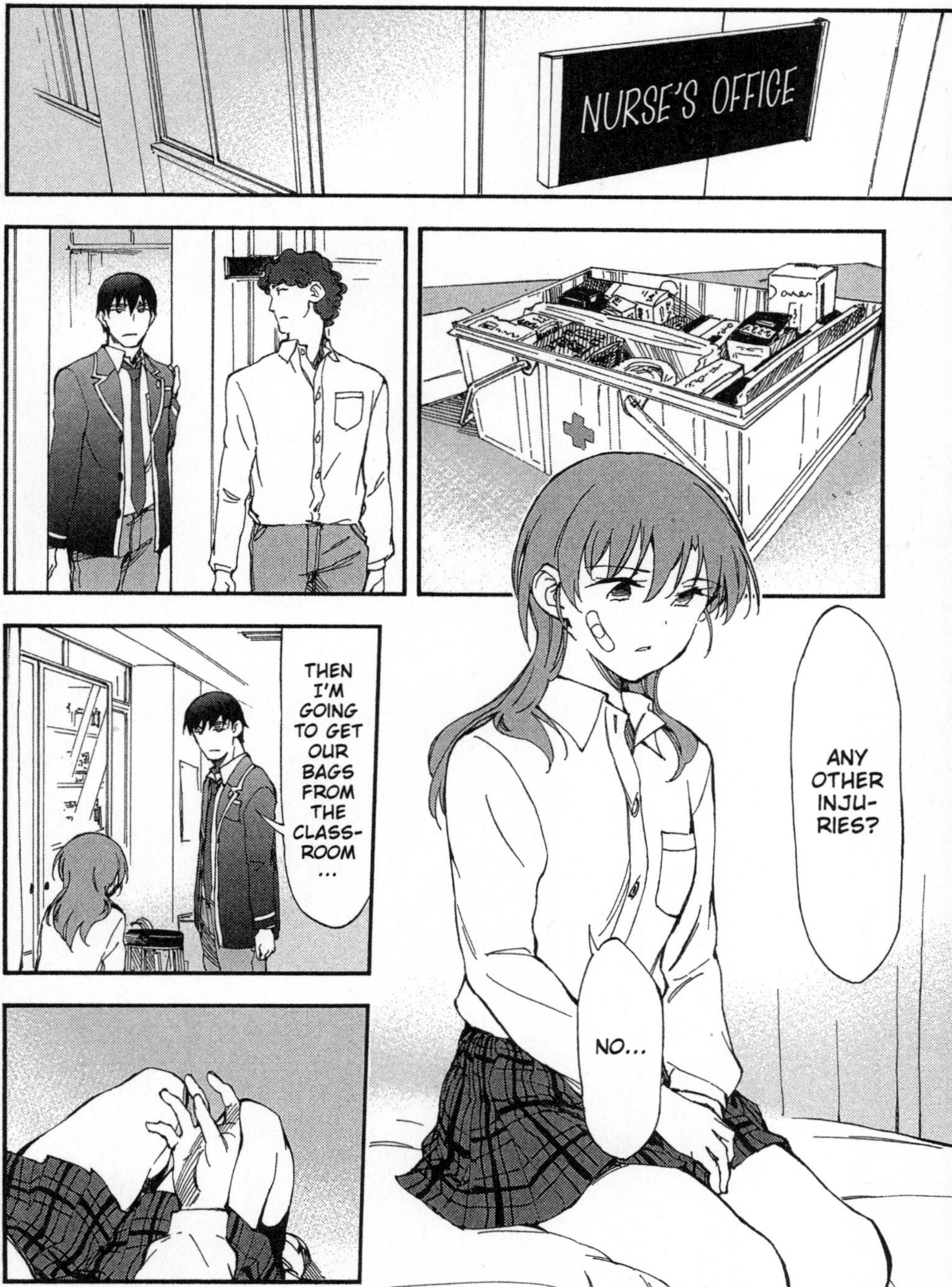
NURSE'S OFFICE
ANY OTHER INJURIES?
NO...
THEN I'M GOING TO GET OUR BAGS FROM THE CLASSROOM...

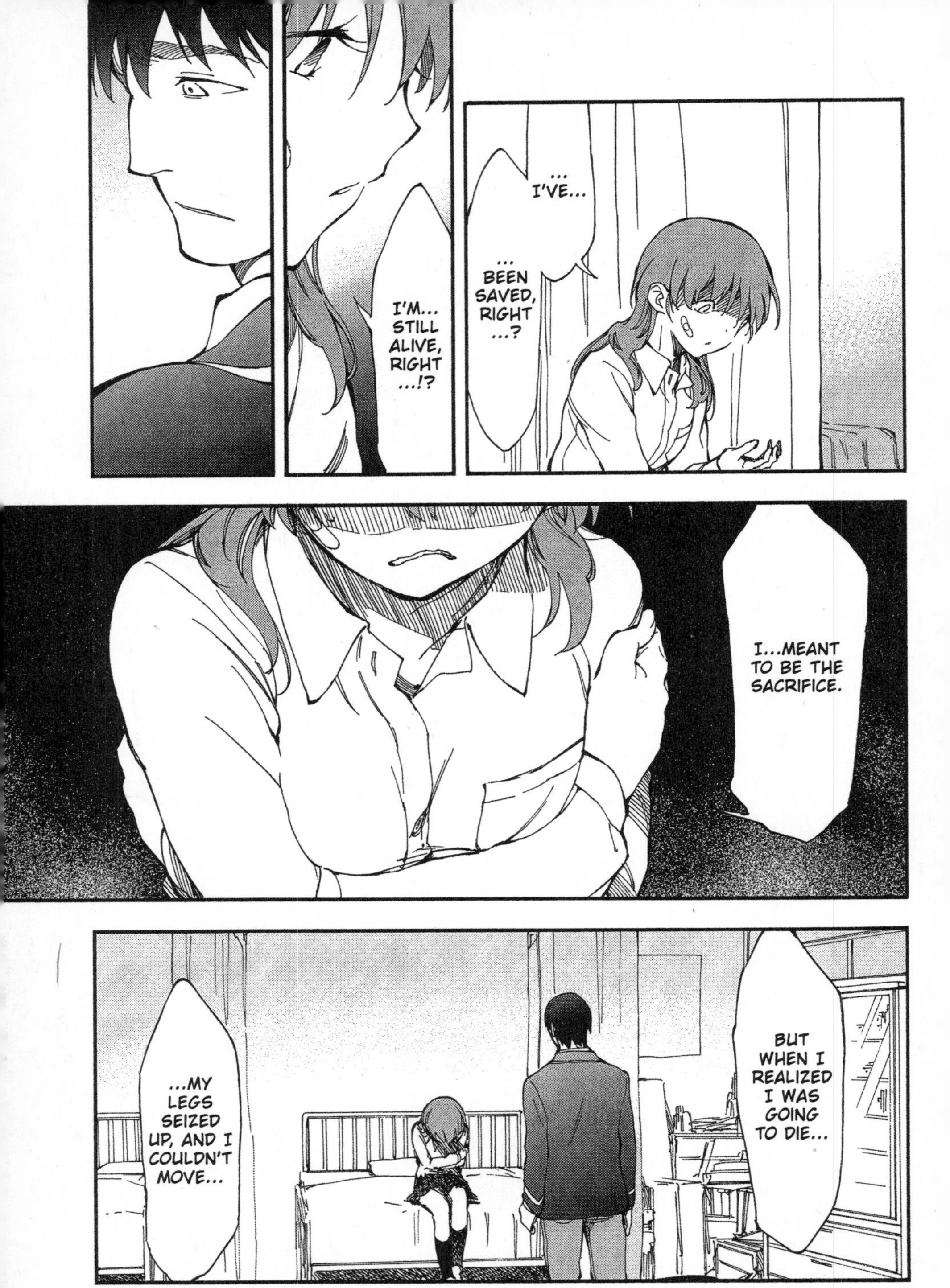
... I'VE...
... BEEN SAVED, RIGHT ...?
I'M... STILL ALIVE, RIGHT ...!?
I...MEANT TO BE THE SACRIFICE.
BUT WHEN I REALIZED I WAS GOING TO DIE...
...MY LEGS SEIZED UP, AND I COULDN'T MOVE...

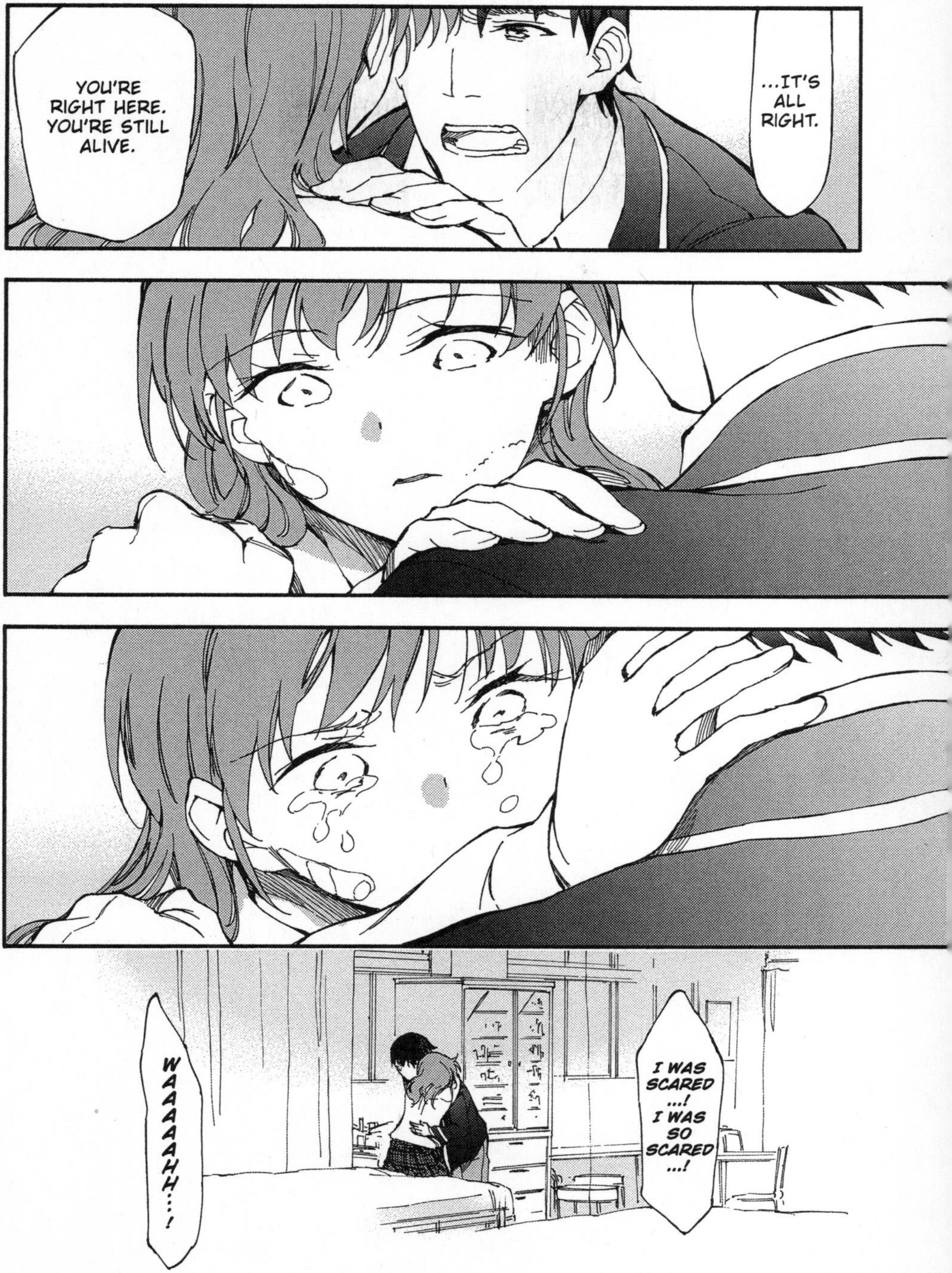
...IT'S ALL RIGHT.
YOU'RE RIGHT HERE. YOU'RE STILL ALIVE.
I WAS SCARED ...! I WAS SO SCARED ...!
WAAAAAAAH...!

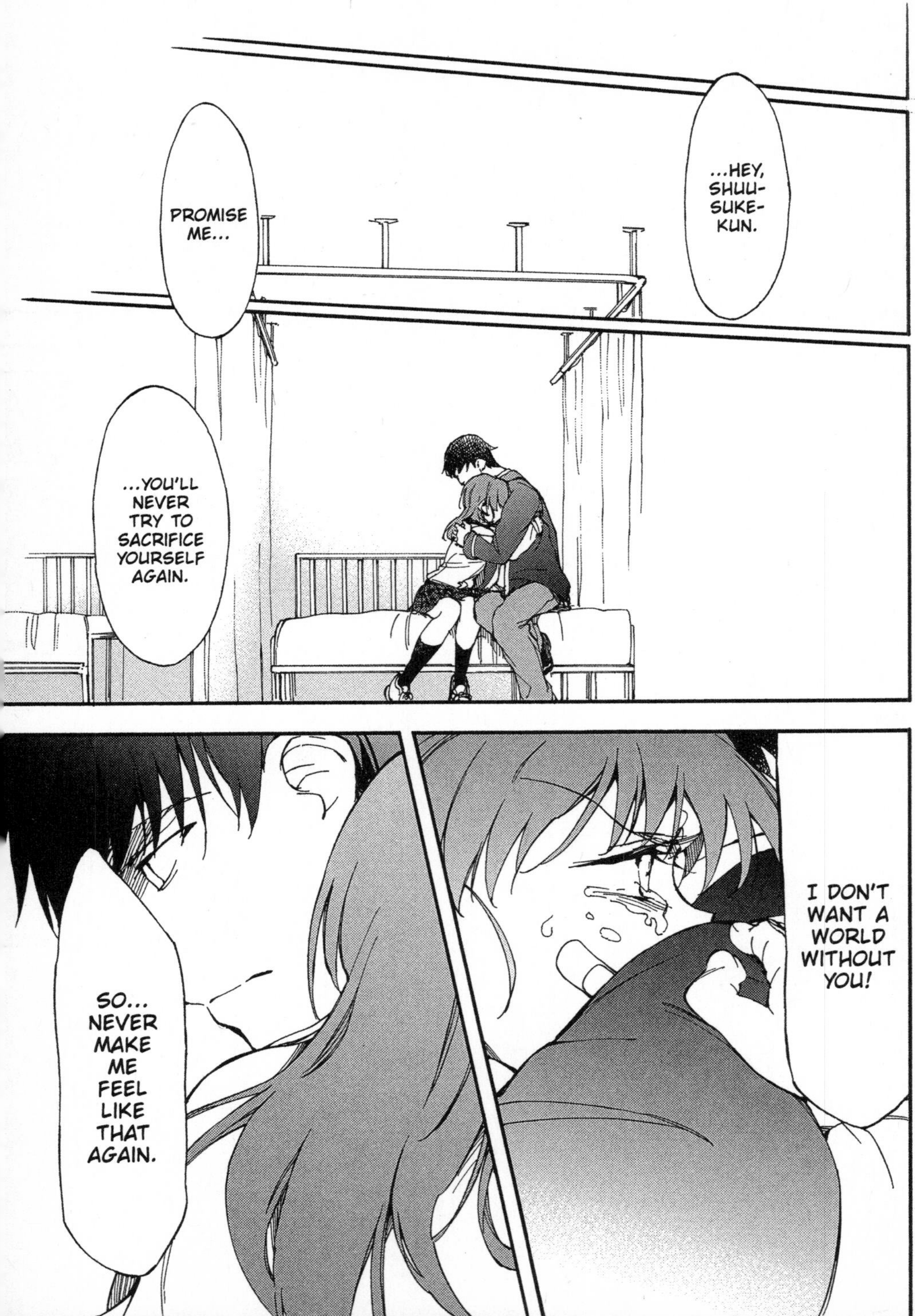
...HEY, SHUU-SUKE-KUN.
PROMISE ME...
...YOU'LL NEVER TRY TO SACRIFICE YOURSELF AGAIN.
I DON'T WANT A WORLD WITHOUT YOU!
SO... NEVER MAKE ME FEEL LIKE THAT AGAIN.

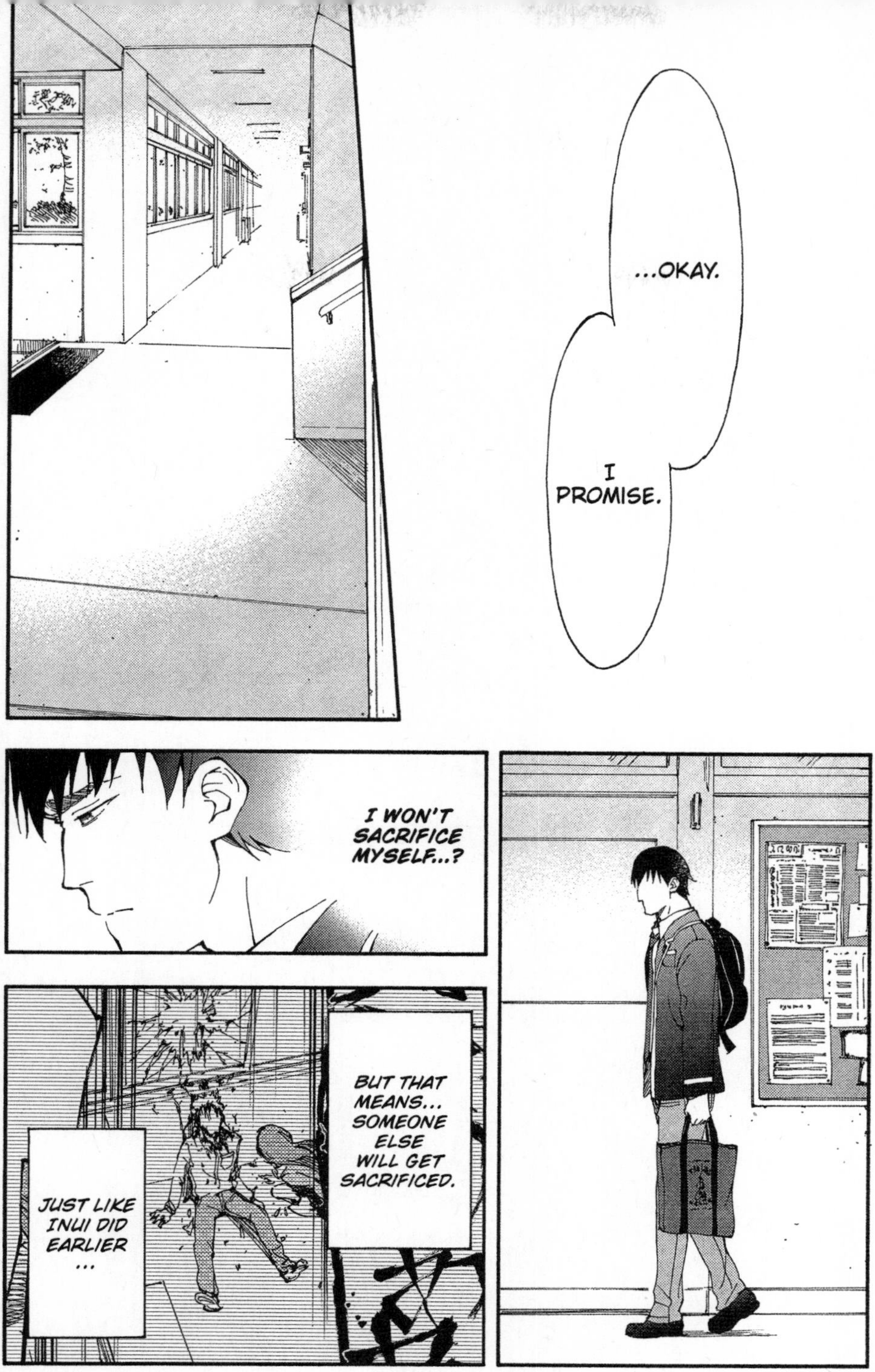
...OKAY.
I PROMISE.
I WON'T SACRIFICE MYSELF...?
BUT THAT MEANS... SOMEONE ELSE WILL GET SACRIFICED.
JUST LIKE INUI DID EARLIER ...

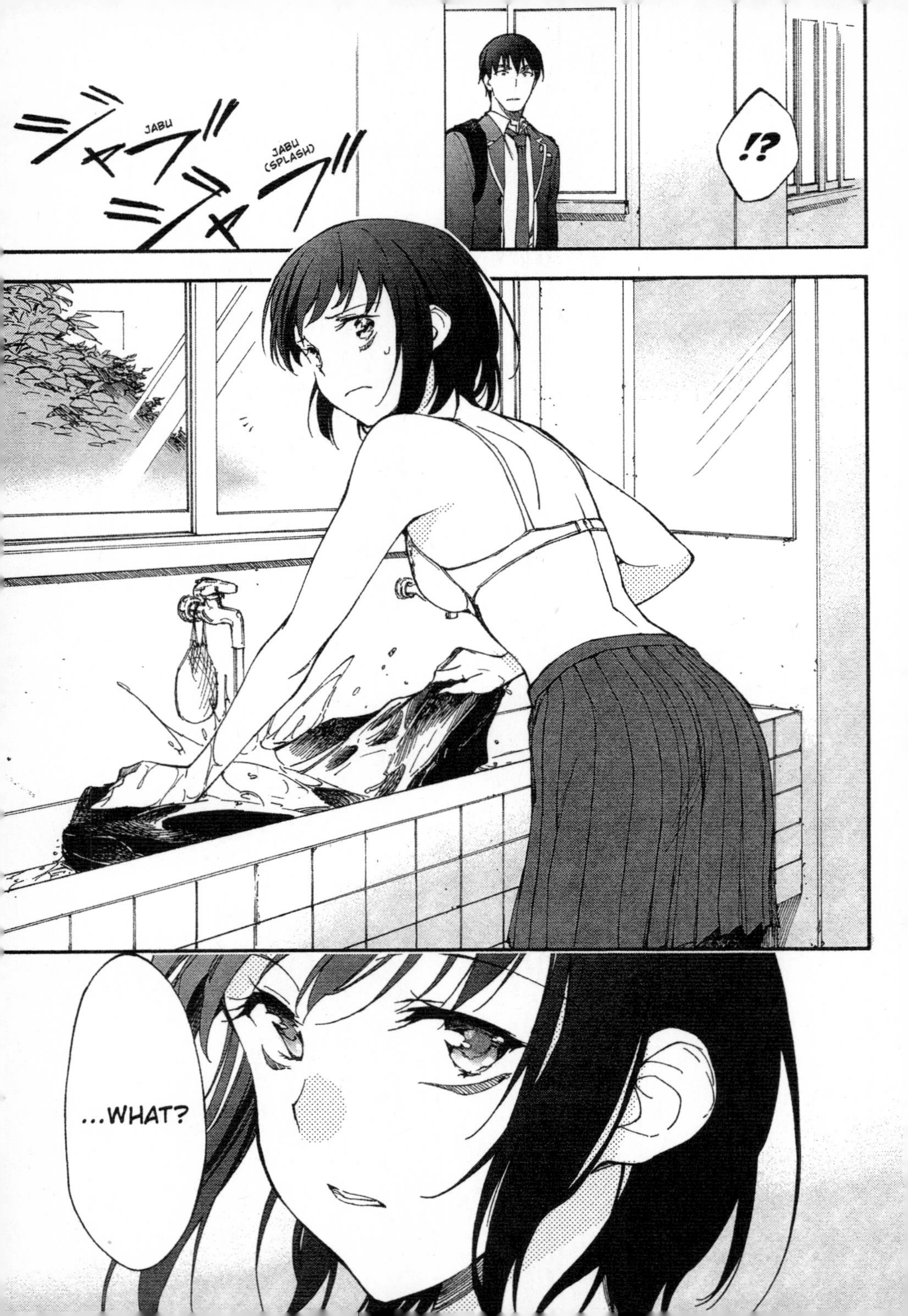
!?
ジャブジャブ
JABU
JABU (SPLASH)
...WHAT?

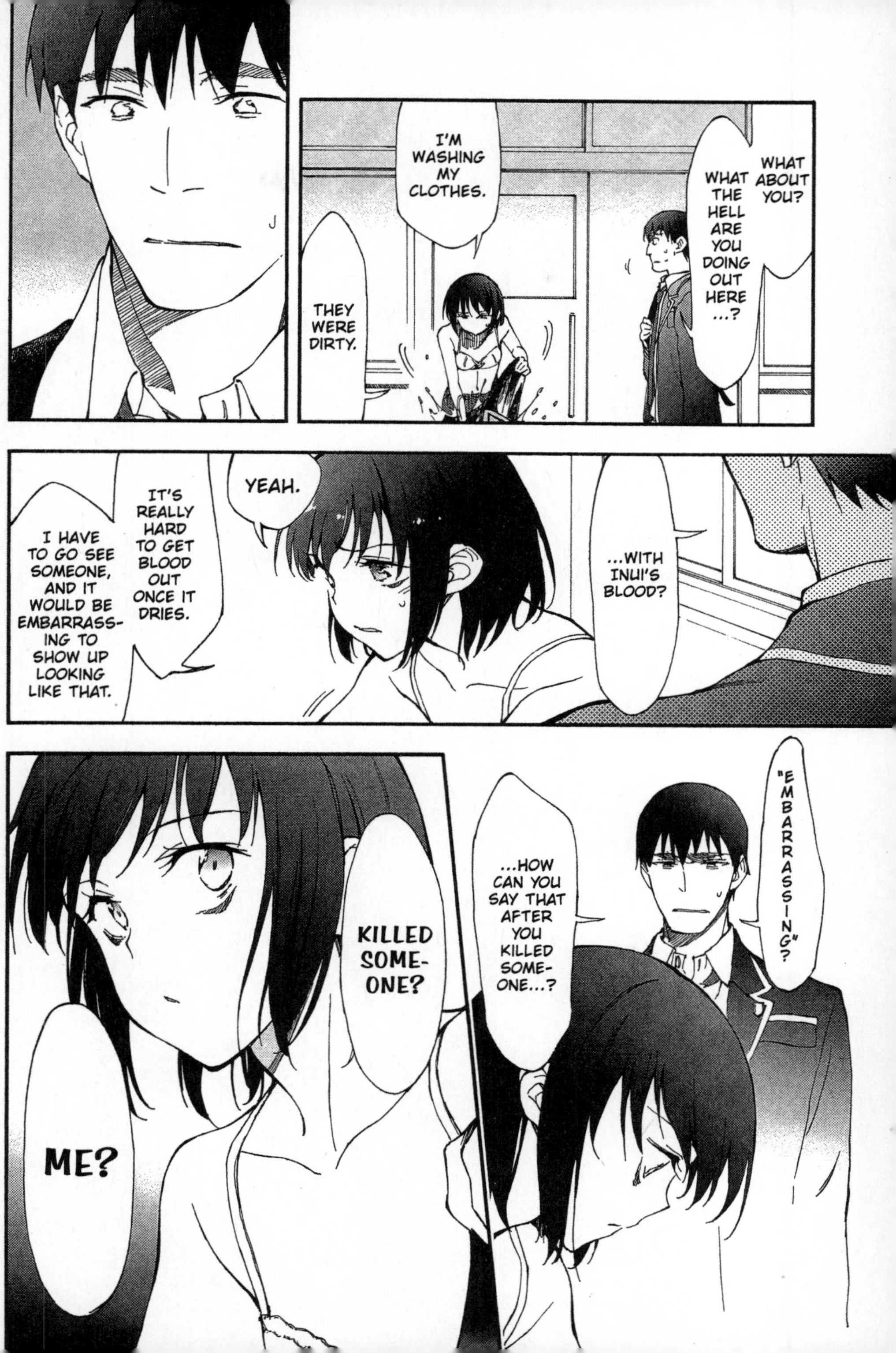
WHAT ABOUT YOU?
WHAT THE HELL ARE YOU DOING OUT HERE...?
I'M WASHING MY CLOTHES.
THEY WERE DIRTY.
...WITH INUI'S BLOOD?
YEAH.
IT'S REALLY HARD TO GET BLOOD OUT ONCE IT DRIES.
I HAVE TO GO SEE SOMEONE, AND IT WOULD BE EMBARRASSING TO SHOW UP LOOKING LIKE THAT.
"EMBARRASSING"?
...HOW CAN YOU SAY THAT AFTER YOU KILLED SOMEONE...?
KILLED SOMEONE?
ME?

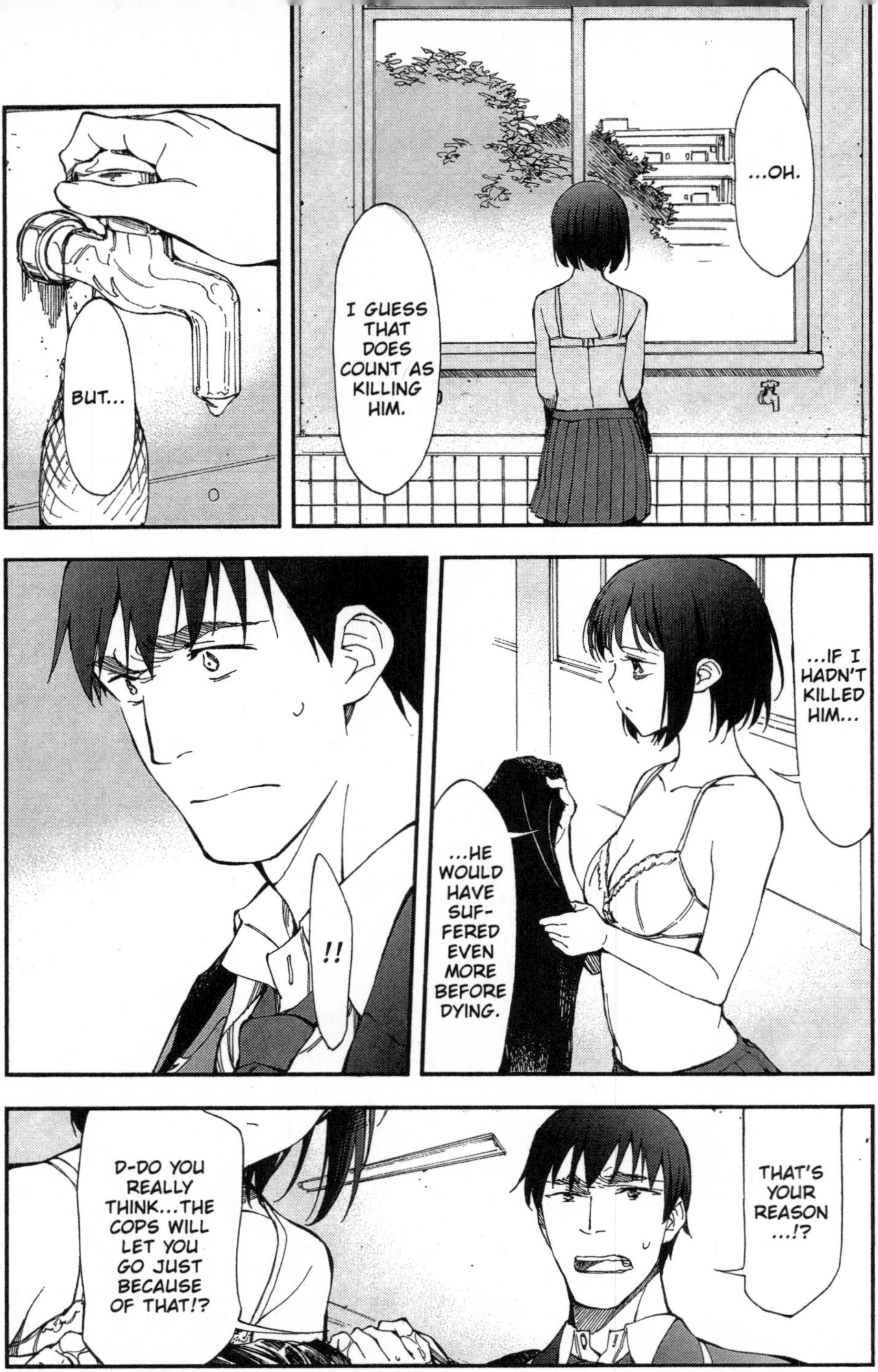
...OH.
I GUESS THAT DOES COUNT AS KILLING HIM.
BUT...
...IF I HADN'T KILLED HIM...
...HE WOULD HAVE SUF-FERED EVEN MORE BEFORE DYING.
!!
THAT'S YOUR REASON ...!?
D-DO YOU REALLY THINK...THE COPS WILL LET YOU GO JUST BECAUSE OF THAT!?

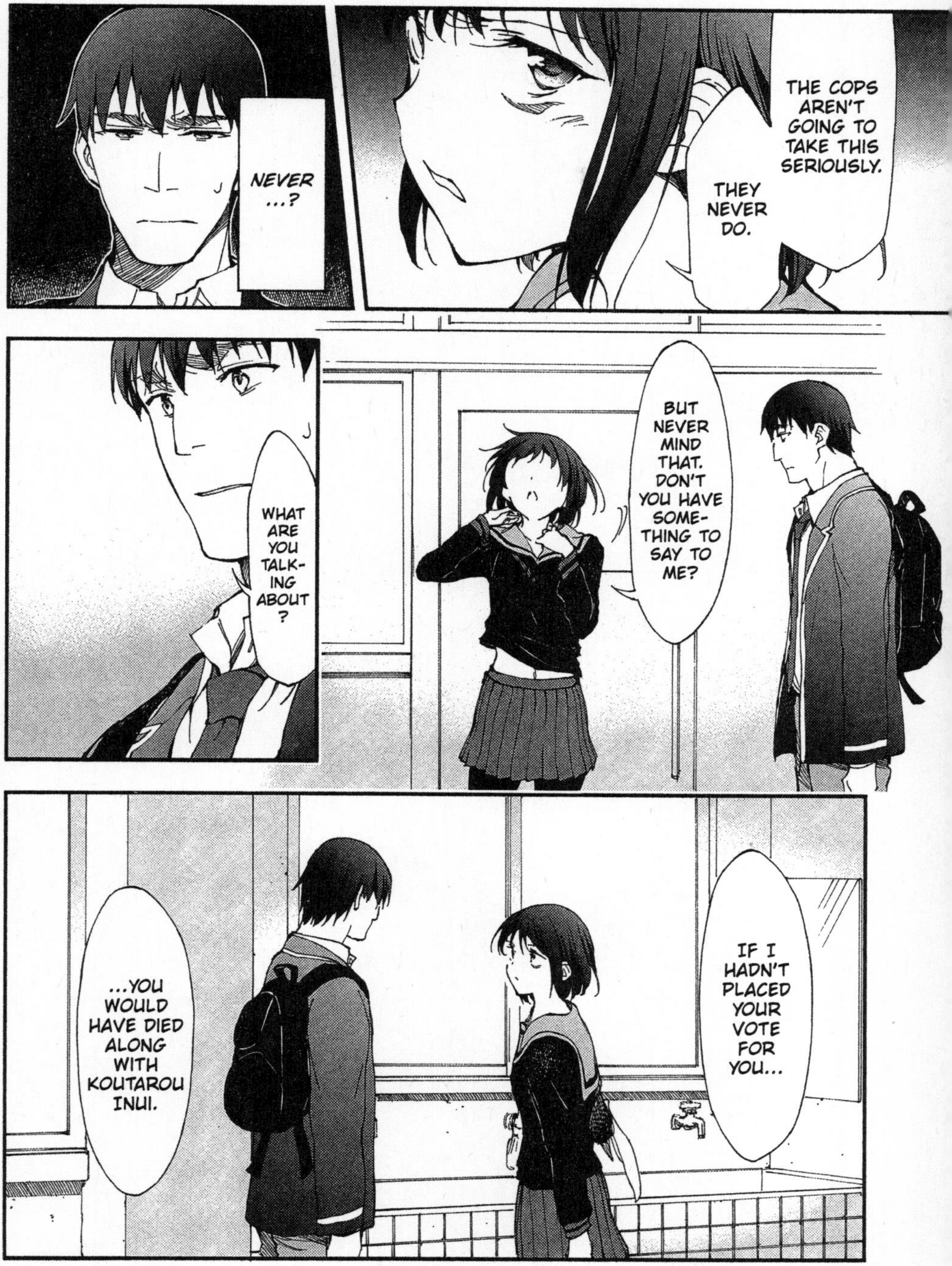
THE COPS AREN'T GOING TO TAKE THIS SERIOUSLY.
THEY NEVER DO.
NEVER ...?
BUT NEVER MIND THAT. DON'T YOU HAVE SOMETHING TO SAY TO ME?
WHAT ARE YOU TALKING ABOUT?
IF I HADN'T PLACED YOUR VOTE FOR YOU...
...YOU WOULD HAVE DIED ALONG WITH KOUTAROU INUI.

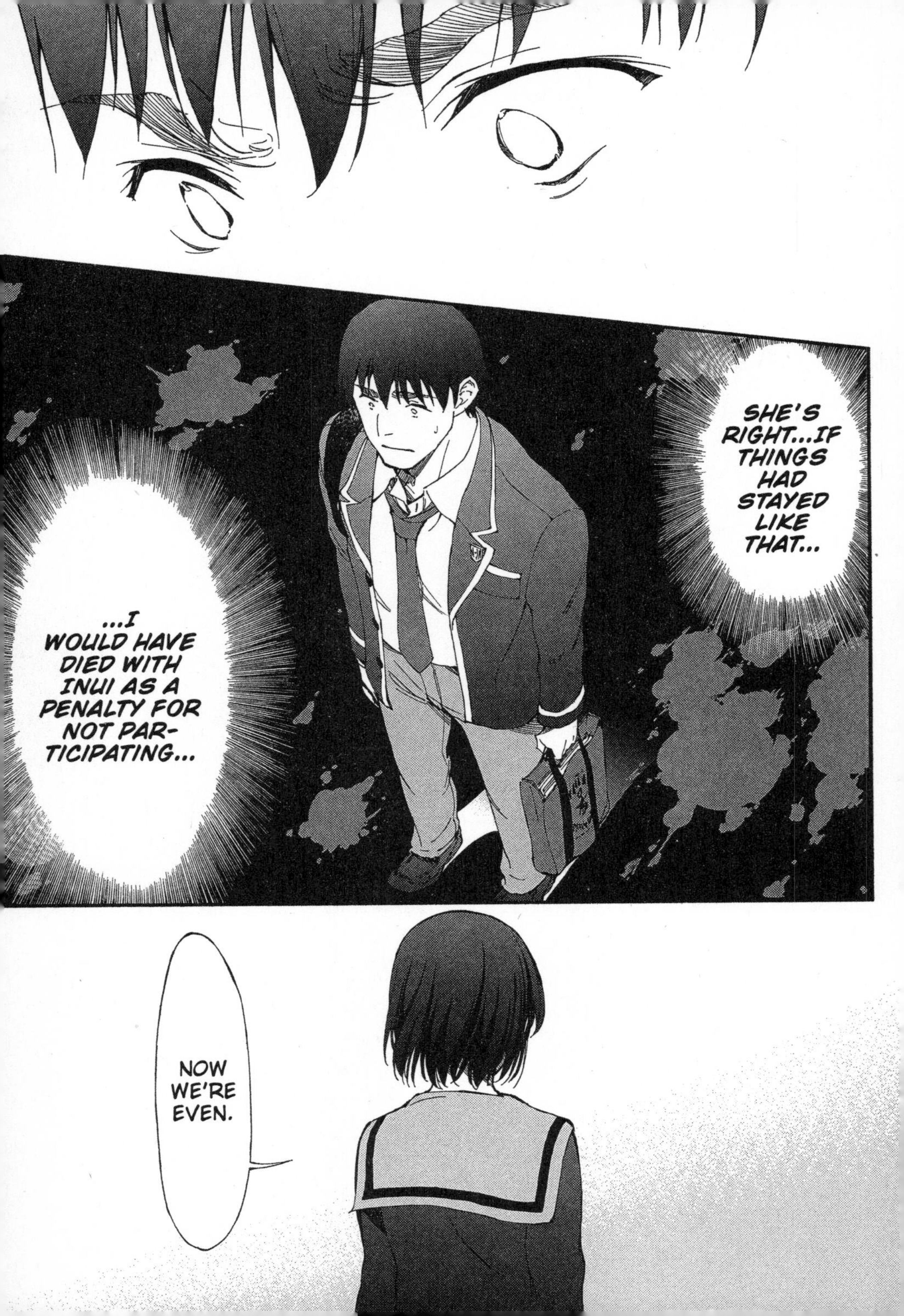
SHE'S RIGHT...IF THINGS HAD STAYED LIKE THAT...
...I WOULD HAVE DIED WITH INUI AS A PENALTY FOR NOT PAR-TICIPATING...
NOW WE'RE EVEN.

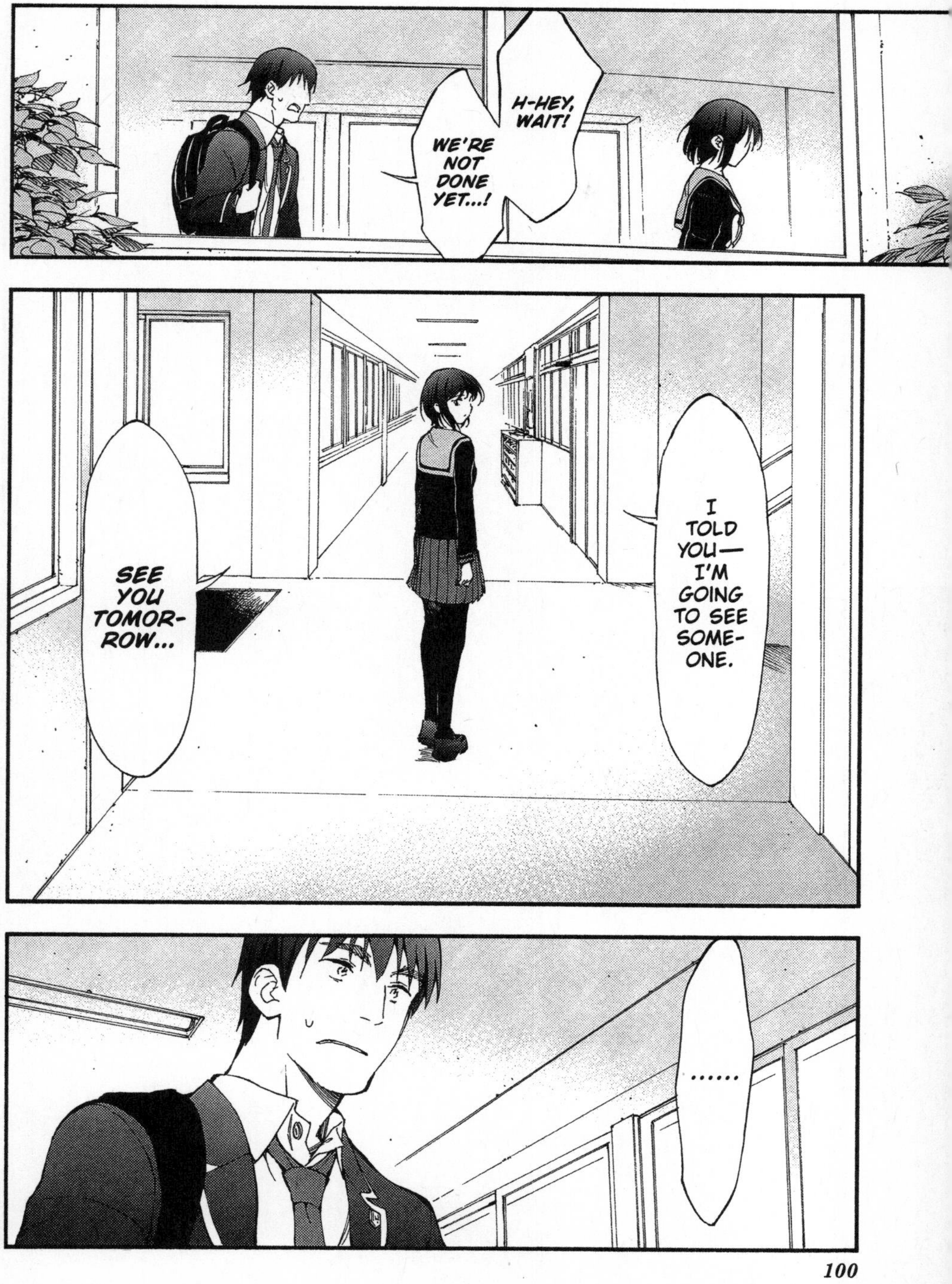
H-HEY, WAIT!
WE'RE NOT DONE YET...!
I TOLD YOU— I'M GOING TO SEE SOME-ONE.
SEE YOU TOMOR-ROW...
......

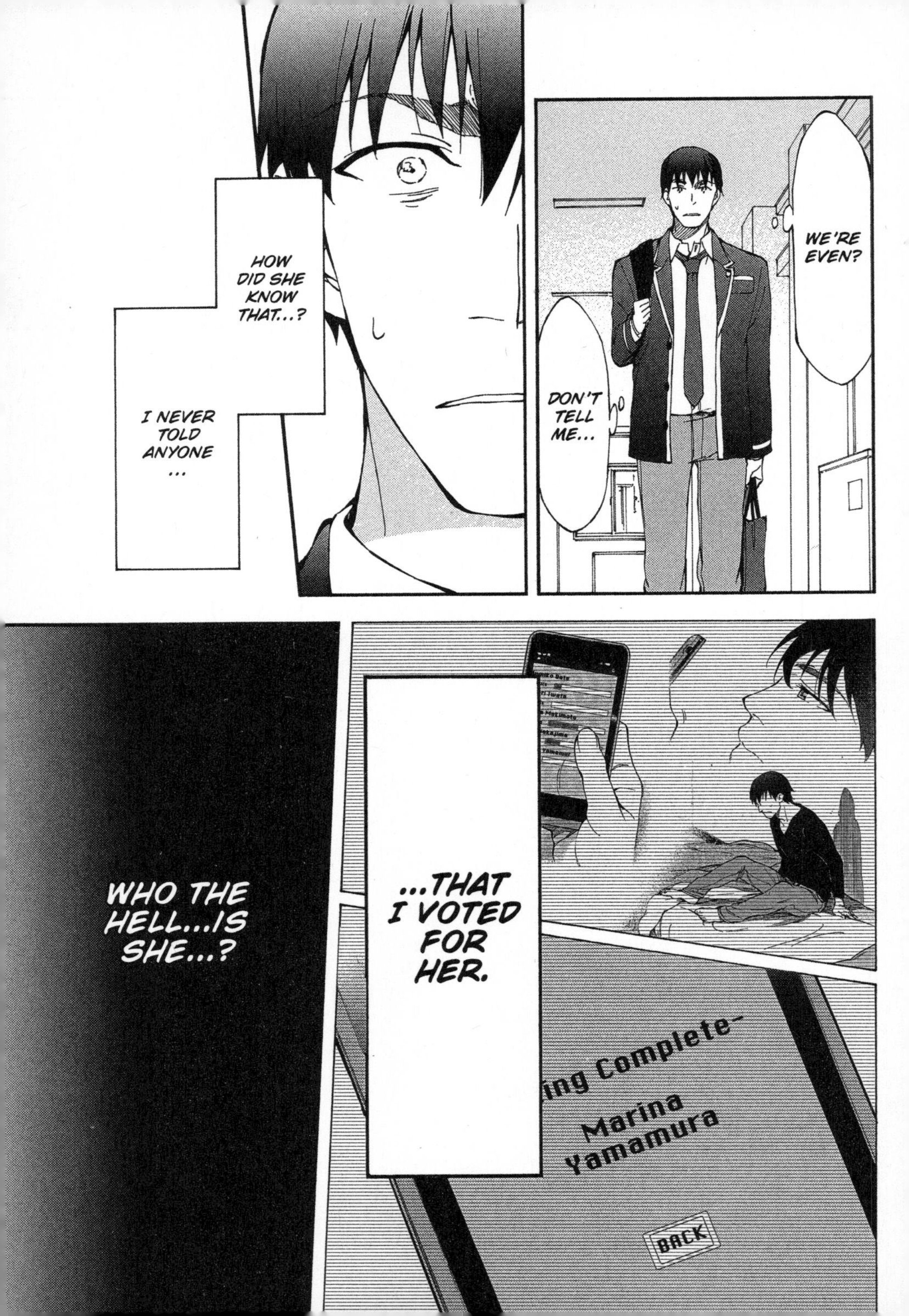
WE'RE EVEN?
DON'T TELL ME...
HOW DID SHE KNOW THAT...?
I NEVER TOLD ANYONE...
...THAT I VOTED FOR HER.
ing Complete-
Marina Yamamura
BACK
WHO THE HELL...IS SHE...?

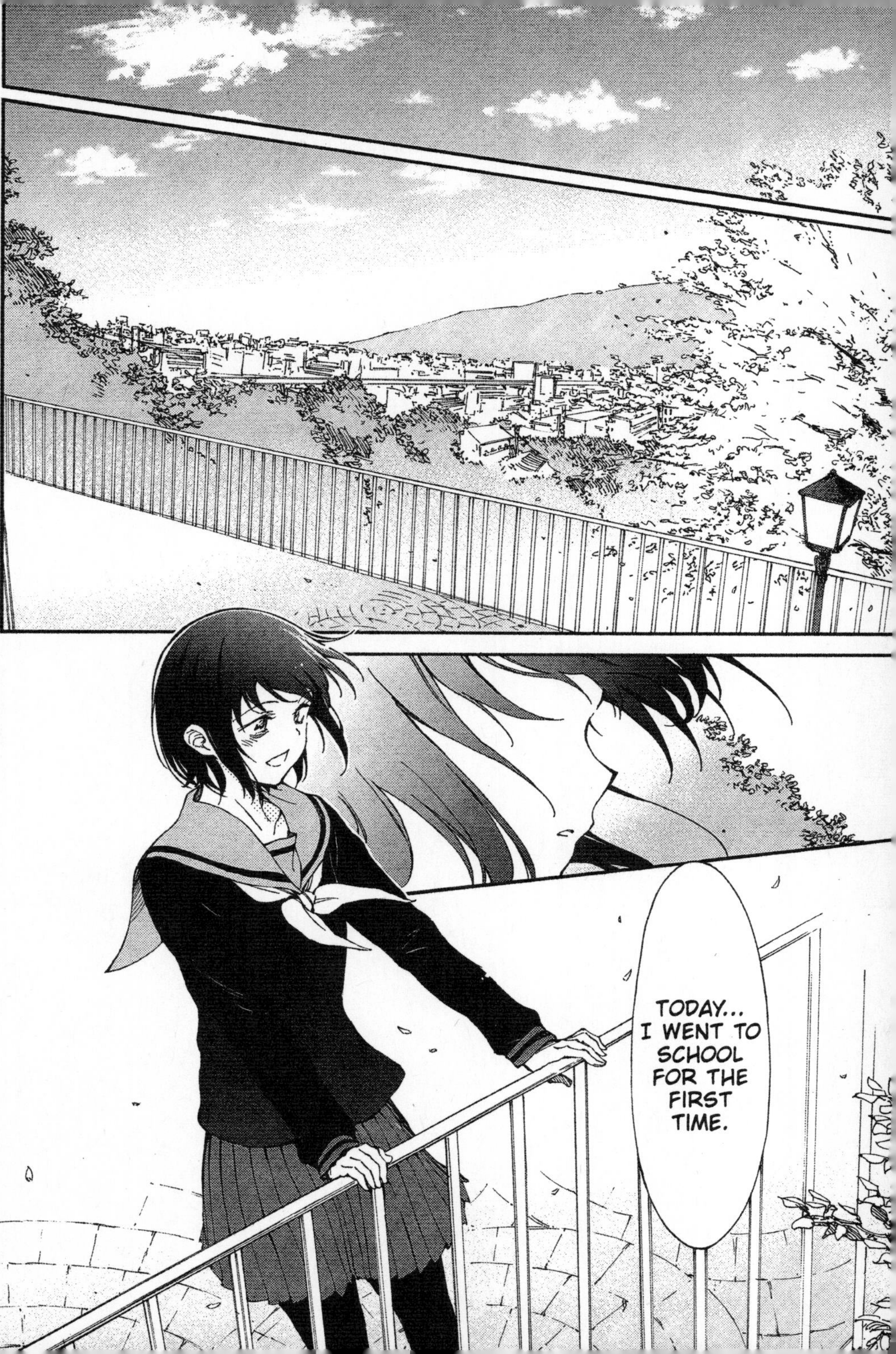
TODAY... I WENT TO SCHOOL FOR THE FIRST TIME.

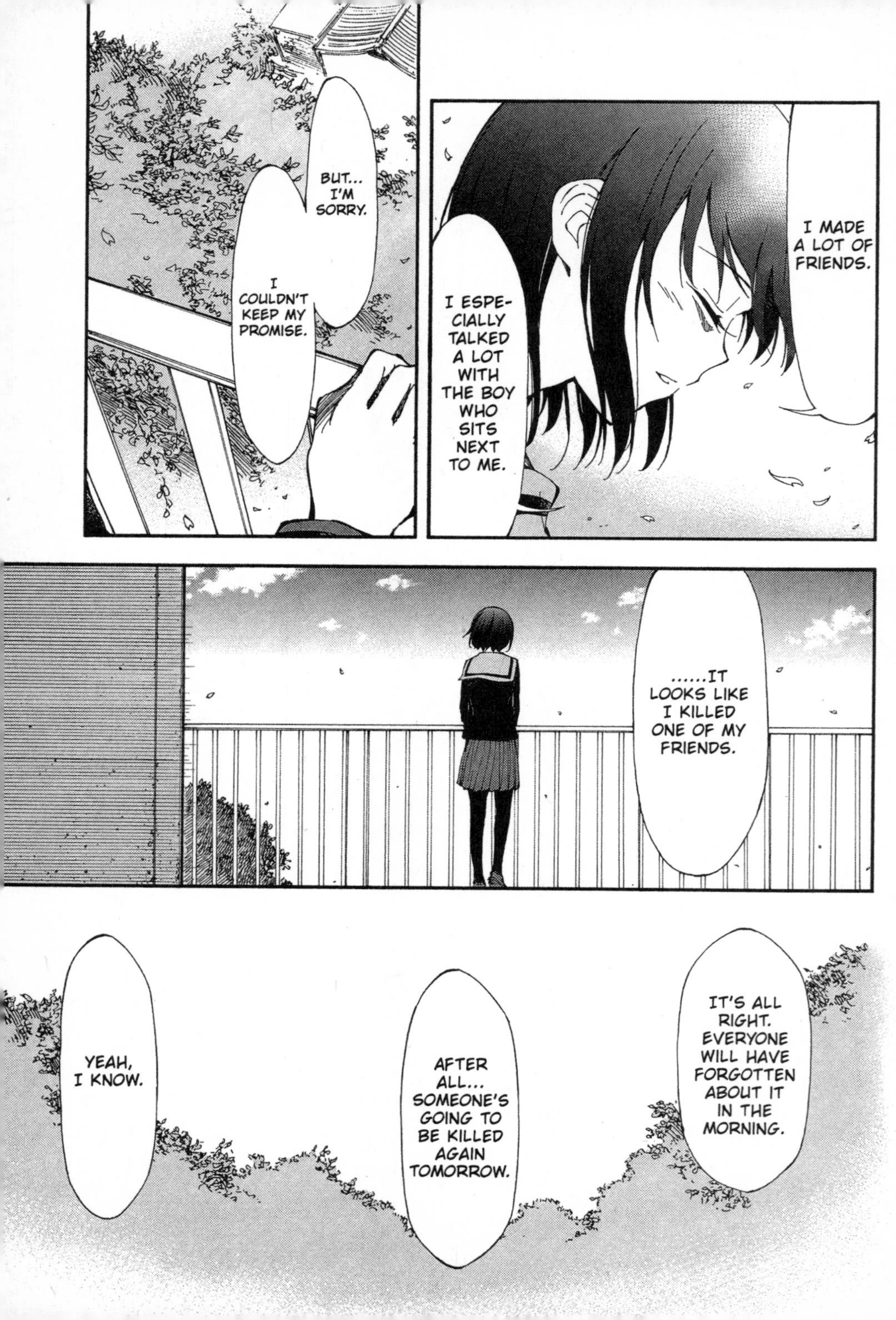
I MADE A LOT OF FRIENDS.
I ESPECIALLY TALKED A LOT WITH THE BOY WHO SITS NEXT TO ME.
BUT... I'M SORRY.
I COULDN'T KEEP MY PROMISE.
......IT LOOKS LIKE I KILLED ONE OF MY FRIENDS.
IT'S ALL RIGHT. EVERYONE WILL HAVE FORGOTTEN ABOUT IT IN THE MORNING.
AFTER ALL... SOMEONE'S GOING TO BE KILLED AGAIN TOMORROW.
YEAH, I KNOW.

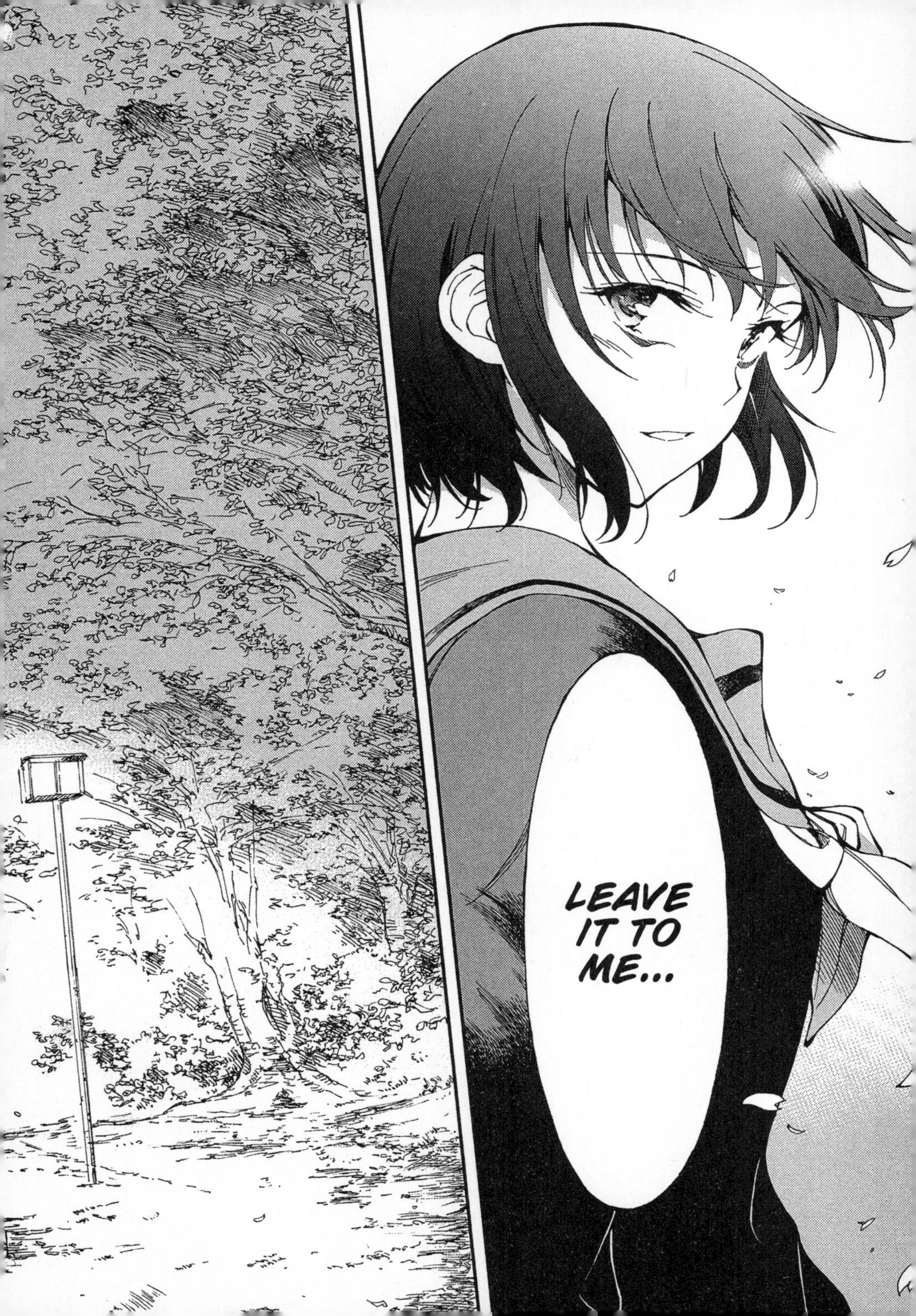
LEAVE IT TO ME...

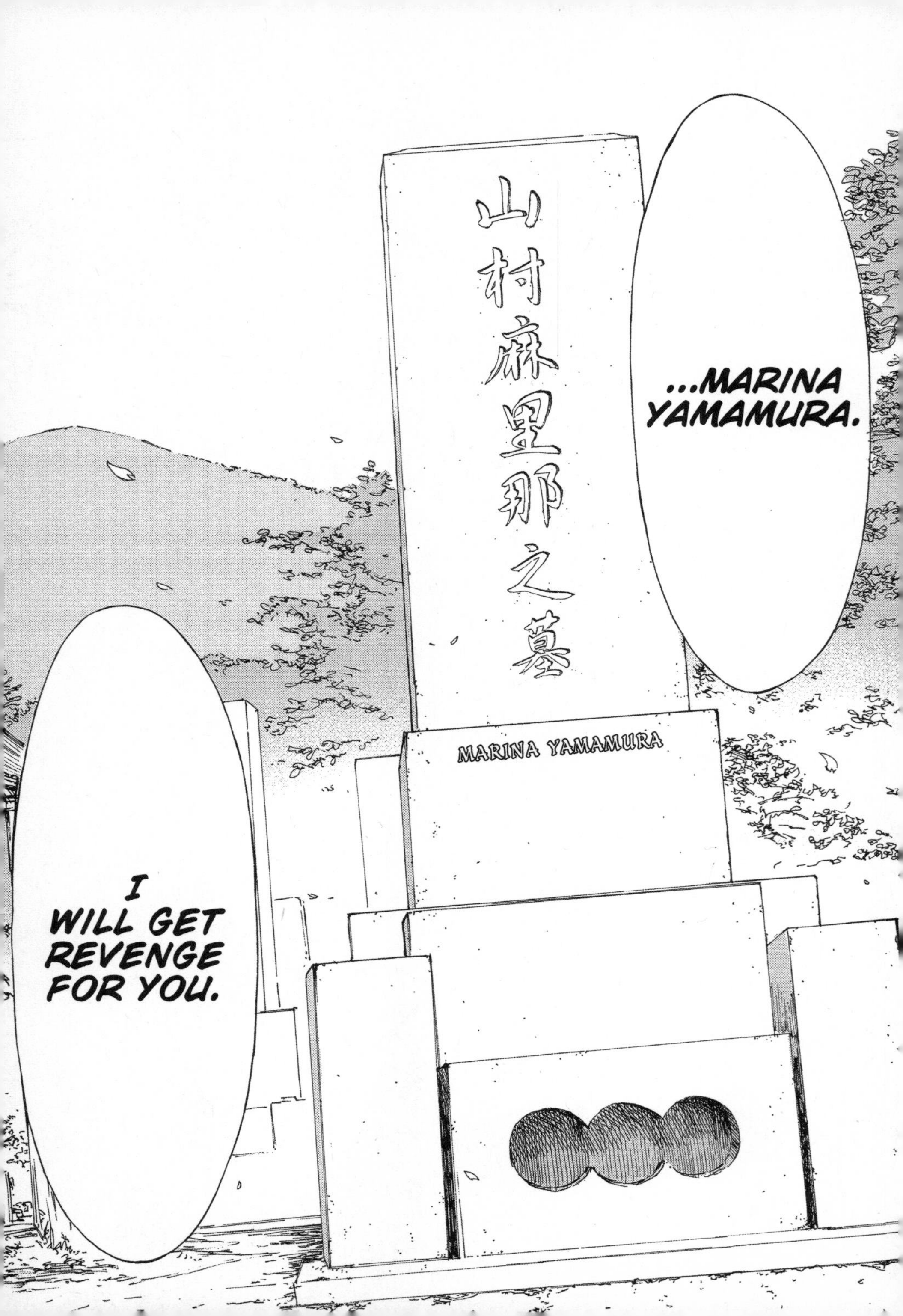
...MARINA YAMAMURA.
山村麻里那之墓
MARINA YAMAMURA
I WILL GET REVENGE FOR YOU.

TOHYO GAME

One **black** ballot ᵗᵒ you

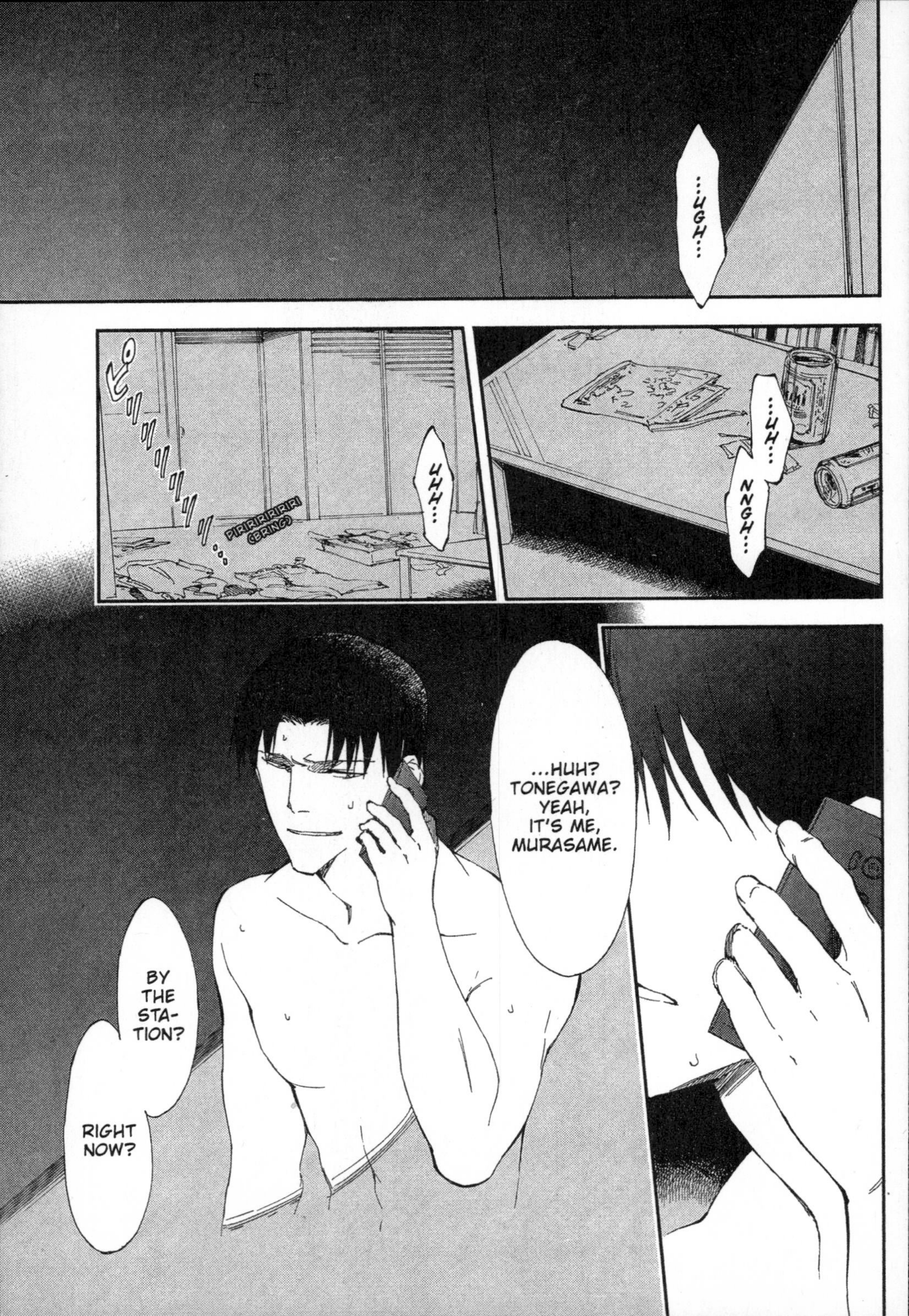
...UGH...
...UH... NNGH...
UHH...
PIRIRIRIRIRI (BRING)
...HUH? TONEGAWA? YEAH, IT'S ME, MURASAME.
BY THE STATION?
RIGHT NOW?

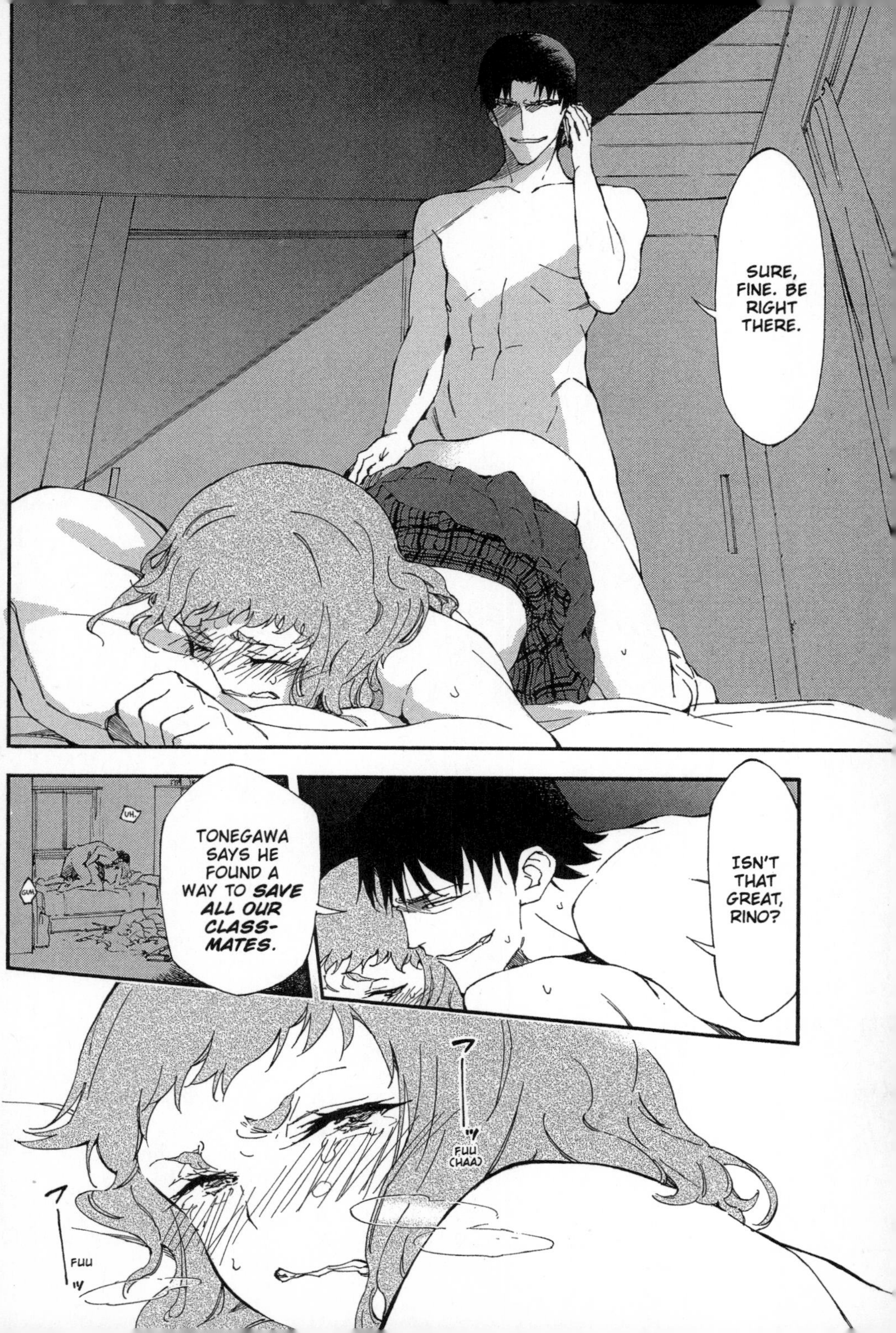
SURE, FINE. BE RIGHT THERE.
ISN'T THAT GREAT, RINO?
TONEGAWA SAYS HE FOUND A WAY TO SAVE ALL OUR CLASSMATES.
UH.
GUH.
FUU (HAA)
FUU

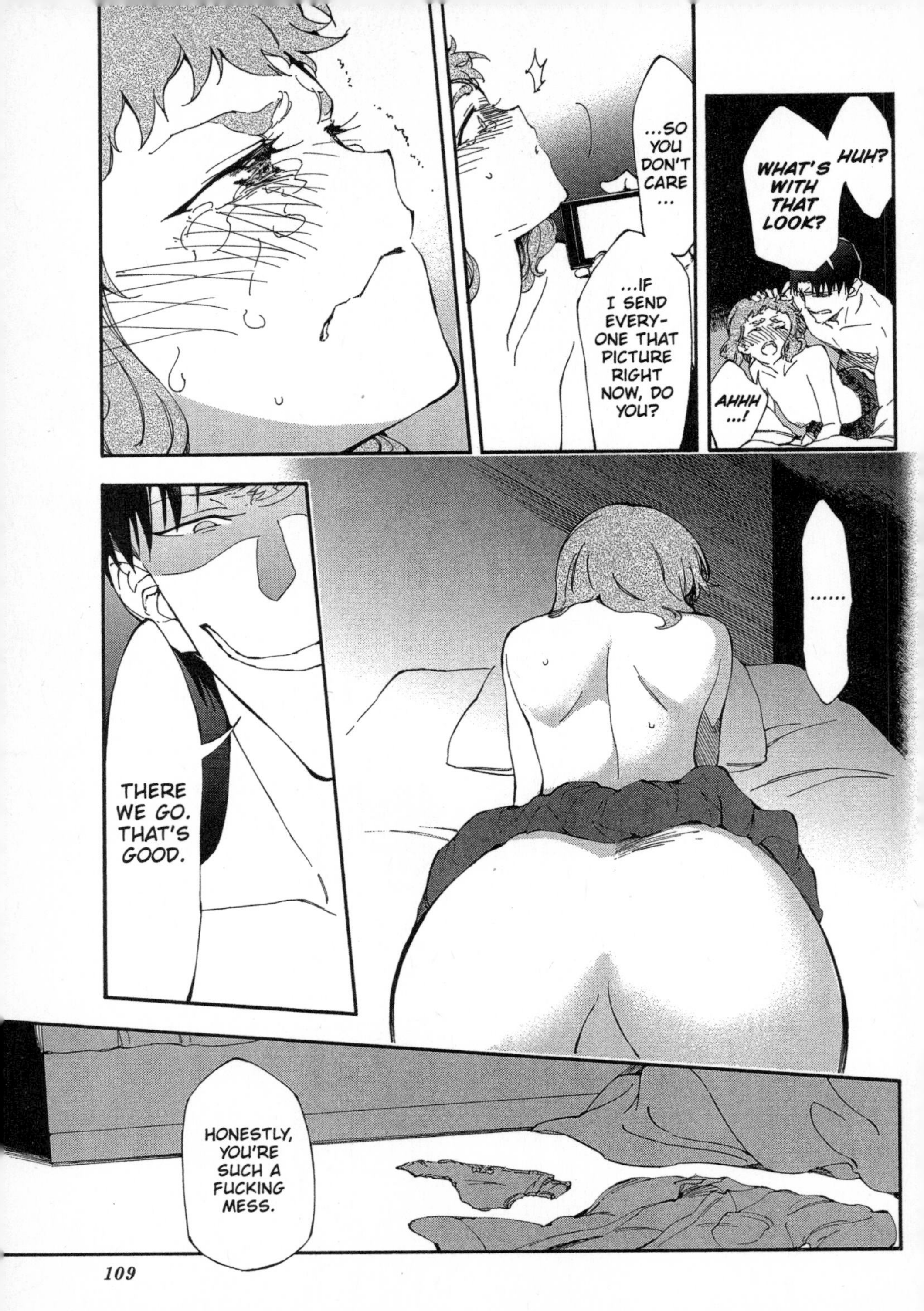
HUH?
WHAT'S WITH THAT LOOK?
AHHH ...!
...SO YOU DON'T CARE ...
...IF I SEND EVERY-ONE THAT PICTURE RIGHT NOW, DO YOU?
......
THERE WE GO. THAT'S GOOD.
HONESTLY, YOU'RE SUCH A FUCKING MESS.

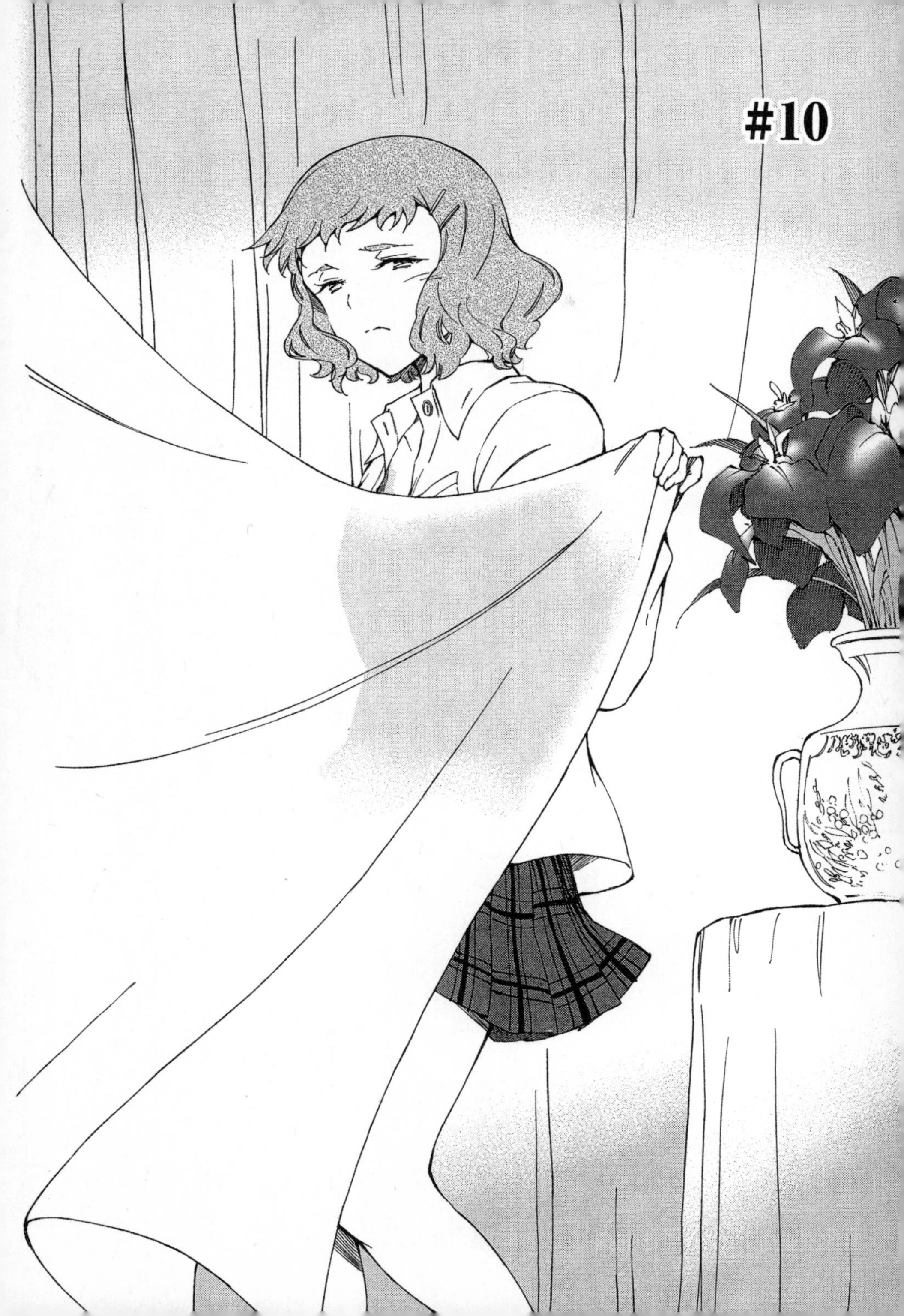
#10

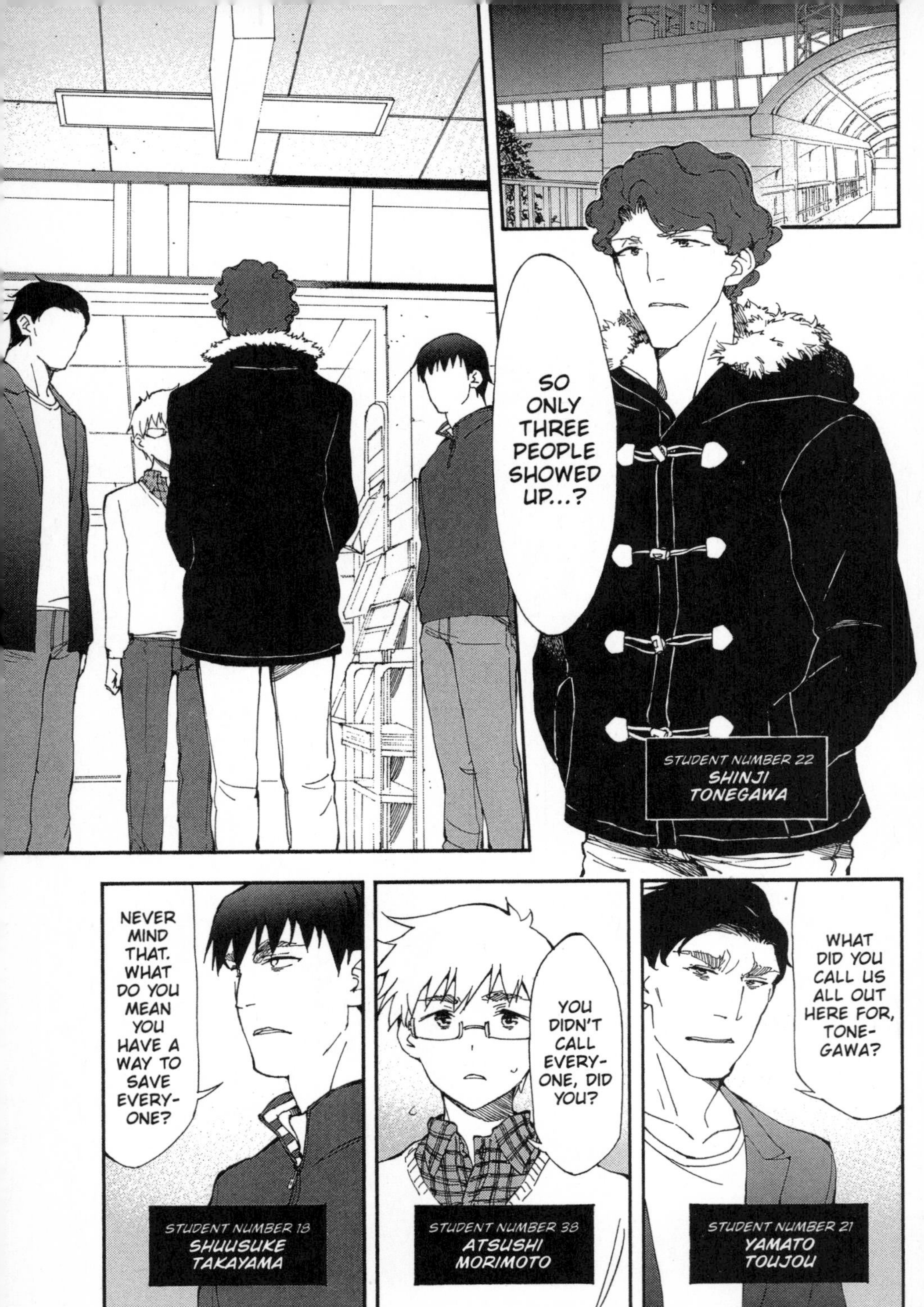
SO ONLY THREE PEOPLE SHOWED UP...?
STUDENT NUMBER 22
SHINJI TONEGAWA
WHAT DID YOU CALL US ALL OUT HERE FOR, TONE-GAWA?
STUDENT NUMBER 21
YAMATO TOUJOU
YOU DIDN'T CALL EVERY-ONE, DID YOU?
STUDENT NUMBER 38
ATSUSHI MORIMOTO
NEVER MIND THAT. WHAT DO YOU MEAN YOU HAVE A WAY TO SAVE EVERY-ONE?
STUDENT NUMBER 18
SHUUSUKE TAKAYAMA

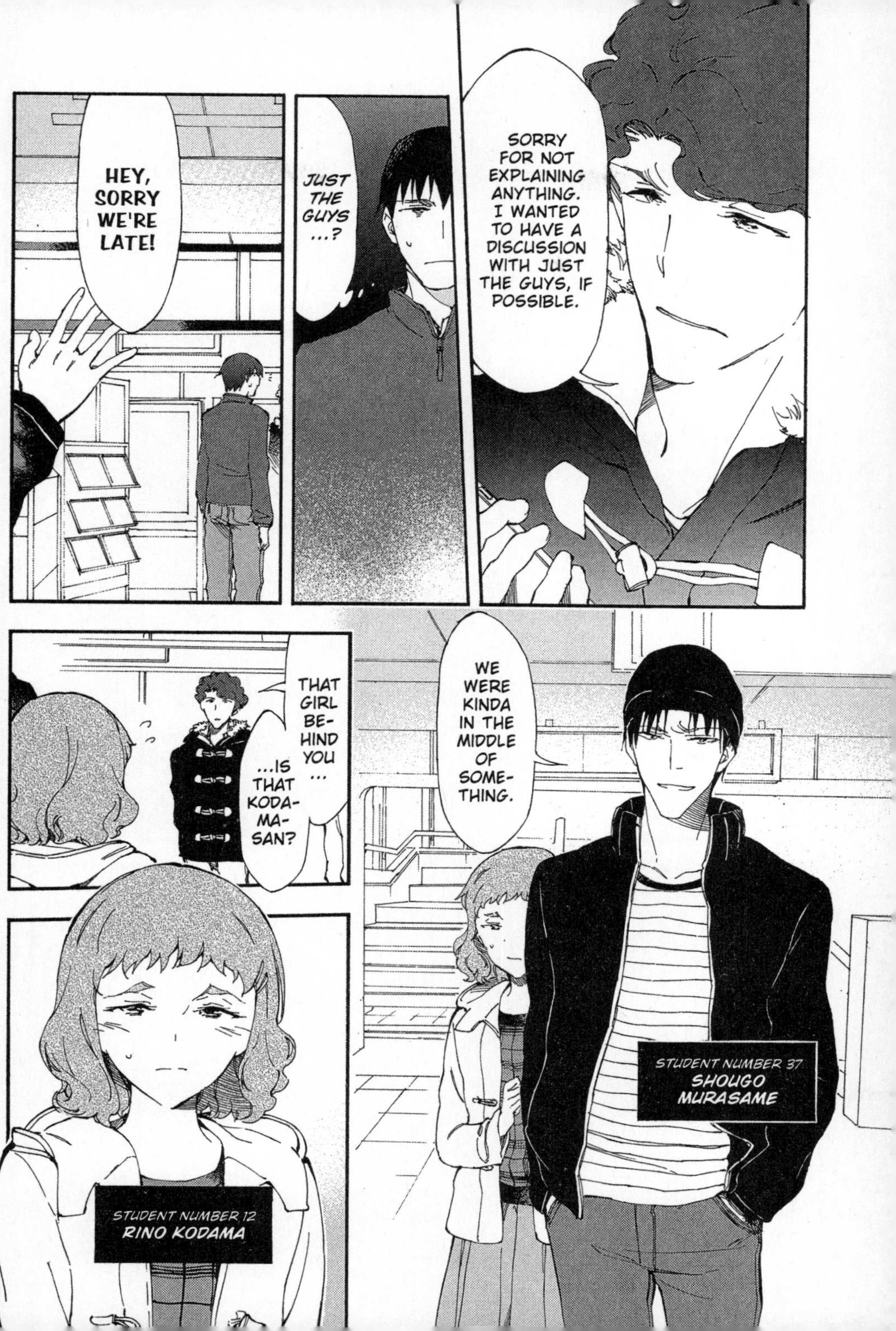
SORRY FOR NOT EXPLAINING ANYTHING. I WANTED TO HAVE A DISCUSSION WITH JUST THE GUYS, IF POSSIBLE.
JUST THE GUYS ...?
HEY, SORRY WE'RE LATE!
WE WERE KINDA IN THE MIDDLE OF SOMETHING.
STUDENT NUMBER 37
SHOUGO MURASAME
THAT GIRL BEHIND YOU ...
...IS THAT KODAMA-SAN?
STUDENT NUMBER 12
RINO KODAMA

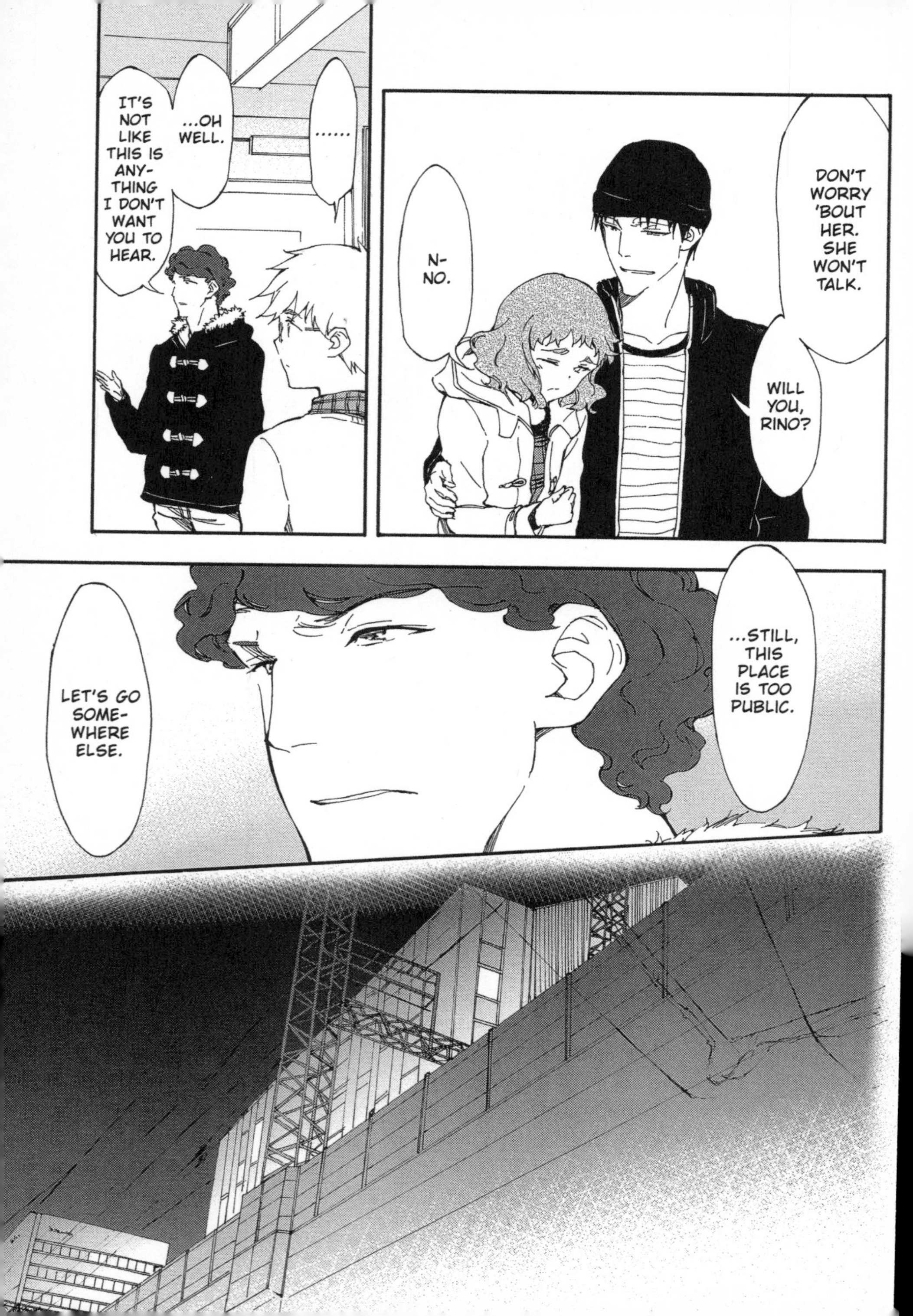
DON'T WORRY 'BOUT HER. SHE WON'T TALK.
WILL YOU, RINO?
N-NO.
......
...OH WELL.
IT'S NOT LIKE THIS IS ANYTHING I DON'T WANT YOU TO HEAR.
...STILL, THIS PLACE IS TOO PUBLIC.
LET'S GO SOMEWHERE ELSE.

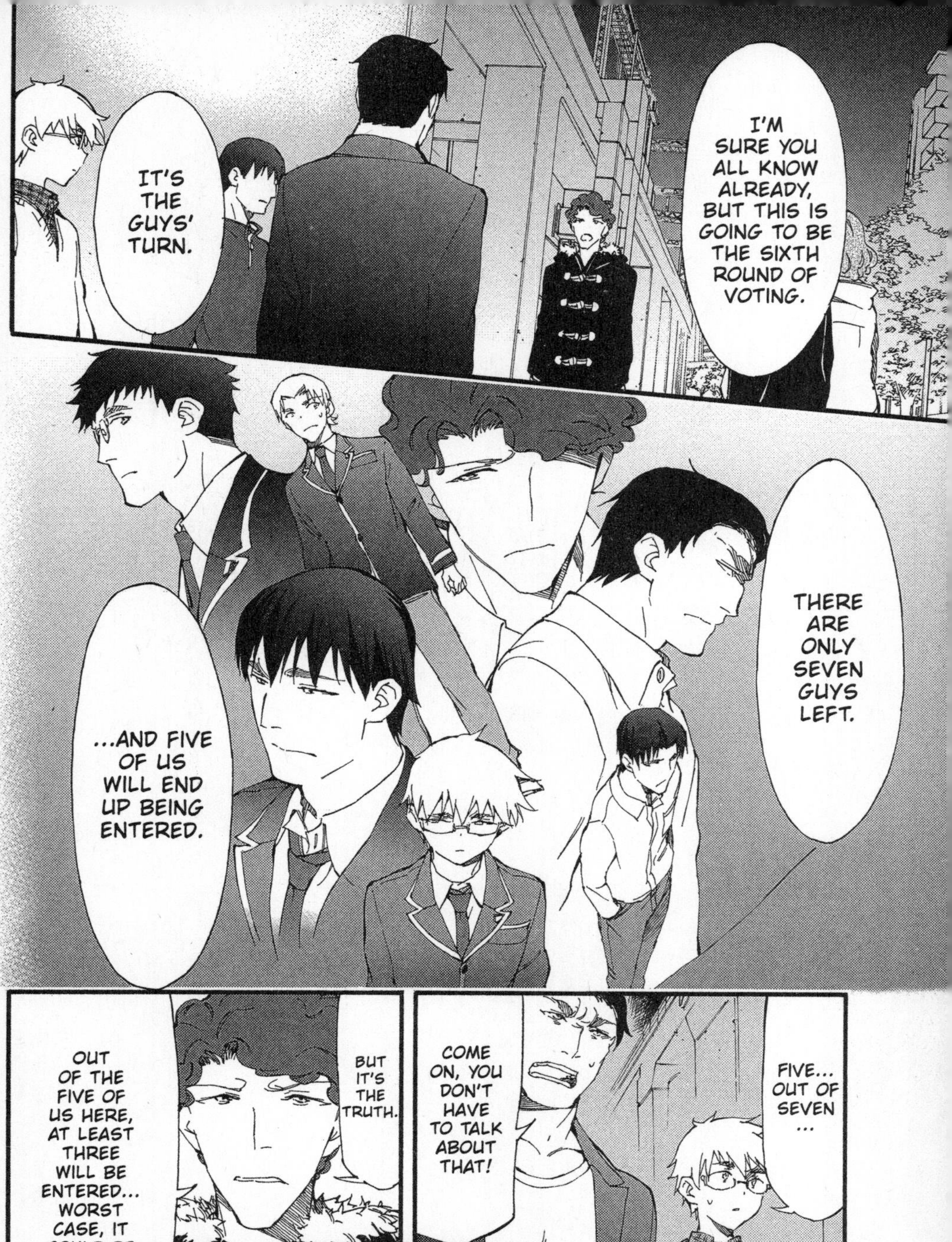
I'M SURE YOU ALL KNOW ALREADY, BUT THIS IS GOING TO BE THE SIXTH ROUND OF VOTING.
IT'S THE GUYS' TURN.
THERE ARE ONLY SEVEN GUYS LEFT.
...AND FIVE OF US WILL END UP BEING ENTERED.
FIVE... OUT OF SEVEN...
COME ON, YOU DON'T HAVE TO TALK ABOUT THAT!
BUT IT'S THE TRUTH.
OUT OF THE FIVE OF US HERE, AT LEAST THREE WILL BE ENTERED... WORST CASE, IT COULD BE ALL OF US.

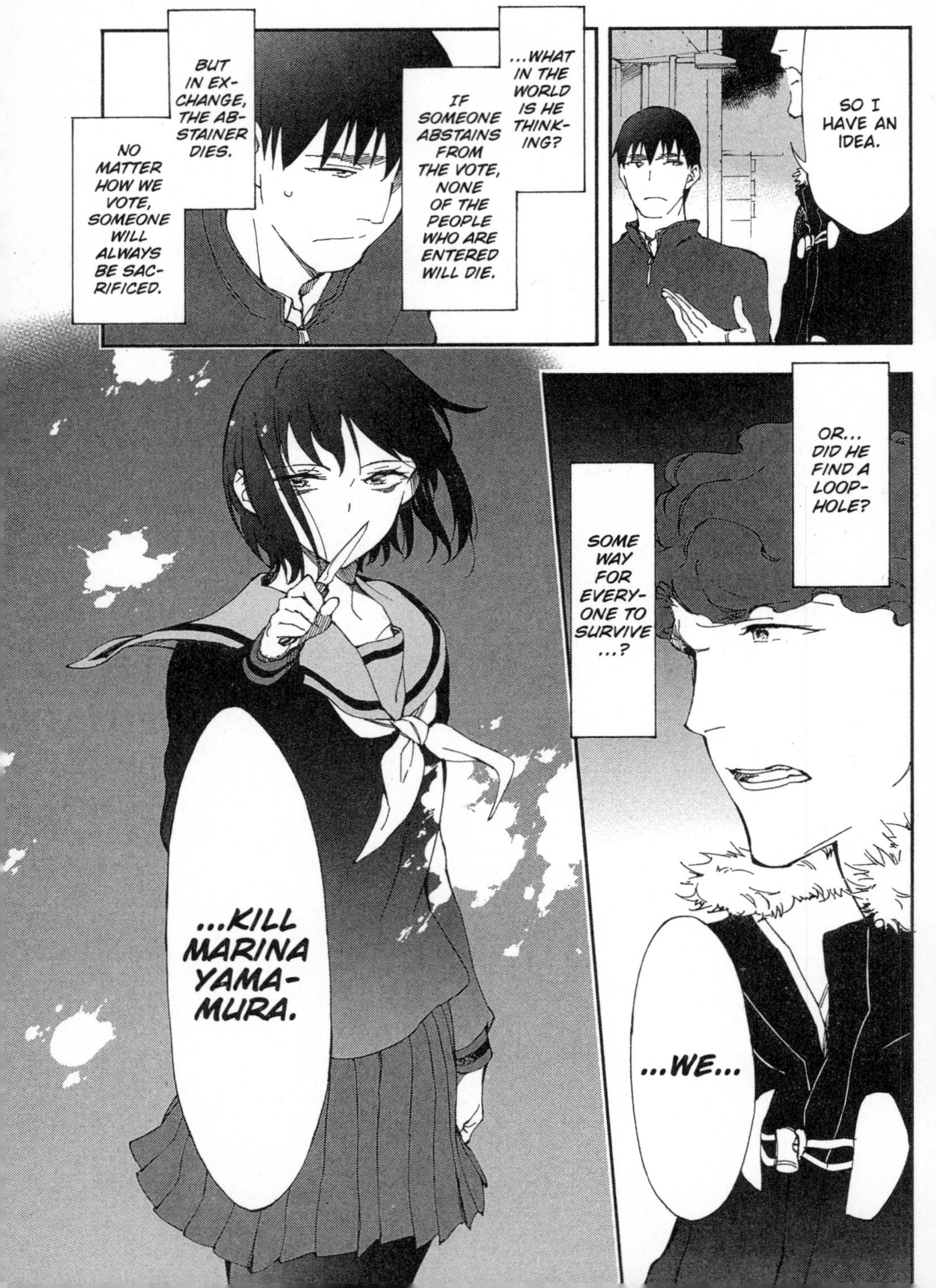
SO I HAVE AN IDEA.
...WHAT IN THE WORLD IS HE THINKING?
IF SOMEONE ABSTAINS FROM THE VOTE, NONE OF THE PEOPLE WHO ARE ENTERED WILL DIE.
BUT IN EXCHANGE, THE ABSTAINER DIES.
NO MATTER HOW WE VOTE, SOMEONE WILL ALWAYS BE SACRIFICED.
OR... DID HE FIND A LOOPHOLE?
SOME WAY FOR EVERYONE TO SURVIVE...?
...WE...
...KILL MARINA YAMAMURA.

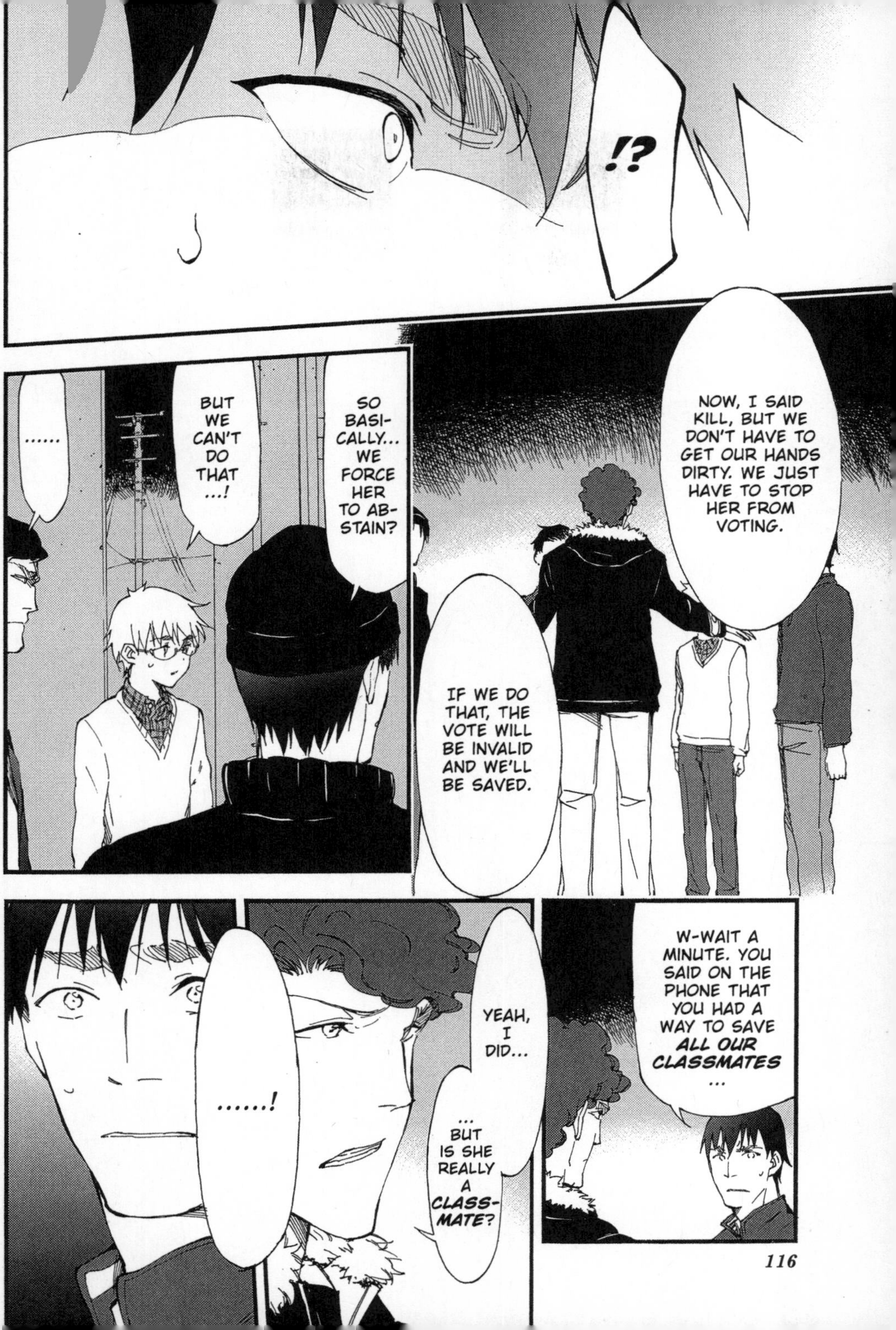
!?
NOW, I SAID KILL, BUT WE DON'T HAVE TO GET OUR HANDS DIRTY. WE JUST HAVE TO STOP HER FROM VOTING.
IF WE DO THAT, THE VOTE WILL BE INVALID AND WE'LL BE SAVED.
SO BASICALLY... WE FORCE HER TO ABSTAIN?
BUT WE CAN'T DO THAT...!
......
W-WAIT A MINUTE. YOU SAID ON THE PHONE THAT YOU HAD A WAY TO SAVE ***ALL OUR CLASSMATES***...
YEAH, I DID...
...BUT IS SHE REALLY A ***CLASSMATE***?
......!

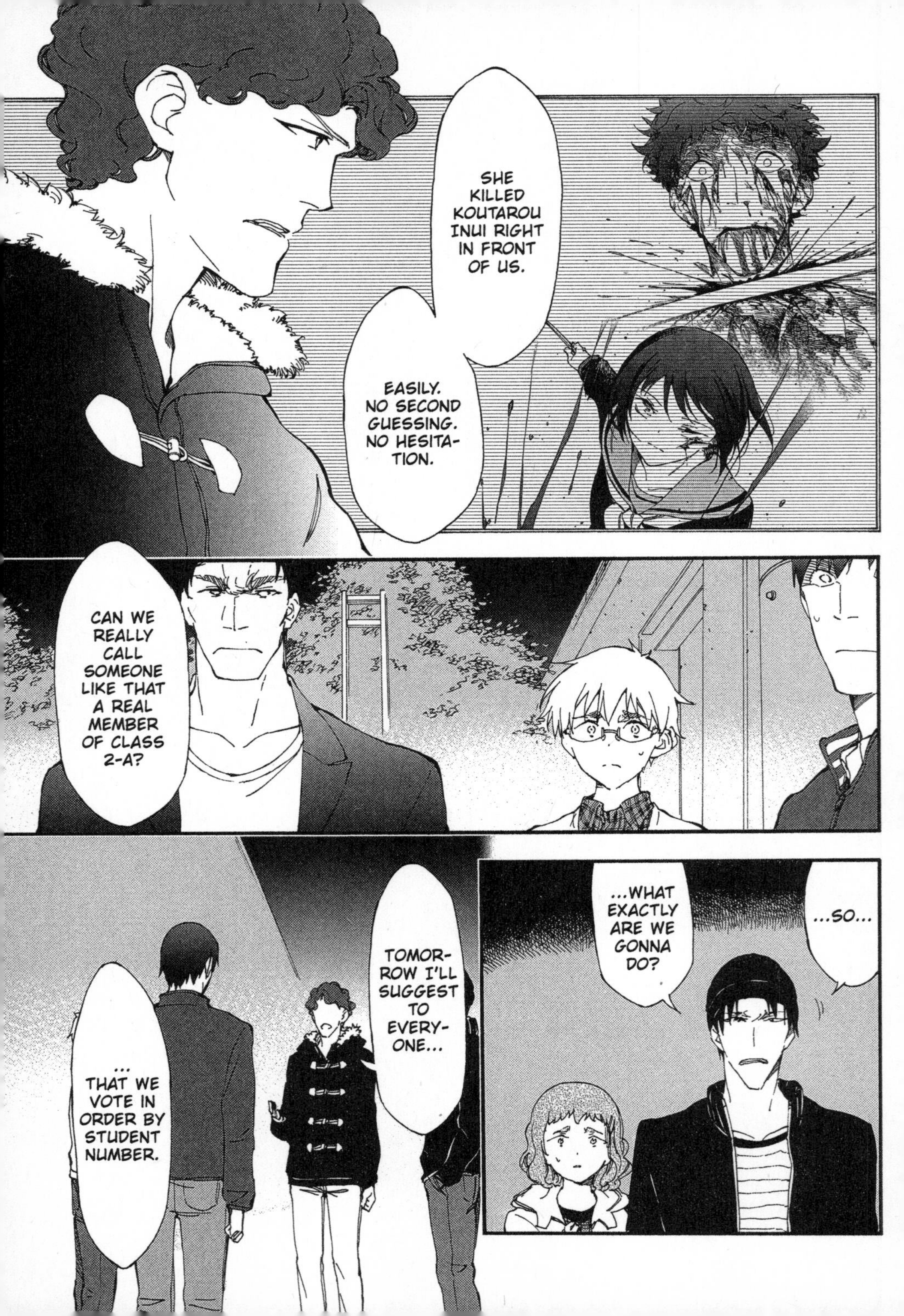
SHE KILLED KOUTAROU INUI RIGHT IN FRONT OF US.
EASILY. NO SECOND GUESSING. NO HESITATION.
CAN WE REALLY CALL SOMEONE LIKE THAT A REAL MEMBER OF CLASS 2-A?
...SO...
...WHAT EXACTLY ARE WE GONNA DO?
TOMORROW I'LL SUGGEST TO EVERYONE...
...THAT WE VOTE IN ORDER BY STUDENT NUMBER.

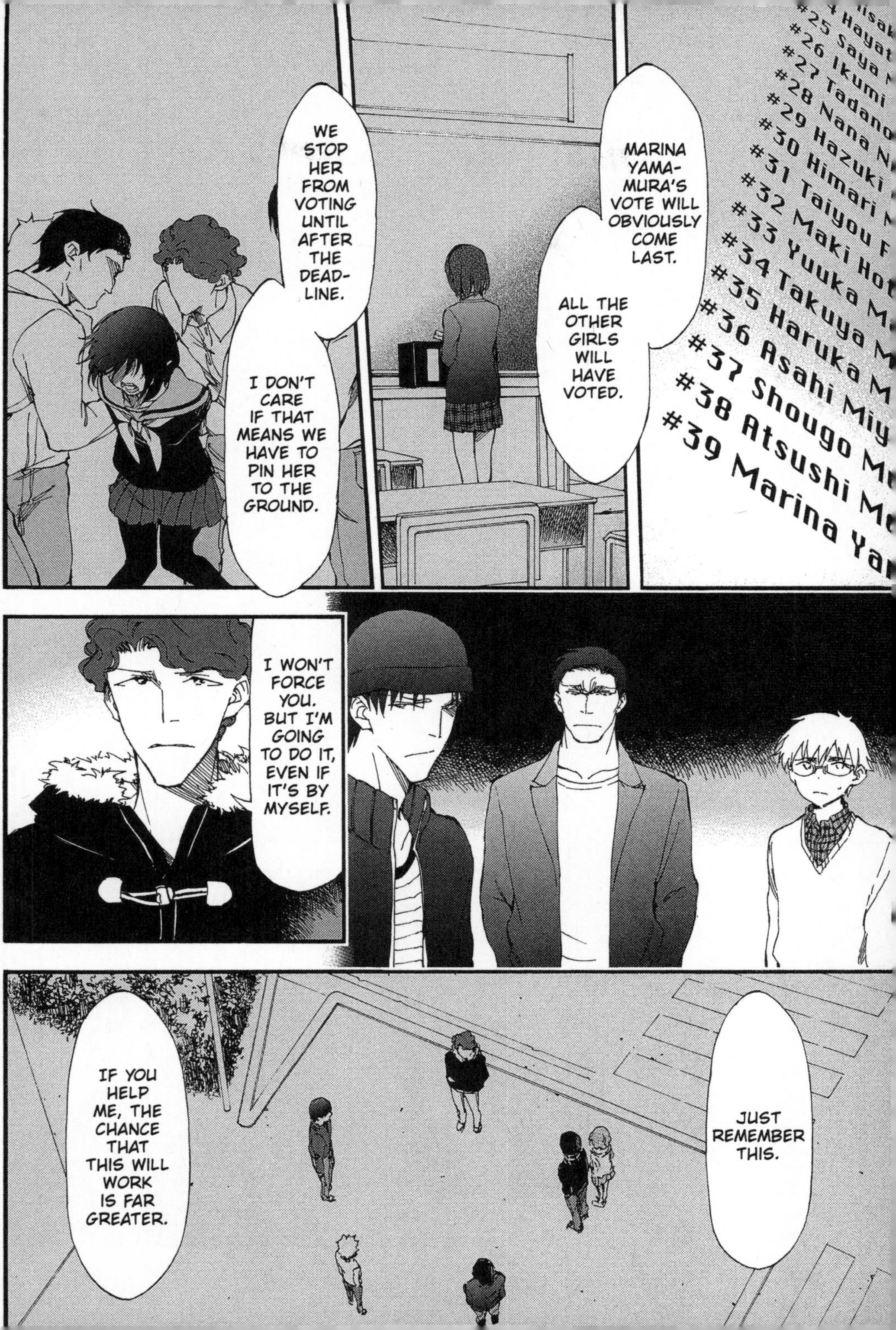
#25 Saya
#26 Ikumi
#27 Tadano
#28 Nana
#29 Hazuki
#30 Himari
#31 Taiyou
#32 Maki
#33 Yuuka
#34 Takuya
#35 Haruka
#36 Asahi
#37 Shougo
#38 Atsushi
#39 Marina
MARINA YAMAMURA'S VOTE WILL OBVIOUSLY COME LAST.
ALL THE OTHER GIRLS WILL HAVE VOTED.
WE STOP HER FROM VOTING UNTIL AFTER THE DEADLINE.
I DON'T CARE IF THAT MEANS WE HAVE TO PIN HER TO THE GROUND.
I WON'T FORCE YOU. BUT I'M GOING TO DO IT, EVEN IF IT'S BY MYSELF.
JUST REMEMBER THIS.
IF YOU HELP ME, THE CHANCE THAT THIS WILL WORK IS FAR GREATER.

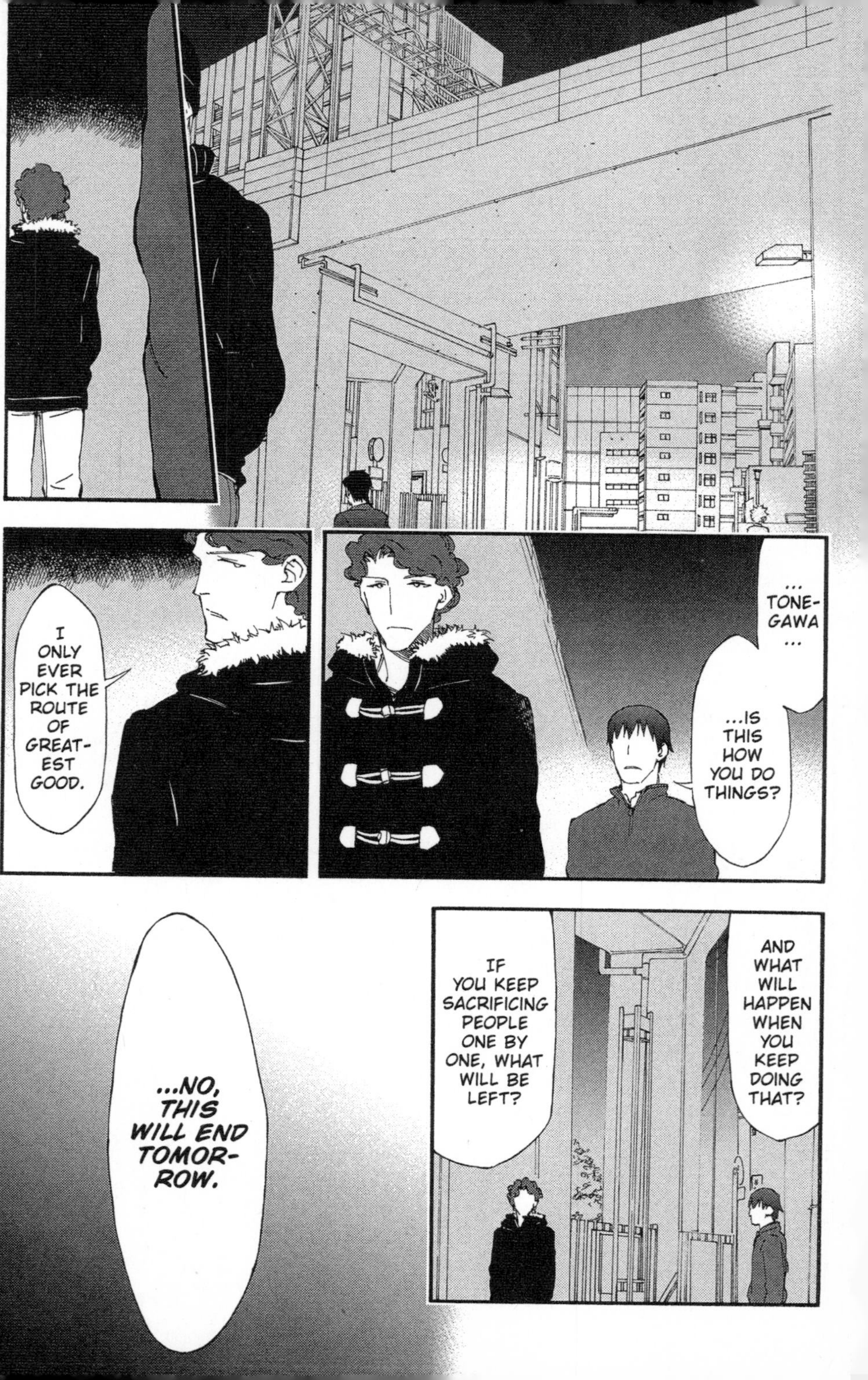

... TONE-GAWA ...
...IS THIS HOW YOU DO THINGS?
I ONLY EVER PICK THE ROUTE OF GREAT-EST GOOD.
AND WHAT WILL HAPPEN WHEN YOU KEEP DOING THAT?
IF YOU KEEP SACRIFICING PEOPLE ONE BY ONE, WHAT WILL BE LEFT?
...NO, THIS WILL END TOMOR-ROW.

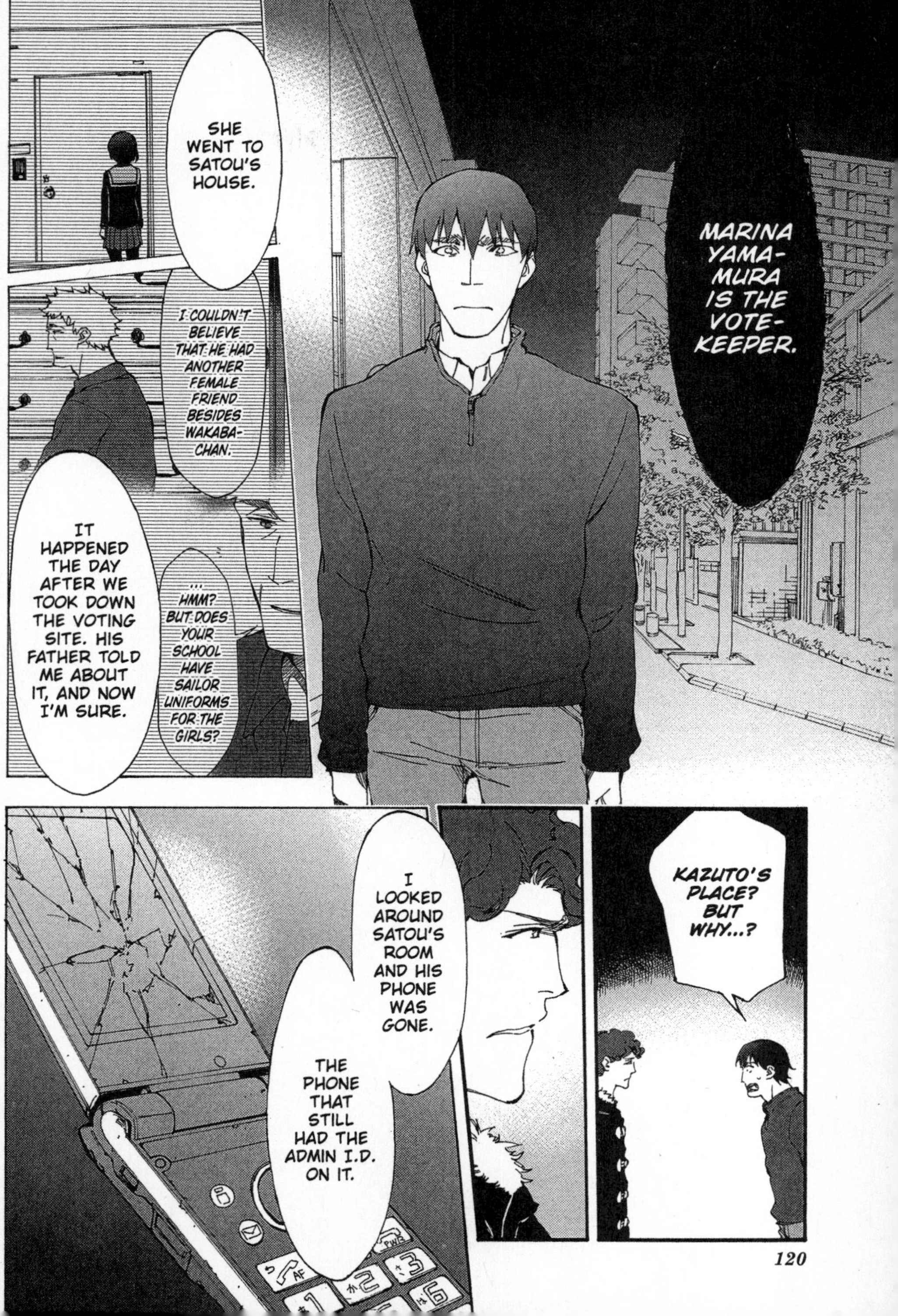
MARINA YAMAMURA IS THE VOTE-KEEPER.
SHE WENT TO SATOU'S HOUSE.
I COULDN'T BELIEVE THAT HE HAD ANOTHER FEMALE FRIEND BESIDES WAKABA-CHAN.
IT HAPPENED THE DAY AFTER WE TOOK DOWN THE VOTING SITE. HIS FATHER TOLD ME ABOUT IT, AND NOW I'M SURE.
... HMM? BUT DOES YOUR SCHOOL HAVE SAILOR UNIFORMS FOR THE GIRLS?
KAZUTO'S PLACE? BUT WHY...?
I LOOKED AROUND SATOU'S ROOM AND HIS PHONE WAS GONE.
THE PHONE THAT STILL HAD THE ADMIN I.D. ON IT.

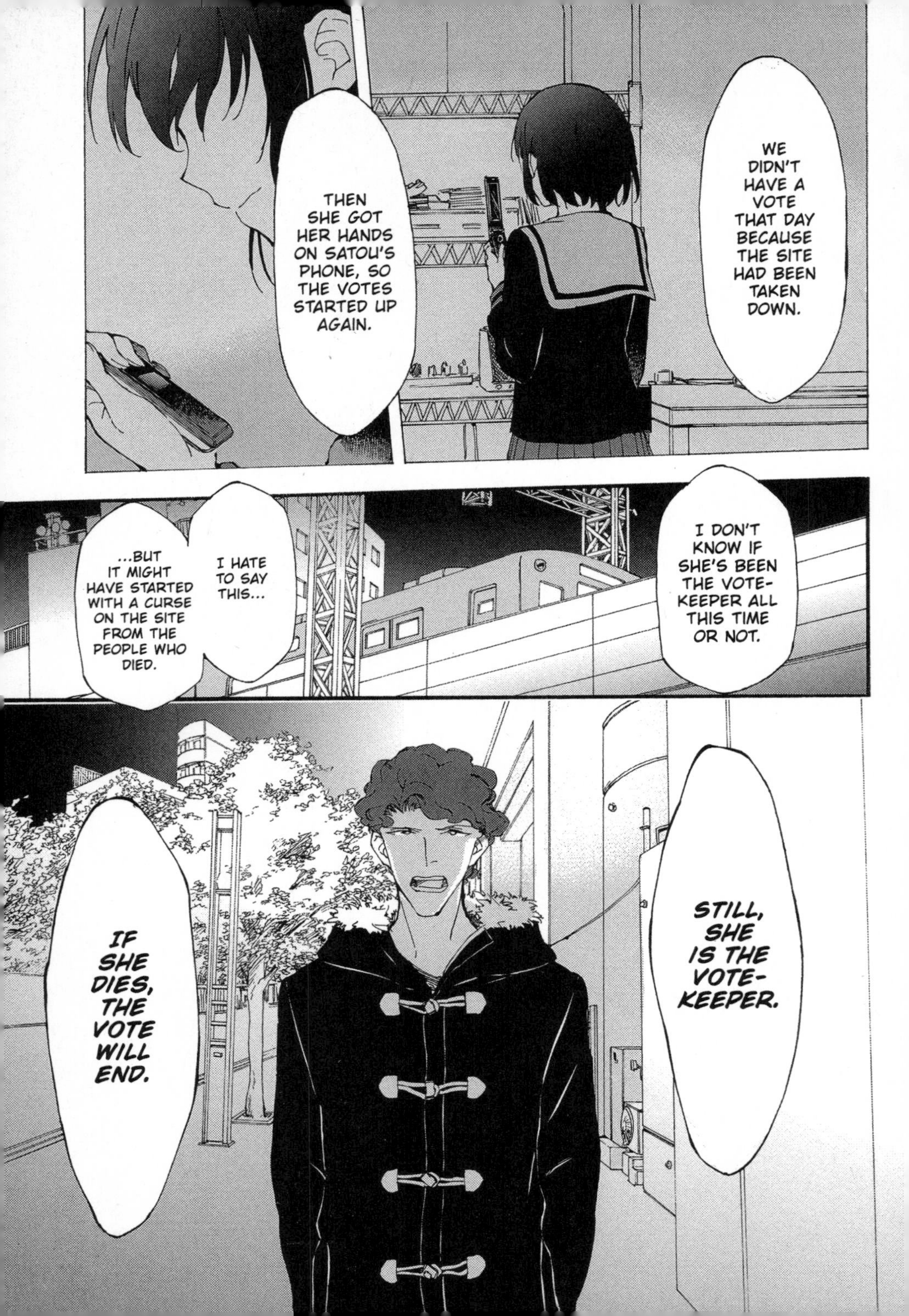
WE DIDN'T HAVE A VOTE THAT DAY BECAUSE THE SITE HAD BEEN TAKEN DOWN.
THEN SHE GOT HER HANDS ON SATOU'S PHONE, SO THE VOTES STARTED UP AGAIN.
I DON'T KNOW IF SHE'S BEEN THE VOTE-KEEPER ALL THIS TIME OR NOT.
I HATE TO SAY THIS...
...BUT IT MIGHT HAVE STARTED WITH A CURSE ON THE SITE FROM THE PEOPLE WHO DIED.
STILL, SHE IS THE VOTE-KEEPER.
IF SHE DIES, THE VOTE WILL END.

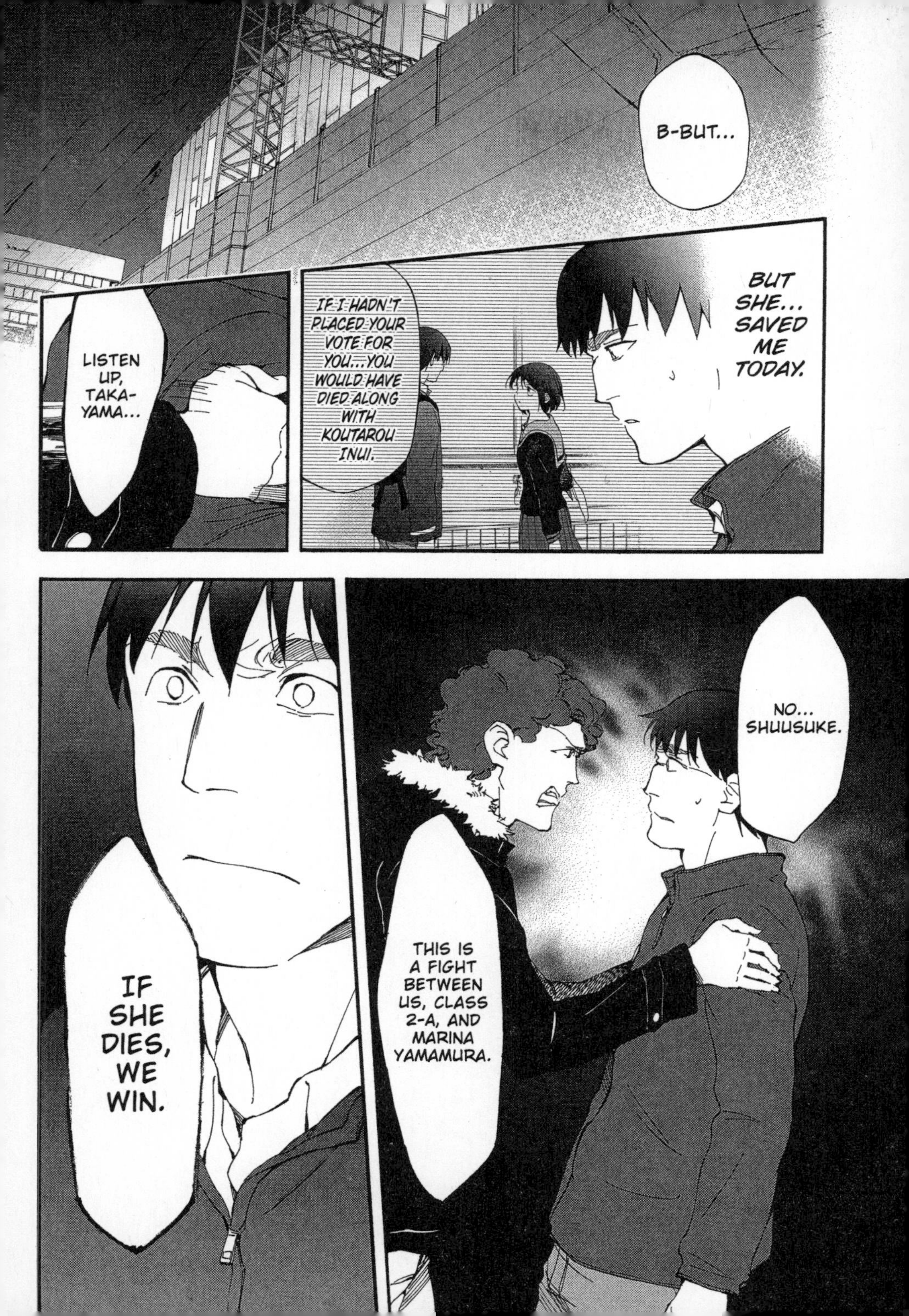
B-BUT...
BUT SHE... SAVED ME TODAY.
IF I HADN'T PLACED YOUR VOTE FOR YOU... YOU WOULD HAVE DIED ALONG WITH KOUTAROU INUI.
LISTEN UP, TAKA-YAMA...
NO... SHUUSUKE.
THIS IS A FIGHT BETWEEN US, CLASS 2-A, AND MARINA YAMAMURA.
IF SHE DIES, WE WIN.

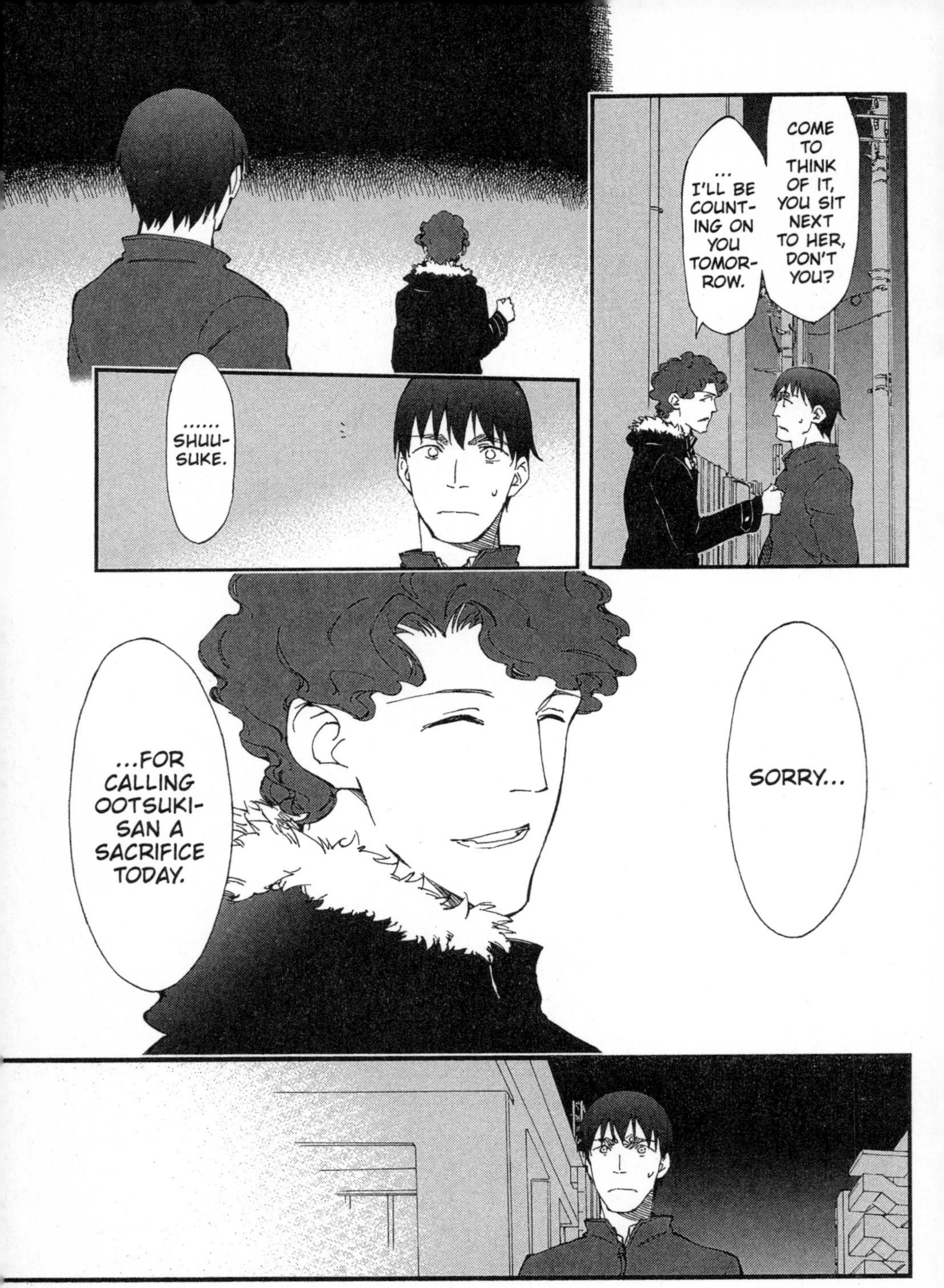
COME TO THINK OF IT, YOU SIT NEXT TO HER, DON'T YOU?
...I'LL BE COUNTING ON YOU TOMORROW.
......SHUUSUKE.
SORRY...
...FOR CALLING OOTSUKI-SAN A SACRIFICE TODAY.

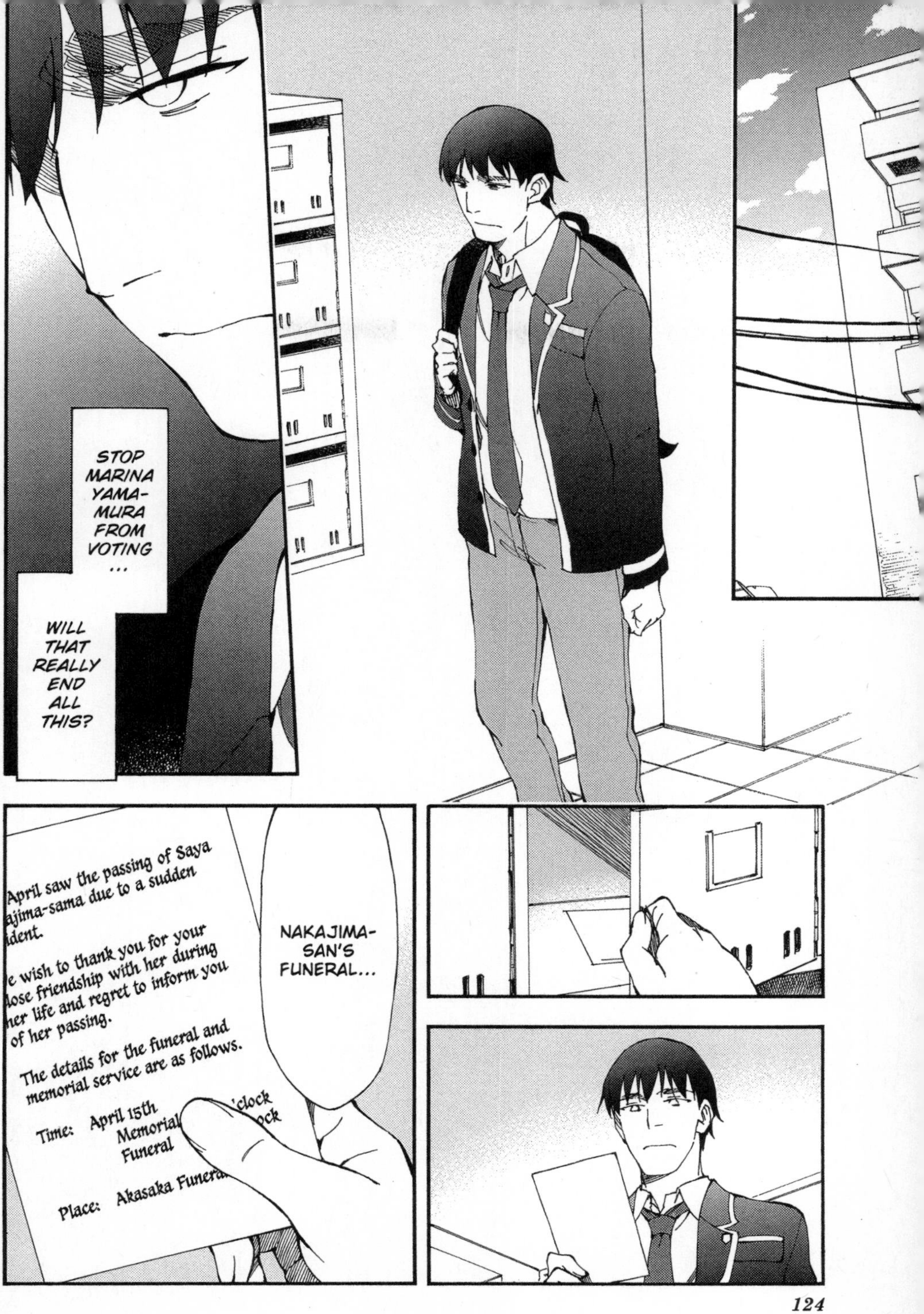
STOP MARINA YAMAMURA FROM VOTING...
WILL THAT REALLY END ALL THIS?
NAKAJIMA-SAN'S FUNERAL...
April saw the passing of Saya
ajima-sama due to a sudden
ident.
e wish to thank you for your
lose friendship with her during
her life and regret to inform you
of her passing.
The details for the funeral and
memorial service are as follows.
Time: April 15th
Memorial
Funeral
'clock
ock
Place: Akasaka Funera

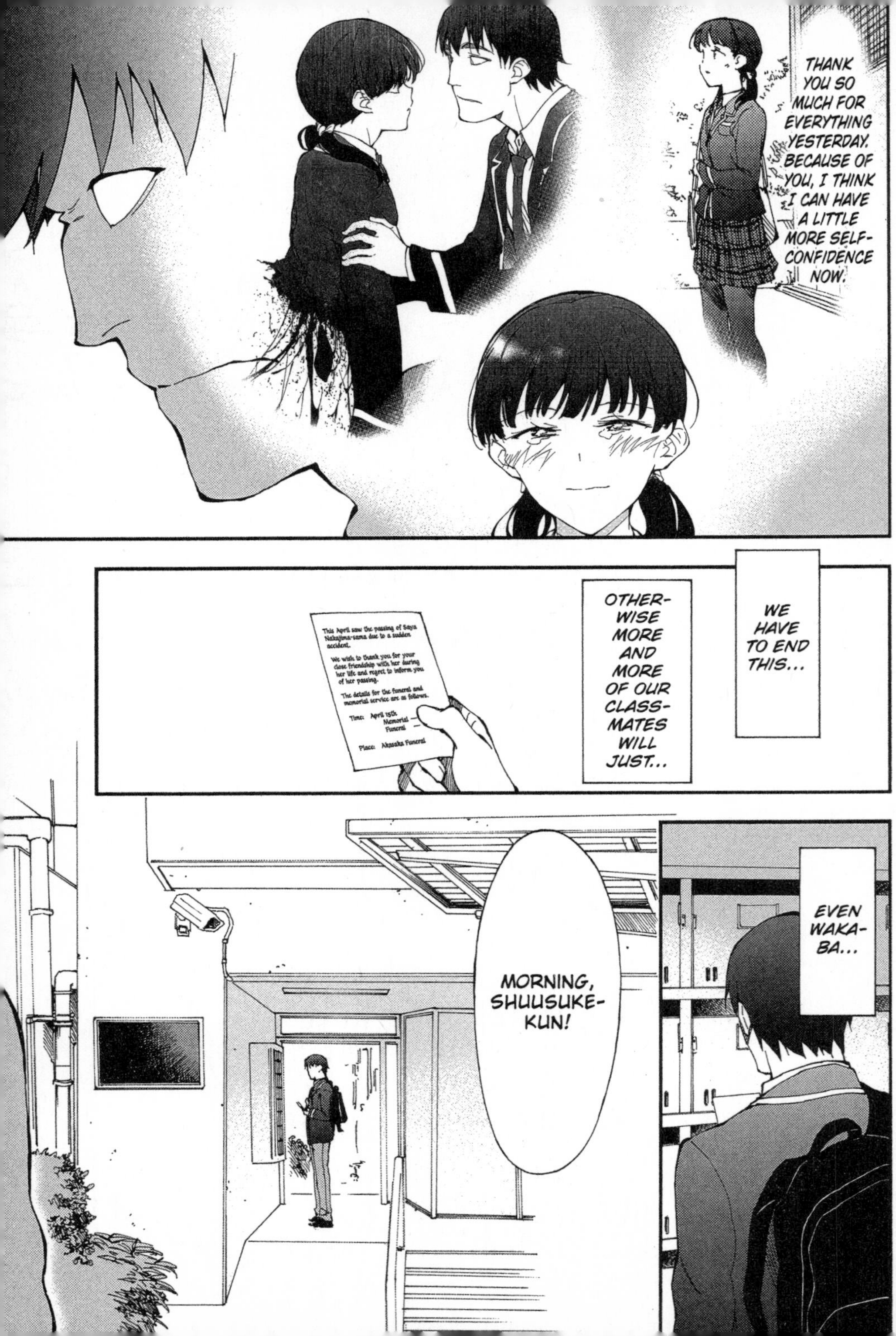
THANK YOU SO MUCH FOR EVERYTHING YESTERDAY. BECAUSE OF YOU, I THINK I CAN HAVE A LITTLE MORE SELF-CONFIDENCE NOW.
WE HAVE TO END THIS...
OTHER-WISE MORE AND MORE OF OUR CLASS-MATES WILL JUST...
This April saw the passing of Saya Nakajima-sama due to a sudden accident.
We wish to thank you for your close friendship with her during her life and regret to inform you of her passing.
The details for the funeral and memorial service are as follows.
Time: April 15th Memorial Funeral
Place: Akasaka Funeral
EVEN WAKA-BA...
MORNING, SHUUSUKE-KUN!

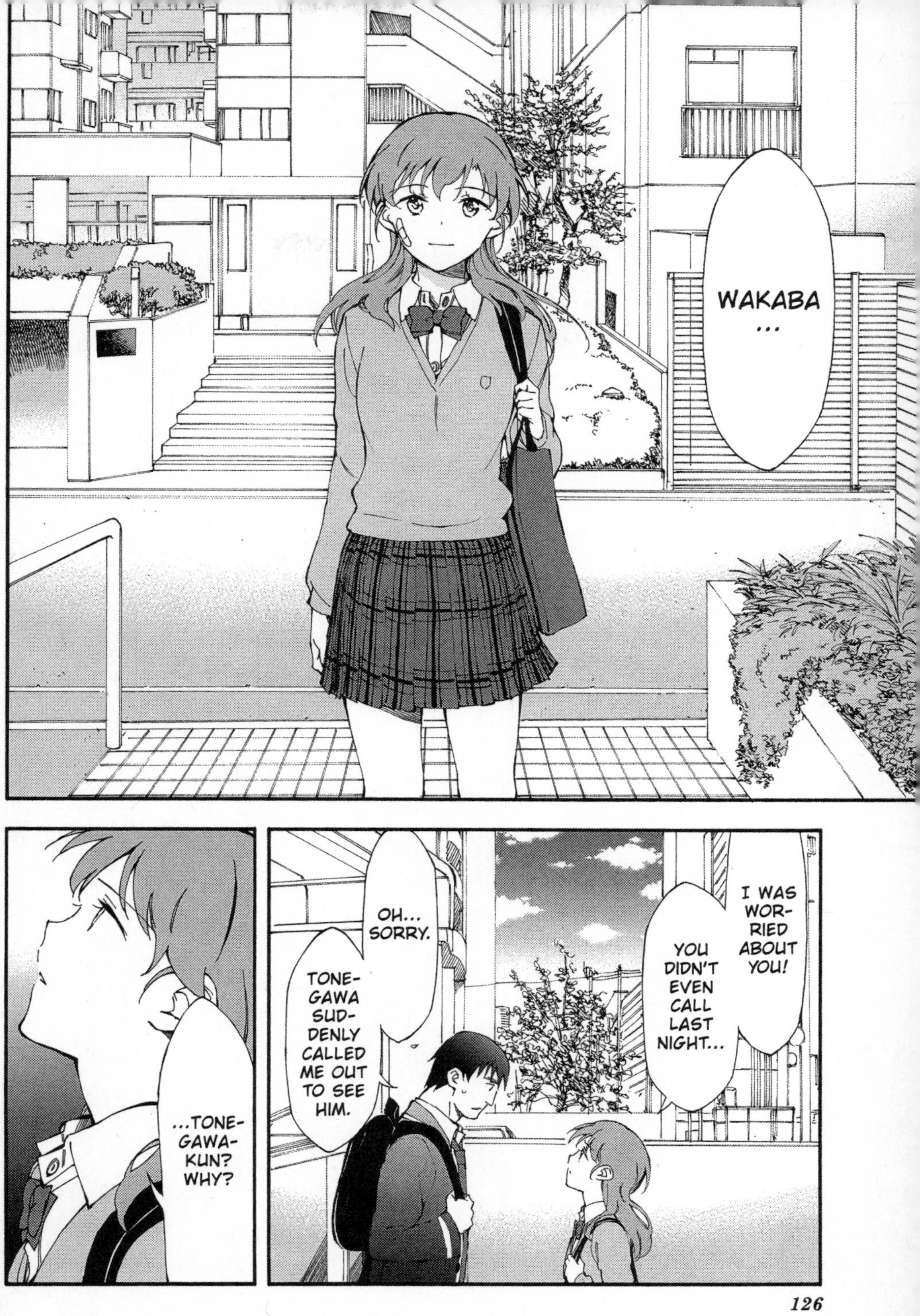
WAKABA ...
I WAS WOR-RIED ABOUT YOU!
YOU DIDN'T EVEN CALL LAST NIGHT...
OH... SORRY.
TONE-GAWA SUD-DENLY CALLED ME OUT TO SEE HIM.
...TONE-GAWA-KUN? WHY?

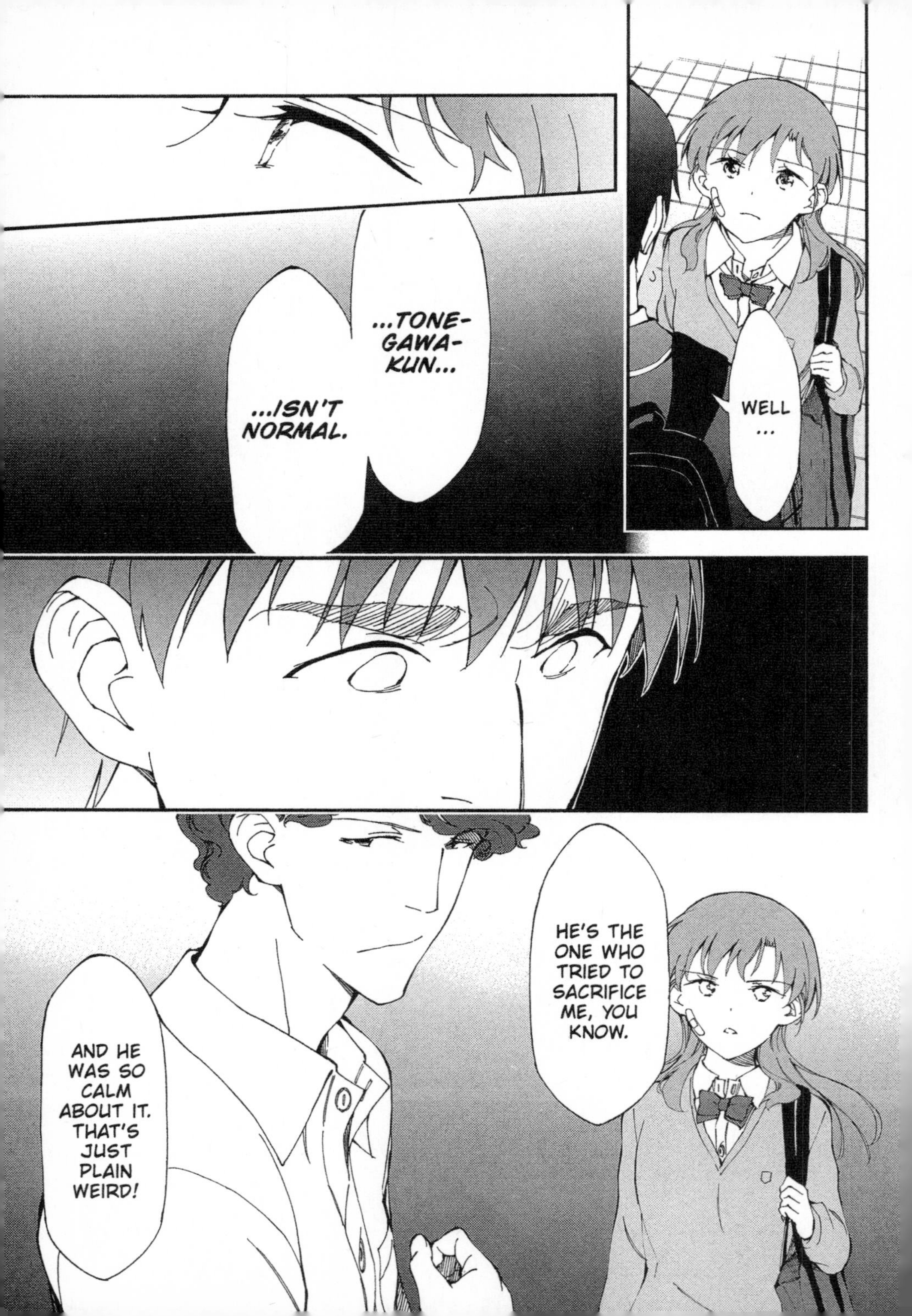
WELL ...
...TONE-GAWA-KUN...
...ISN'T NORMAL.
HE'S THE ONE WHO TRIED TO SACRIFICE ME, YOU KNOW.
AND HE WAS SO CALM ABOUT IT. THAT'S JUST PLAIN WEIRD!

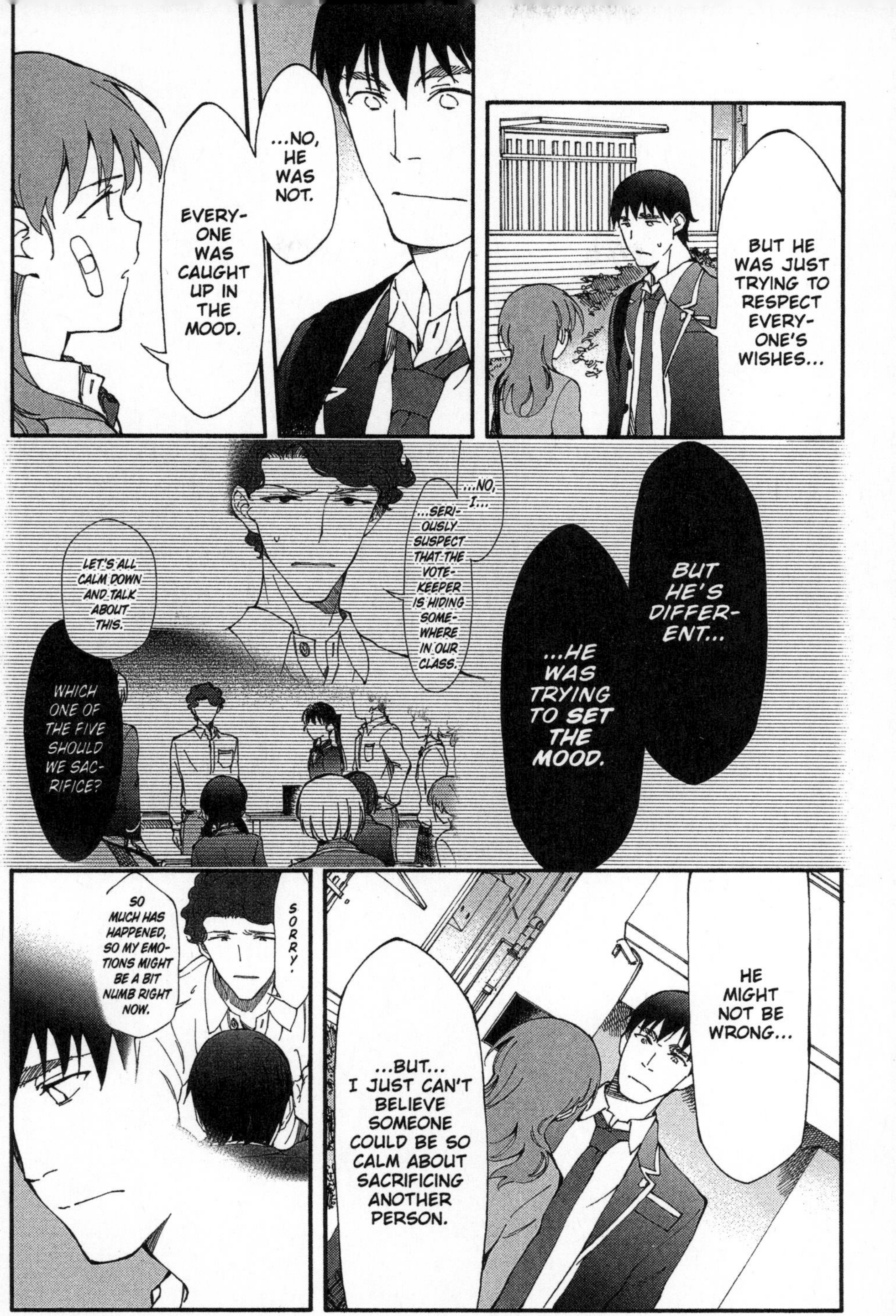
BUT HE WAS JUST TRYING TO RESPECT EVERY-ONE'S WISHES...
...NO, HE WAS NOT.
EVERY-ONE WAS CAUGHT UP IN THE MOOD.
BUT HE'S DIFFER-ENT...
...HE WAS TRYING TO SET THE MOOD.
...NO, I...
...SERI-OUSLY SUSPECT THAT THE VOTE-KEEPER IS HIDING SOME-WHERE IN OUR CLASS.
LET'S ALL CALM DOWN AND TALK ABOUT THIS.
WHICH ONE OF THE FIVE SHOULD WE SAC-RIFICE?
HE MIGHT NOT BE WRONG...
...BUT... I JUST CAN'T BELIEVE SOMEONE COULD BE SO CALM ABOUT SACRIFICING ANOTHER PERSON.
SORRY.
SO MUCH HAS HAPPENED, SO MY EMO-TIONS MIGHT BE A BIT NUMB RIGHT NOW.

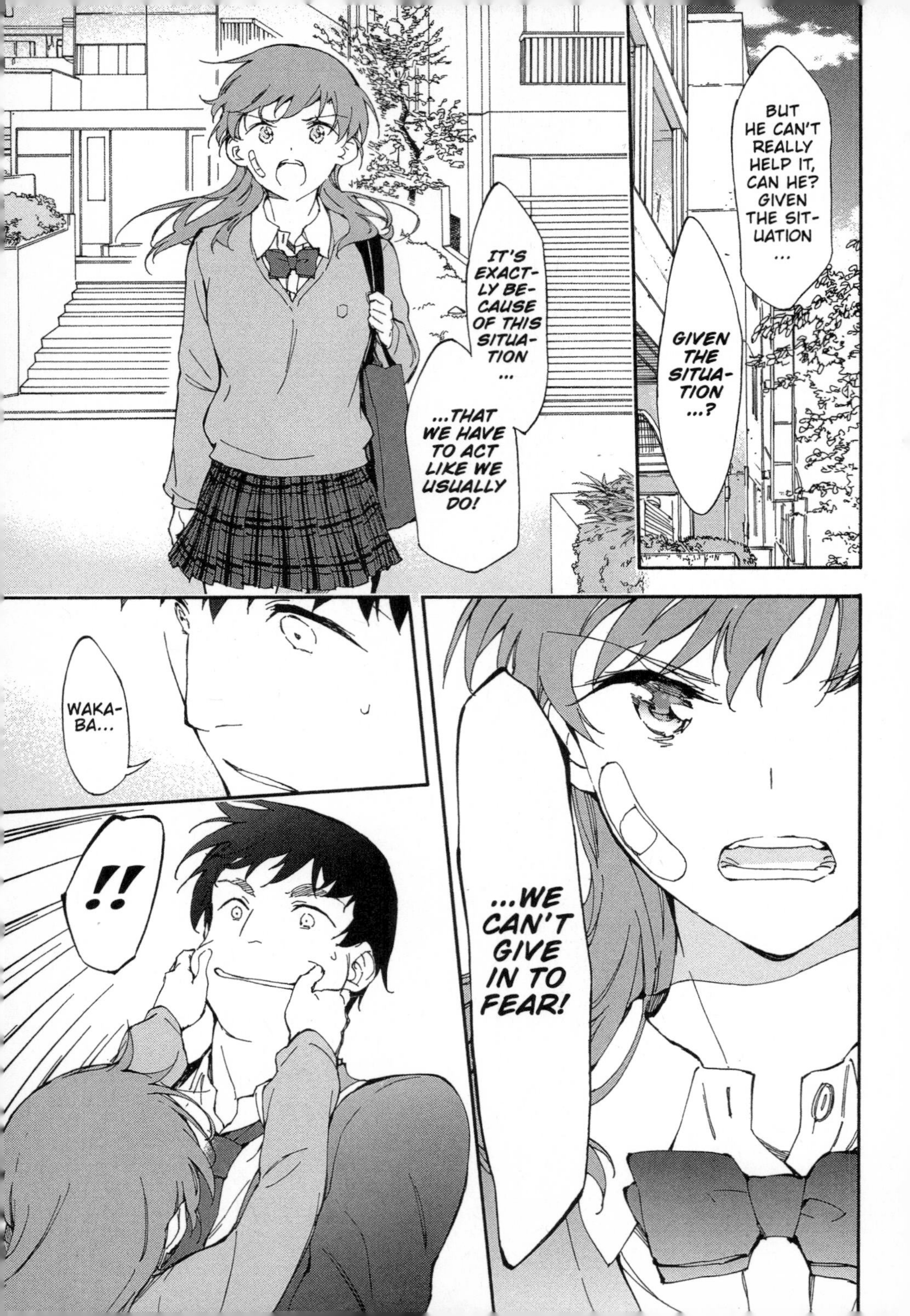
BUT HE CAN'T REALLY HELP IT, CAN HE? GIVEN THE SITUATION...
GIVEN THE SITUATION...?
IT'S EXACTLY BECAUSE OF THIS SITUATION...
...THAT WE HAVE TO ACT LIKE WE USUALLY DO!
...WE CAN'T GIVE IN TO FEAR!
WAKABA...
!!

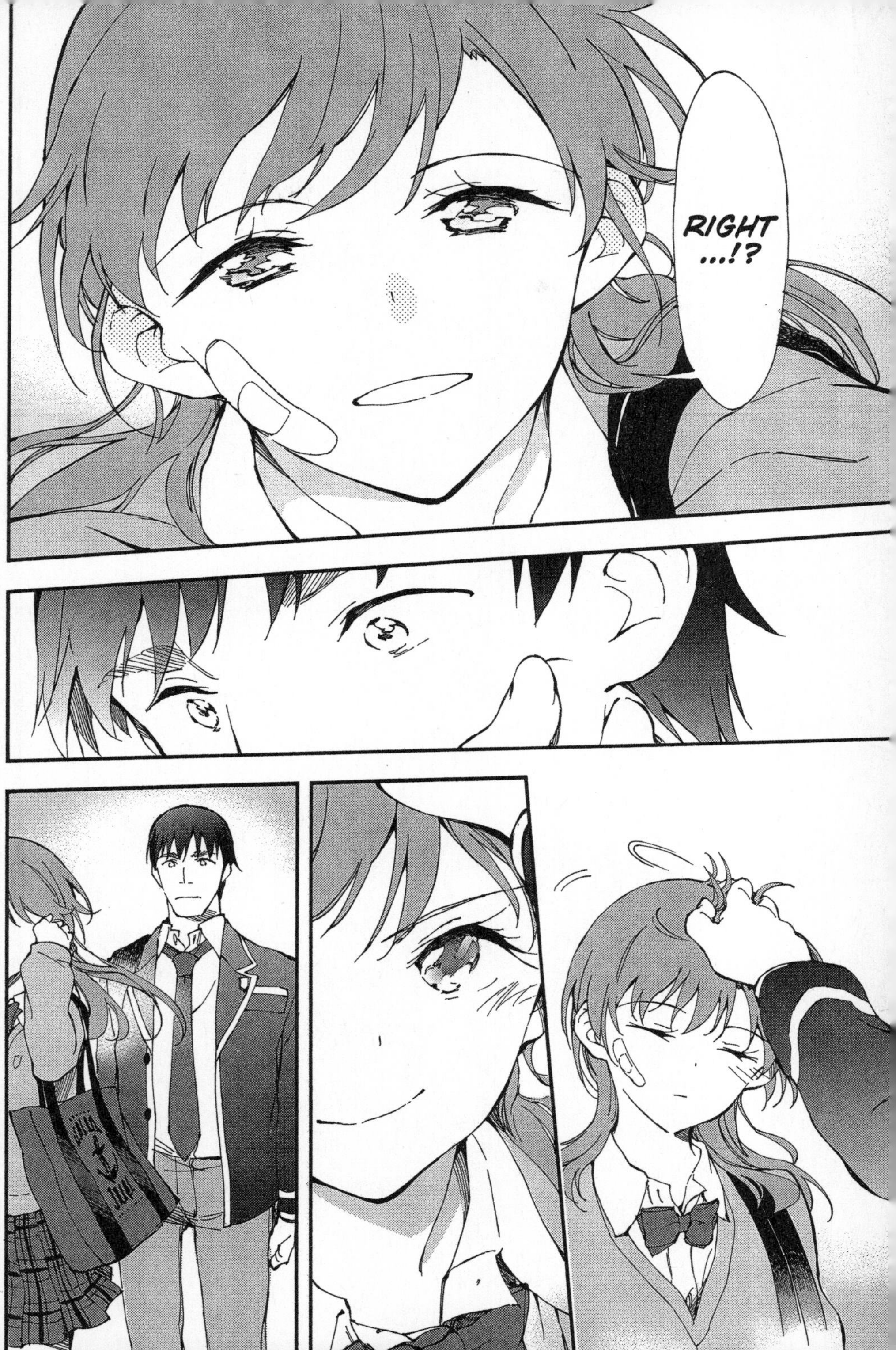
RIGHT ...!?

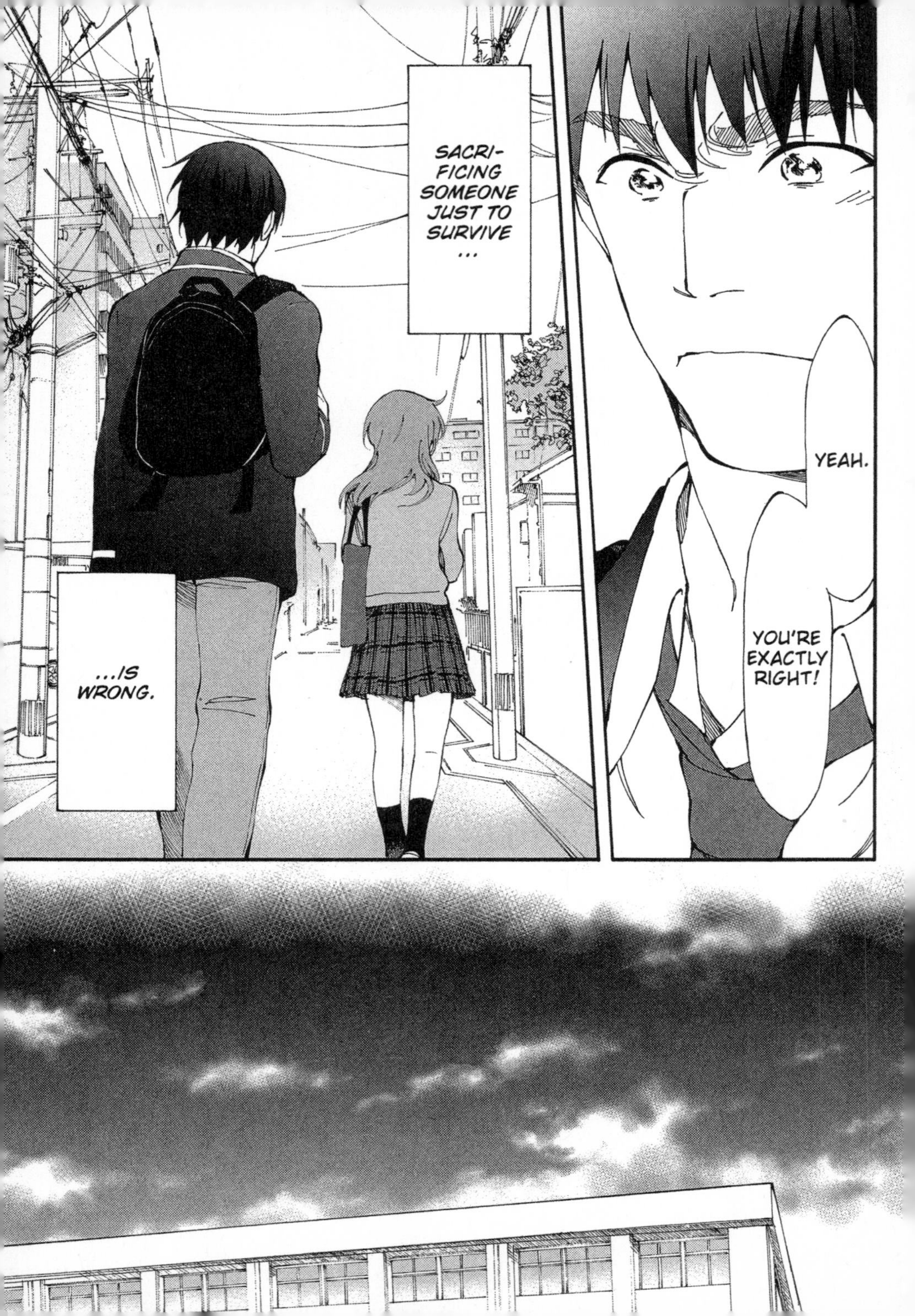
YEAH.
YOU'RE EXACTLY RIGHT!
SACRI-FICING SOMEONE JUST TO SURVIVE...
...IS WRONG.

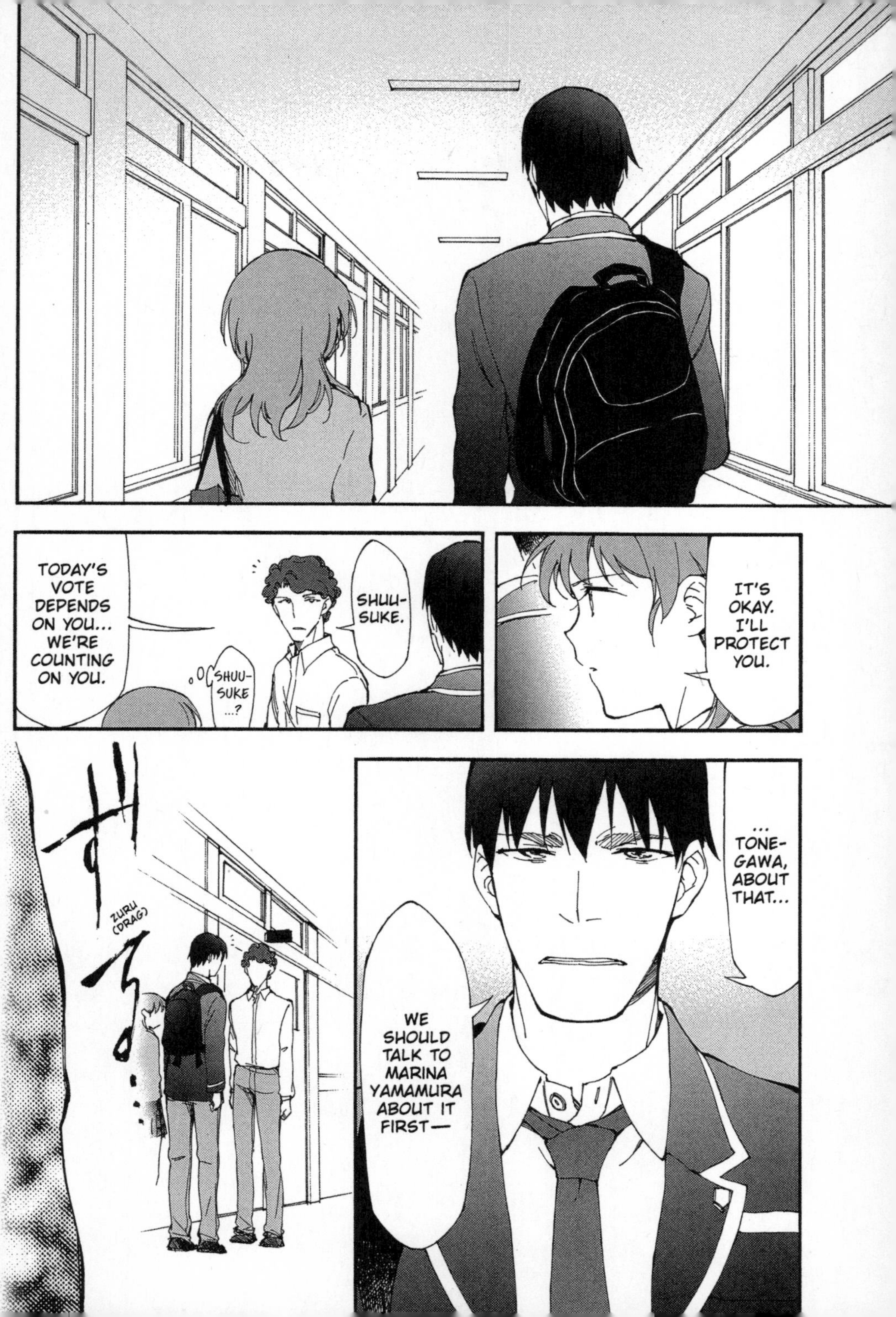
IT'S OKAY. I'LL PROTECT YOU.
SHUU-SUKE.
TODAY'S VOTE DEPENDS ON YOU... WE'RE COUNTING ON YOU.
SHUU-SUKE ...?
... TONE-GAWA, ABOUT THAT...
WE SHOULD TALK TO MARINA YAMAMURA ABOUT IT FIRST—
ZURU (DRAG)

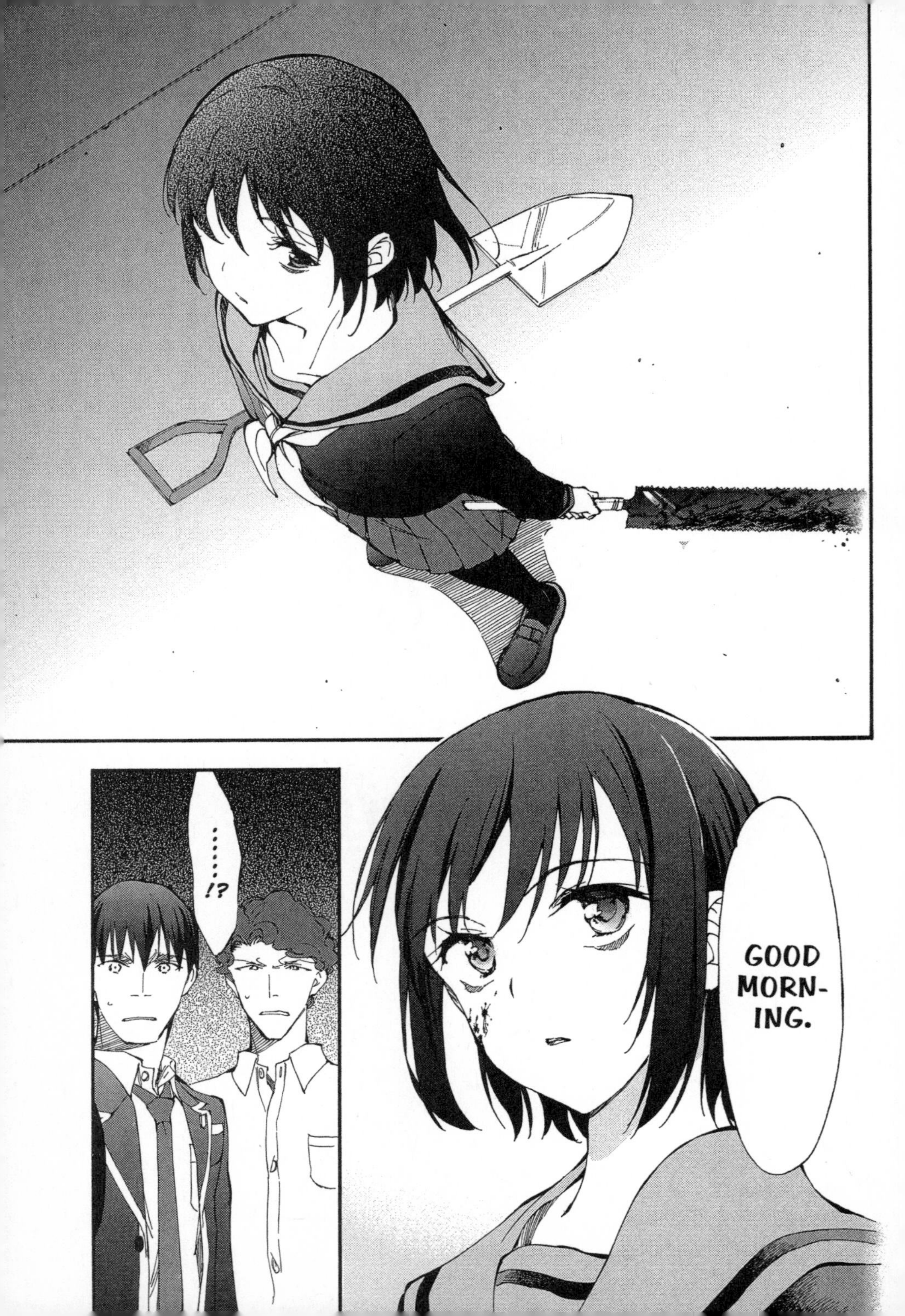
GOOD MORN-ING.
......!?

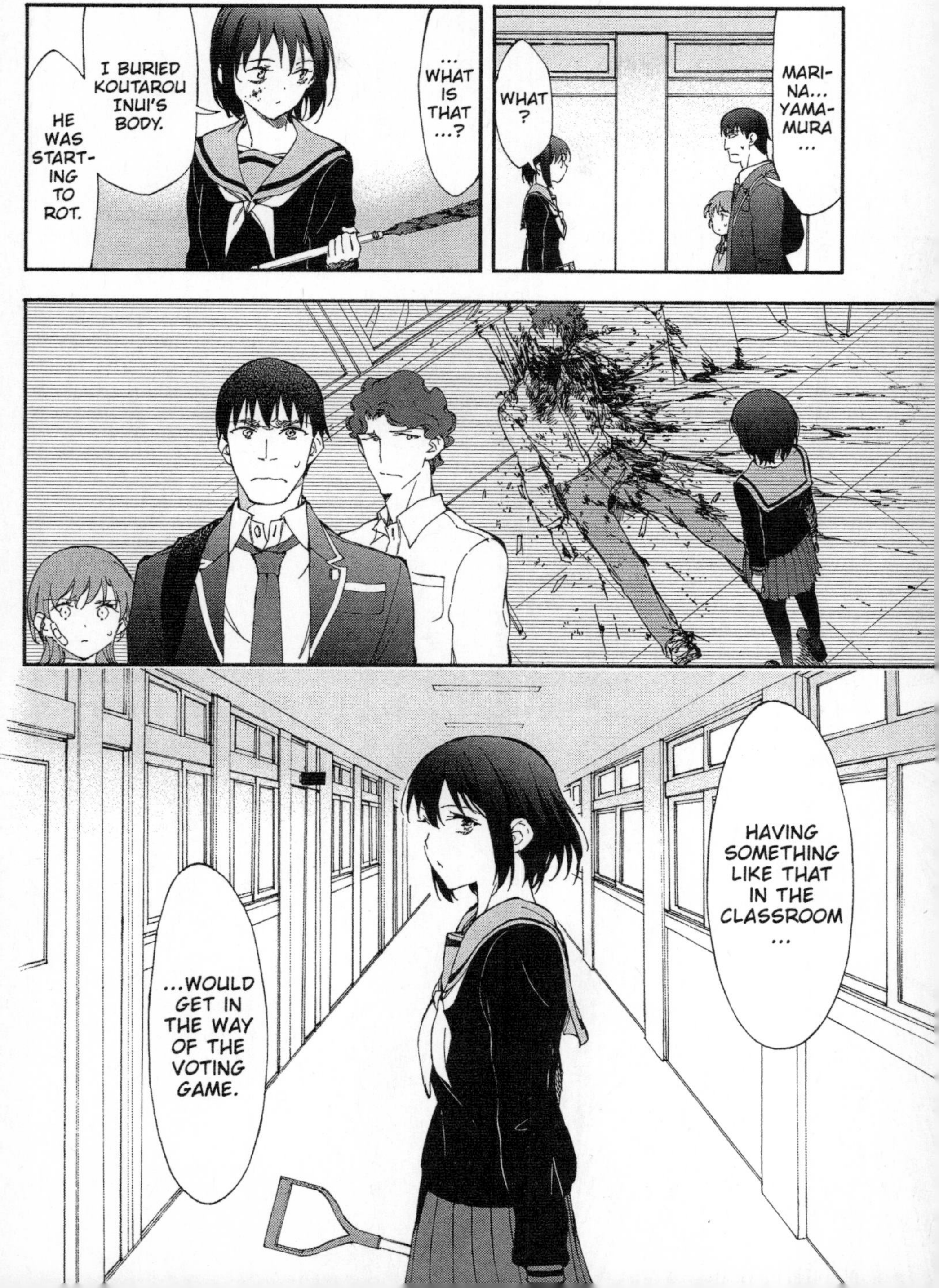
MARI-NA... YAMA-MURA...
WHAT?
...WHAT IS THAT...?
I BURIED KOUTAROU INUI'S BODY.
HE WAS START-ING TO ROT.
HAVING SOMETHING LIKE THAT IN THE CLASSROOM...
...WOULD GET IN THE WAY OF THE VOTING GAME.

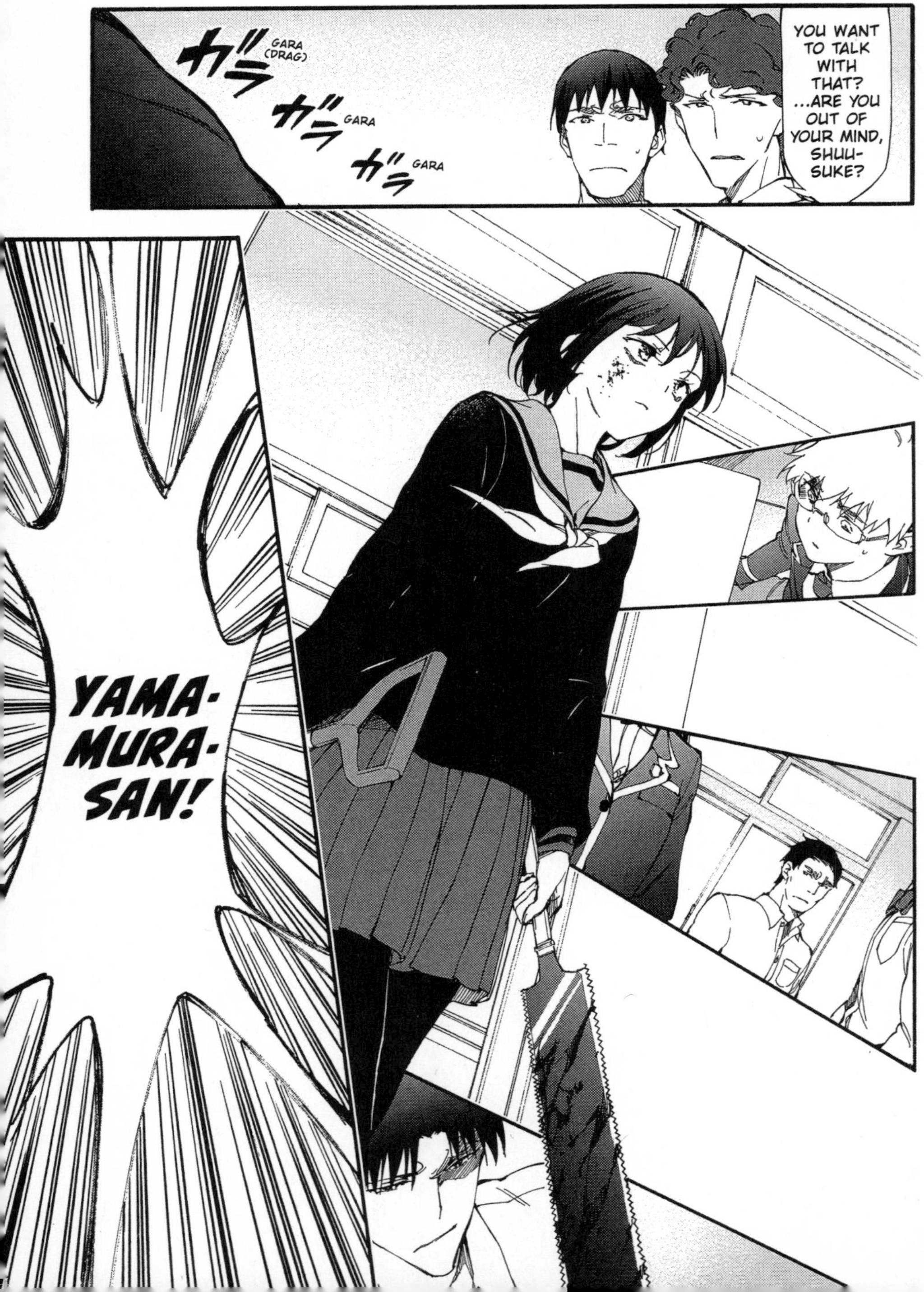
YOU WANT TO TALK WITH THAT? ...ARE YOU OUT OF YOUR MIND, SHUU-SUKE?
ガラ GARA (DRAG)
ガラ GARA
ガラ GARA
YAMA-MURA-SAN!

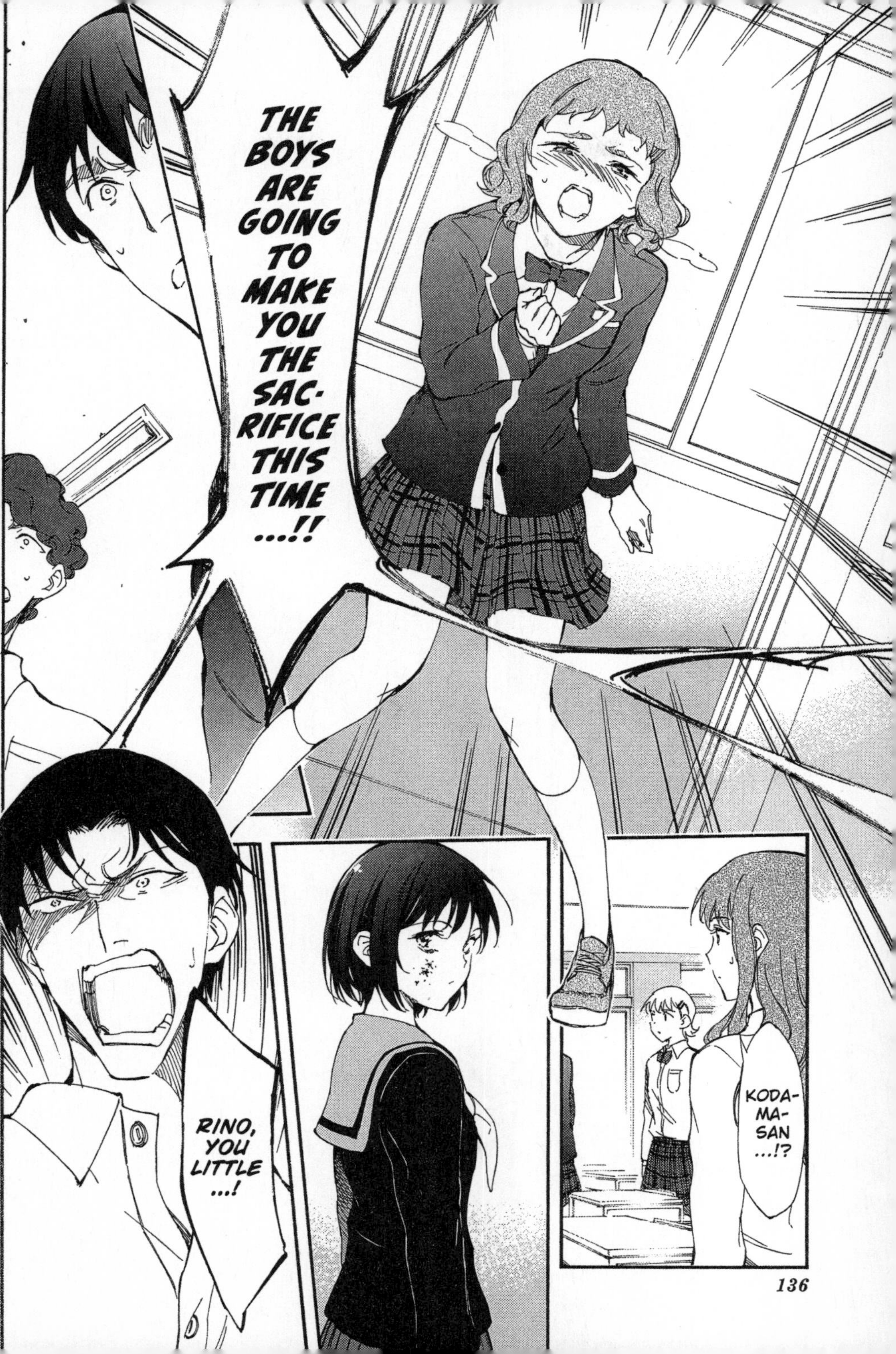
THE BOYS ARE GOING TO MAKE YOU THE SAC-RIFICE THIS TIME ...!!
KODA-MA-SAN ...!?
RINO, YOU LITTLE ...!

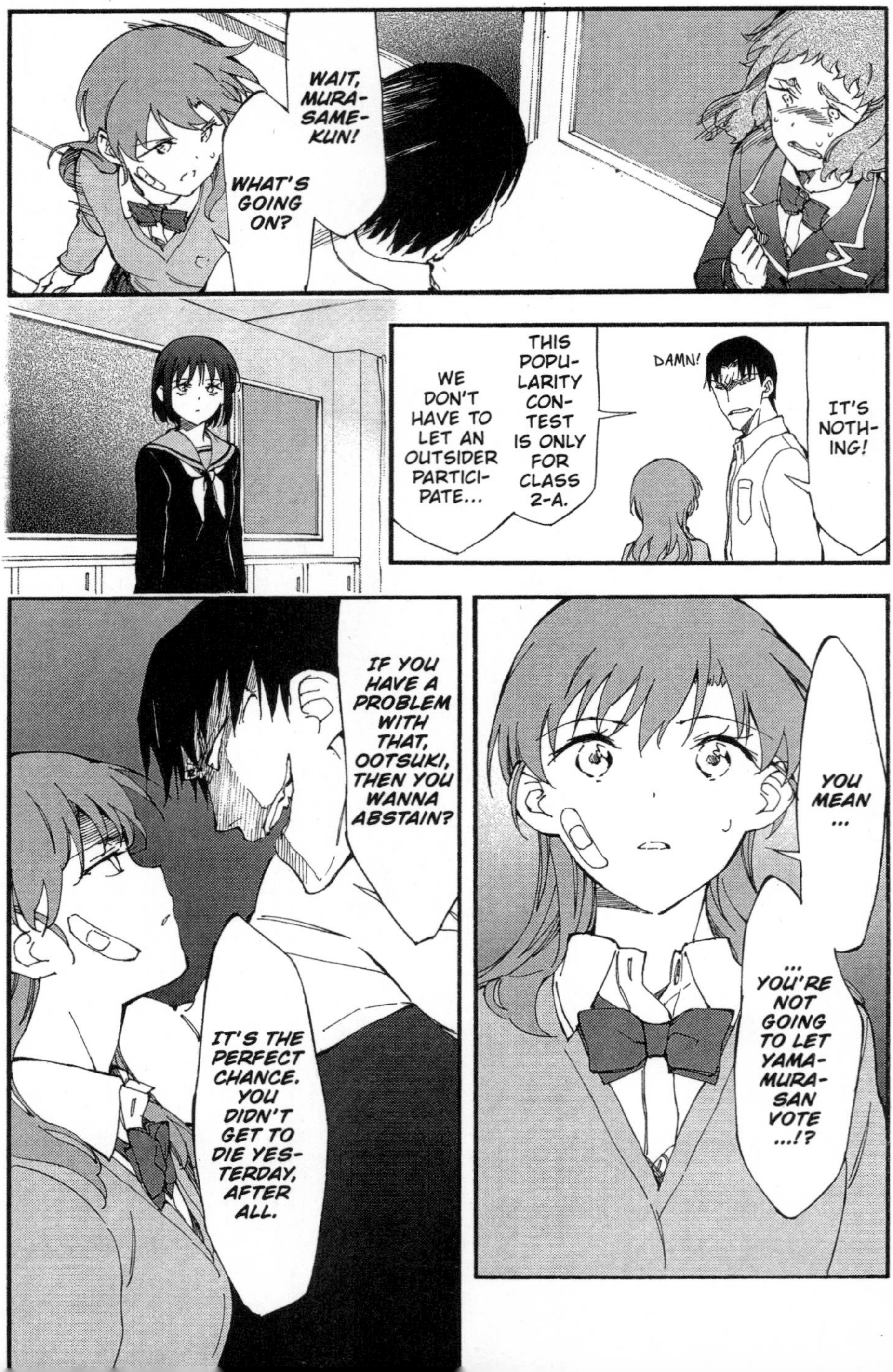
WAIT, MURA-SAME-KUN!
WHAT'S GOING ON?
IT'S NOTH-ING!
DAMN!
THIS POPU-LARITY CON-TEST IS ONLY FOR CLASS 2-A.
WE DON'T HAVE TO LET AN OUTSIDER PARTICI-PATE...
YOU MEAN...
...YOU'RE NOT GOING TO LET YAMA-MURA-SAN VOTE...!?
IF YOU HAVE A PROBLEM WITH THAT, OOTSUKI, THEN YOU WANNA ABSTAIN?
IT'S THE PERFECT CHANCE. YOU DIDN'T GET TO DIE YES-TERDAY, AFTER ALL.

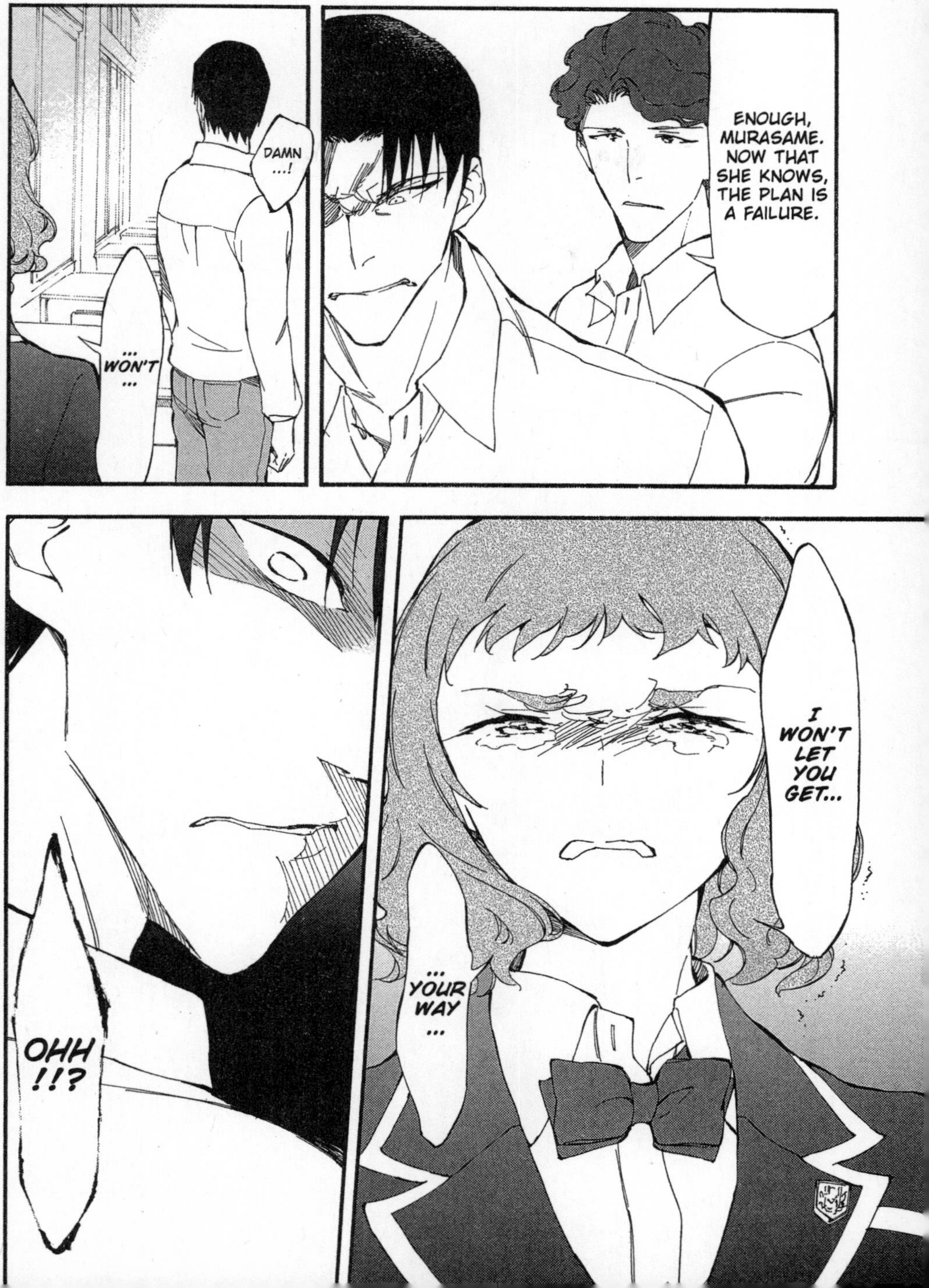
ENOUGH, MURASAME. NOW THAT SHE KNOWS, THE PLAN IS A FAILURE.
DAMN ...!
... WON'T ...
I WON'T LET YOU GET...
... YOUR WAY ...
OHH !!?

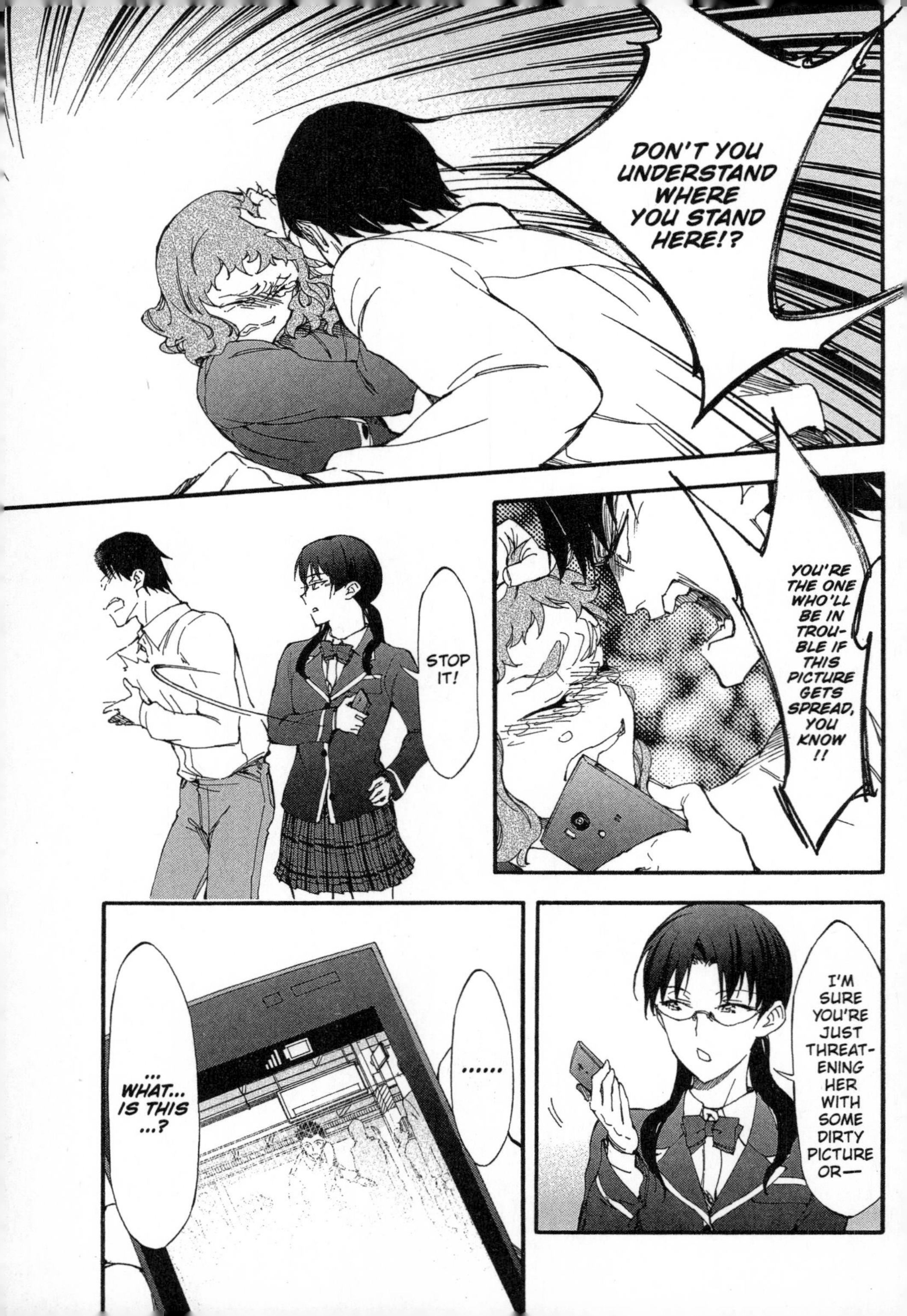
DON'T YOU UNDERSTAND WHERE YOU STAND HERE!?
YOU'RE THE ONE WHO'LL BE IN TROUBLE IF THIS PICTURE GETS SPREAD, YOU KNOW!!
STOP IT!
I'M SURE YOU'RE JUST THREATENING HER WITH SOME DIRTY PICTURE OR—
......
...WHAT... IS THIS ...?

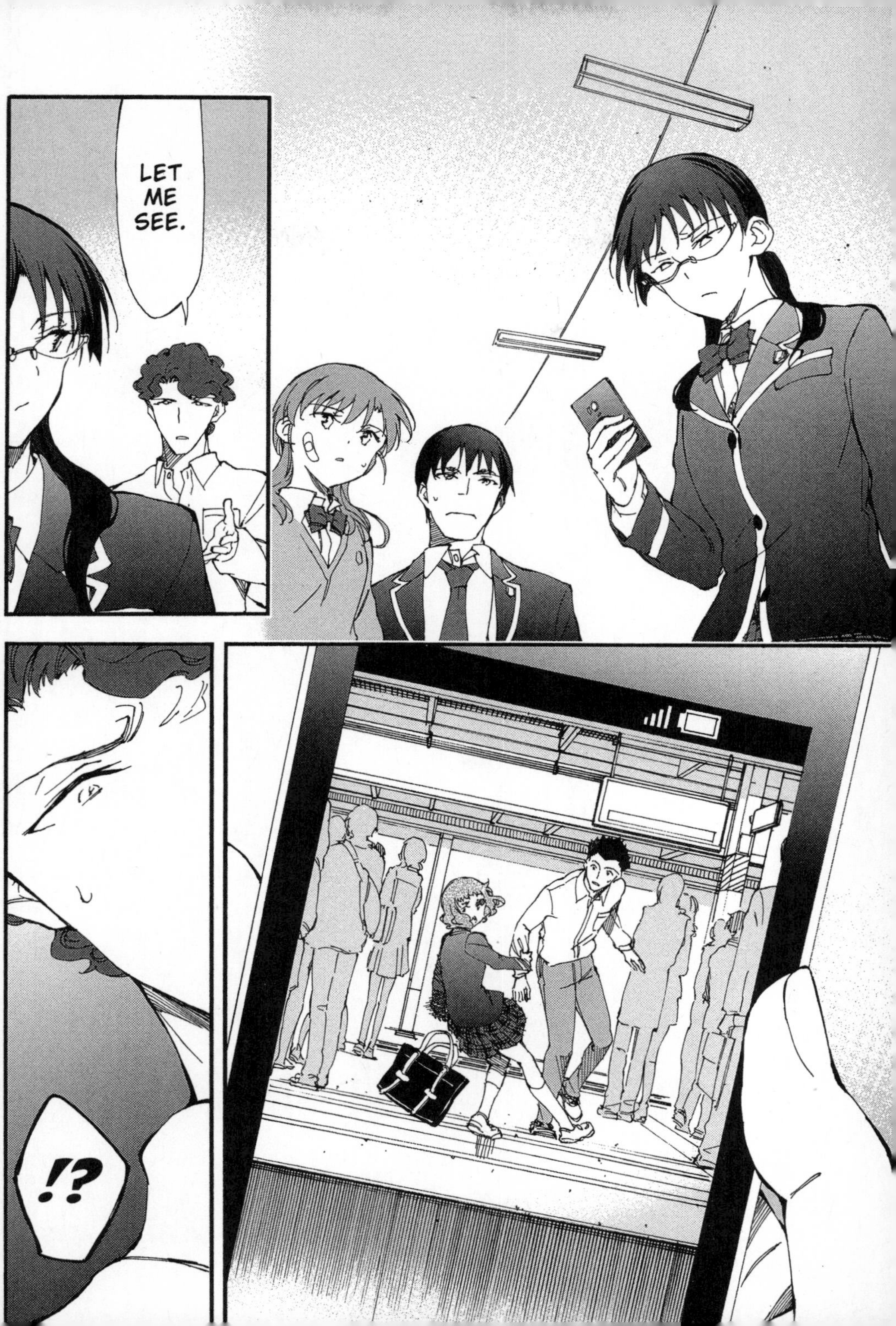
LET ME SEE.
!?

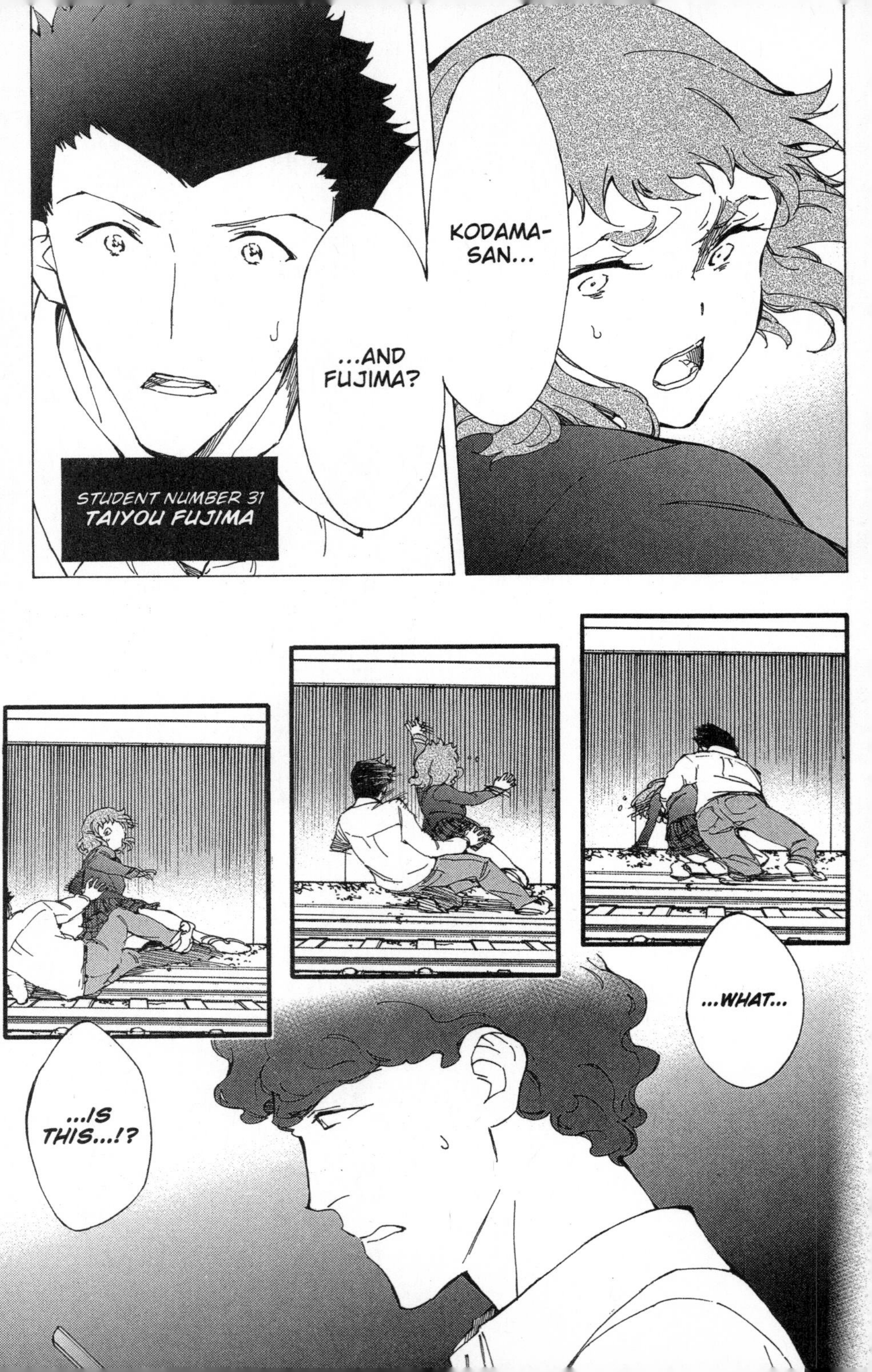
KODAMA-SAN...
...AND FUJIMA?
STUDENT NUMBER 31 TAIYOU FUJIMA
...WHAT...
...IS THIS...!?

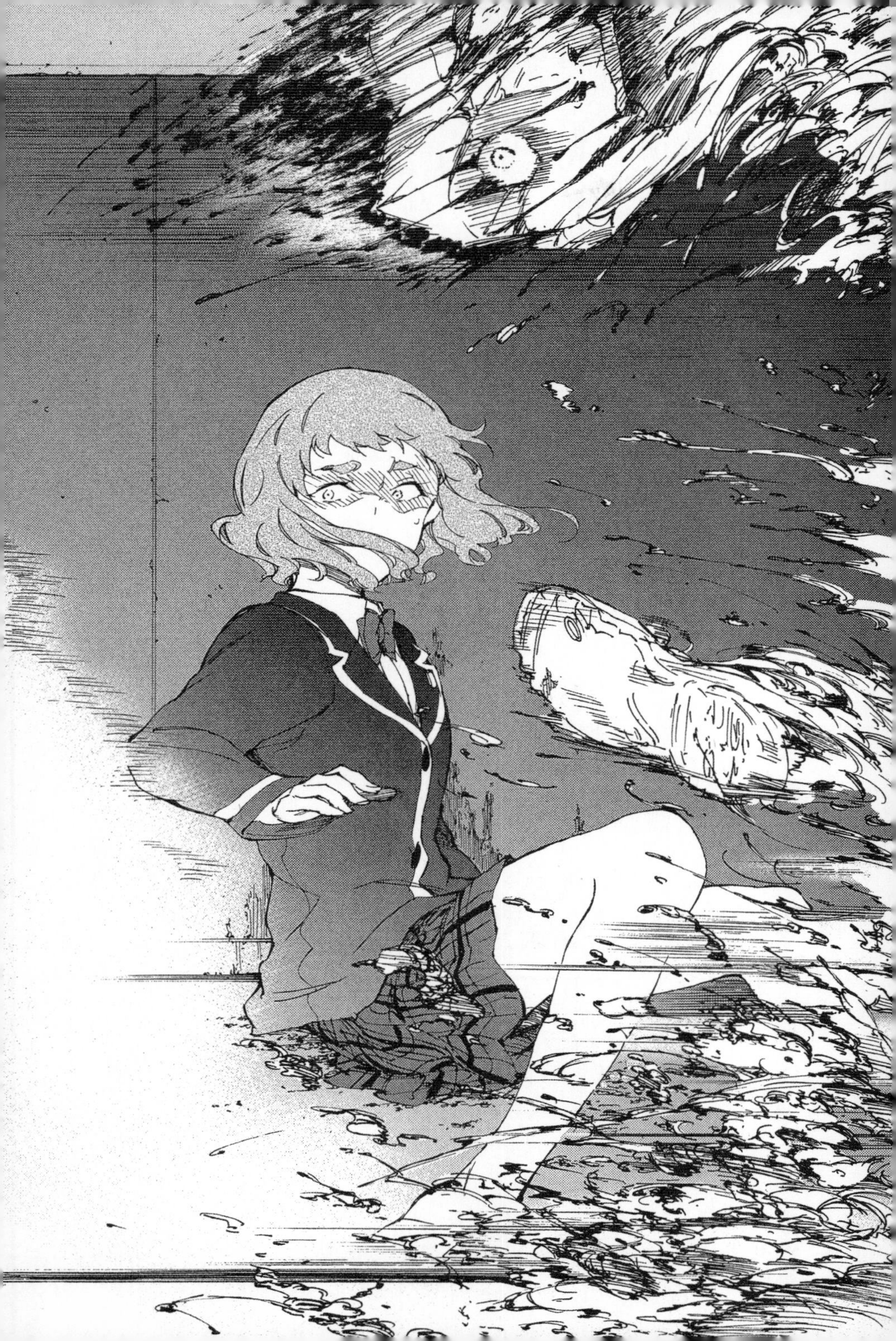

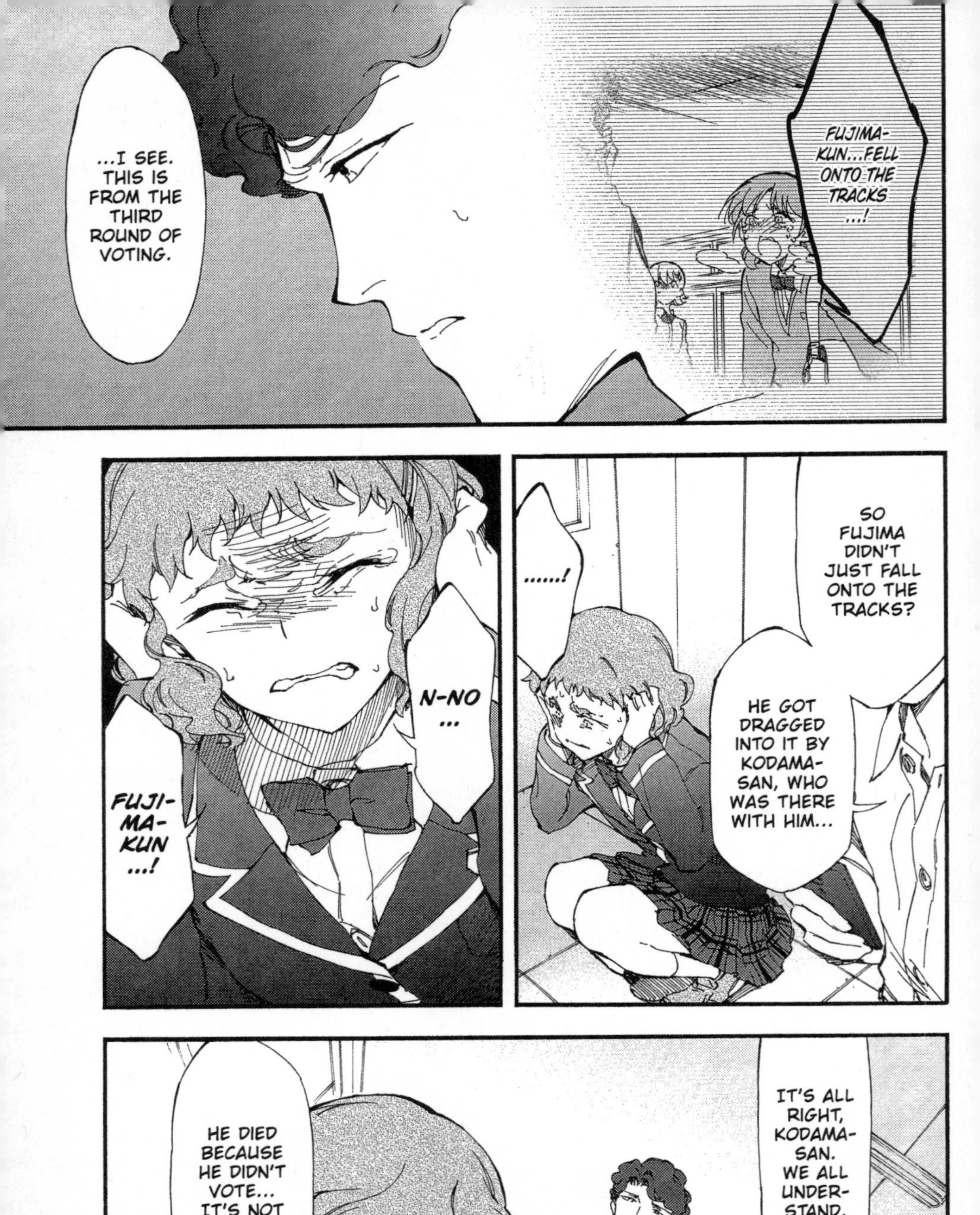
FUJIMA-KUN...FELL ONTO THE TRACKS ...!
...I SEE. THIS IS FROM THE THIRD ROUND OF VOTING.
SO FUJIMA DIDN'T JUST FALL ONTO THE TRACKS?
HE GOT DRAGGED INTO IT BY KODAMA-SAN, WHO WAS THERE WITH HIM...
......!
N-NO ...
FUJI-MA-KUN ...!
IT'S ALL RIGHT, KODAMA-SAN. WE ALL UNDER-STAND.
HE DIED BECAUSE HE DIDN'T VOTE... IT'S NOT YOUR FAULT.

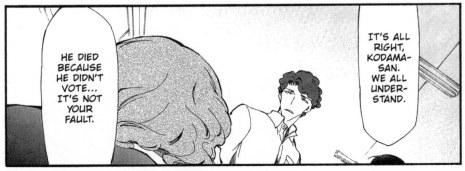

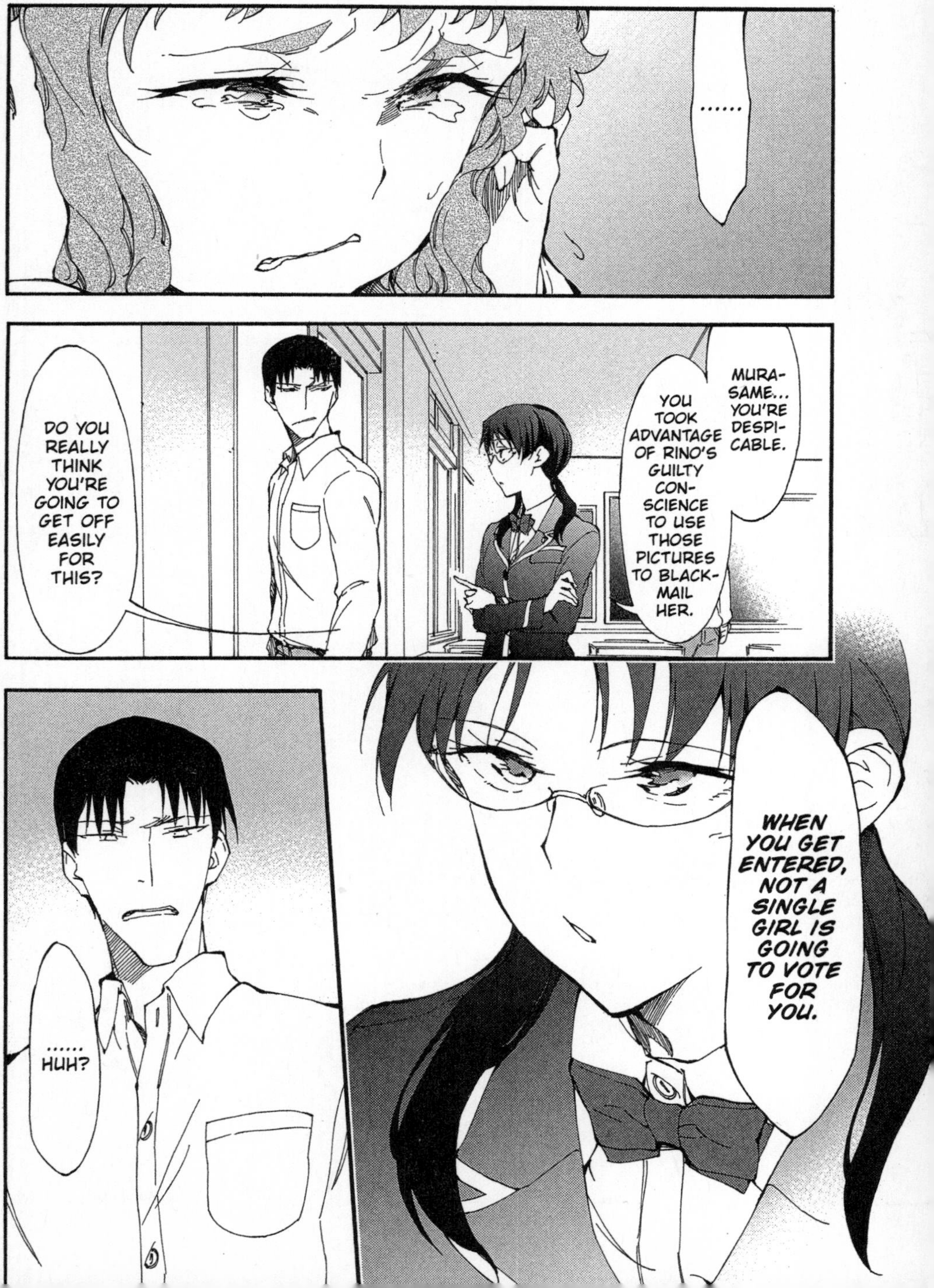
......
MURA-SAME... YOU'RE DESPI-CABLE.
YOU TOOK ADVANTAGE OF RINO'S GUILTY CON-SCIENCE TO USE THOSE PICTURES TO BLACK-MAIL HER.
DO YOU REALLY THINK YOU'RE GOING TO GET OFF EASILY FOR THIS?
WHEN YOU GET ENTERED, NOT A SINGLE GIRL IS GOING TO VOTE FOR YOU.
...... HUH?

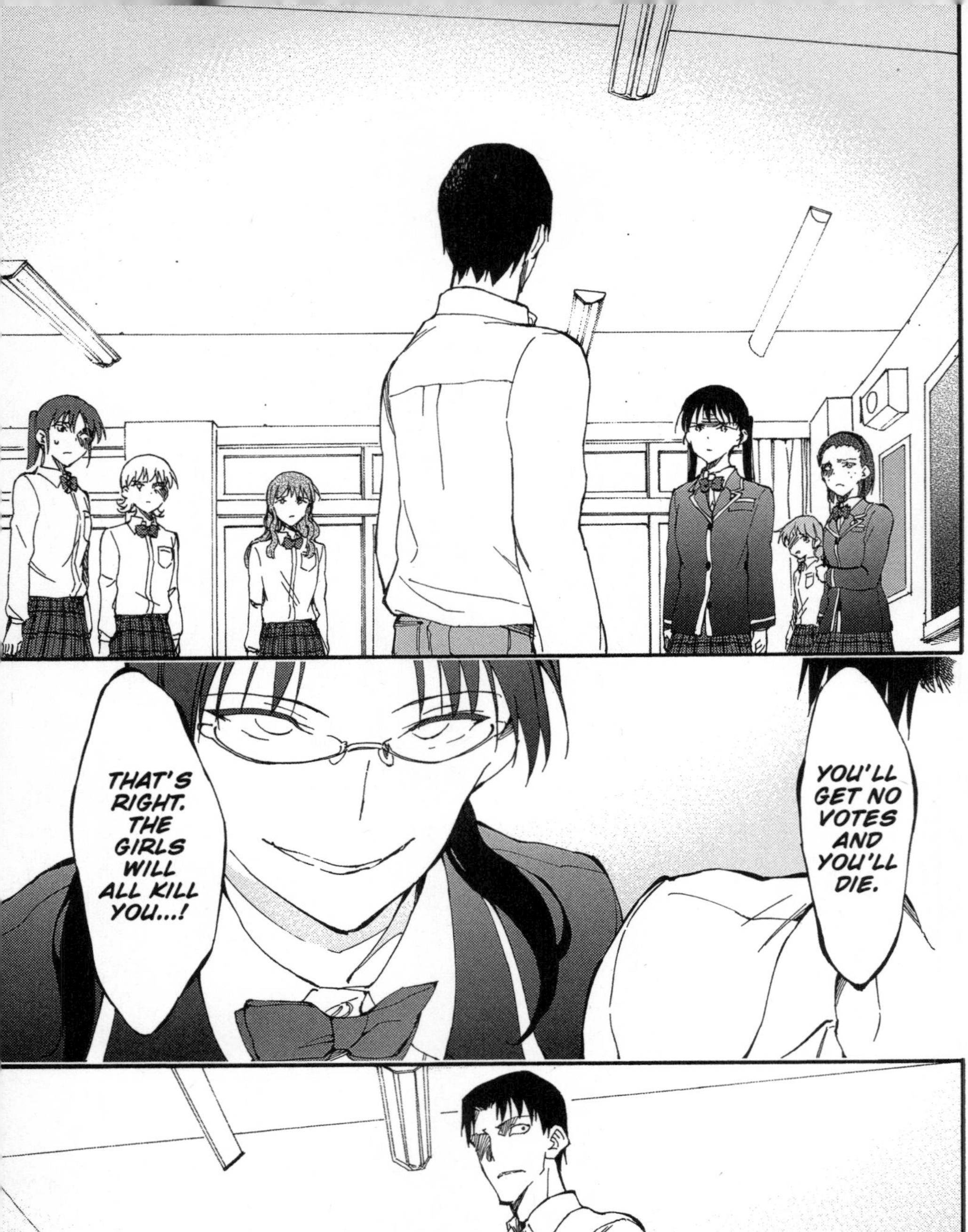
YOU'LL GET NO VOTES AND YOU'LL DIE.
THAT'S RIGHT. THE GIRLS WILL ALL KILL YOU...!

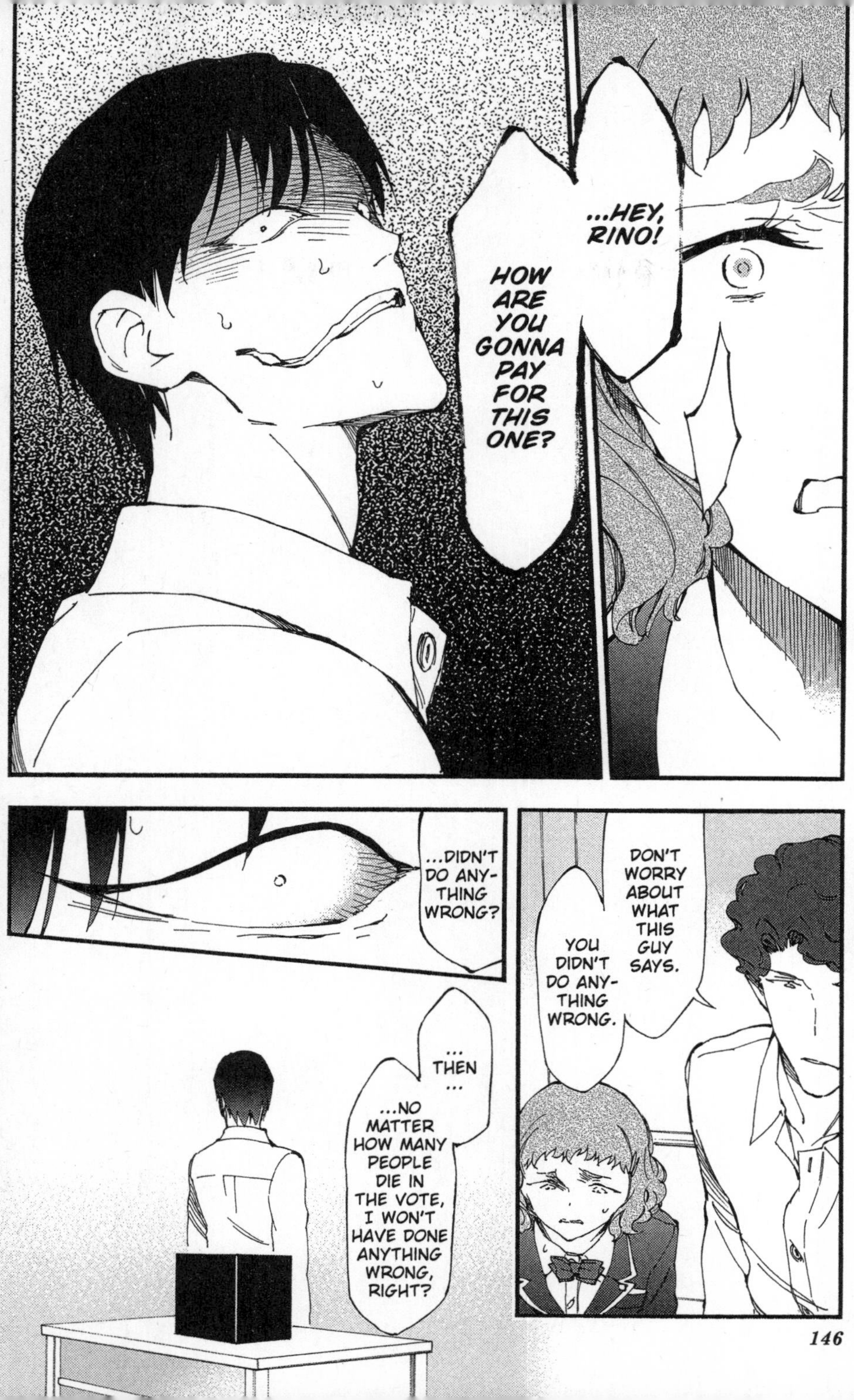
...HEY, RINO!
HOW ARE YOU GONNA PAY FOR THIS ONE?
DON'T WORRY ABOUT WHAT THIS GUY SAYS.
YOU DIDN'T DO ANY-THING WRONG.
...DIDN'T DO ANY-THING WRONG?
... THEN ...
...NO MATTER HOW MANY PEOPLE DIE IN THE VOTE, I WON'T HAVE DONE ANYTHING WRONG, RIGHT?

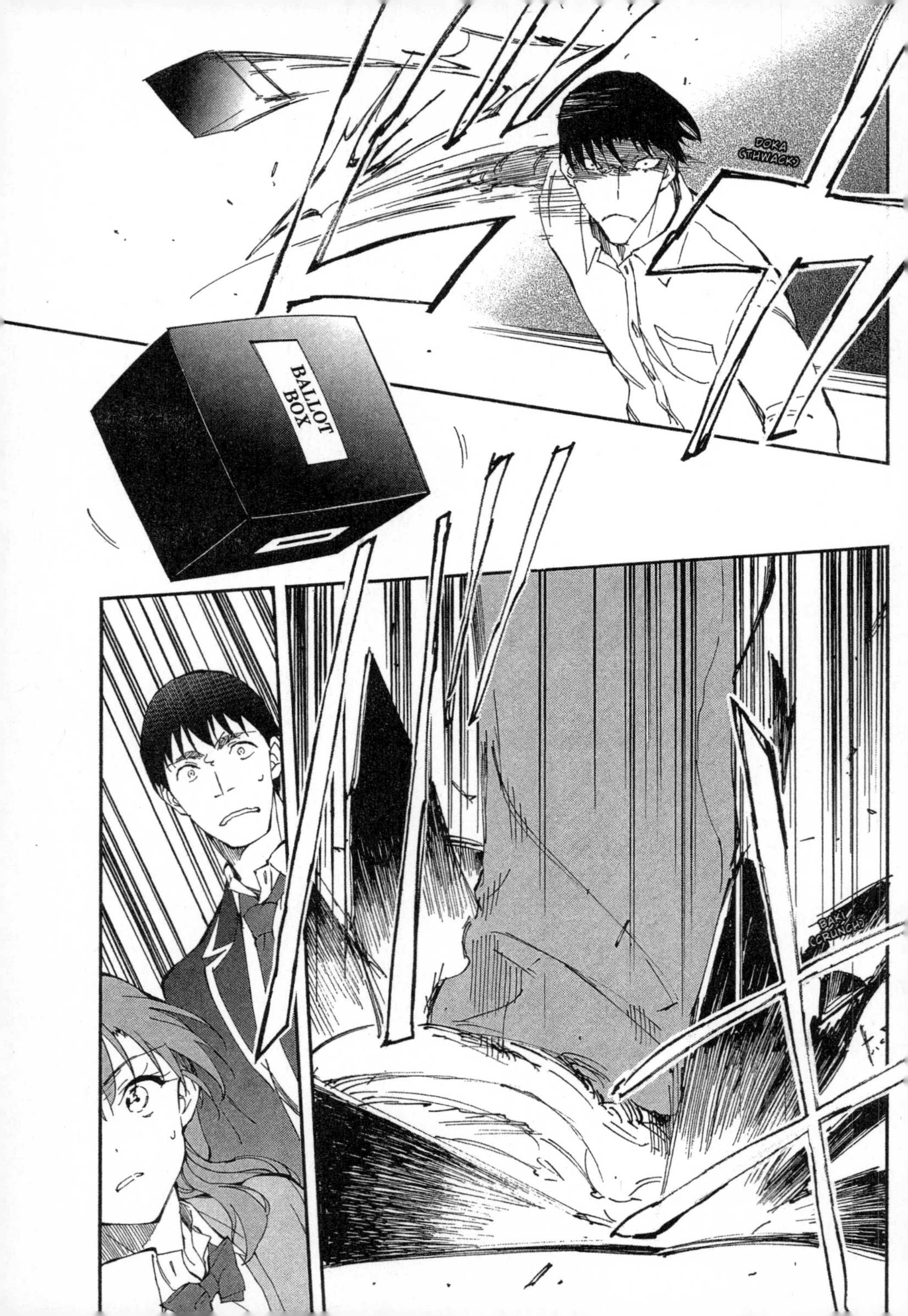
DOKA (THWACK)
BALLOT BOX
BAKI (CRUNCH)

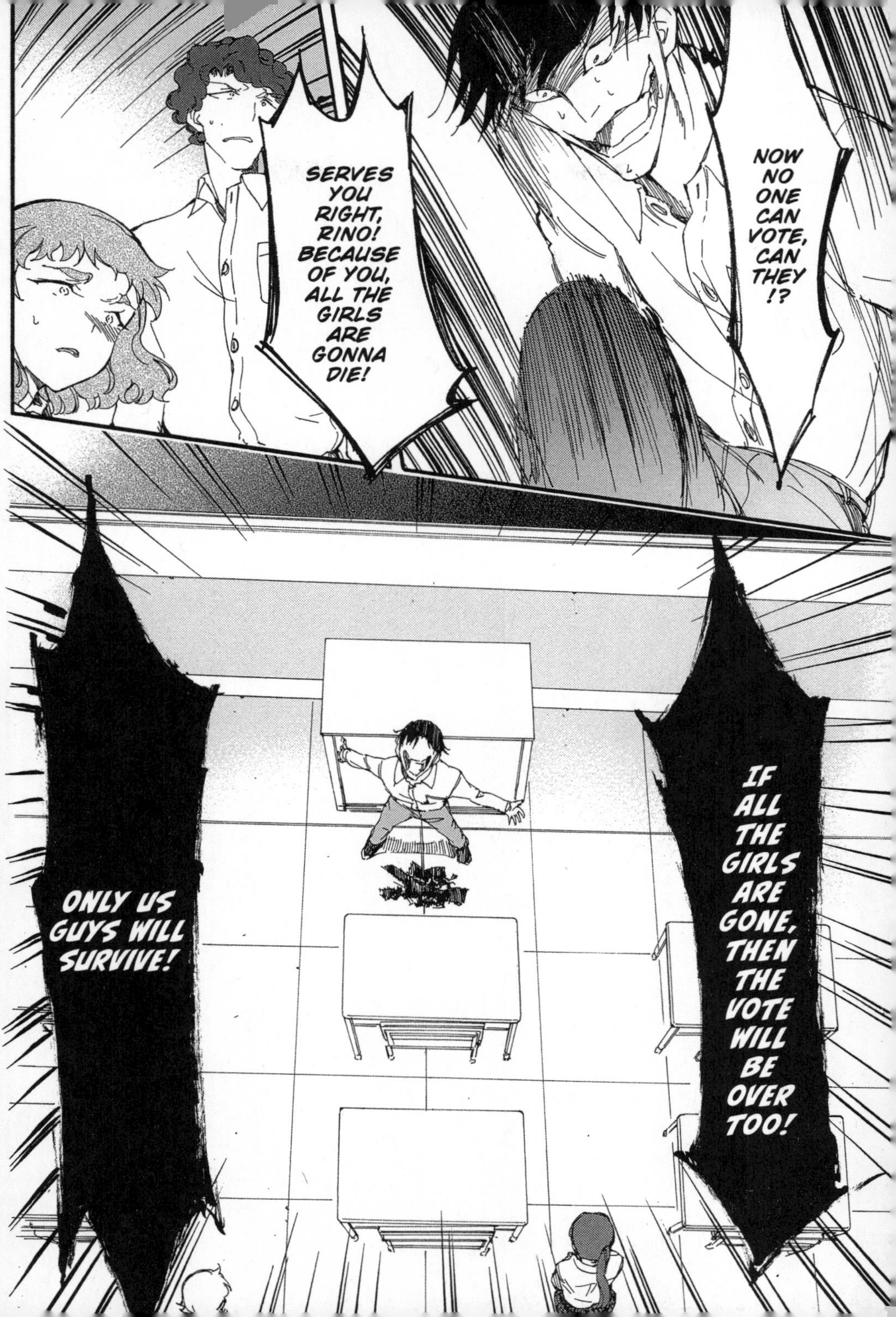
NOW NO ONE CAN VOTE, CAN THEY!?
SERVES YOU RIGHT, RINO! BECAUSE OF YOU, ALL THE GIRLS ARE GONNA DIE!
IF ALL THE GIRLS ARE GONE, THEN THE VOTE WILL BE OVER TOO!
ONLY US GUYS WILL SURVIVE!

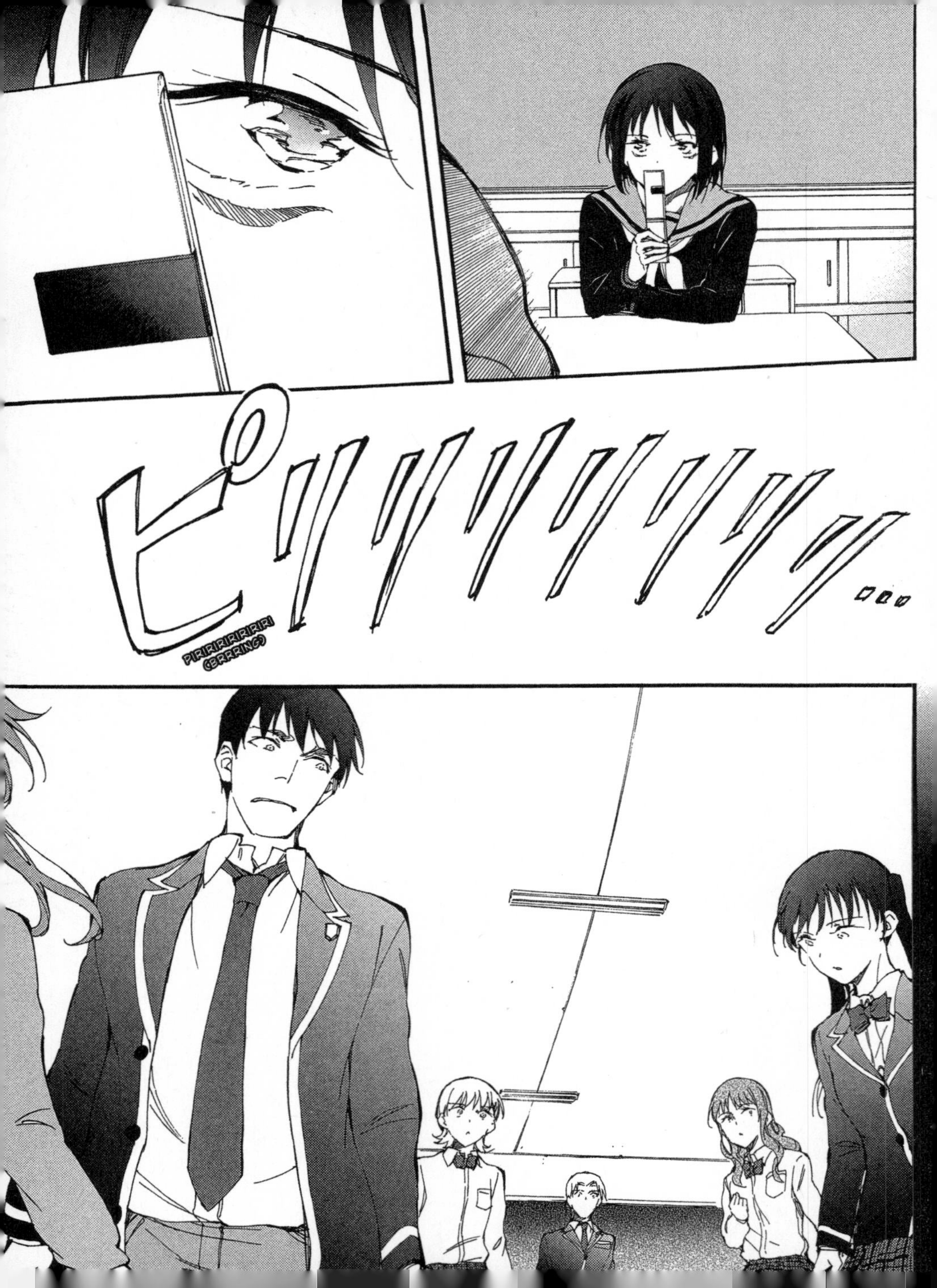
ピリリリリリリリ...
PIRIRIRIRIRIRIRI
(BRRRING)

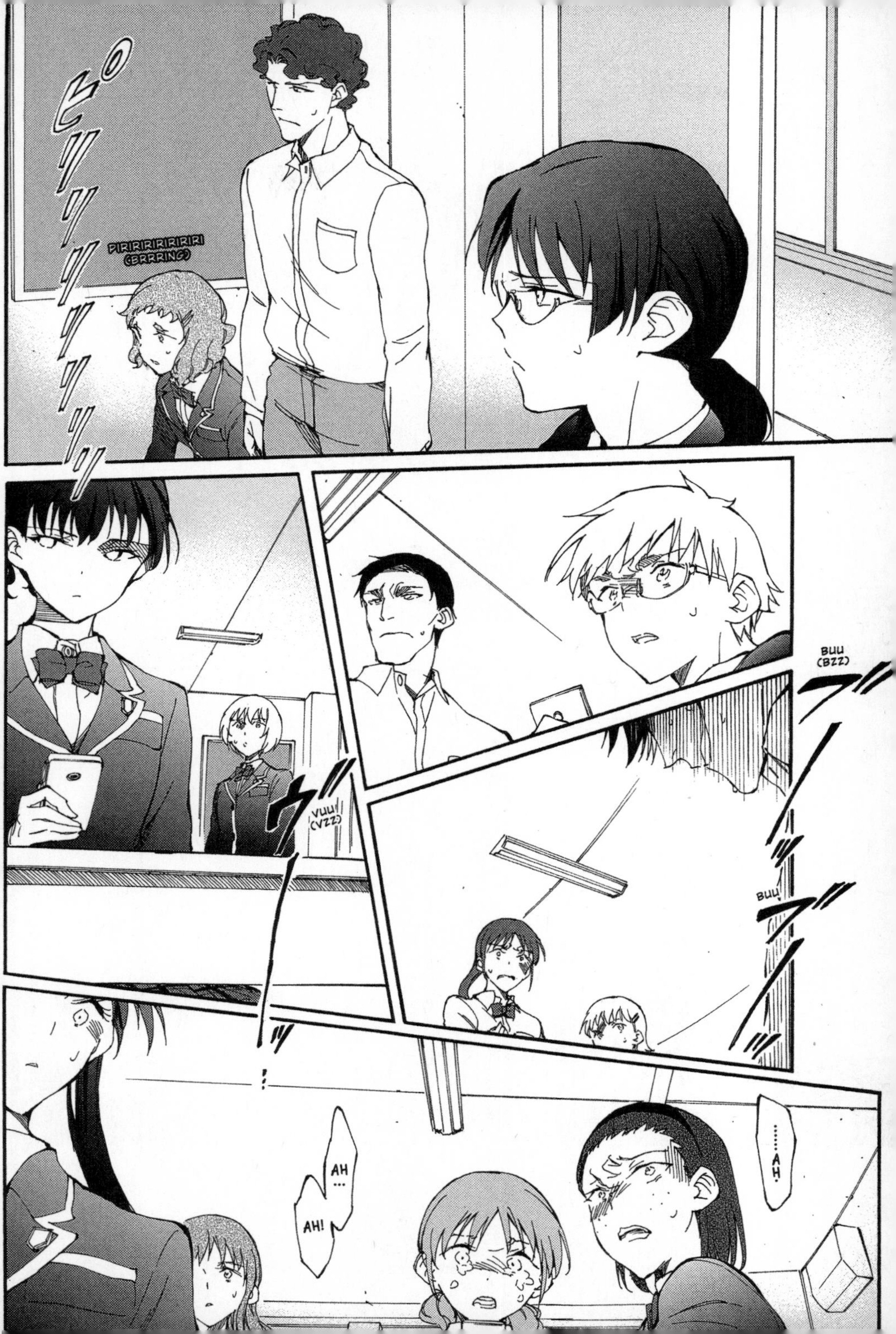
PIRIRIRIRIRIRIRI (BRRRING)
BUU (BZZ)
BUU
VUU (VZZ)
......AH!
!
AH...
AH!

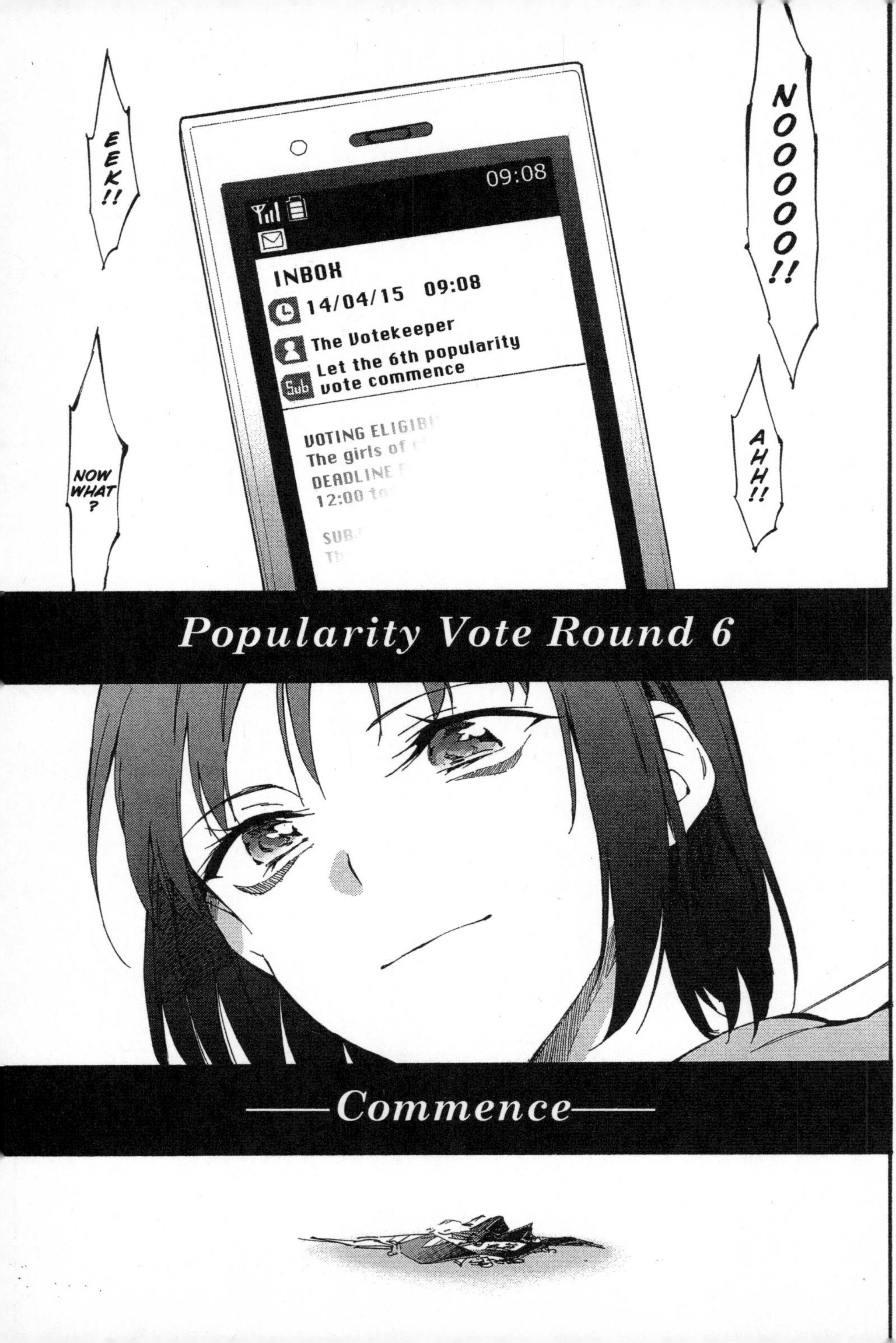
NOOOOOO!!
AHH!!
09:08
INBOX
14/04/15 09:08
The Votekeeper
Let the 6th popularity vote commence
EEK!!
NOW WHAT?

Popularity Vote Round 6

—Commence—

TOHYO GAME

One **black** ballot to you

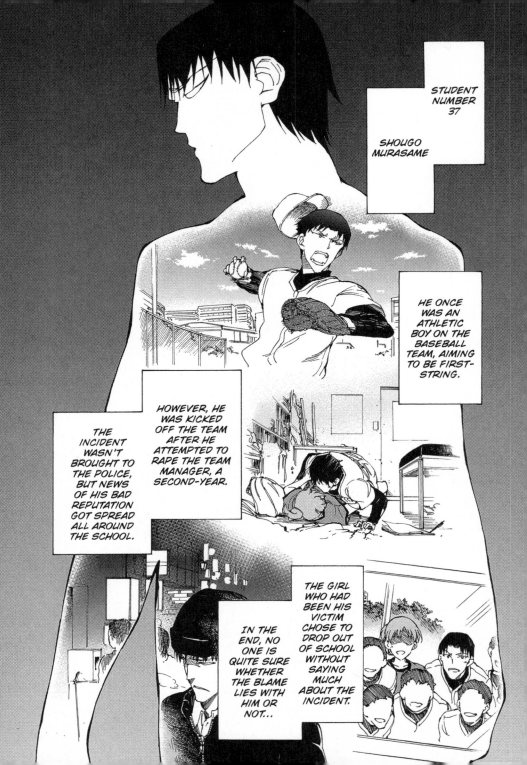

STUDENT NUMBER 37

SHOUGO MURASAME

HE ONCE WAS AN ATHLETIC BOY ON THE BASEBALL TEAM, AIMING TO BE FIRST-STRING.

HOWEVER, HE WAS KICKED OFF THE TEAM AFTER HE ATTEMPTED TO RAPE THE TEAM MANAGER, A SECOND-YEAR.

THE INCIDENT WASN'T BROUGHT TO THE POLICE, BUT NEWS OF HIS BAD REPUTATION GOT SPREAD ALL AROUND THE SCHOOL.

THE GIRL WHO HAD BEEN HIS VICTIM CHOSE TO DROP OUT OF SCHOOL WITHOUT SAYING MUCH ABOUT THE INCIDENT.

IN THE END, NO ONE IS QUITE SURE WHETHER THE BLAME LIES WITH HIM OR NOT...

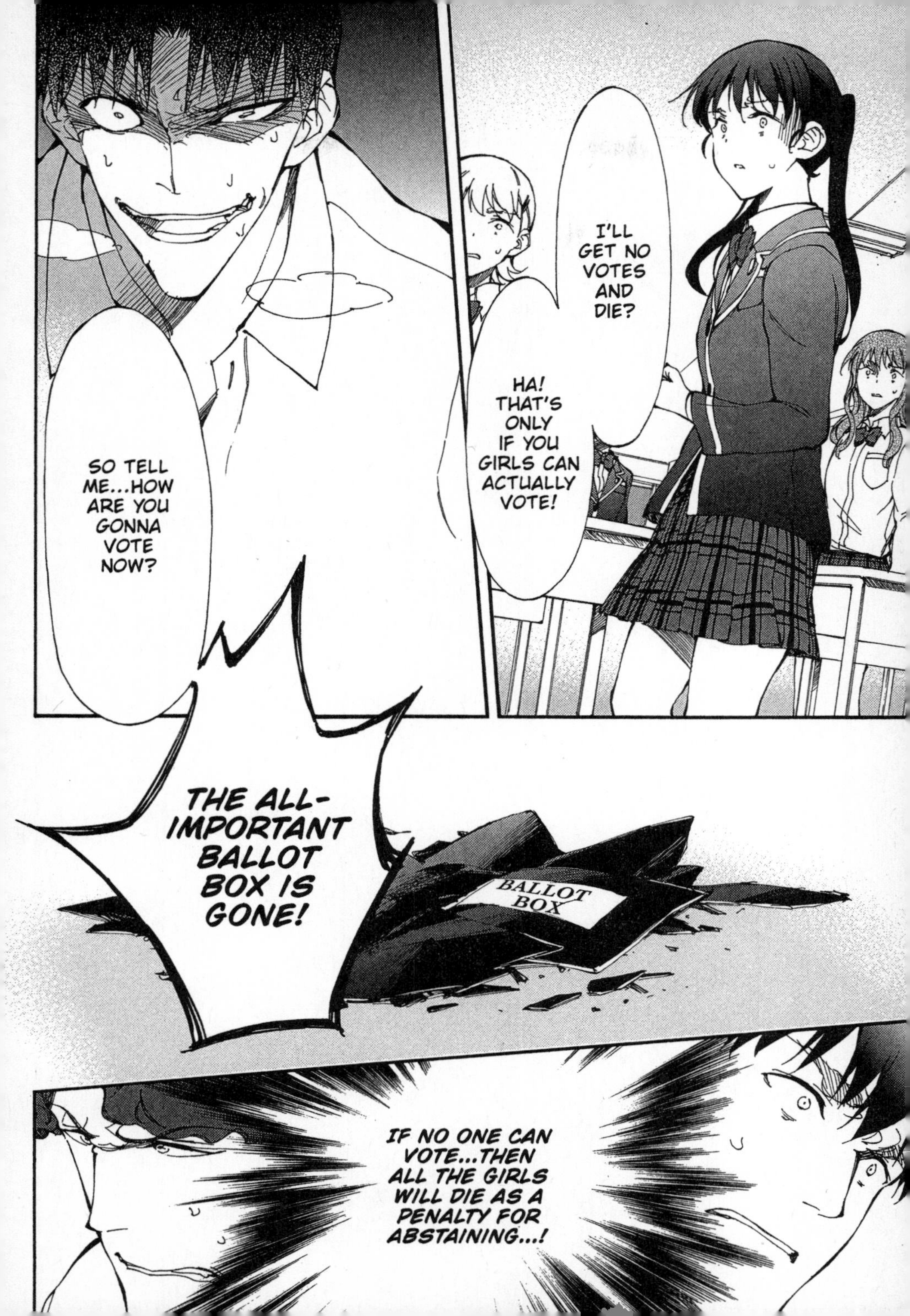

I'LL GET NO VOTES AND DIE?
HA! THAT'S ONLY IF YOU GIRLS CAN ACTUALLY VOTE!
SO TELL ME...HOW ARE YOU GONNA VOTE NOW?
THE ALL-IMPORTANT BALLOT BOX IS GONE!
BALLOT BOX
IF NO ONE CAN VOTE...THEN ALL THE GIRLS WILL DIE AS A PENALTY FOR ABSTAINING...!

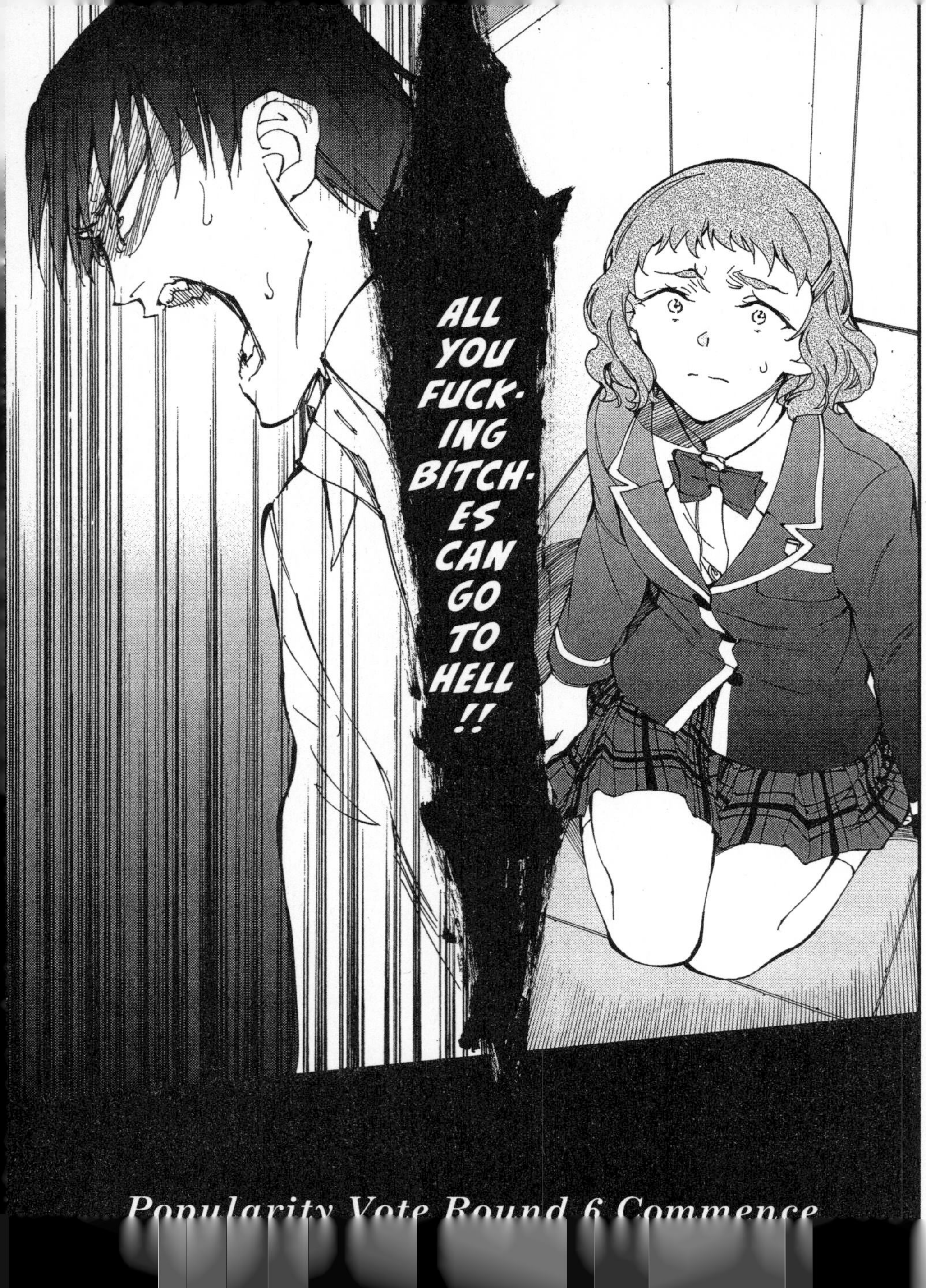
ALL YOU FUCK-ING BITCH-ES CAN GO TO HELL!!
Popularity Vote Round 6 Commence

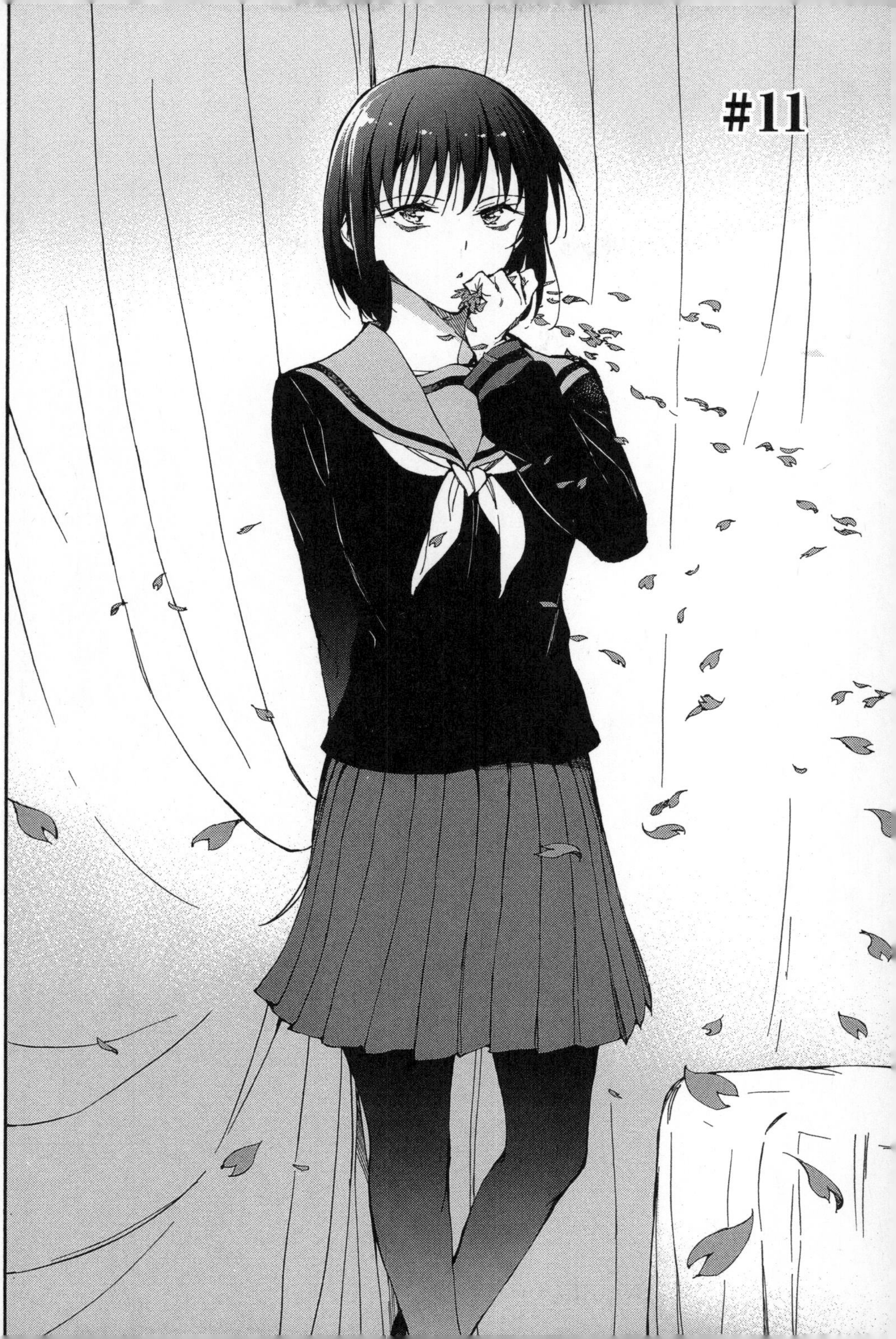
#11

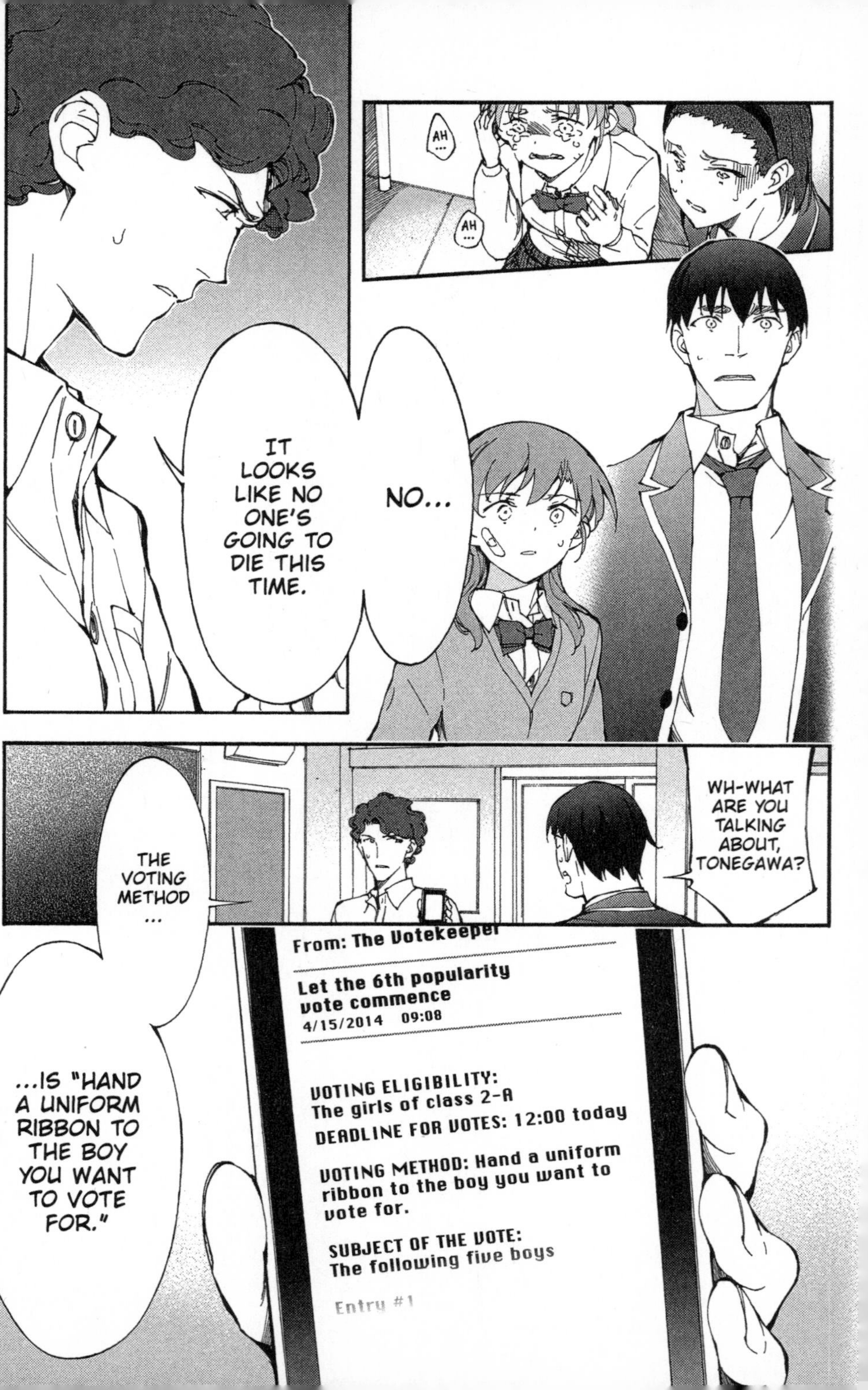
AH...
AH...
NO...
IT LOOKS LIKE NO ONE'S GOING TO DIE THIS TIME.
WH-WHAT ARE YOU TALKING ABOUT, TONEGAWA?
THE VOTING METHOD ...
From: The Votekeeper
Let the 6th popularity vote commence
4/15/2014 09:08
VOTING ELIGIBILITY:
The girls of class 2-A
DEADLINE FOR VOTES: 12:00 today
VOTING METHOD: Hand a uniform ribbon to the boy you want to vote for.
SUBJECT OF THE VOTE:
The following five boys
Entry #1
...IS "HAND A UNIFORM RIBBON TO THE BOY YOU WANT TO VOTE FOR."

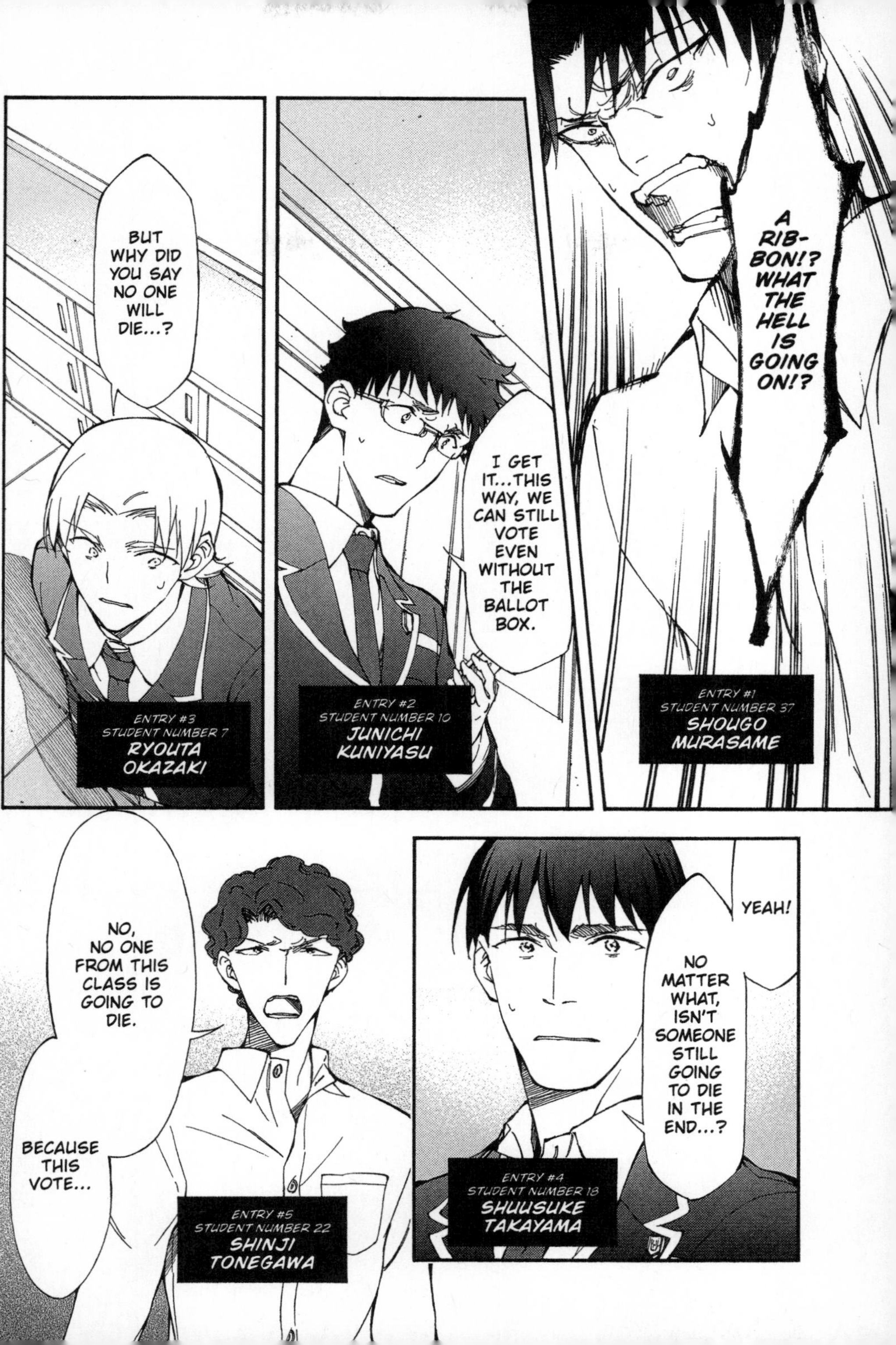
A RIB-BON!? WHAT THE HELL IS GOING ON!?
ENTRY #1 STUDENT NUMBER 37 SHOUGO MURASAME
I GET IT...THIS WAY, WE CAN STILL VOTE EVEN WITHOUT THE BALLOT BOX.
ENTRY #2 STUDENT NUMBER 10 JUNICHI KUNIYASU
BUT WHY DID YOU SAY NO ONE WILL DIE...?
ENTRY #3 STUDENT NUMBER 7 RYOUTA OKAZAKI
YEAH!
NO MATTER WHAT, ISN'T SOMEONE STILL GOING TO DIE IN THE END...?
ENTRY #4 STUDENT NUMBER 18 SHUUSUKE TAKAYAMA
NO, NO ONE FROM THIS CLASS IS GOING TO DIE.
BECAUSE THIS VOTE...
ENTRY #5 STUDENT NUMBER 22 SHINJI TONEGAWA

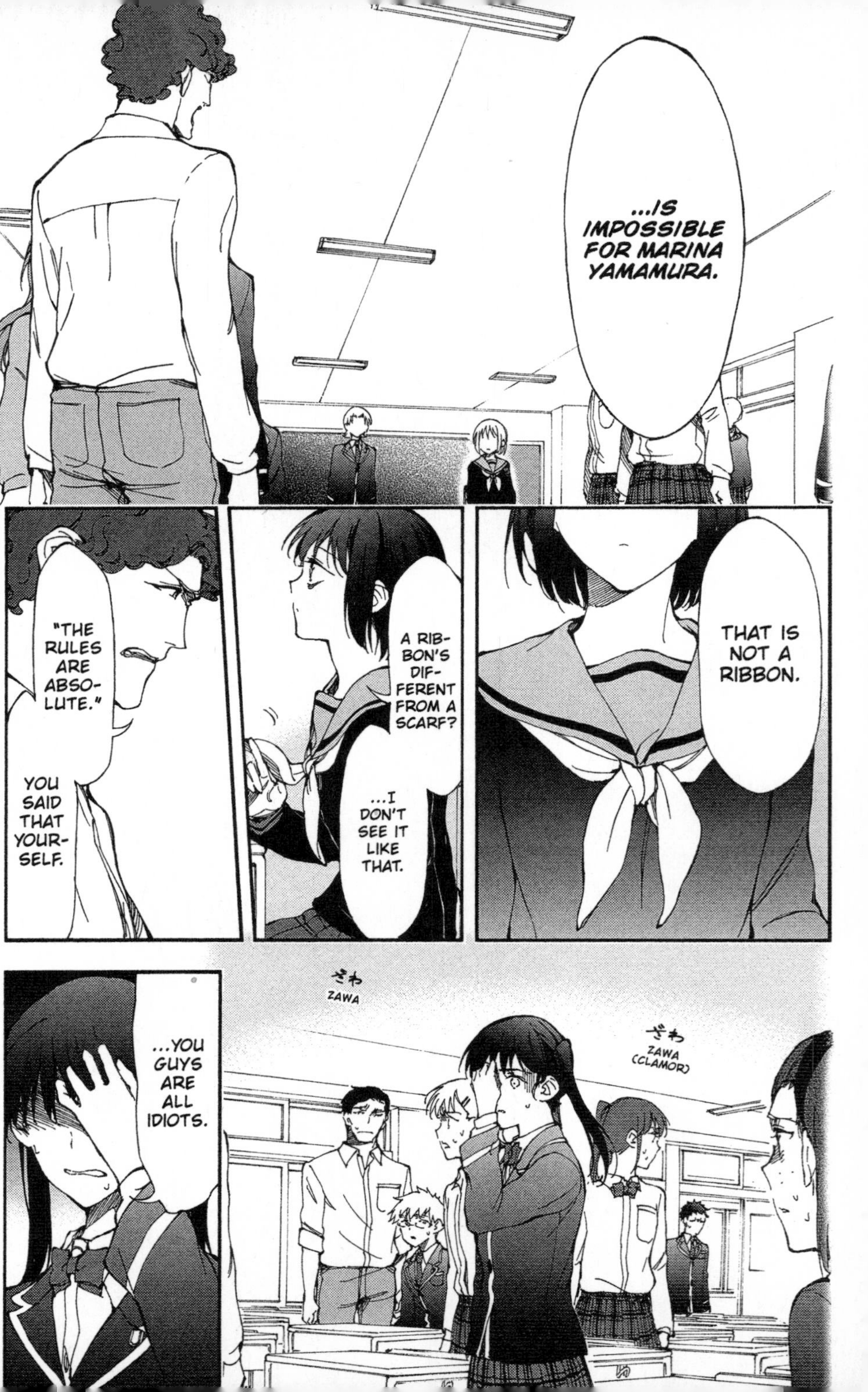
...IS IMPOSSIBLE FOR MARINA YAMAMURA.
THAT IS NOT A RIBBON.
A RIBBON'S DIFFERENT FROM A SCARF?
...I DON'T SEE IT LIKE THAT.
"THE RULES ARE ABSOLUTE."
YOU SAID THAT YOURSELF.
ざわ
ZAWA (CLAMOR)
ざわ
ZAWA
...YOU GUYS ARE ALL IDIOTS.

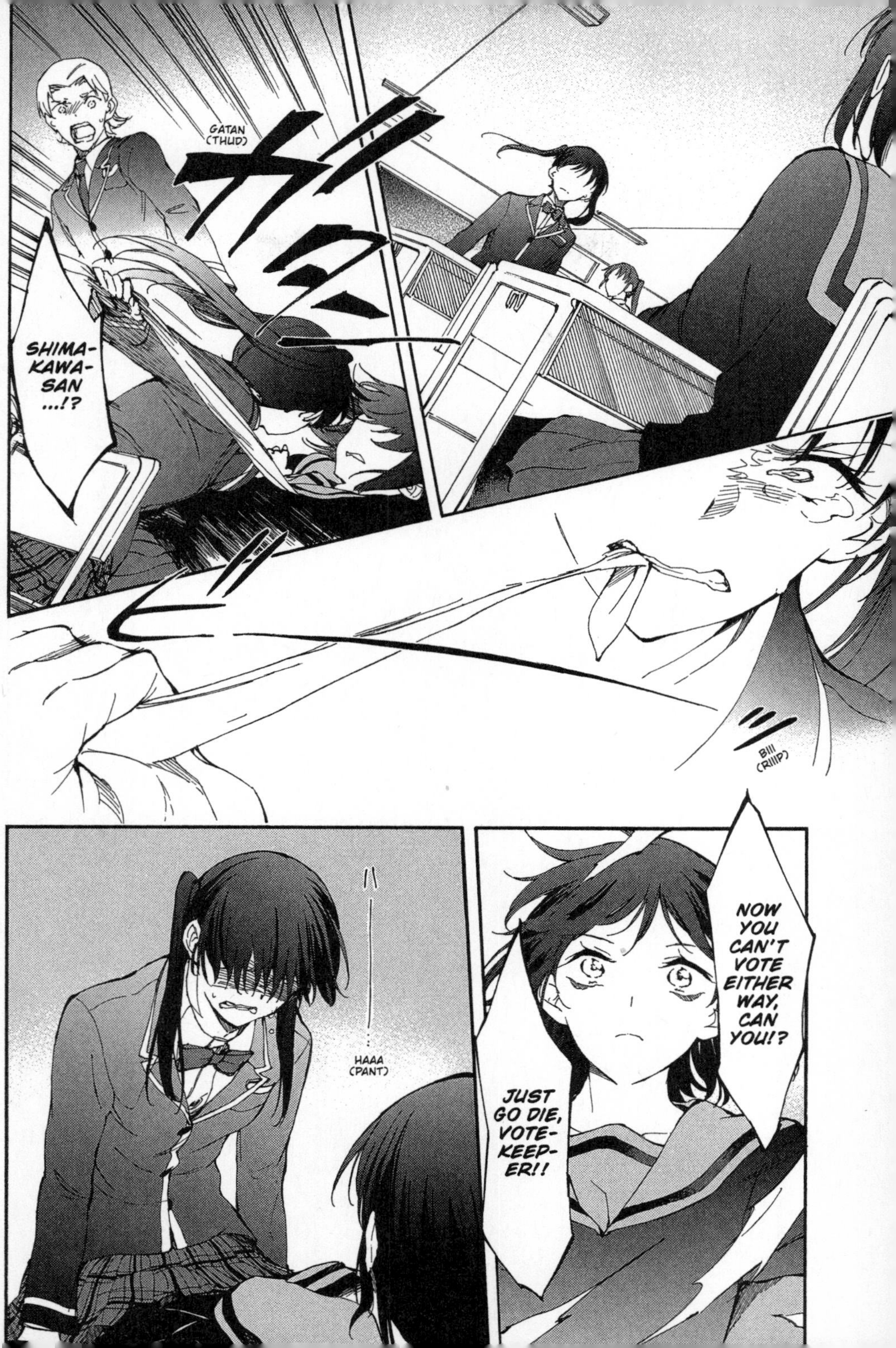
GATAN (THUD)
SHIMAKAWA-SAN ...!?
BIII (RIIIP)
NOW YOU CAN'T VOTE EITHER WAY, CAN YOU!?
JUST GO DIE, VOTE-KEEPER!!
HAAA (PANT)

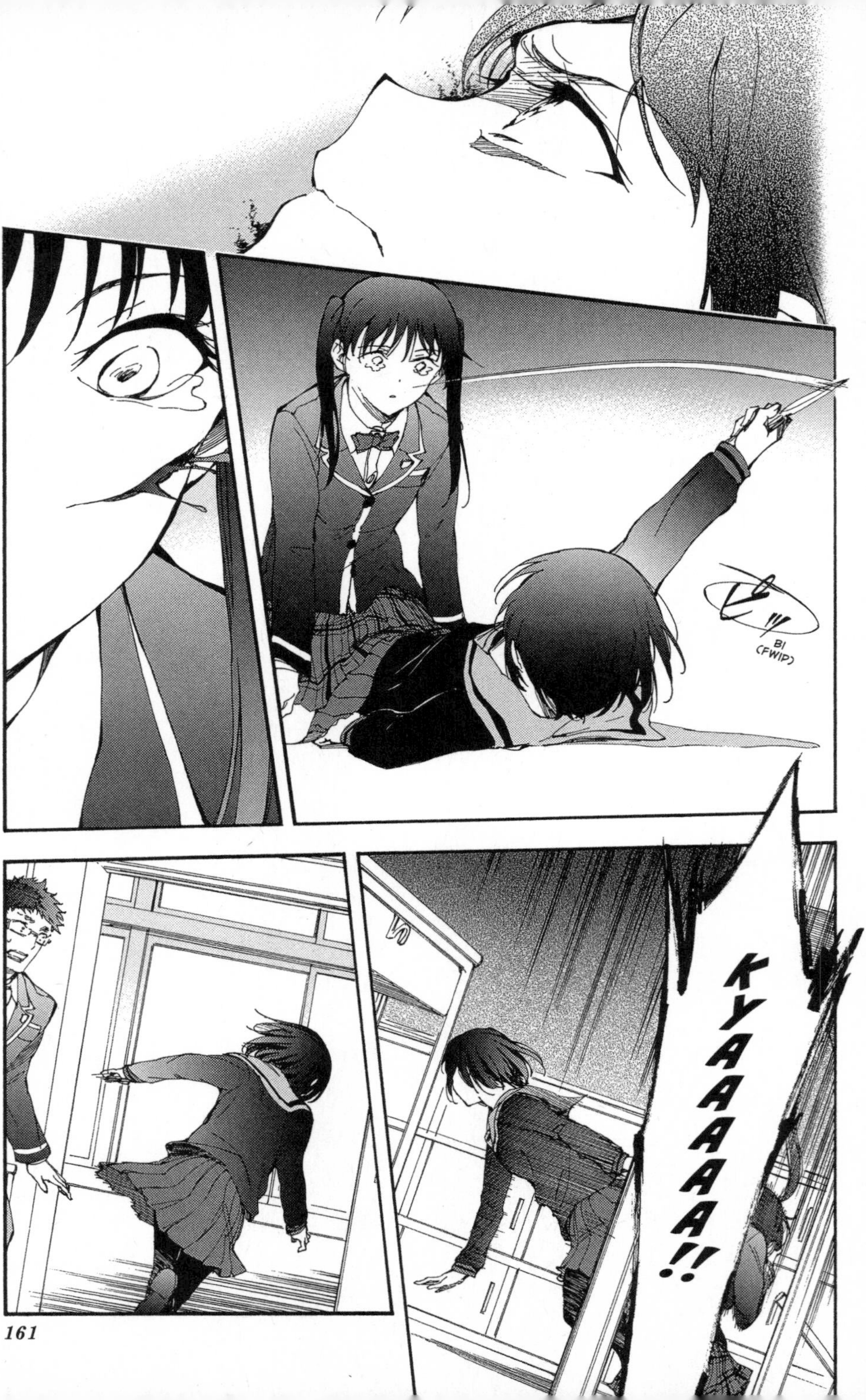
BI
(FWIP)
KYAAAAAAA!!

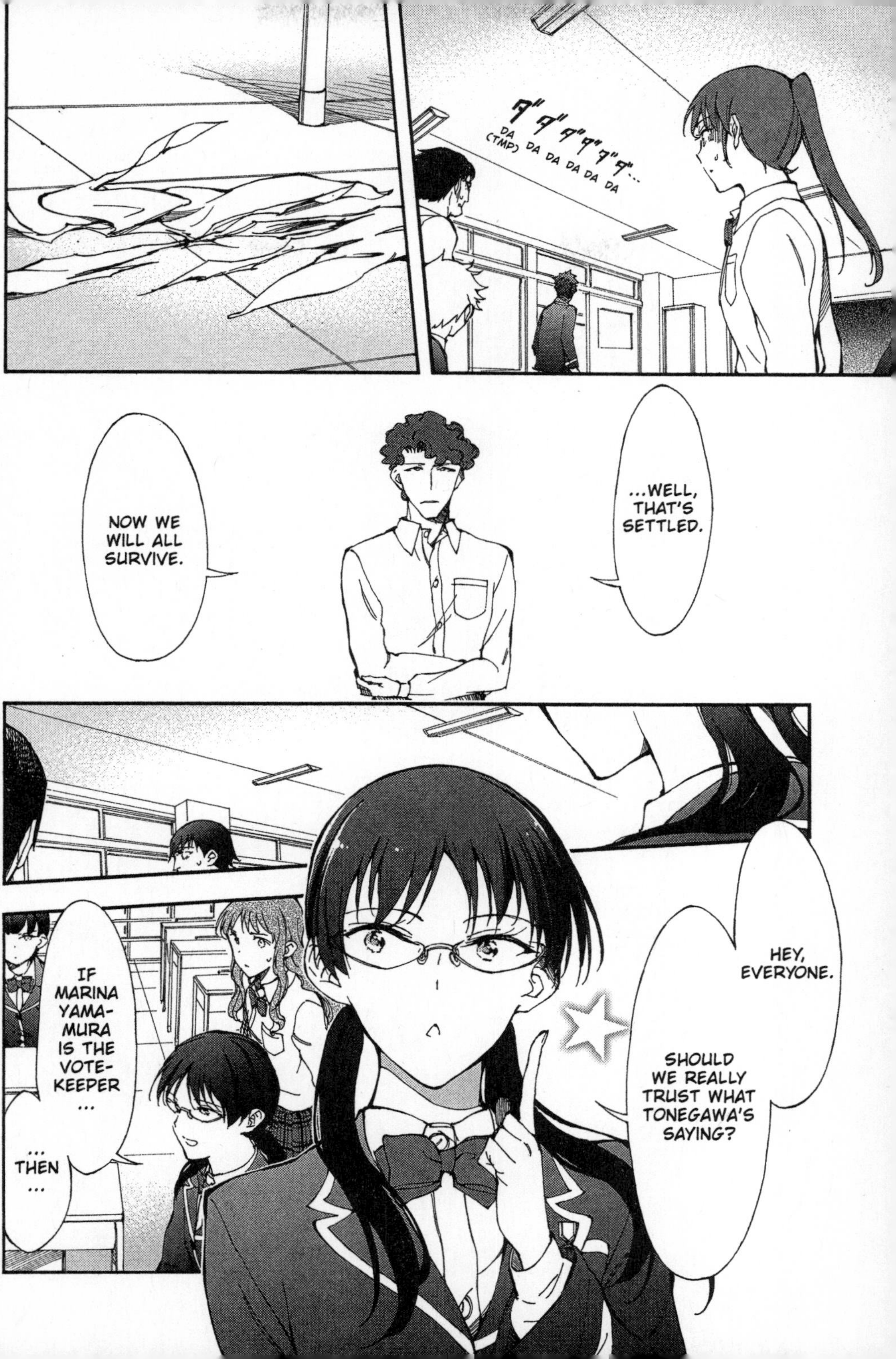
DA DA DA DA DA DA (TMP)
...WELL, THAT'S SETTLED.
NOW WE WILL ALL SURVIVE.
HEY, EVERYONE.
SHOULD WE REALLY TRUST WHAT TONEGAWA'S SAYING?
IF MARINA YAMAMURA IS THE VOTE-KEEPER...
...THEN...

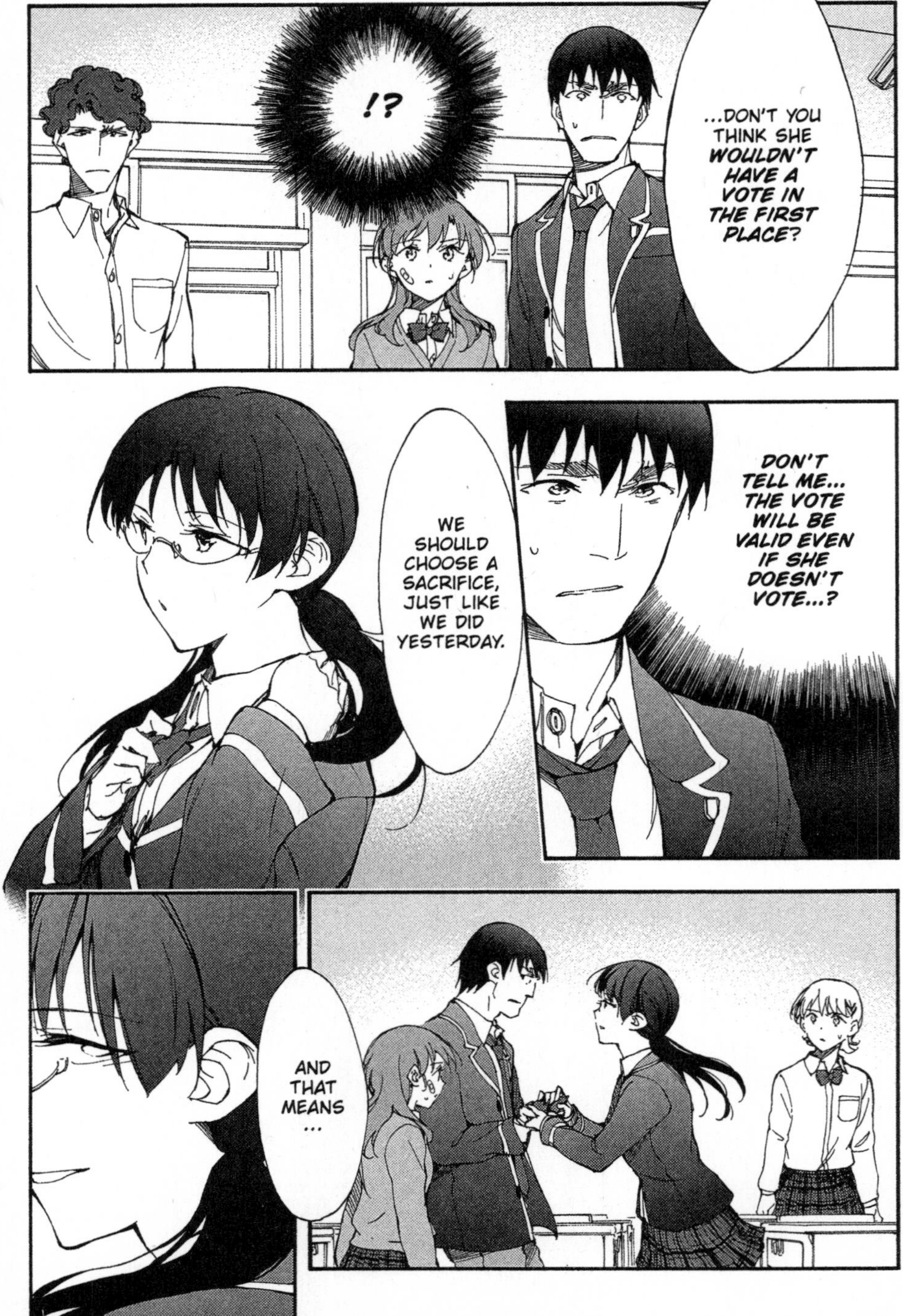
...DON'T YOU THINK SHE WOULDN'T HAVE A VOTE IN THE FIRST PLACE?
!?
DON'T TELL ME... THE VOTE WILL BE VALID EVEN IF SHE DOESN'T VOTE...?
WE SHOULD CHOOSE A SACRIFICE, JUST LIKE WE DID YESTERDAY.
AND THAT MEANS...

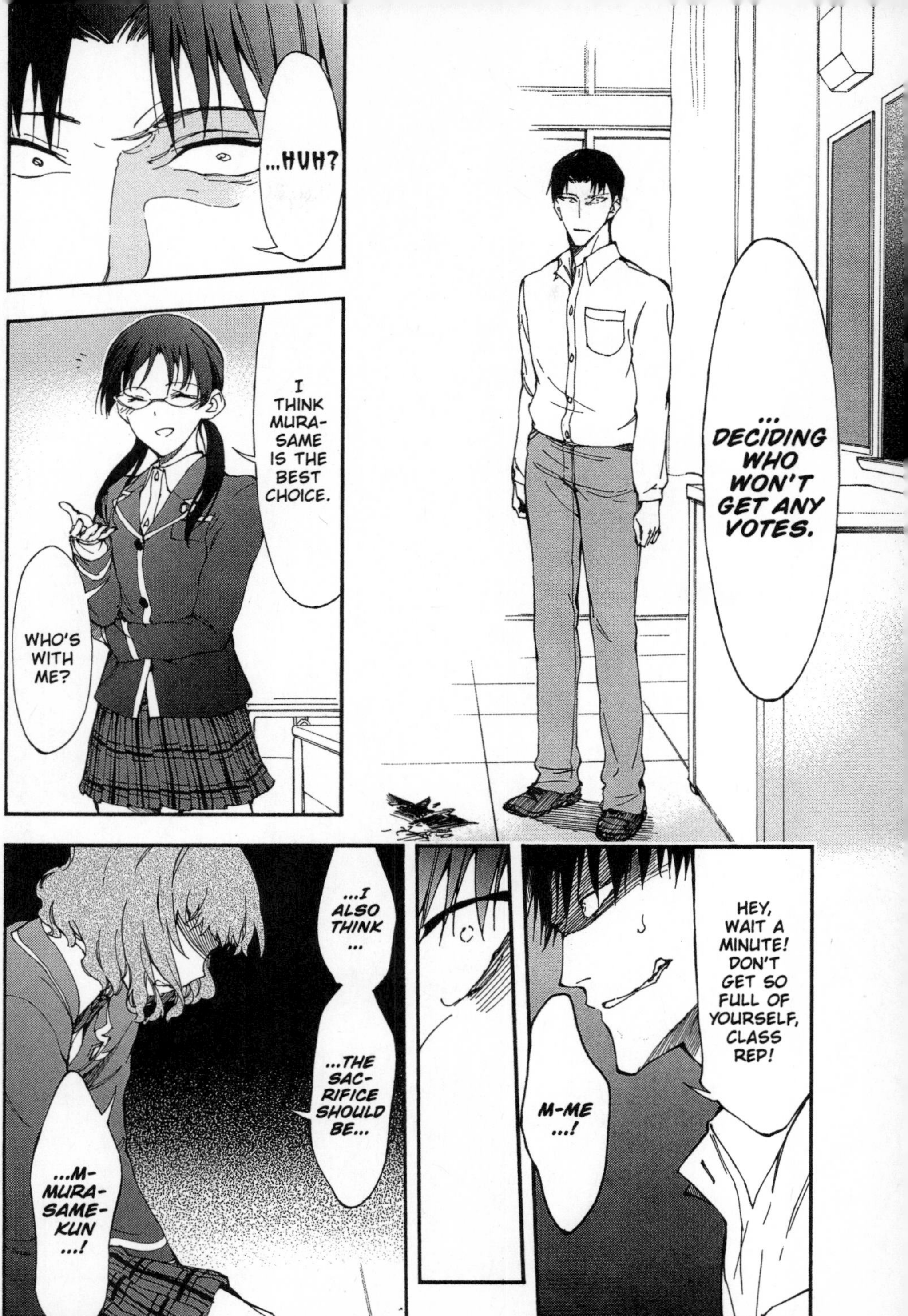
...DECIDING WHO WON'T GET ANY VOTES.
...HUH?
I THINK MURA-SAME IS THE BEST CHOICE.
WHO'S WITH ME?
HEY, WAIT A MINUTE! DON'T GET SO FULL OF YOURSELF, CLASS REP!
M-ME ...!
...I ALSO THINK ...
...THE SAC-RIFICE SHOULD BE...
...M-MURA-SAME-KUN ...!

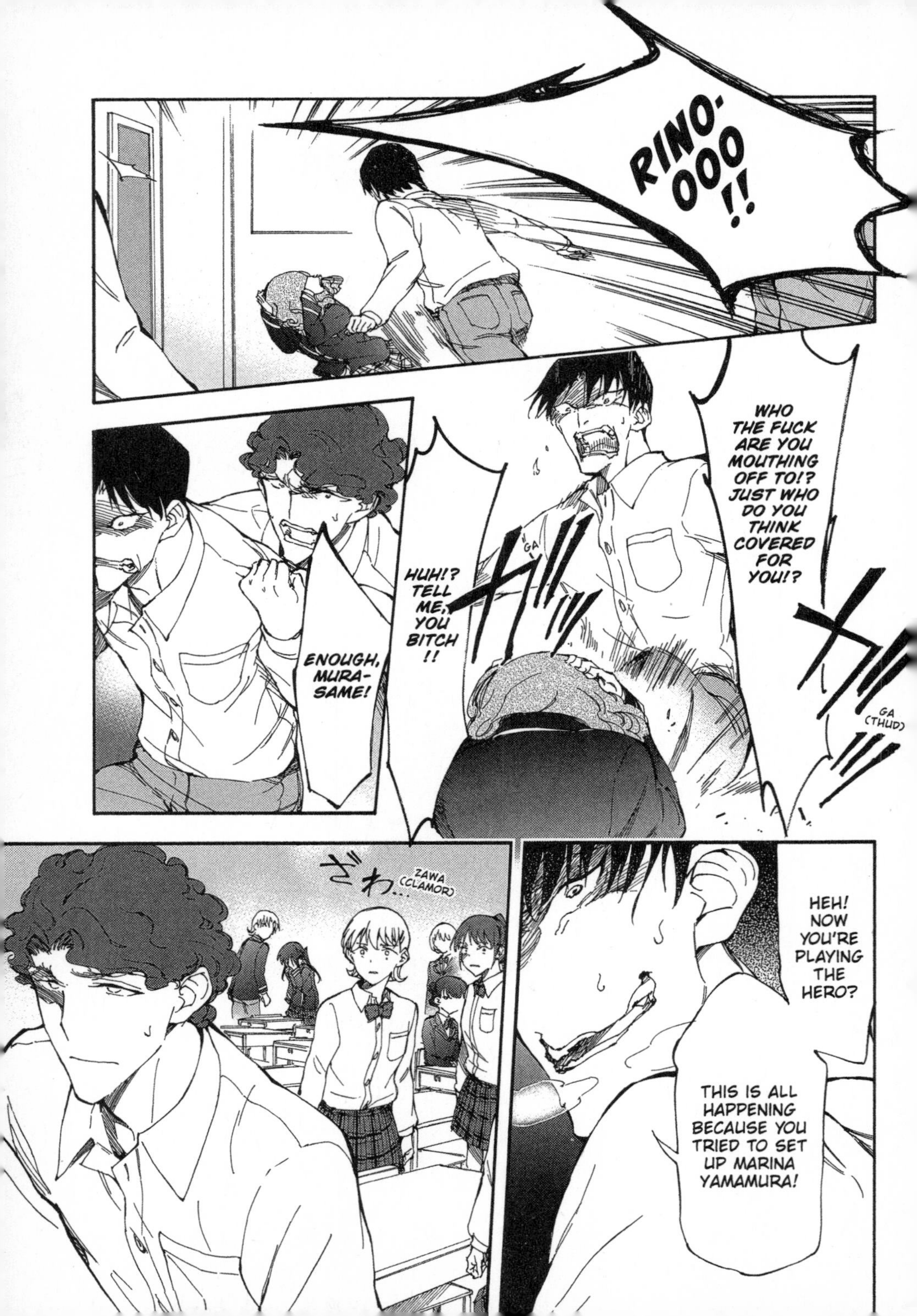

RINO-OOO!!
WHO THE FUCK ARE YOU MOUTHING OFF TO!? JUST WHO DO YOU THINK COVERED FOR YOU!?
GA (THUD)
GA
HUH!? TELL ME, YOU BITCH!!
ENOUGH, MURASAME!
HEH! NOW YOU'RE PLAYING THE HERO?
THIS IS ALL HAPPENING BECAUSE YOU TRIED TO SET UP MARINA YAMAMURA!
ざわ…
ZAWA (CLAMOR)

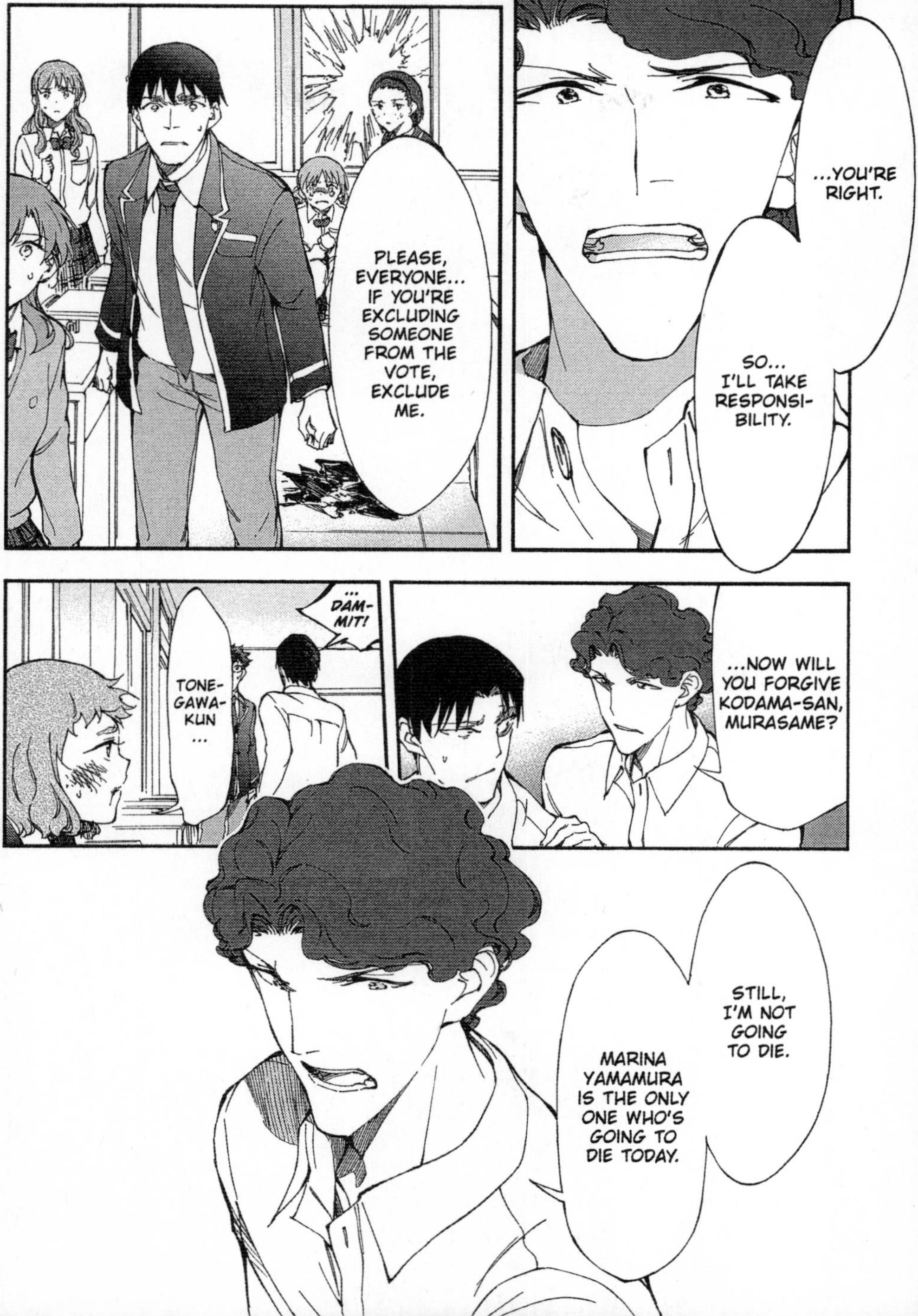
...YOU'RE RIGHT.
SO... I'LL TAKE RESPONSI-BILITY.
PLEASE, EVERYONE... IF YOU'RE EXCLUDING SOMEONE FROM THE VOTE, EXCLUDE ME.
...NOW WILL YOU FORGIVE KODAMA-SAN, MURASAME?
...DAM-MIT!
TONE-GAWA-KUN...
STILL, I'M NOT GOING TO DIE.
MARINA YAMAMURA IS THE ONLY ONE WHO'S GOING TO DIE TODAY.

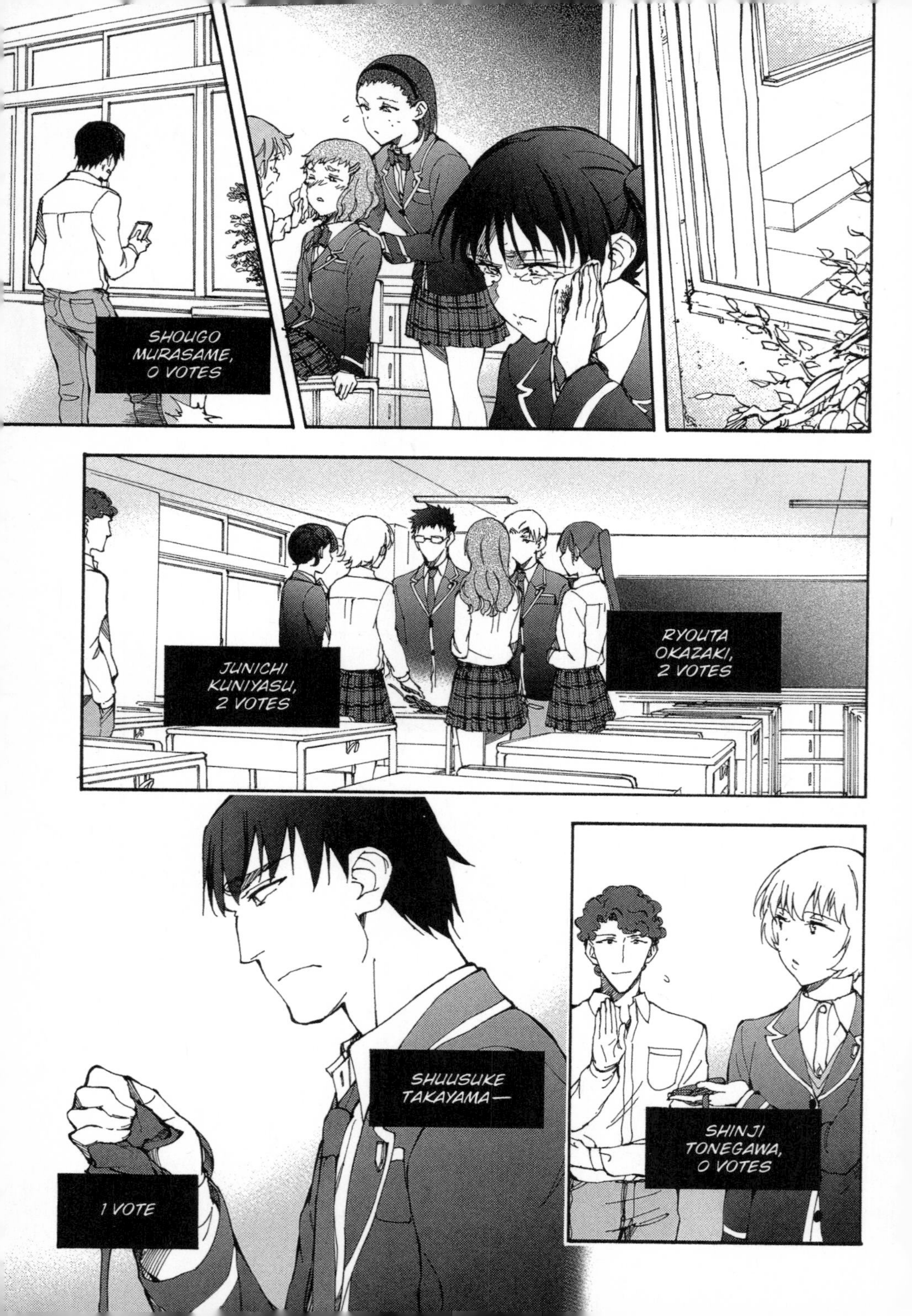
SHOUGO MURASAME, 0 VOTES
RYOUTA OKAZAKI, 2 VOTES
JUNICHI KUNIYASU, 2 VOTES
SHINJI TONEGAWA, 0 VOTES
SHUUSUKE TAKAYAMA—
1 VOTE

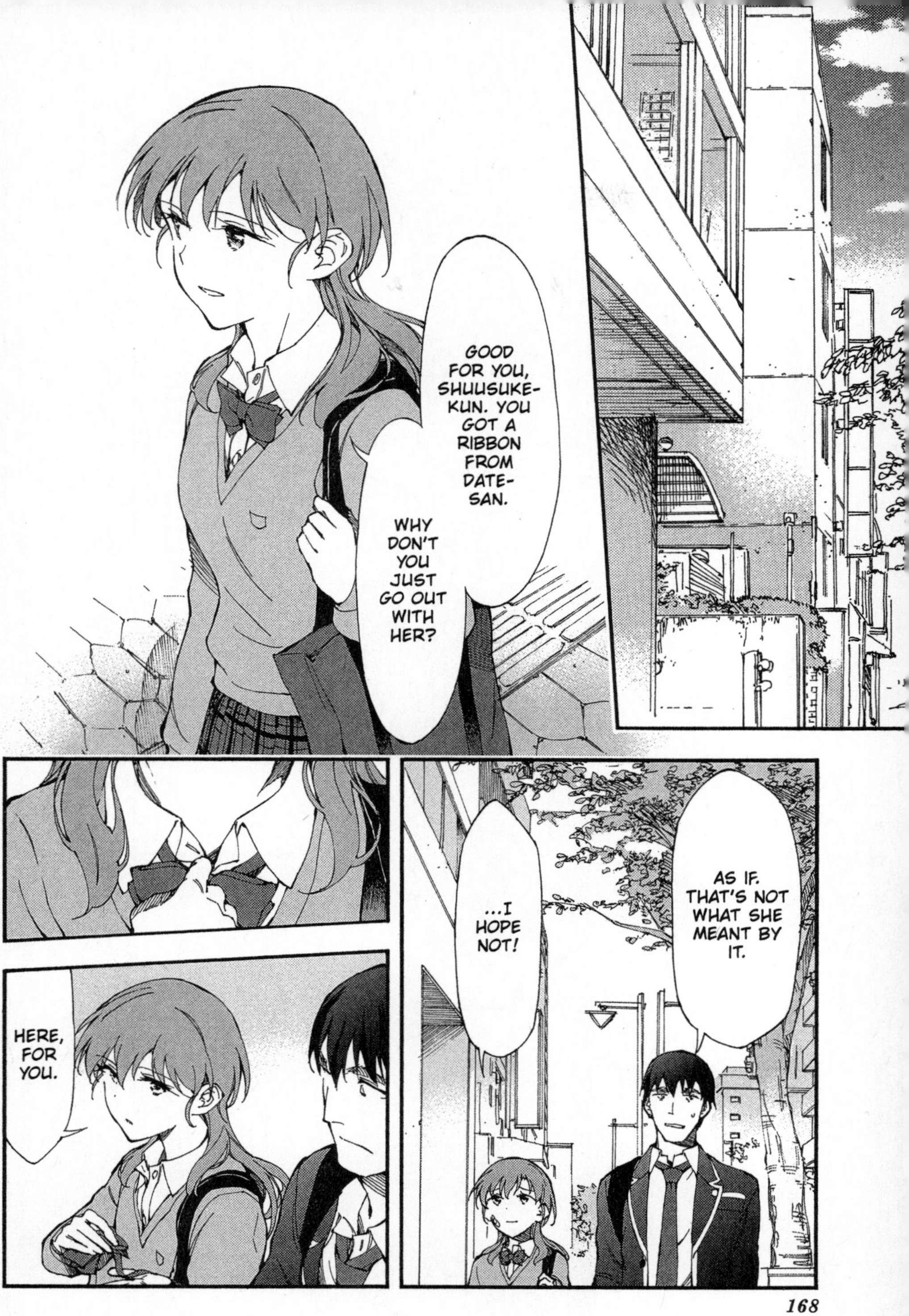
GOOD FOR YOU, SHUUSUKE-KUN. YOU GOT A RIBBON FROM DATE-SAN.
WHY DON'T YOU JUST GO OUT WITH HER?
AS IF. THAT'S NOT WHAT SHE MEANT BY IT.
...I HOPE NOT!
HERE, FOR YOU.

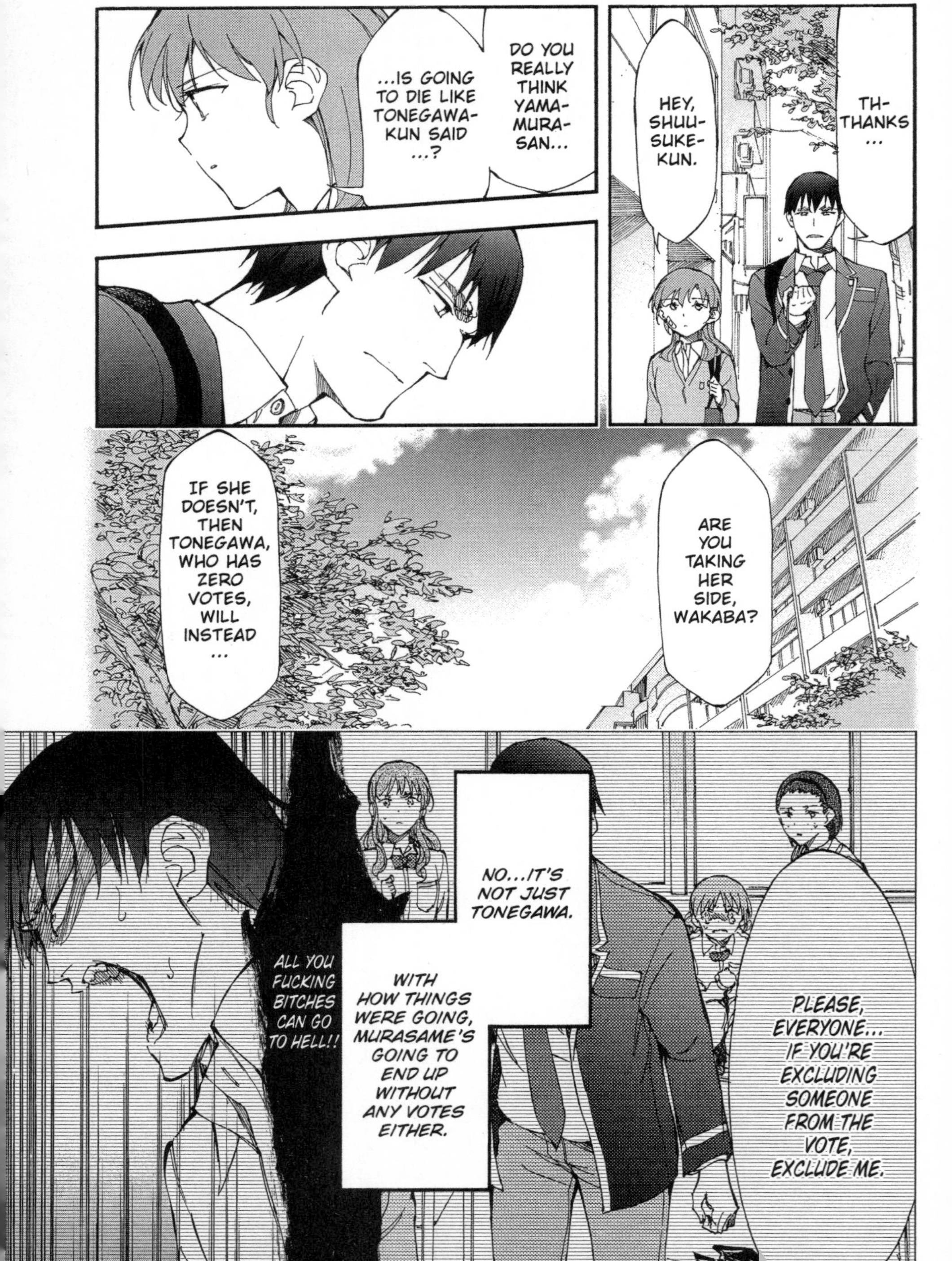
TH-THANKS...
HEY, SHUUSUKE-KUN.
DO YOU REALLY THINK YAMAMURA-SAN...
...IS GOING TO DIE LIKE TONEGAWA-KUN SAID...?
ARE YOU TAKING HER SIDE, WAKABA?
IF SHE DOESN'T, THEN TONEGAWA, WHO HAS ZERO VOTES, WILL INSTEAD...
PLEASE, EVERYONE... IF YOU'RE EXCLUDING SOMEONE FROM THE VOTE, EXCLUDE ME.
NO...IT'S NOT JUST TONEGAWA.
WITH HOW THINGS WERE GOING, MURASAME'S GOING TO END UP WITHOUT ANY VOTES EITHER.
ALL YOU FUCKING BITCHES CAN GO TO HELL!!

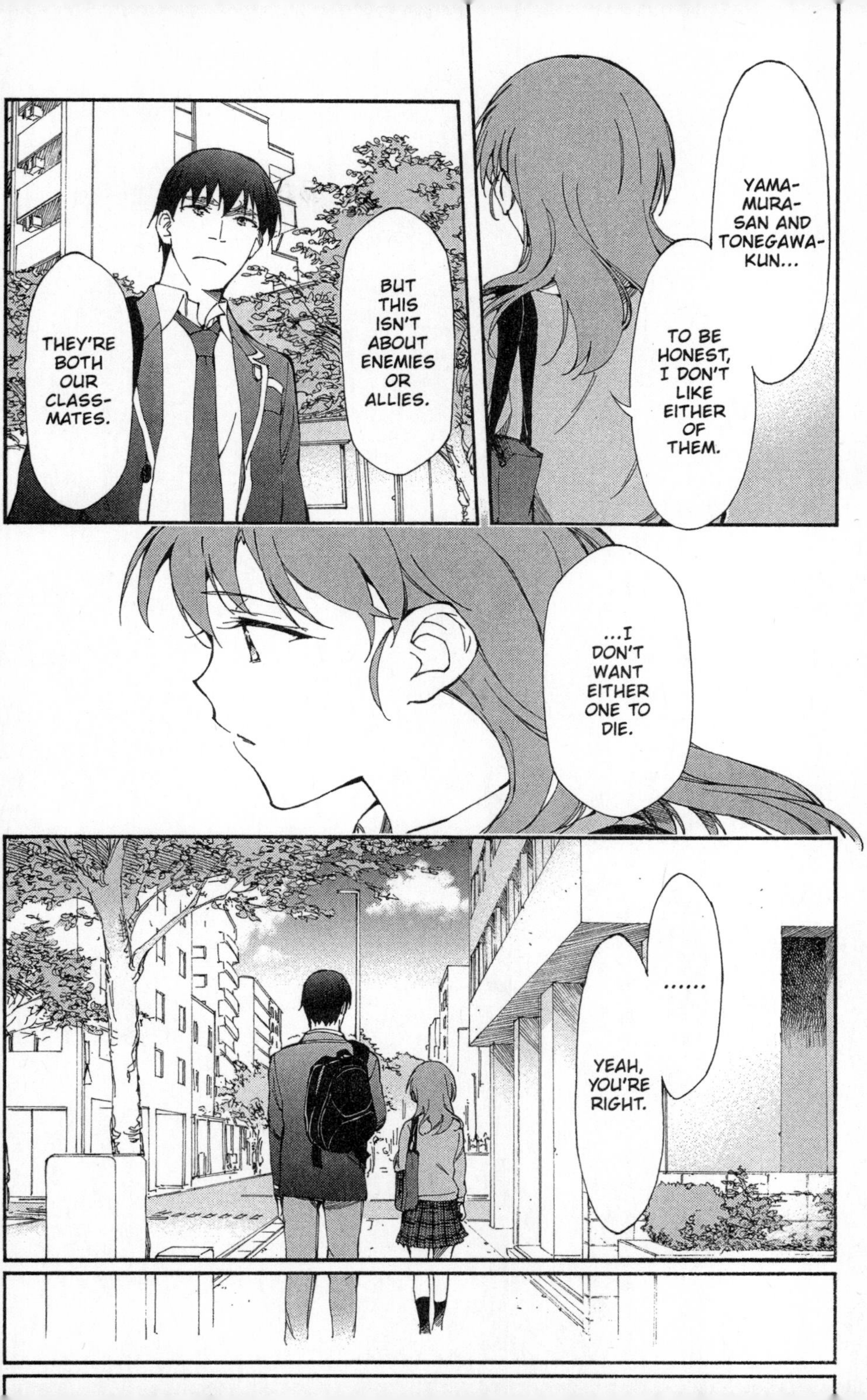
YAMA-MURA-SAN AND TONEGAWA-KUN...
TO BE HONEST, I DON'T LIKE EITHER OF THEM.
BUT THIS ISN'T ABOUT ENEMIES OR ALLIES.
THEY'RE BOTH OUR CLASS-MATES.
...I DON'T WANT EITHER ONE TO DIE.
......
YEAH, YOU'RE RIGHT.

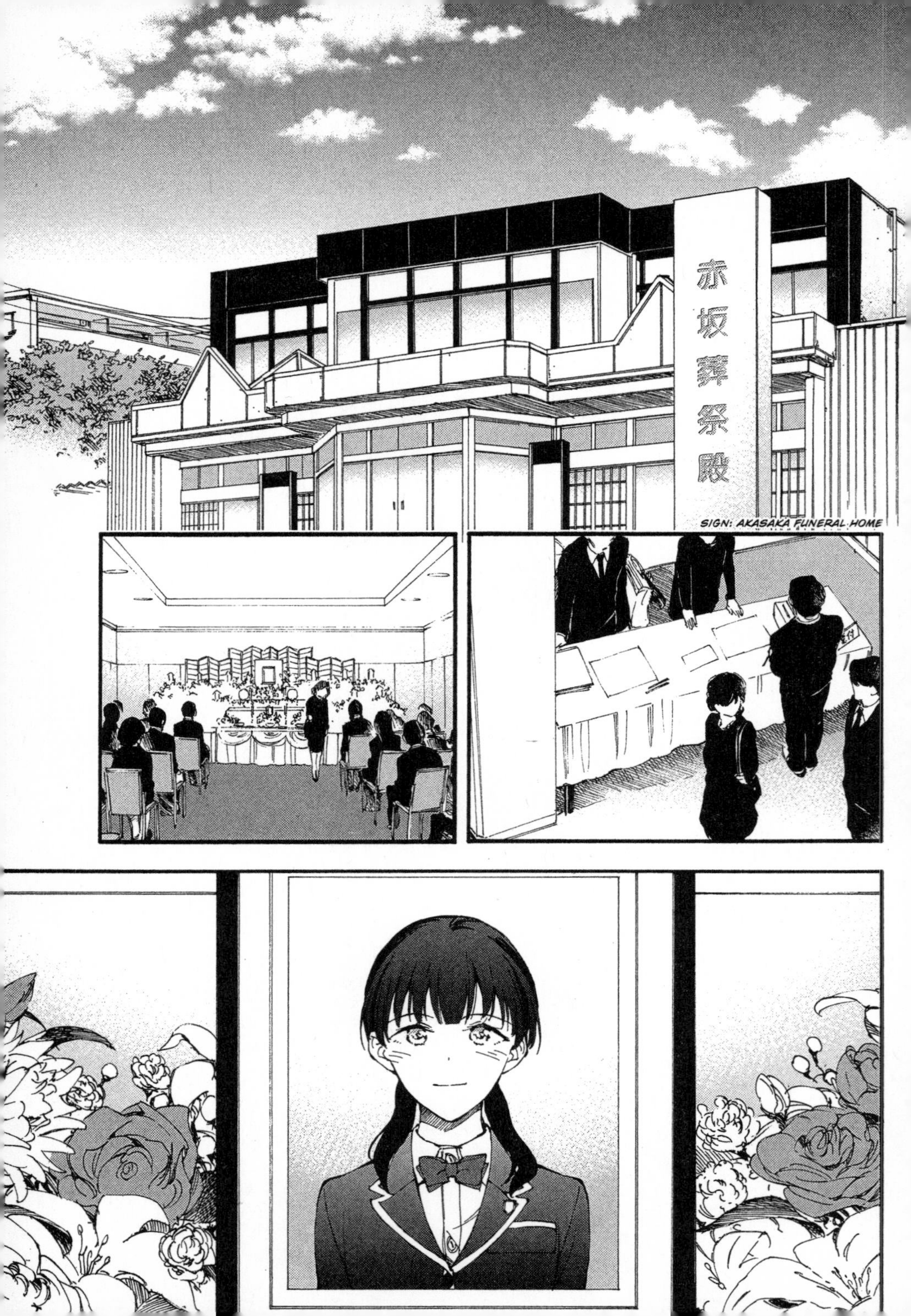
赤坂葬祭殿
SIGN: AKASAKA FUNERAL HOME

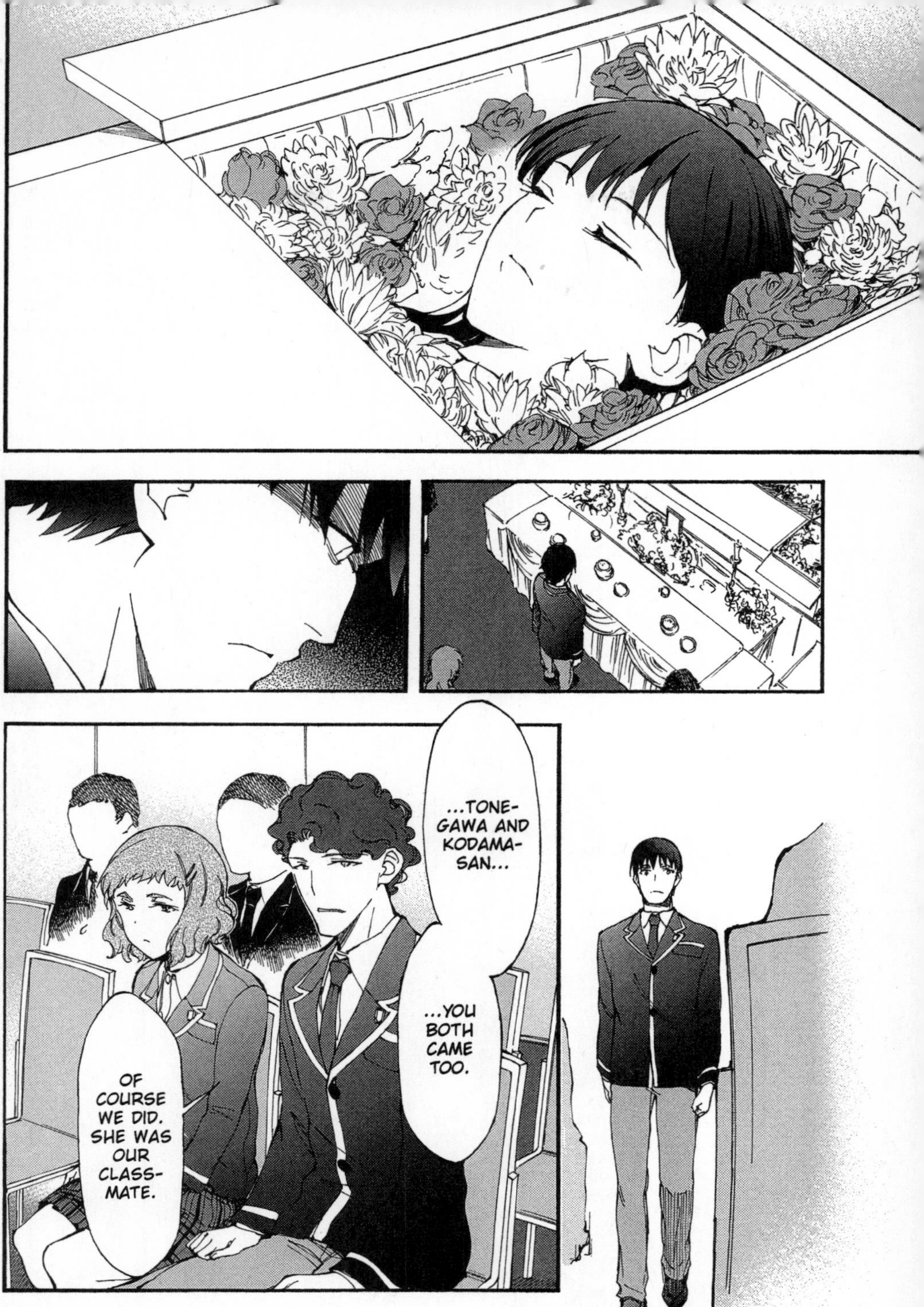
...TONE-GAWA AND KODAMA-SAN...
...YOU BOTH CAME TOO.
OF COURSE WE DID. SHE WAS OUR CLASSMATE.

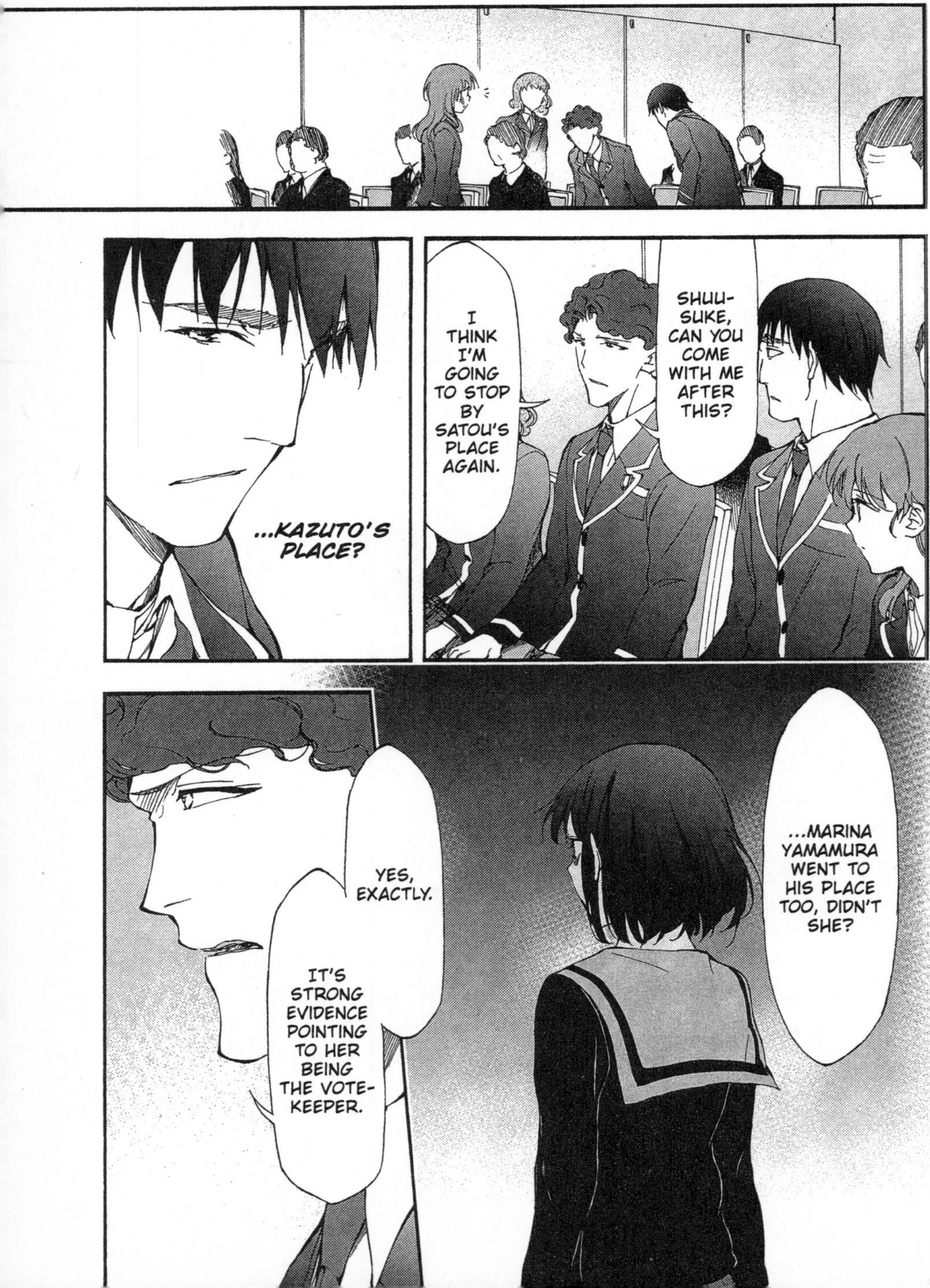
SHUU-SUKE, CAN YOU COME WITH ME AFTER THIS?
I THINK I'M GOING TO STOP BY SATOU'S PLACE AGAIN.
...KAZUTO'S PLACE?
...MARINA YAMAMURA WENT TO HIS PLACE TOO, DIDN'T SHE?
YES, EXACTLY.
IT'S STRONG EVIDENCE POINTING TO HER BEING THE VOTE-KEEPER.

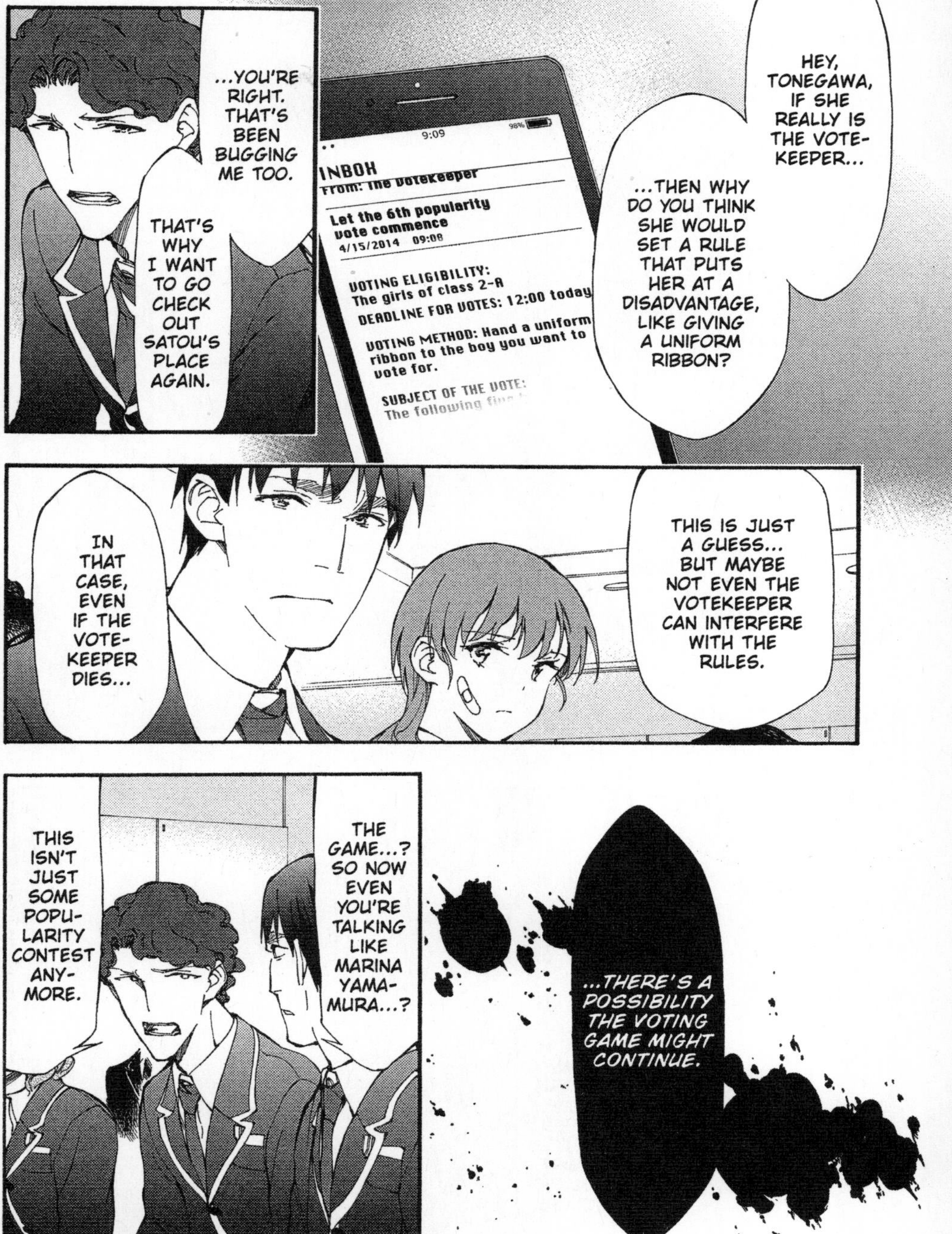
HEY, TONEGAWA, IF SHE REALLY IS THE VOTE-KEEPER...
...THEN WHY DO YOU THINK SHE WOULD SET A RULE THAT PUTS HER AT A DISADVANTAGE, LIKE GIVING A UNIFORM RIBBON?
9:09
98%
INBOX
From: The Votekeeper
Let the 6th popularity vote commence
4/15/2014 09:08
VOTING ELIGIBILITY: The girls of class 2-A
DEADLINE FOR VOTES: 12:00 today
VOTING METHOD: Hand a uniform ribbon to the boy you want to vote for.
SUBJECT OF THE VOTE:
...YOU'RE RIGHT. THAT'S BEEN BUGGING ME TOO.
THAT'S WHY I WANT TO GO CHECK OUT SATOU'S PLACE AGAIN.
THIS IS JUST A GUESS... BUT MAYBE NOT EVEN THE VOTEKEEPER CAN INTERFERE WITH THE RULES.
IN THAT CASE, EVEN IF THE VOTE-KEEPER DIES...
...THERE'S A POSSIBILITY THE VOTING GAME MIGHT CONTINUE.
THE GAME...? SO NOW EVEN YOU'RE TALKING LIKE MARINA YAMA-MURA...?
THIS ISN'T JUST SOME POPU-LARITY CONTEST ANY-MORE.

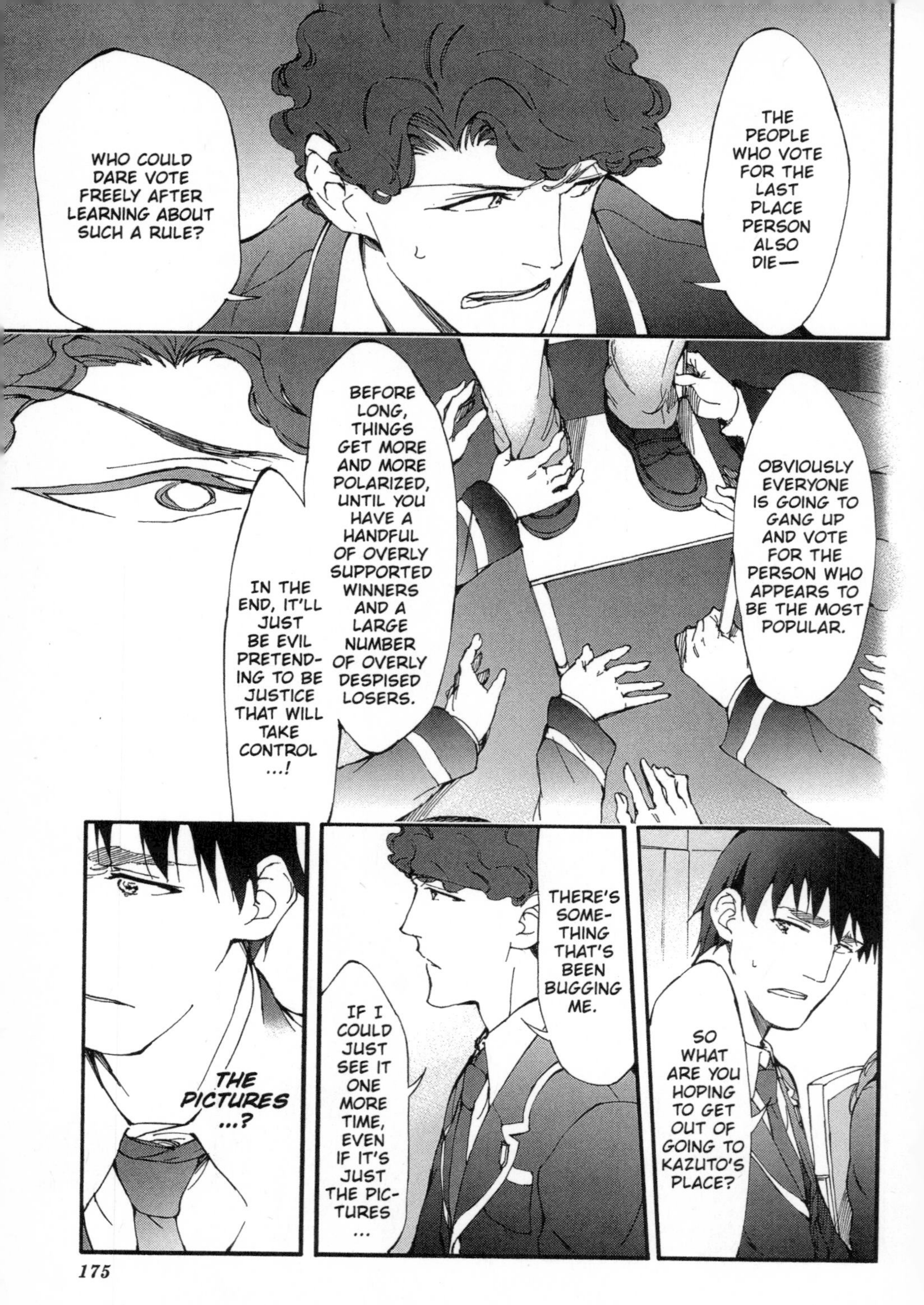
THE PEOPLE WHO VOTE FOR THE LAST PLACE PERSON ALSO DIE—
WHO COULD DARE VOTE FREELY AFTER LEARNING ABOUT SUCH A RULE?
OBVIOUSLY EVERYONE IS GOING TO GANG UP AND VOTE FOR THE PERSON WHO APPEARS TO BE THE MOST POPULAR.
BEFORE LONG, THINGS GET MORE AND MORE POLARIZED, UNTIL YOU HAVE A HANDFUL OF OVERLY SUPPORTED WINNERS AND A LARGE NUMBER OF OVERLY DESPISED LOSERS.
IN THE END, IT'LL JUST BE EVIL PRETENDING TO BE JUSTICE THAT WILL TAKE CONTROL ...!
SO WHAT ARE YOU HOPING TO GET OUT OF GOING TO KAZUTO'S PLACE?
THERE'S SOMETHING THAT'S BEEN BUGGING ME.
IF I COULD JUST SEE IT ONE MORE TIME, EVEN IF IT'S JUST THE PICTURES ...
THE PICTURES ...?

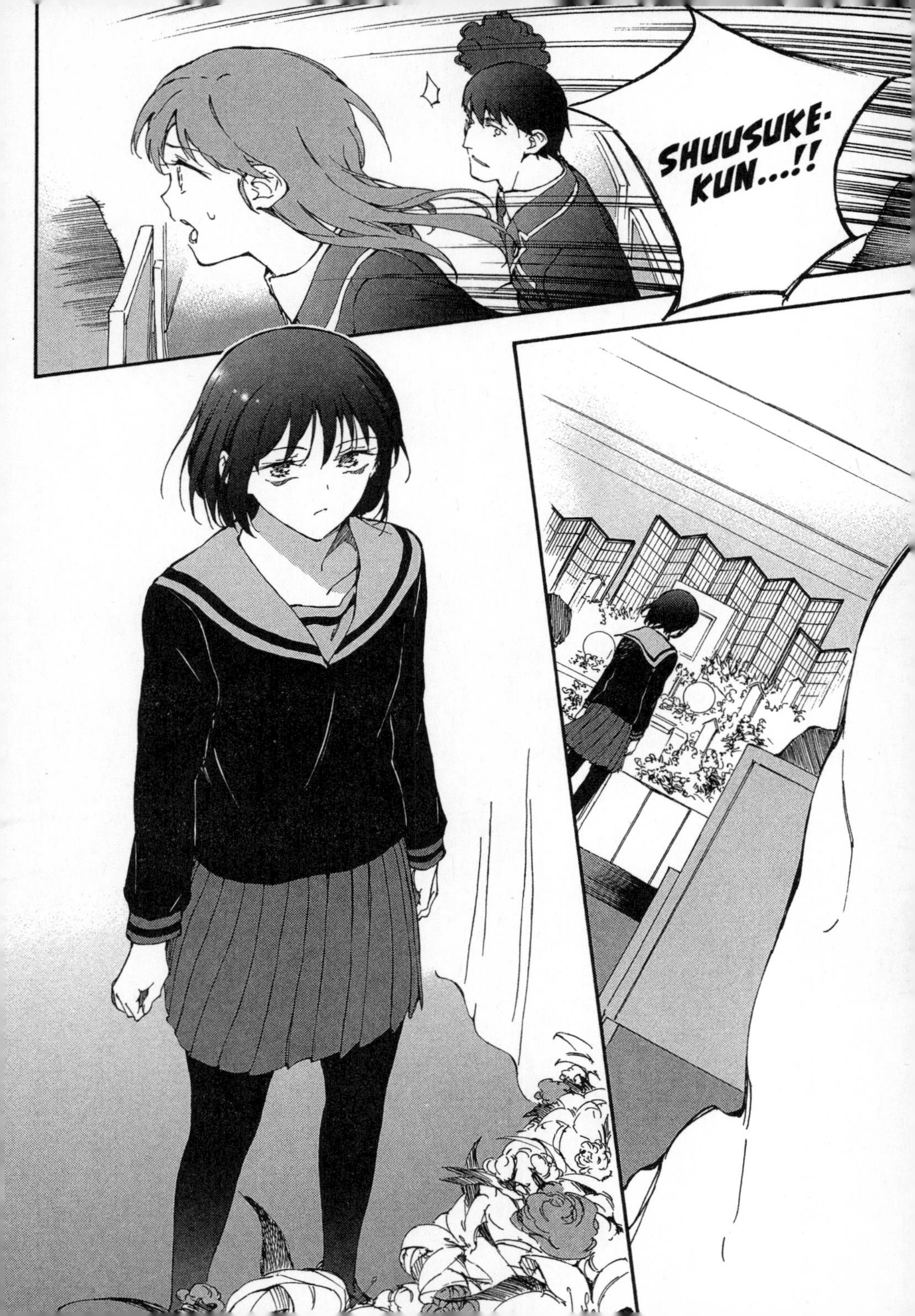
SHUUSUKE-KUN...!!

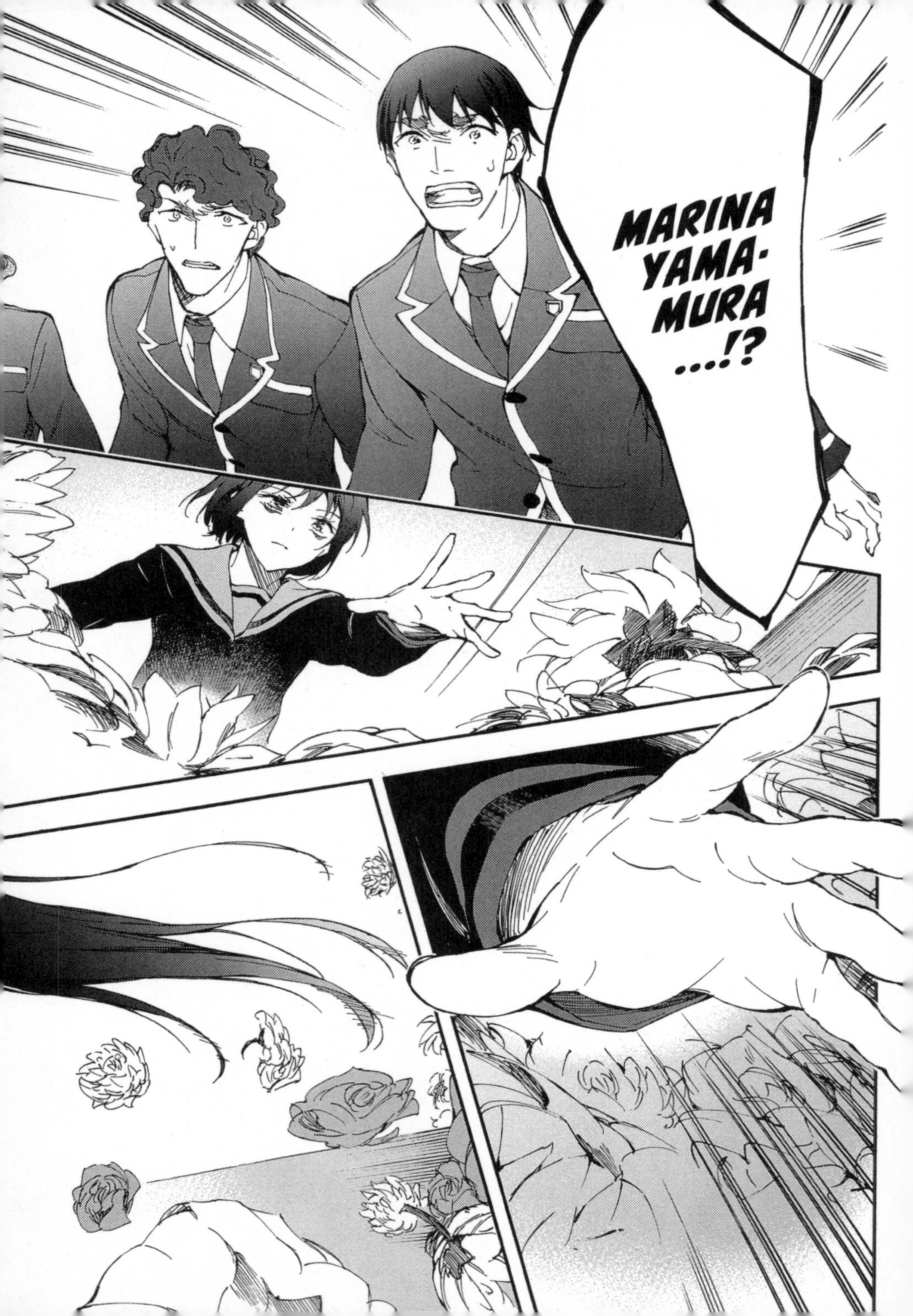
MARINA YAMA-MURA ...!?

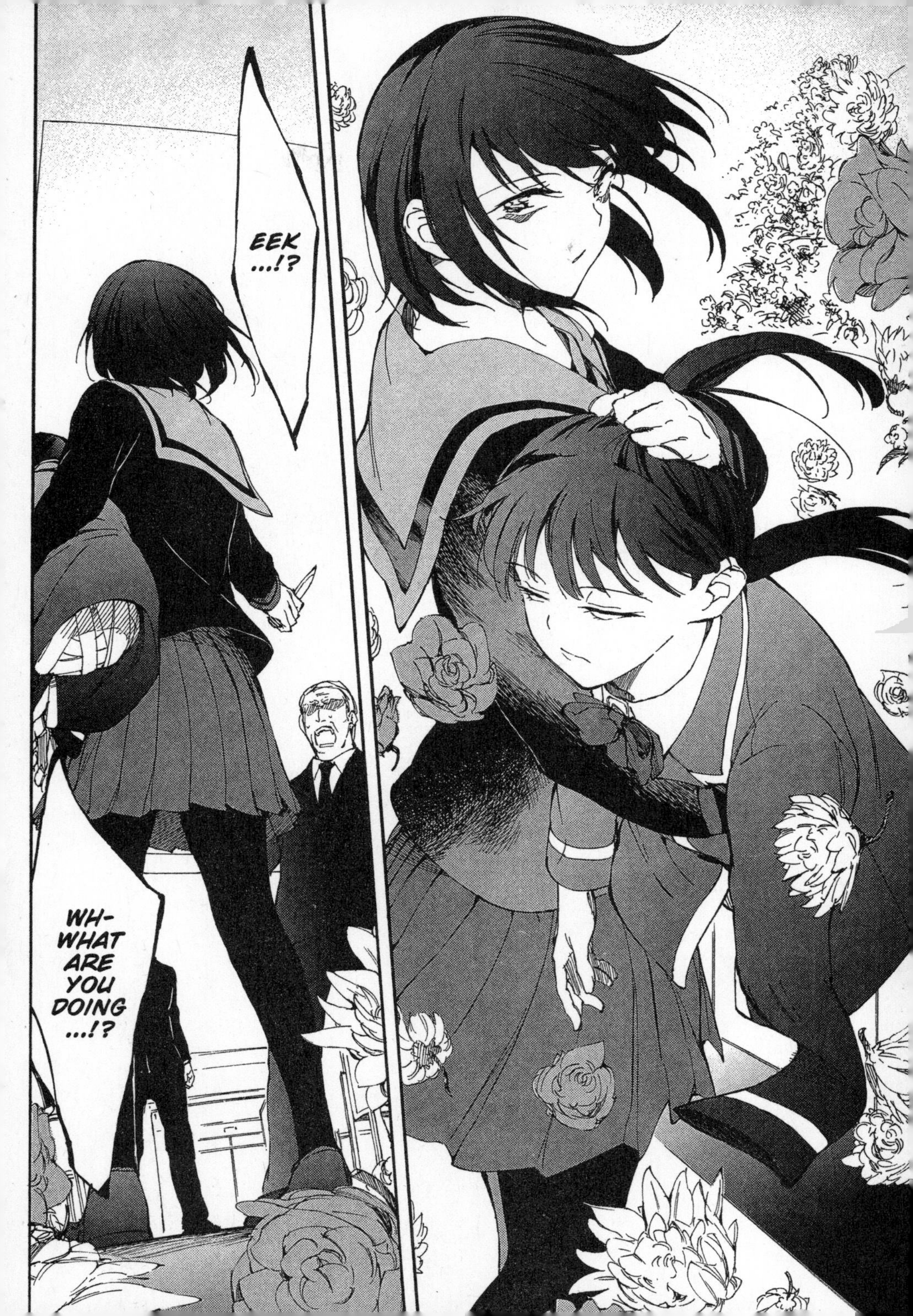
EEK ...!?
WH-WHAT ARE YOU DOING ...!?

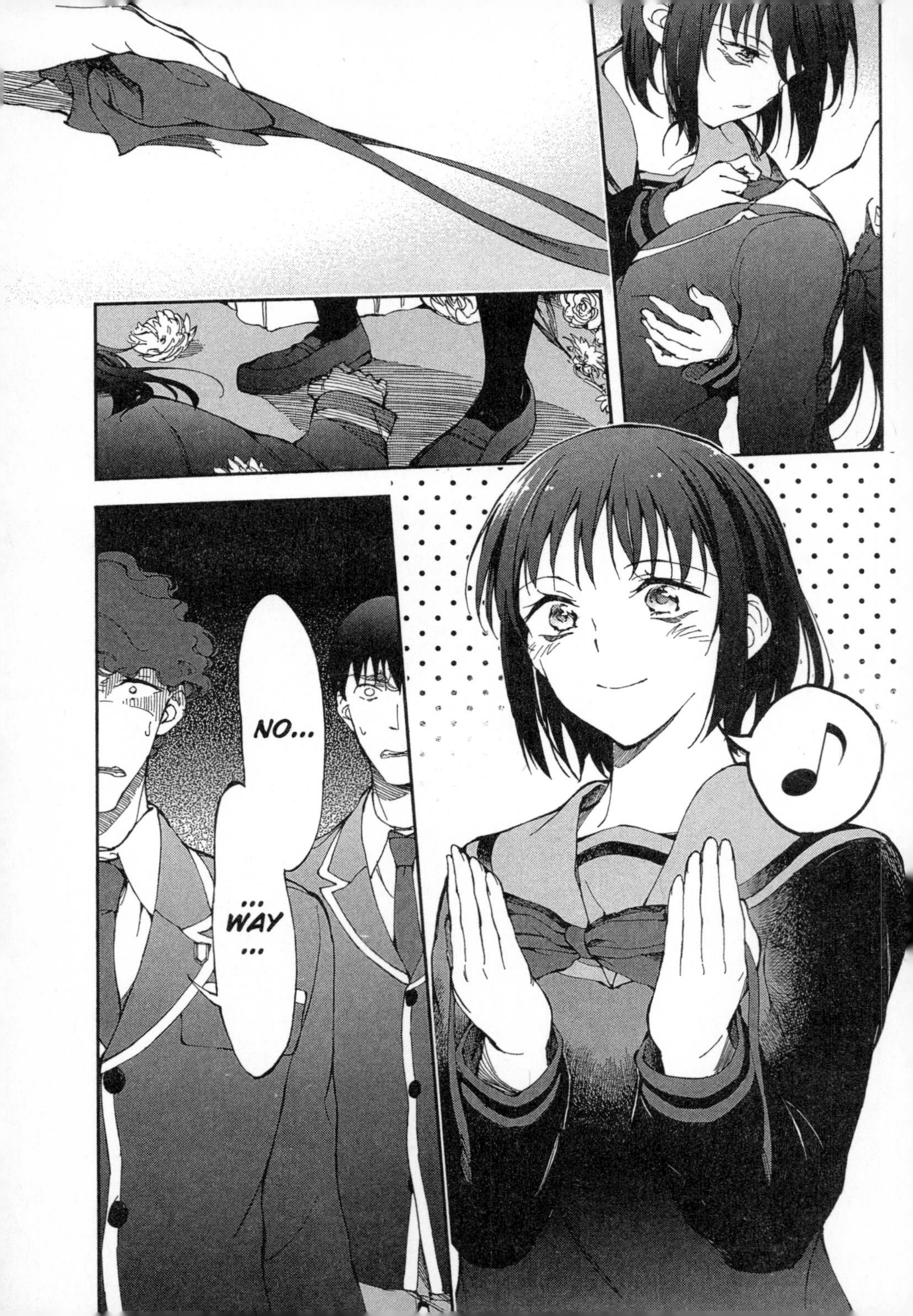
NO...
...WAY...

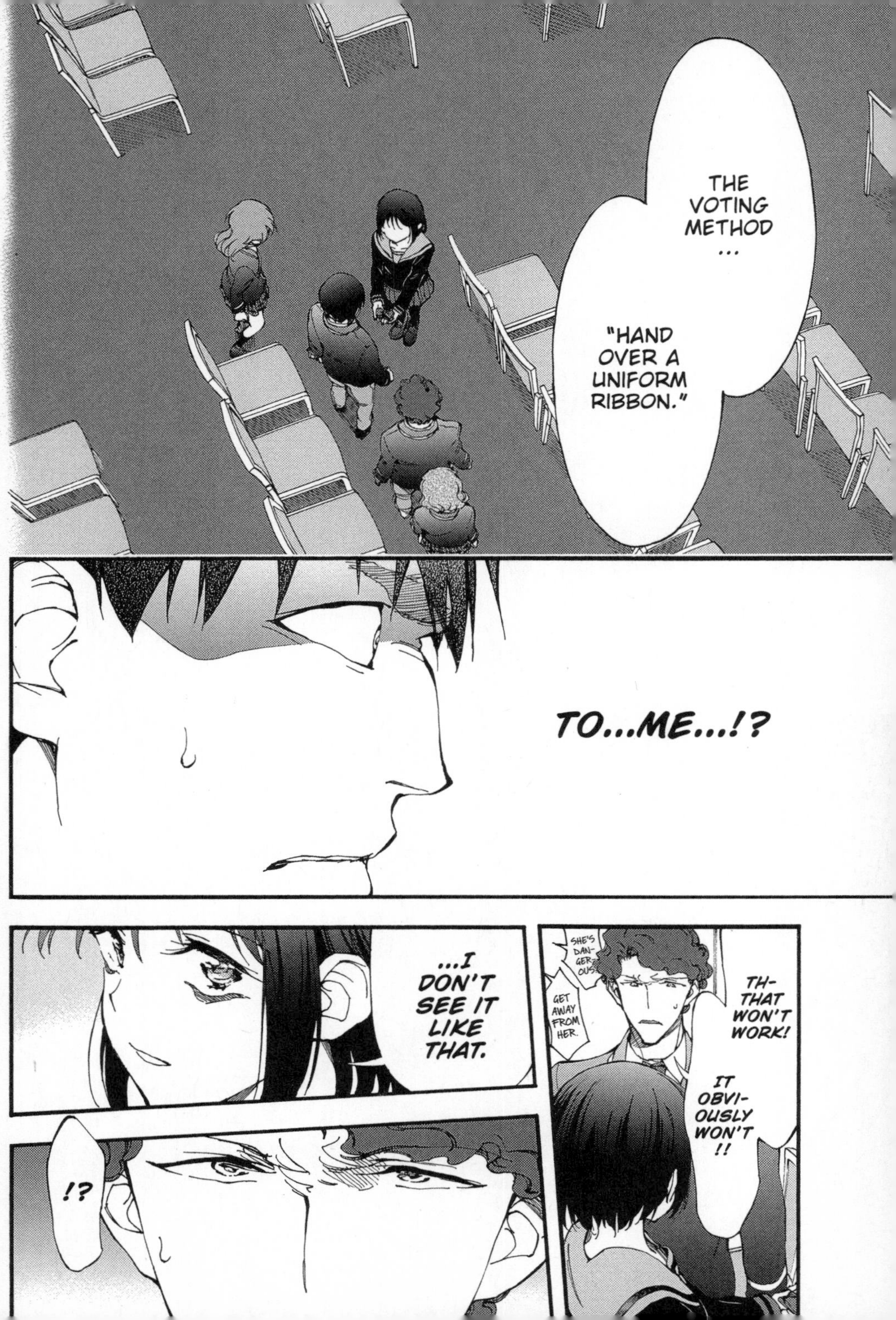
THE VOTING METHOD ...
"HAND OVER A UNIFORM RIBBON."
TO...ME...!?
SHE'S DANGEROUS
GET AWAY FROM HER.
TH-THAT WON'T WORK!
IT OBVIOUSLY WON'T!!
...I DON'T SEE IT LIKE THAT.
!?

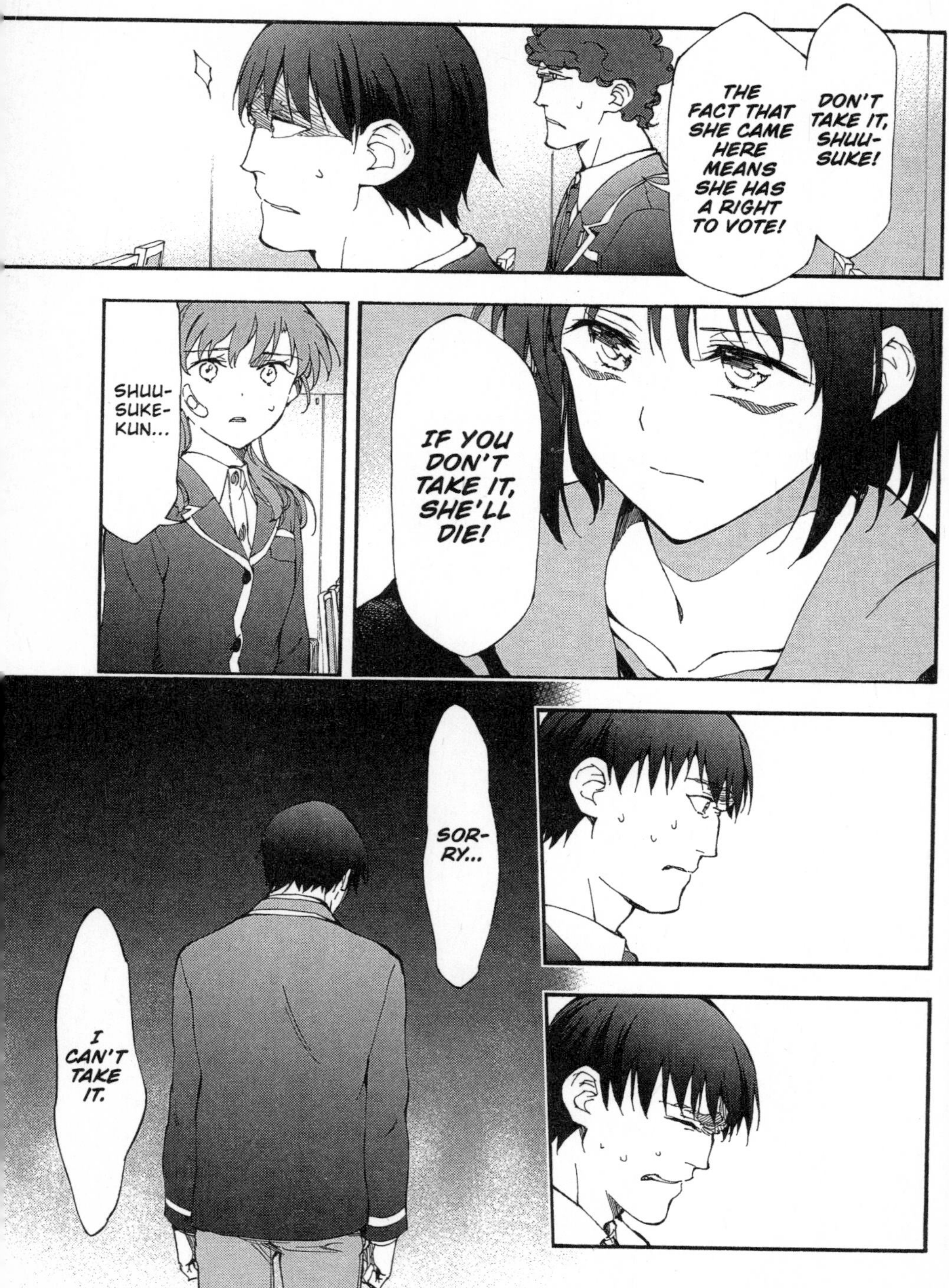
DON'T TAKE IT, SHUU-SUKE!
THE FACT THAT SHE CAME HERE MEANS SHE HAS A RIGHT TO VOTE!
IF YOU DON'T TAKE IT, SHE'LL DIE!
SHUU-SUKE-KUN...
SOR-RY...
I CAN'T TAKE IT.

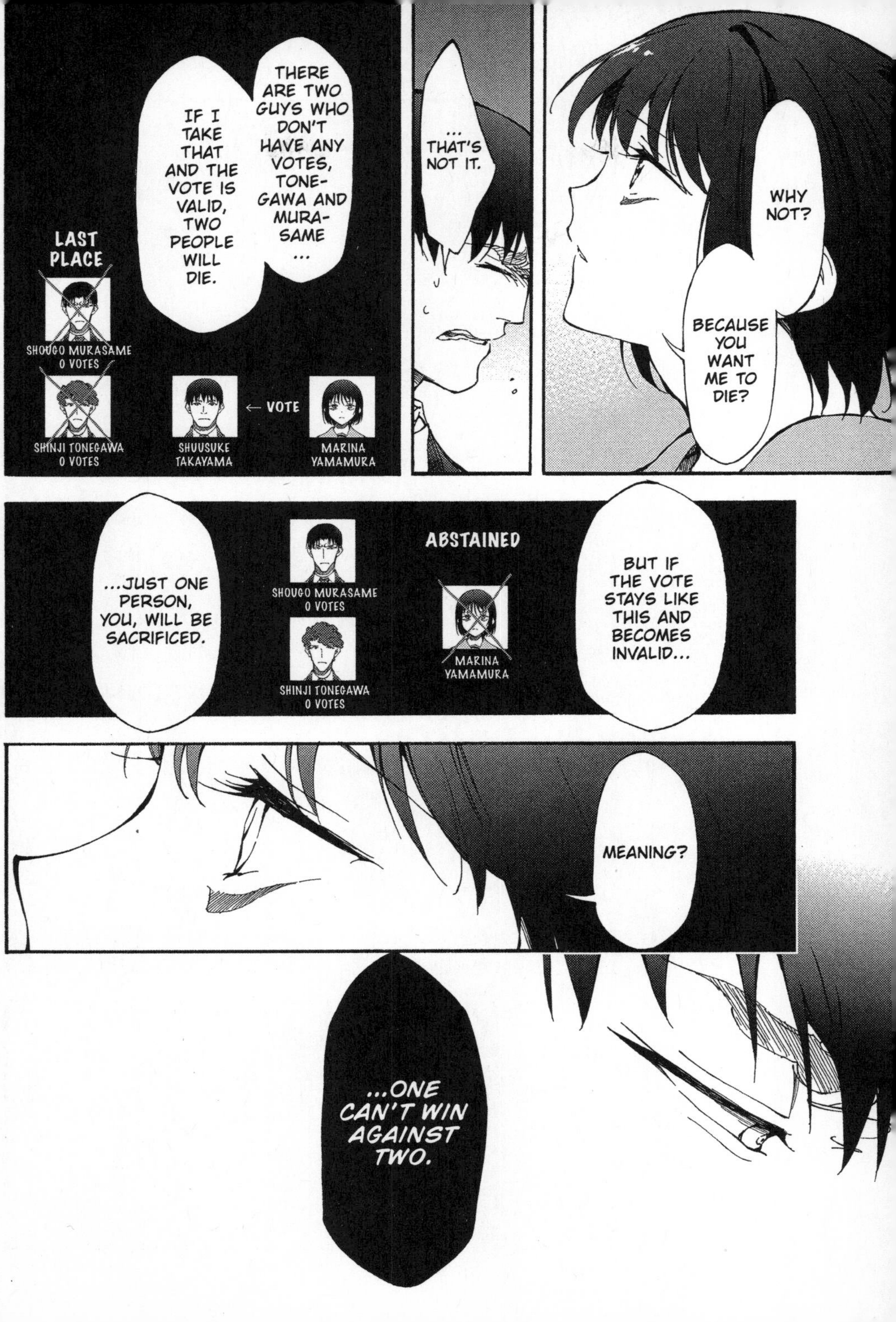
WHY NOT?
BECAUSE YOU WANT ME TO DIE?
...THAT'S NOT IT.
THERE ARE TWO GUYS WHO DON'T HAVE ANY VOTES, TONE-GAWA AND MURA-SAME...
IF I TAKE THAT AND THE VOTE IS VALID, TWO PEOPLE WILL DIE.
LAST PLACE
SHOUGO MURASAME 0 VOTES
SHINJI TONEGAWA 0 VOTES
← VOTE
MARINA YAMAMURA
SHUUSUKE TAKAYAMA
BUT IF THE VOTE STAYS LIKE THIS AND BECOMES INVALID...
ABSTAINED
MARINA YAMAMURA
SHOUGO MURASAME 0 VOTES
SHINJI TONEGAWA 0 VOTES
...JUST ONE PERSON, YOU, WILL BE SACRIFICED.
MEANING?
...ONE CAN'T WIN AGAINST TWO.

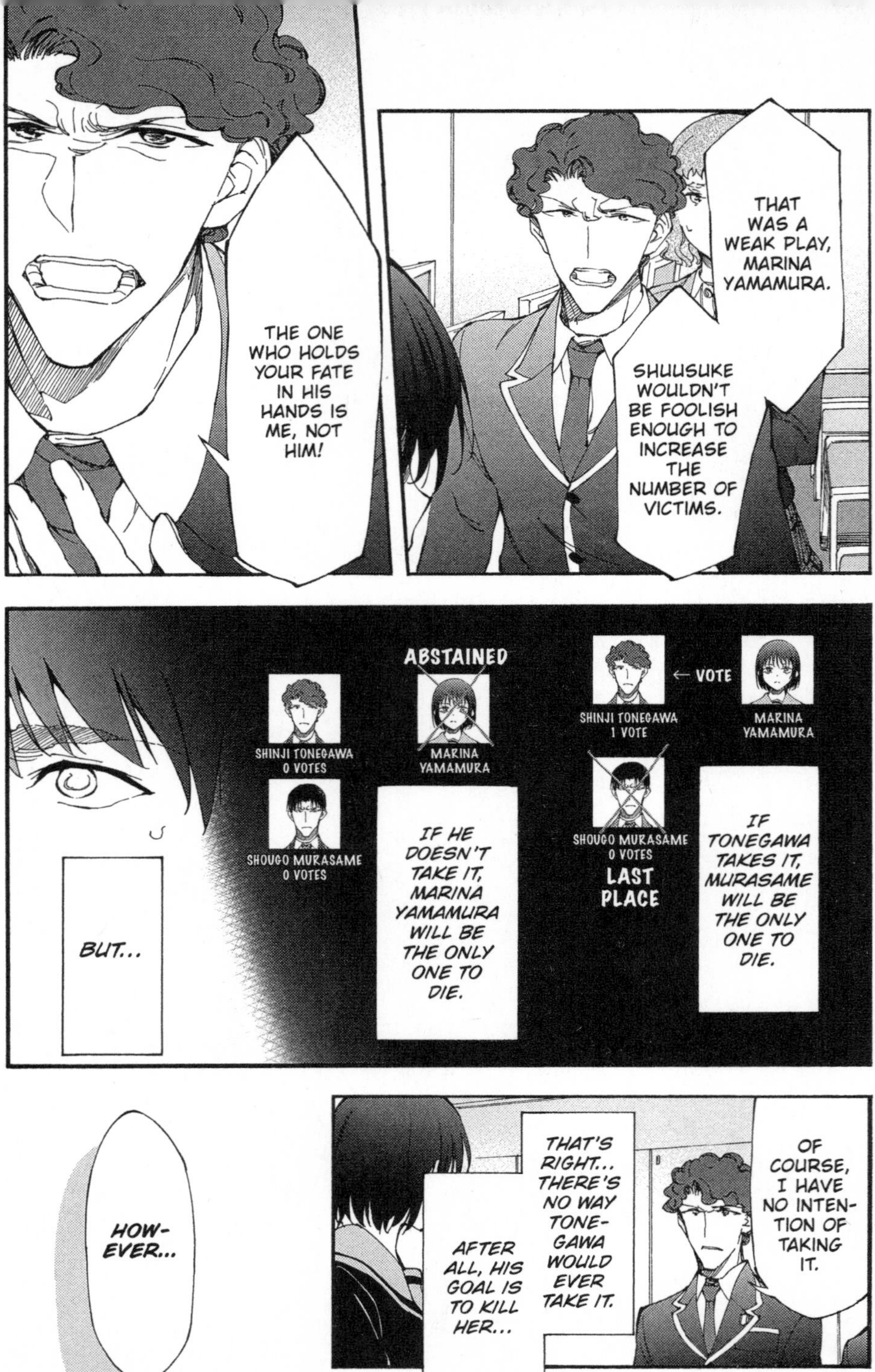
THAT WAS A WEAK PLAY, MARINA YAMAMURA.
SHUUSUKE WOULDN'T BE FOOLISH ENOUGH TO INCREASE THE NUMBER OF VICTIMS.
THE ONE WHO HOLDS YOUR FATE IN HIS HANDS IS ME, NOT HIM!
MARINA YAMAMURA
← VOTE
SHINJI TONEGAWA 1 VOTE
SHOUGO MURASAME 0 VOTES
LAST PLACE
IF TONEGAWA TAKES IT, MURASAME WILL BE THE ONLY ONE TO DIE.
ABSTAINED
MARINA YAMAMURA
SHINJI TONEGAWA 0 VOTES
SHOUGO MURASAME 0 VOTES
IF HE DOESN'T TAKE IT, MARINA YAMAMURA WILL BE THE ONLY ONE TO DIE.
BUT...
OF COURSE, I HAVE NO INTENTION OF TAKING IT.
THAT'S RIGHT... THERE'S NO WAY TONEGAWA WOULD EVER TAKE IT.
AFTER ALL, HIS GOAL IS TO KILL HER...
HOWEVER...

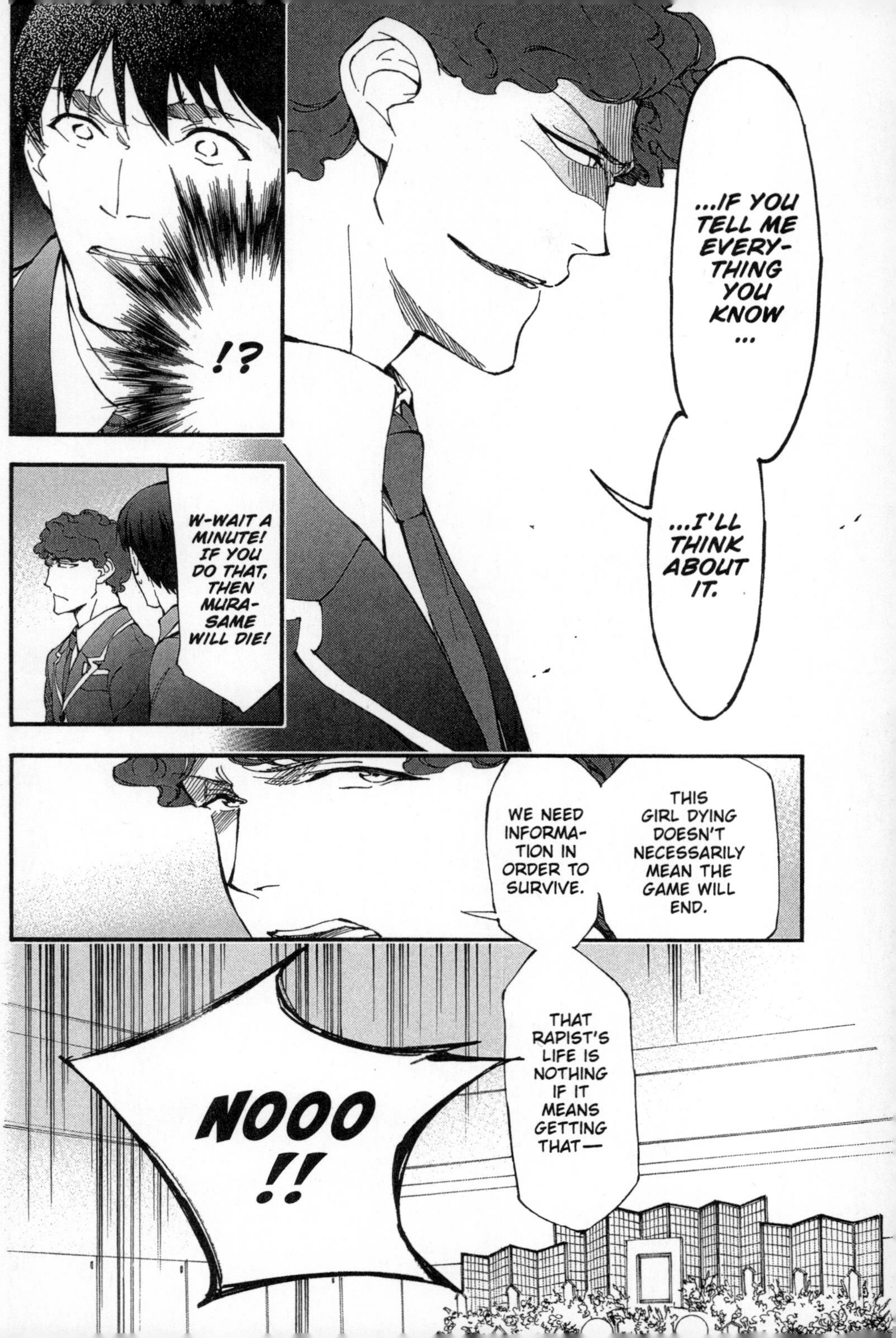
...IF YOU TELL ME EVERY-THING YOU KNOW...
...I'LL THINK ABOUT IT.
!?
W-WAIT A MINUTE! IF YOU DO THAT, THEN MURA-SAME WILL DIE!
THIS GIRL DYING DOESN'T NECESSARILY MEAN THE GAME WILL END.
WE NEED INFORMA-TION IN ORDER TO SURVIVE.
THAT RAPIST'S LIFE IS NOTHING IF IT MEANS GETTING THAT—
NOOO!!

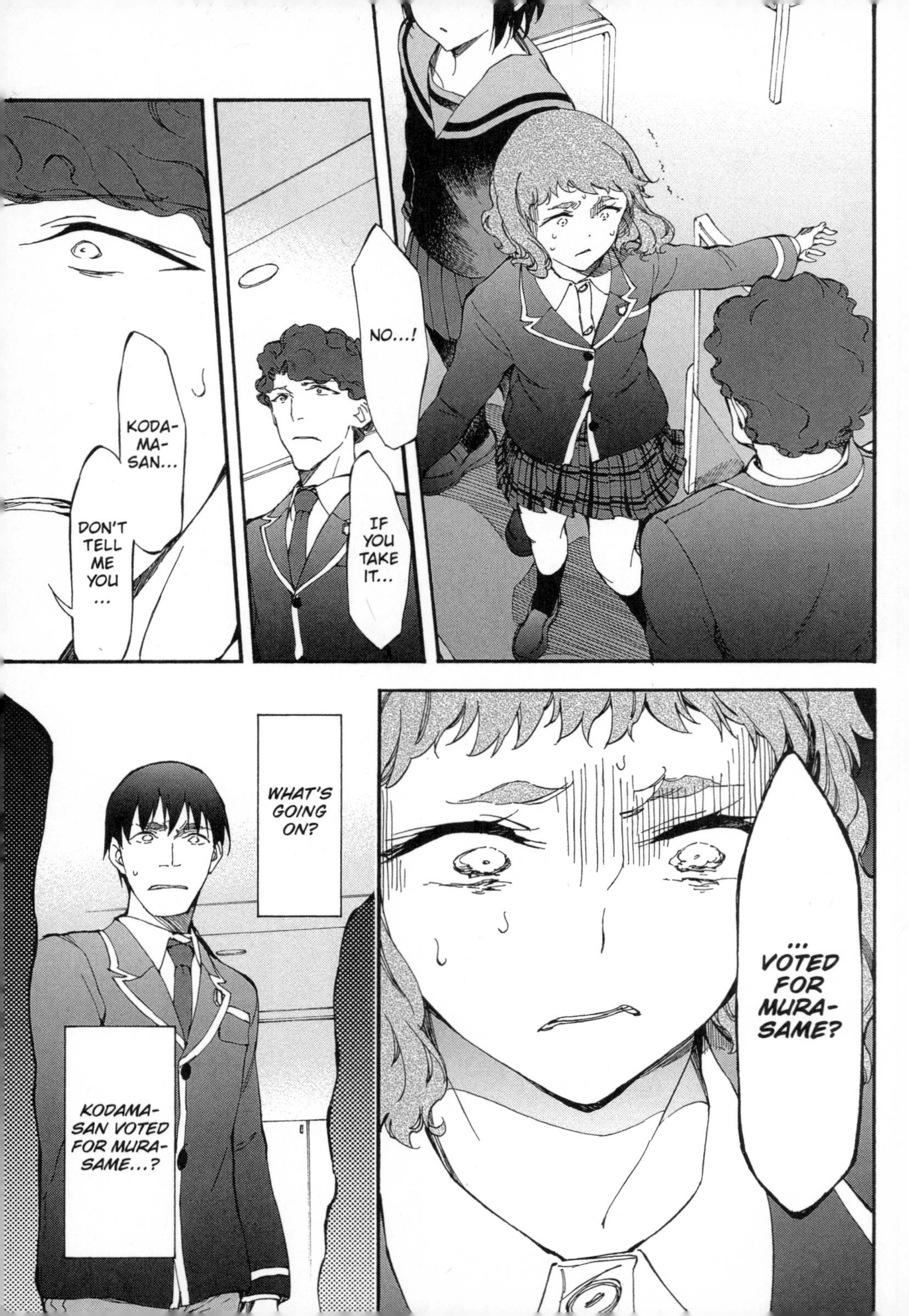
NO...!
IF YOU TAKE IT...
KODAMA-SAN...
DON'T TELL ME YOU ...
... VOTED FOR MURASAME?
WHAT'S GOING ON?
KODAMA-SAN VOTED FOR MURASAME...?

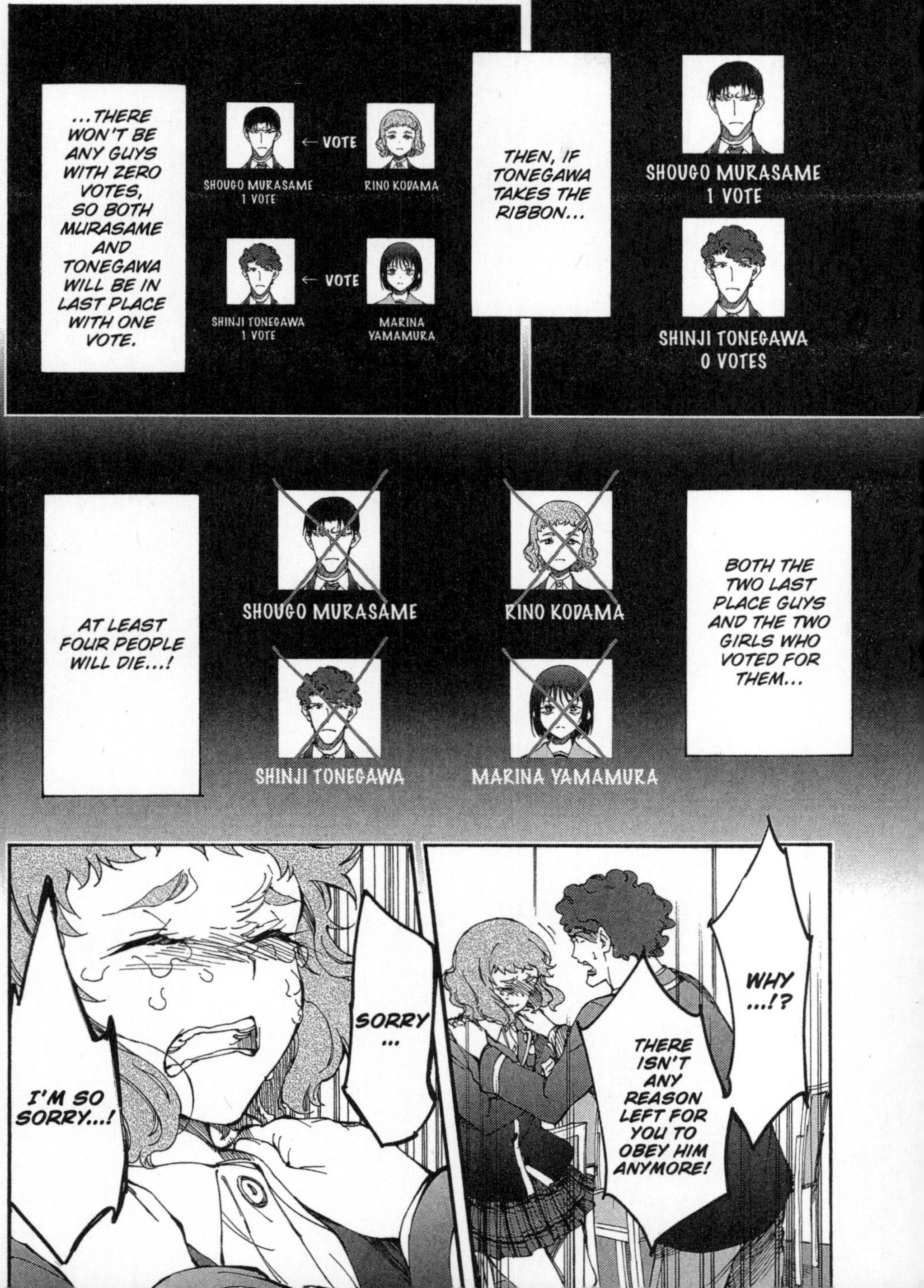
THEN, IF TONEGAWA TAKES THE RIBBON...
SHOUGO MURASAME
1 VOTE
SHINJI TONEGAWA
0 VOTES
...THERE WON'T BE ANY GUYS WITH ZERO VOTES, SO BOTH MURASAME AND TONEGAWA WILL BE IN LAST PLACE WITH ONE VOTE.
RINO KODAMA
← VOTE
SHOUGO MURASAME
1 VOTE
MARINA YAMAMURA
← VOTE
SHINJI TONEGAWA
1 VOTE
BOTH THE TWO LAST PLACE GUYS AND THE TWO GIRLS WHO VOTED FOR THEM...
RINO KODAMA
SHOUGO MURASAME
MARINA YAMAMURA
SHINJI TONEGAWA
AT LEAST FOUR PEOPLE WILL DIE...!
WHY ...!?
THERE ISN'T ANY REASON LEFT FOR YOU TO OBEY HIM ANYMORE!
SORRY ...
I'M SO SORRY...!

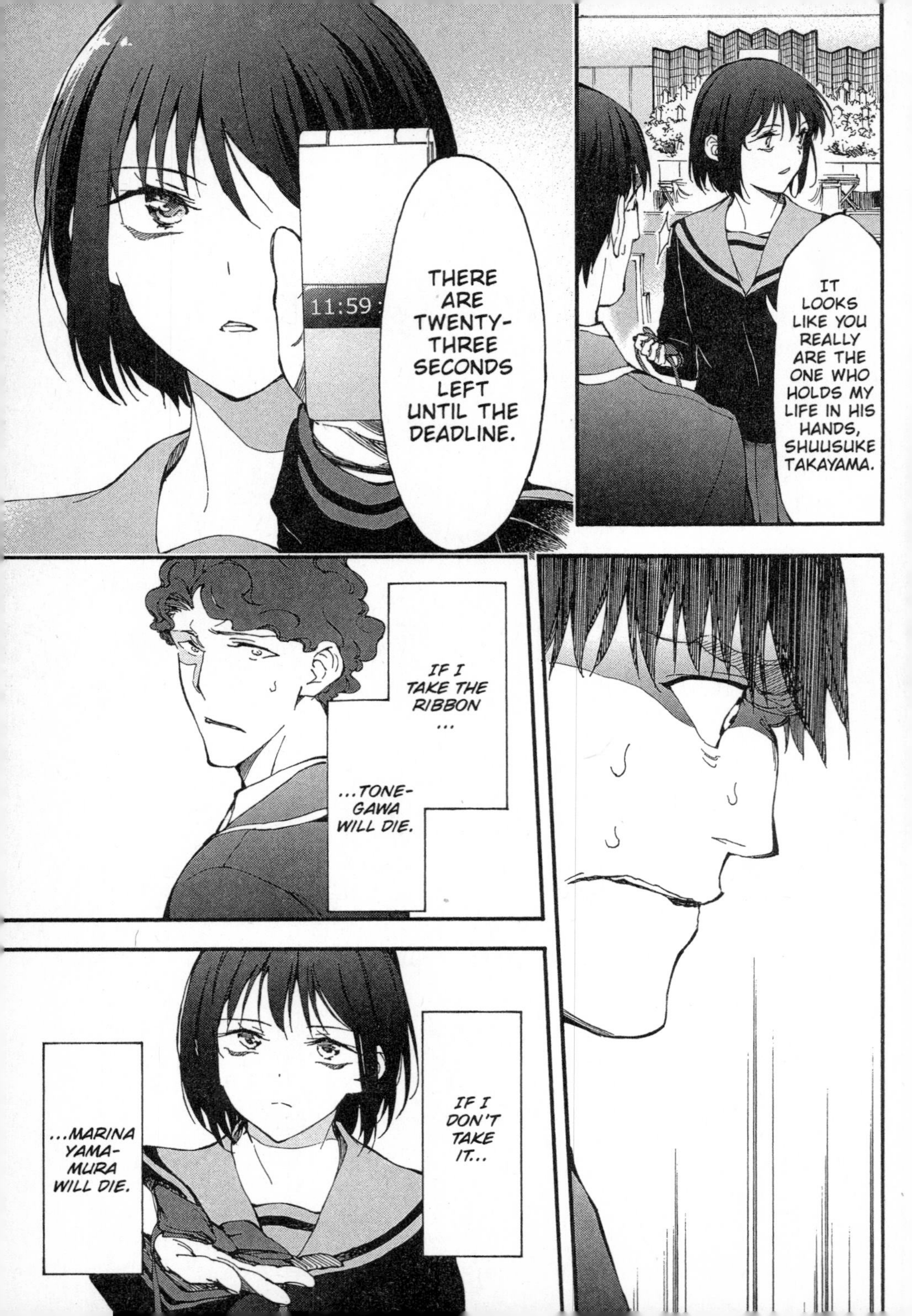
IT LOOKS LIKE YOU REALLY ARE THE ONE WHO HOLDS MY LIFE IN HIS HANDS, SHUUSUKE TAKAYAMA.
11:59
THERE ARE TWENTY-THREE SECONDS LEFT UNTIL THE DEADLINE.
IF I TAKE THE RIBBON...
...TONE-GAWA WILL DIE.
IF I DON'T TAKE IT...
...MARINA YAMA-MURA WILL DIE.

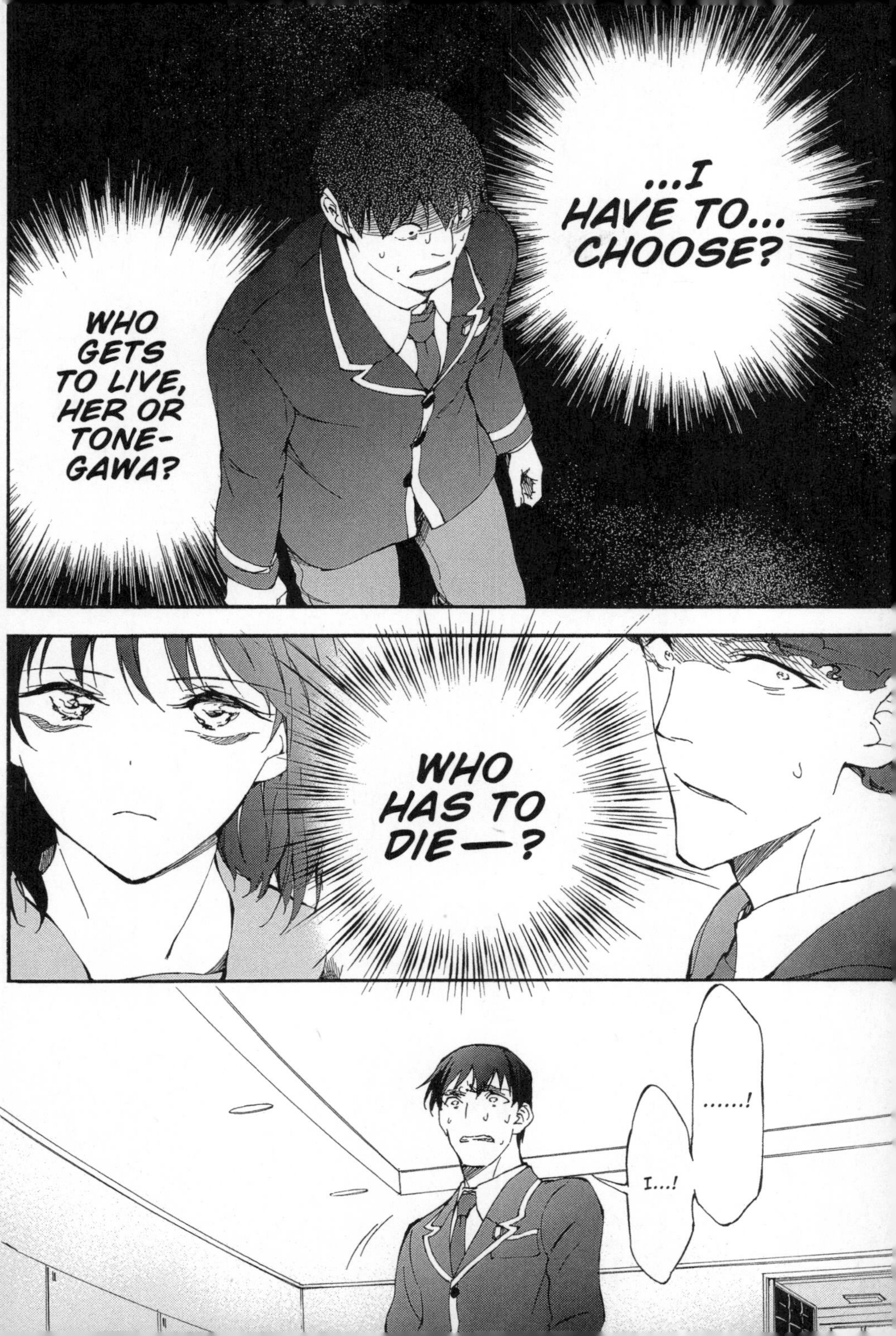
...I HAVE TO... CHOOSE?
WHO GETS TO LIVE, HER OR TONE-GAWA?
WHO HAS TO DIE—?
......!
I...!

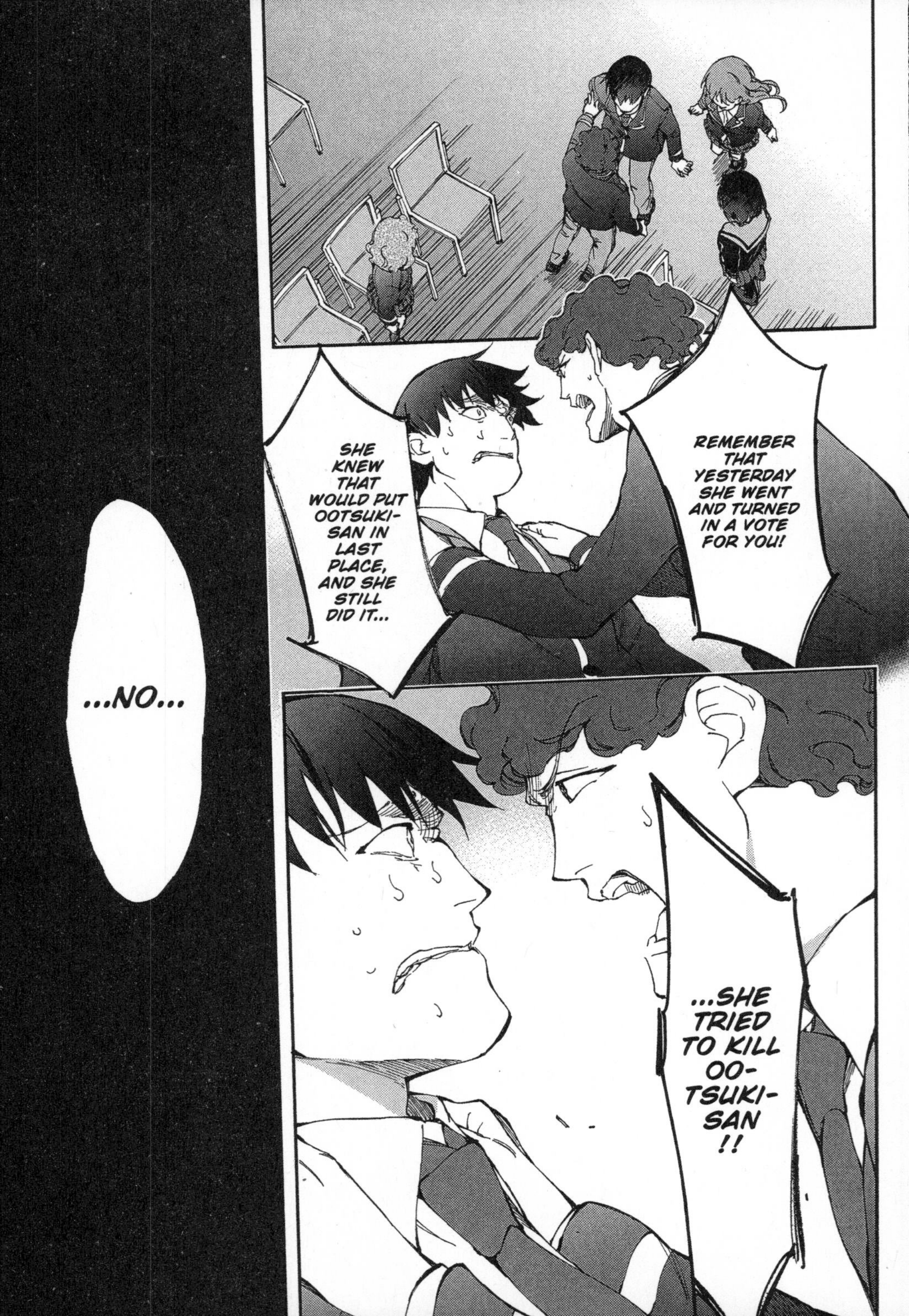
REMEMBER THAT YESTERDAY SHE WENT AND TURNED IN A VOTE FOR YOU!
SHE KNEW THAT WOULD PUT OOTSUKI-SAN IN LAST PLACE, AND SHE STILL DID IT...
...SHE TRIED TO KILL OO-TSUKI-SAN!!
...NO...

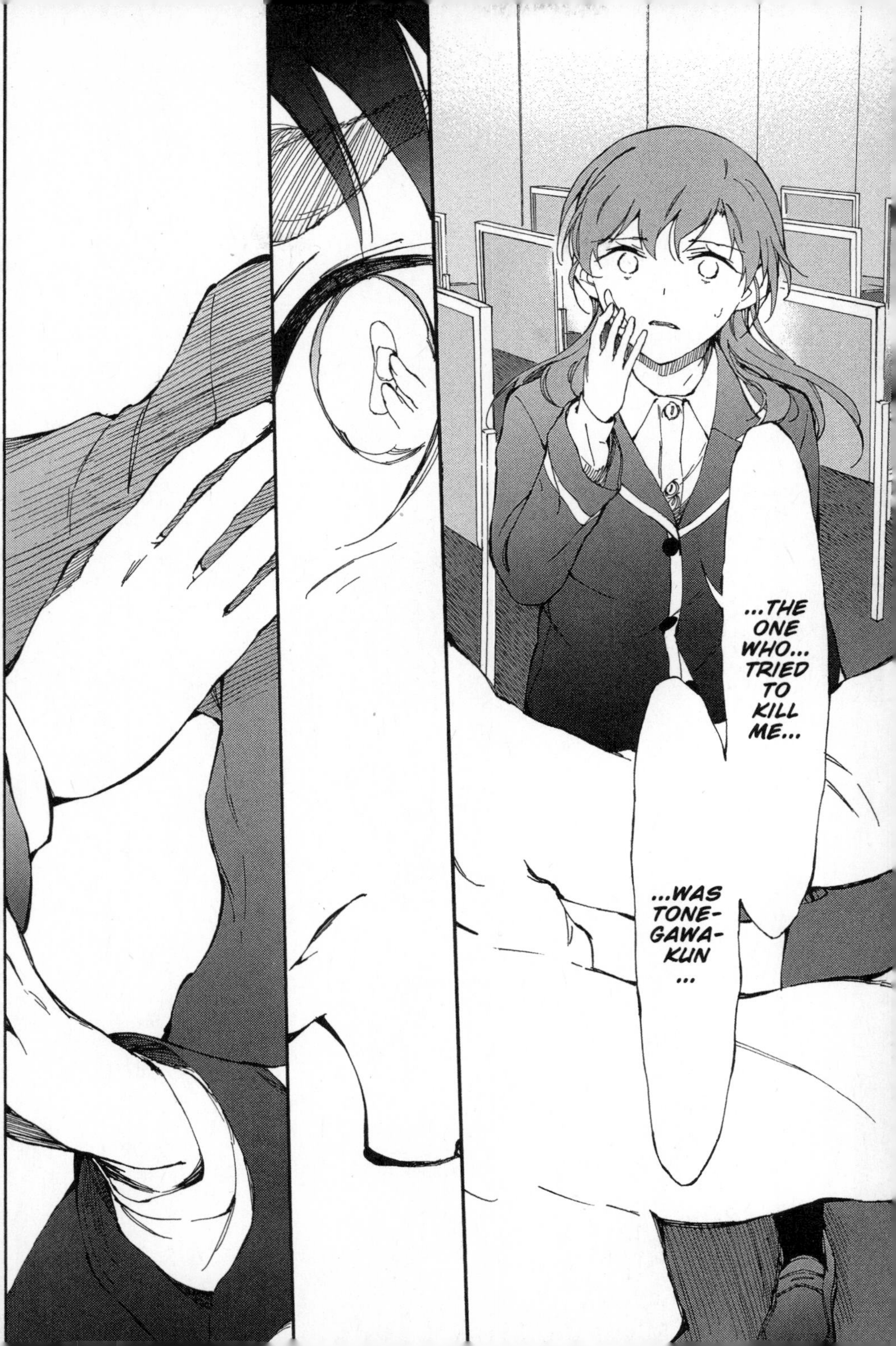
...THE ONE WHO... TRIED TO KILL ME...
...WAS TONE-GAWA-KUN ...

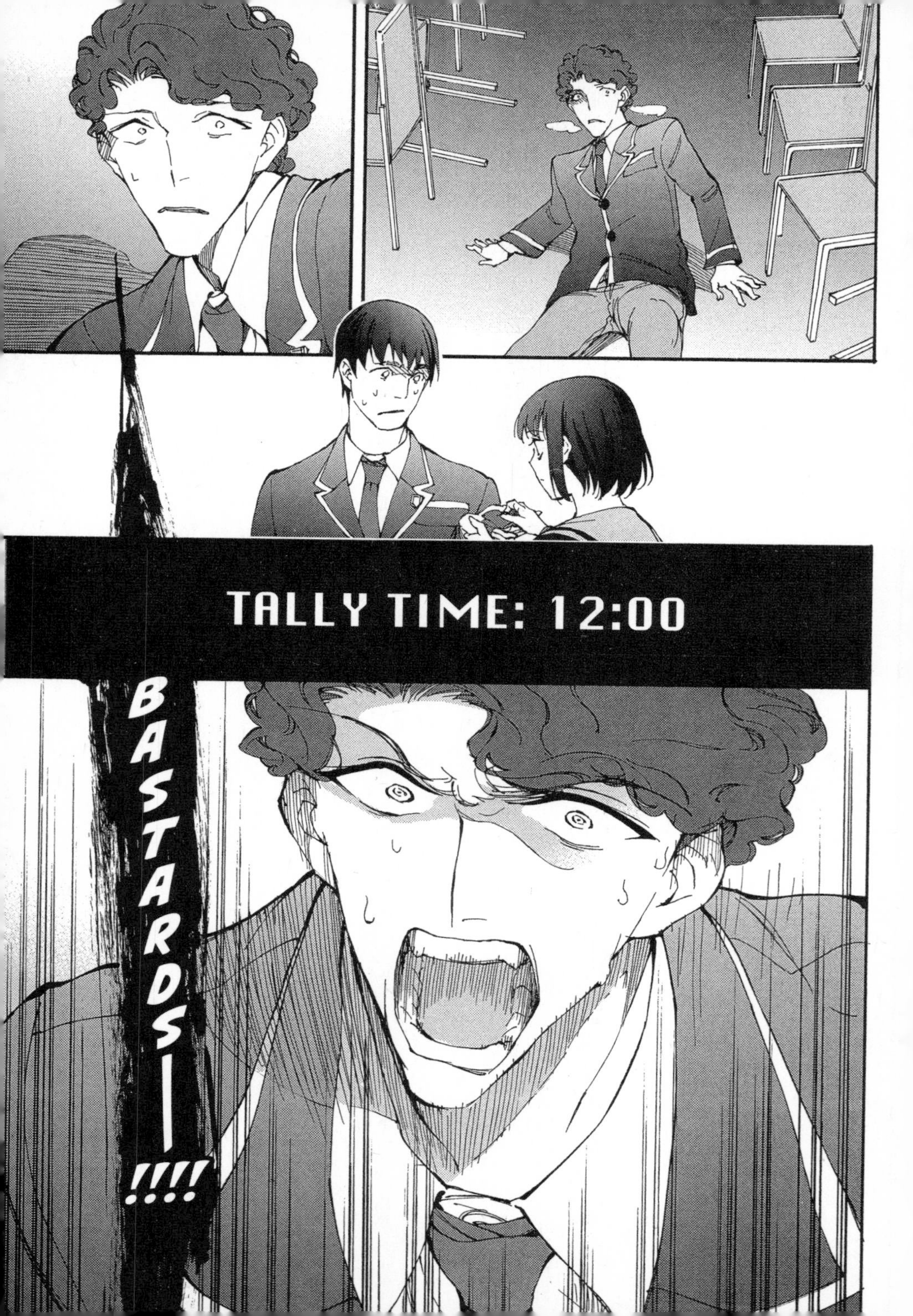
TALLY TIME: 12:00
BASTARDS—!!!!

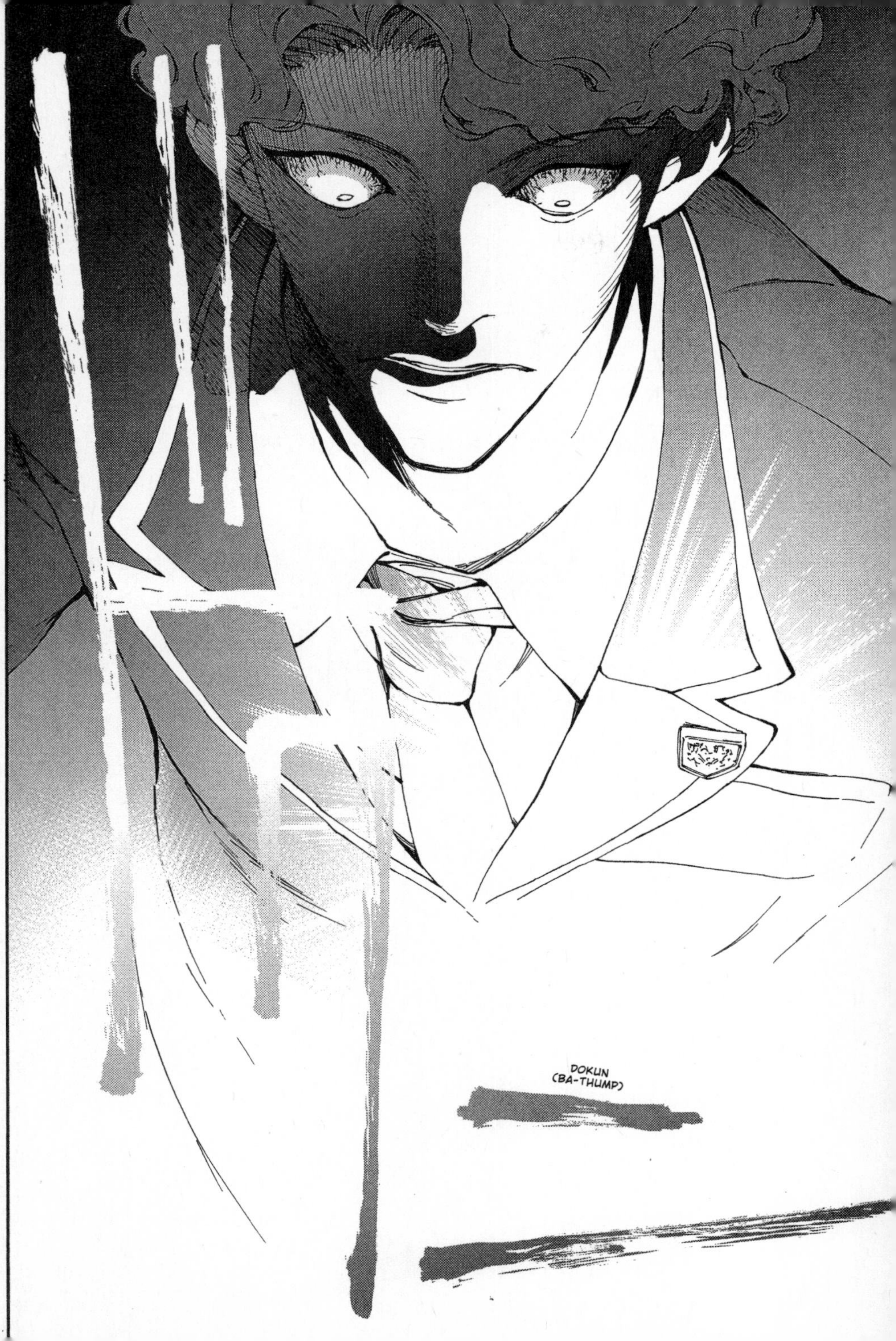
DOKUN
(BA-THUMP)

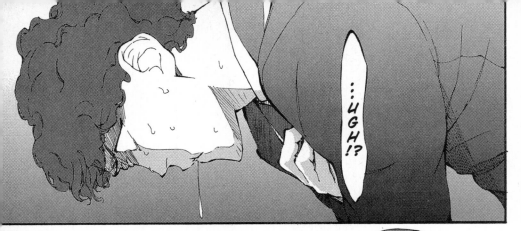

...UGH!?

....I...
WAS
JUST
...

...
TRYING
TO...
SAVE
...

...
EVERY-
ONE
...

WHY
...?

......?

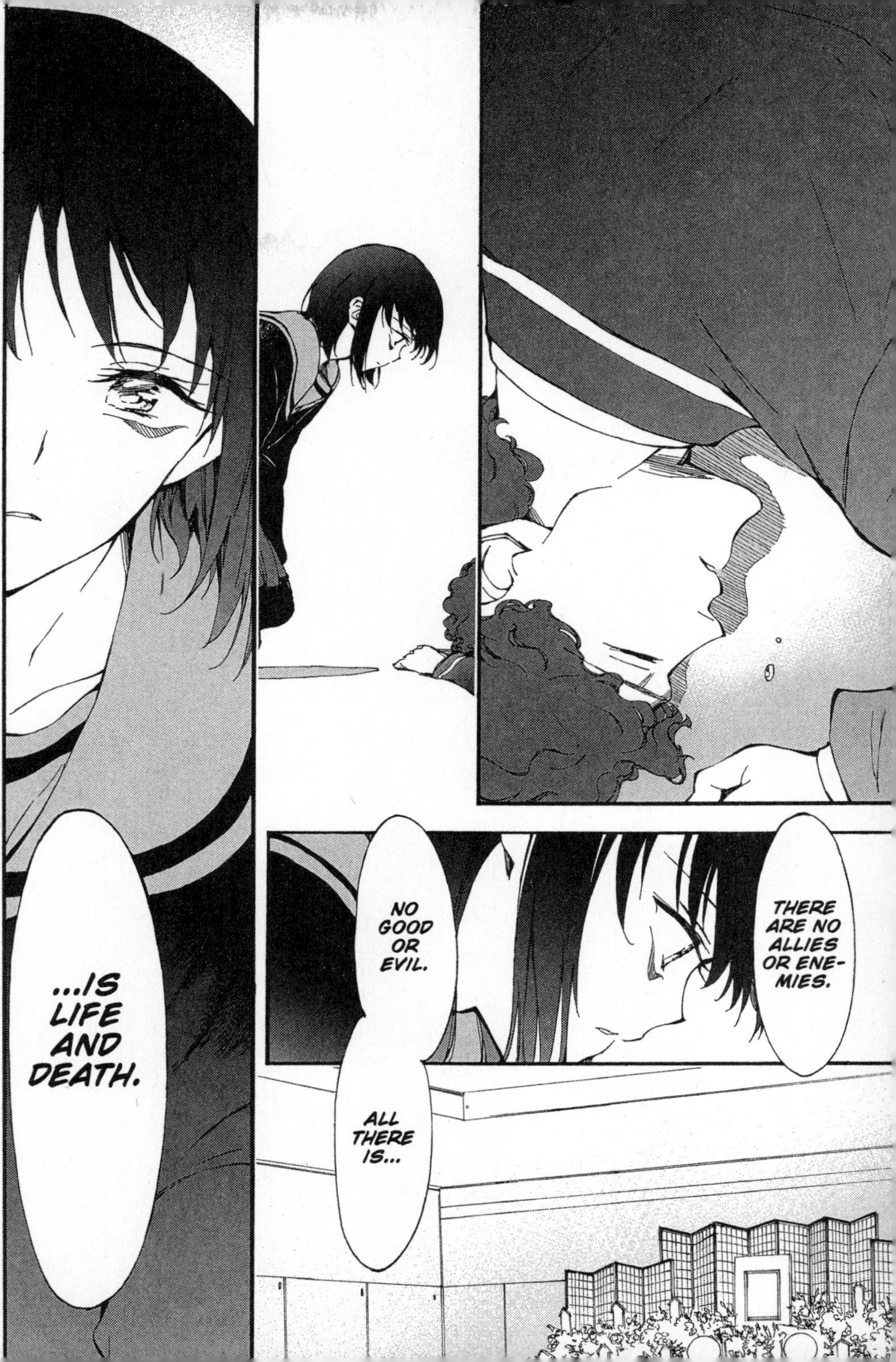
THERE ARE NO ALLIES OR ENEMIES.
NO GOOD OR EVIL.
ALL THERE IS...
...IS LIFE AND DEATH.

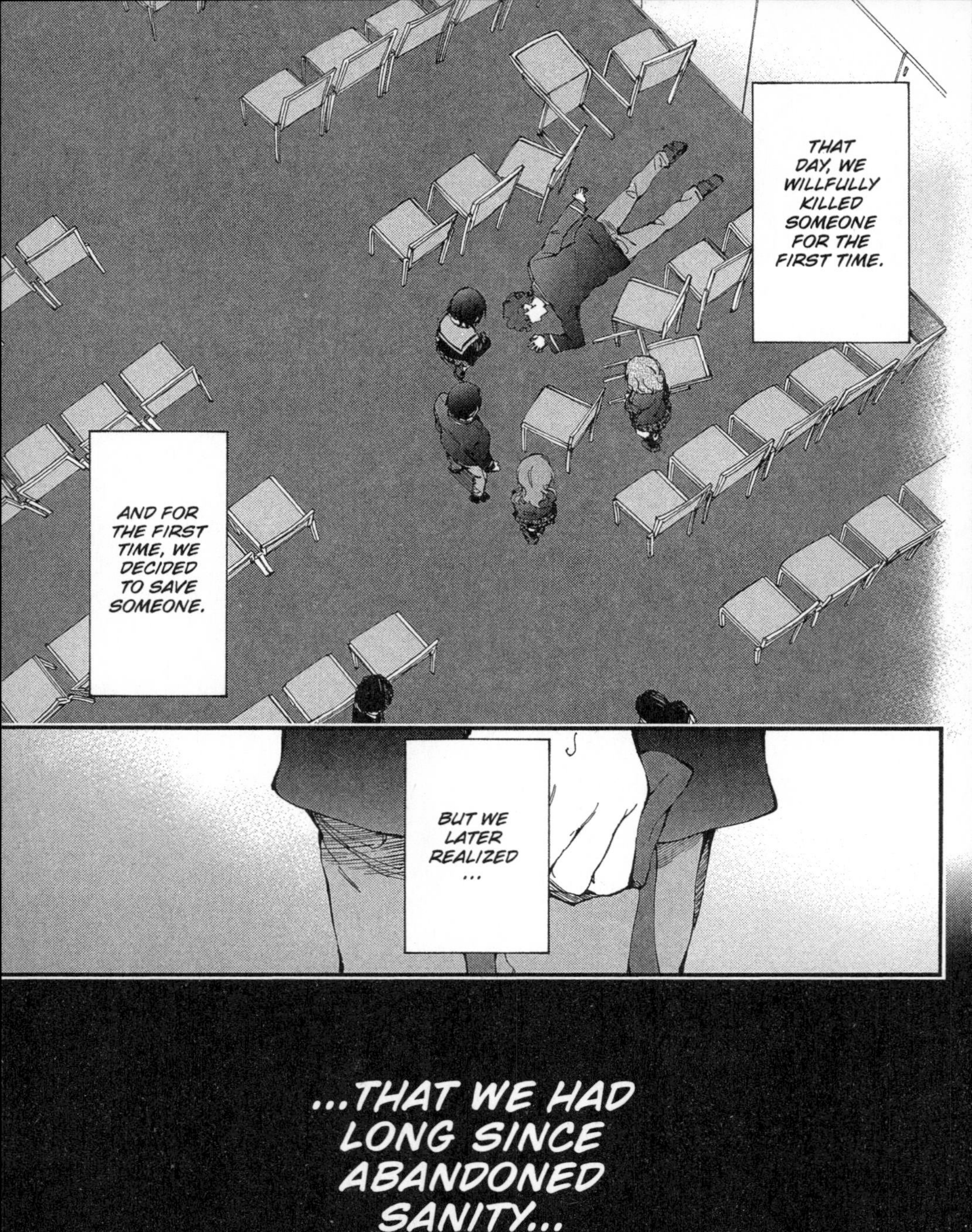
THAT DAY, WE WILLFULLY KILLED SOMEONE FOR THE FIRST TIME.
AND FOR THE FIRST TIME, WE DECIDED TO SAVE SOMEONE.
BUT WE LATER REALIZED...
...THAT WE HAD LONG SINCE ABANDONED SANITY...

TOHYO GAME
One **black** ballot to you

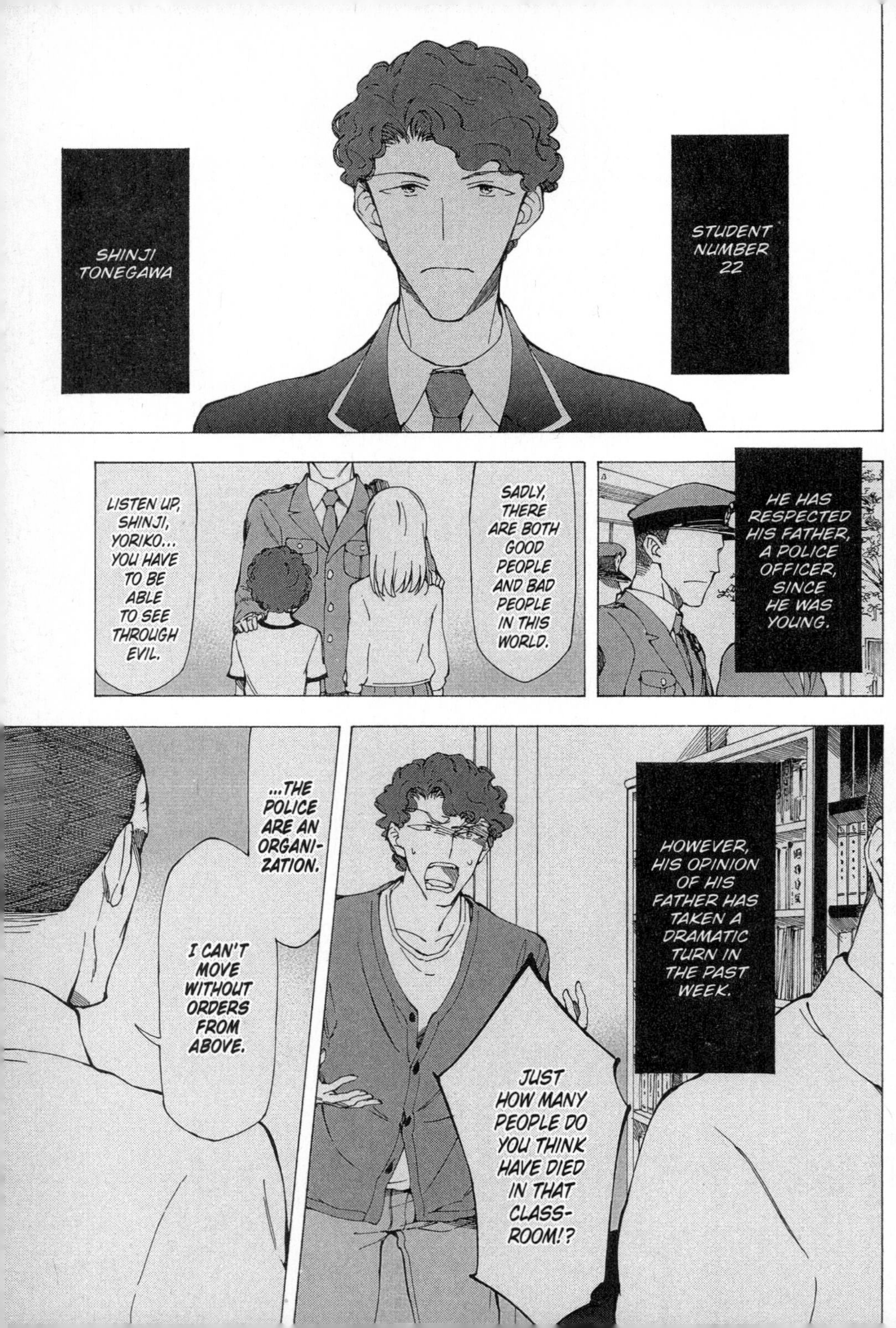
STUDENT NUMBER 22
SHINJI TONEGAWA
HE HAS RESPECTED HIS FATHER, A POLICE OFFICER, SINCE HE WAS YOUNG.
SADLY, THERE ARE BOTH GOOD PEOPLE AND BAD PEOPLE IN THIS WORLD.
LISTEN UP, SHINJI, YORIKO... YOU HAVE TO BE ABLE TO SEE THROUGH EVIL.
HOWEVER, HIS OPINION OF HIS FATHER HAS TAKEN A DRAMATIC TURN IN THE PAST WEEK.
JUST HOW MANY PEOPLE DO YOU THINK HAVE DIED IN THAT CLASS-ROOM!?
...THE POLICE ARE AN ORGANI-ZATION.
I CAN'T MOVE WITHOUT ORDERS FROM ABOVE.

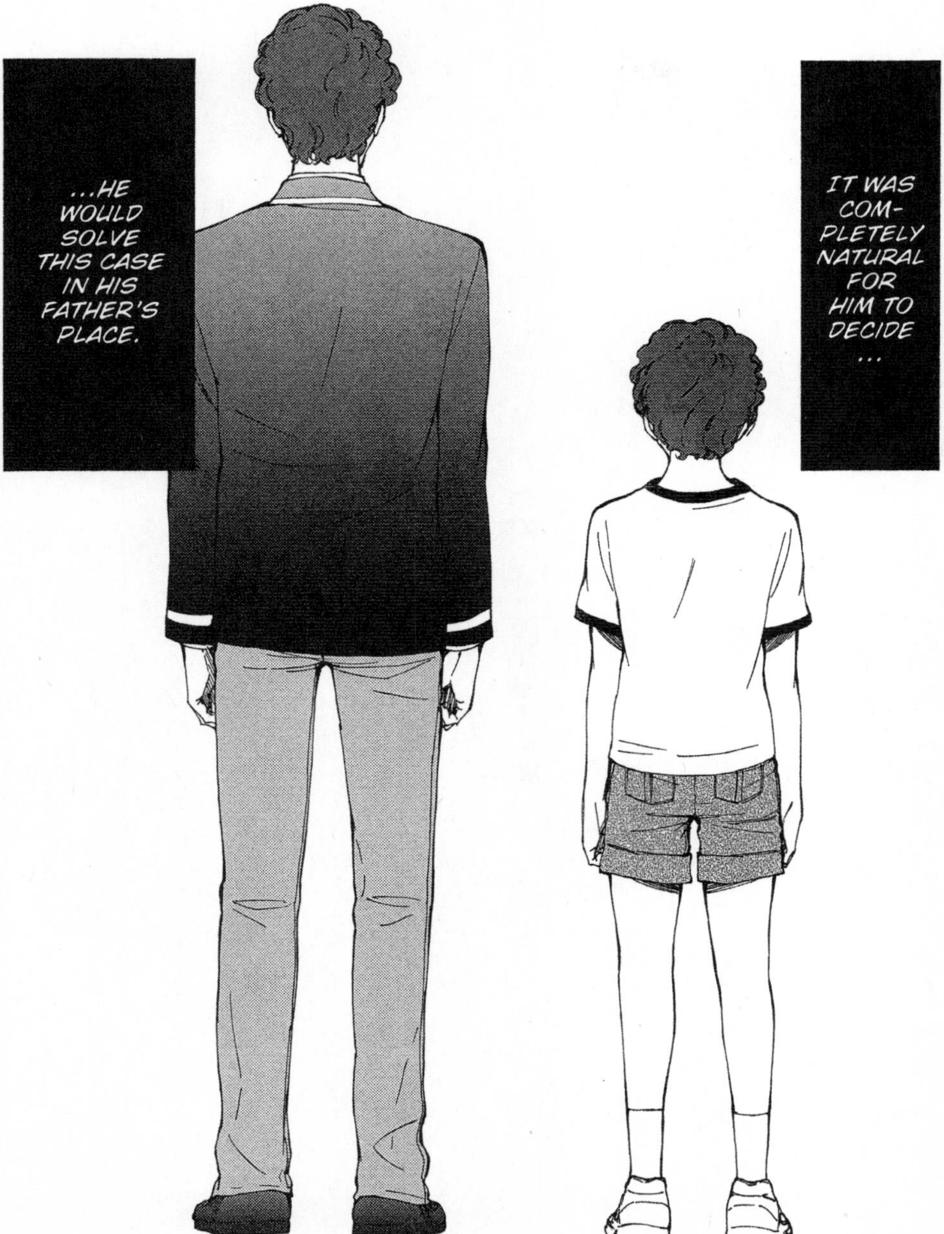
IT WAS COM-PLETELY NATURAL FOR HIM TO DECIDE...
...HE WOULD SOLVE THIS CASE IN HIS FATHER'S PLACE.

#12

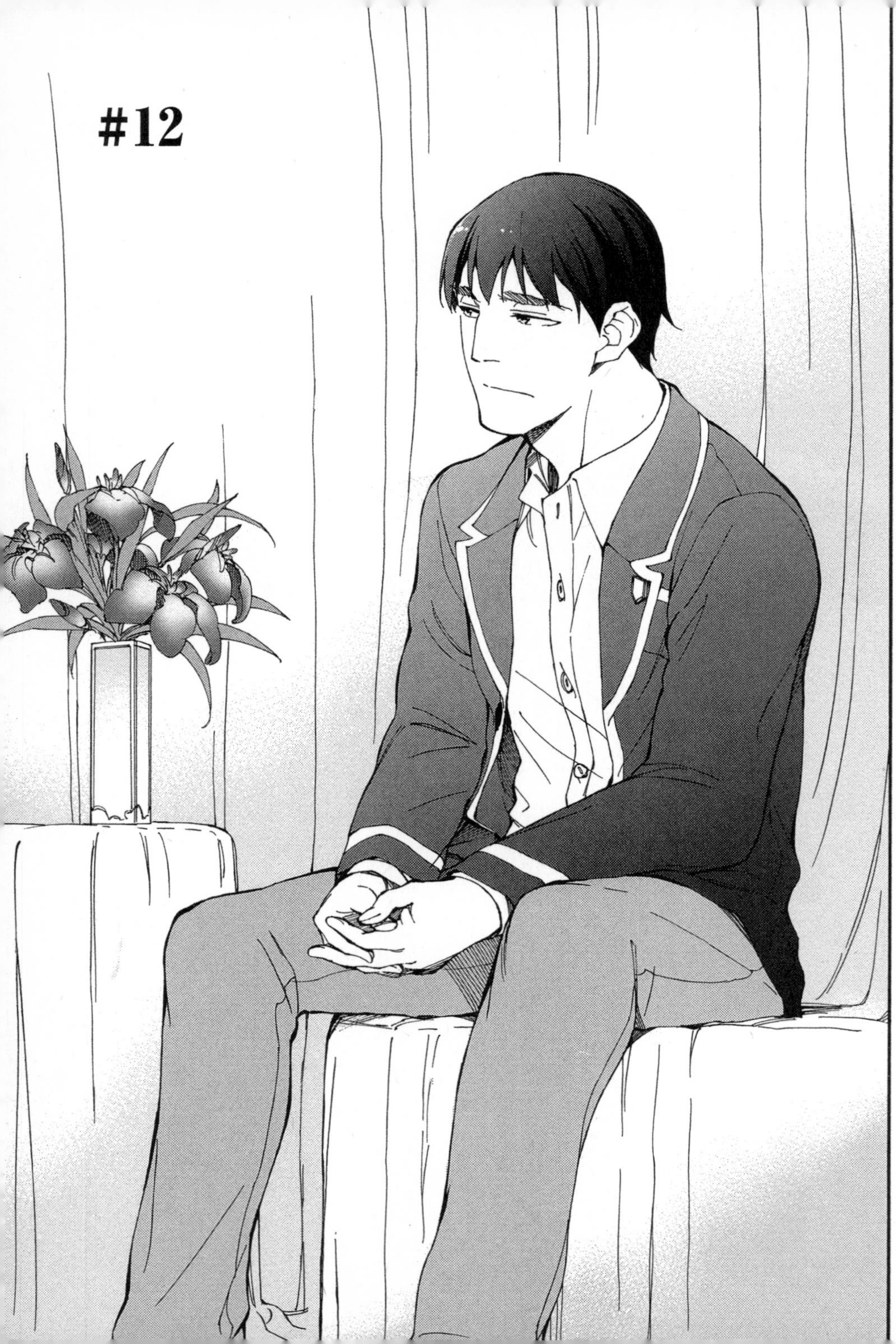

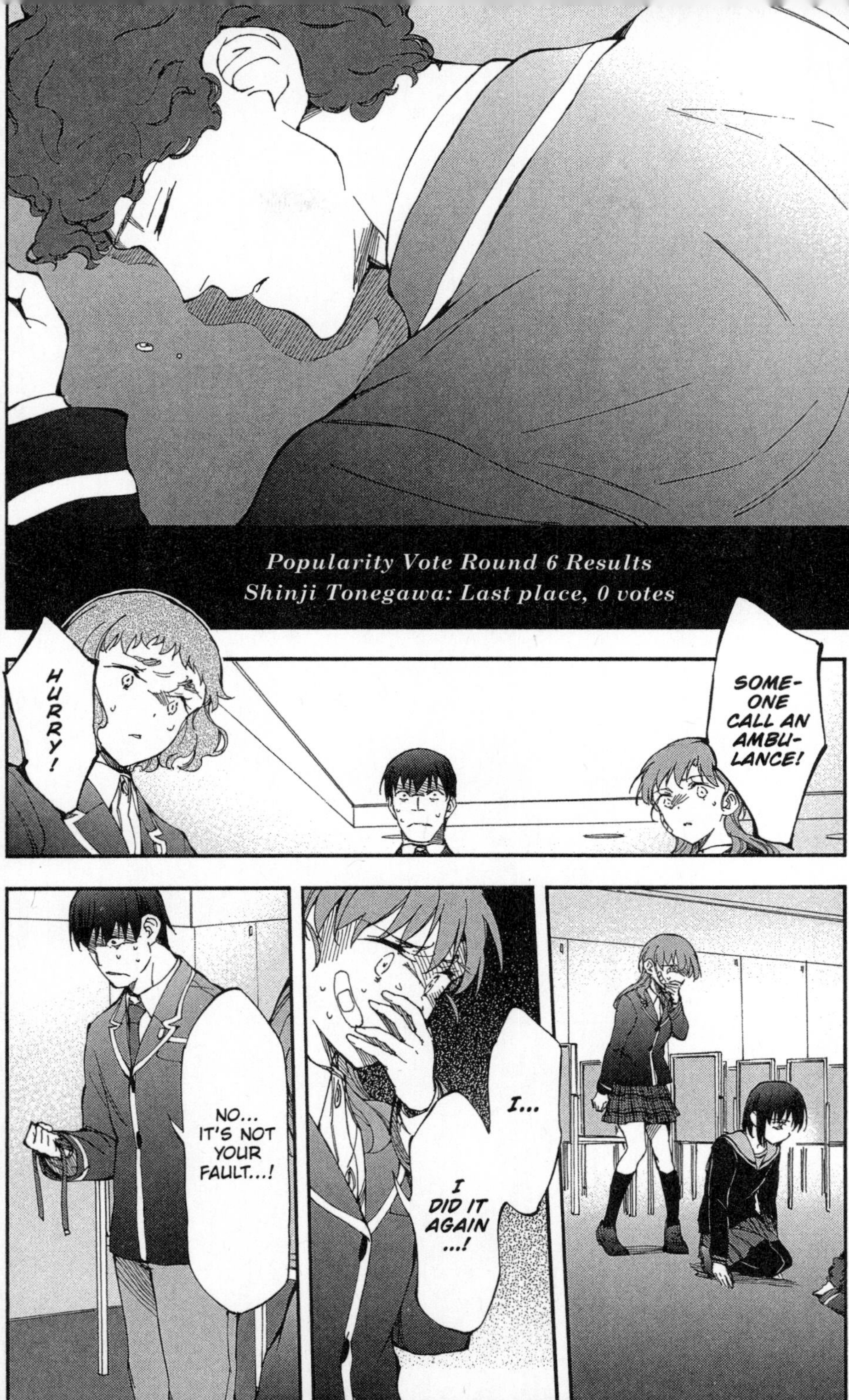
Popularity Vote Round 6 Results
Shinji Tonegawa: Last place, 0 votes
SOME-ONE CALL AN AMBU-LANCE!
HURRY!
I...
I DID IT AGAIN...!
NO... IT'S NOT YOUR FAULT...!

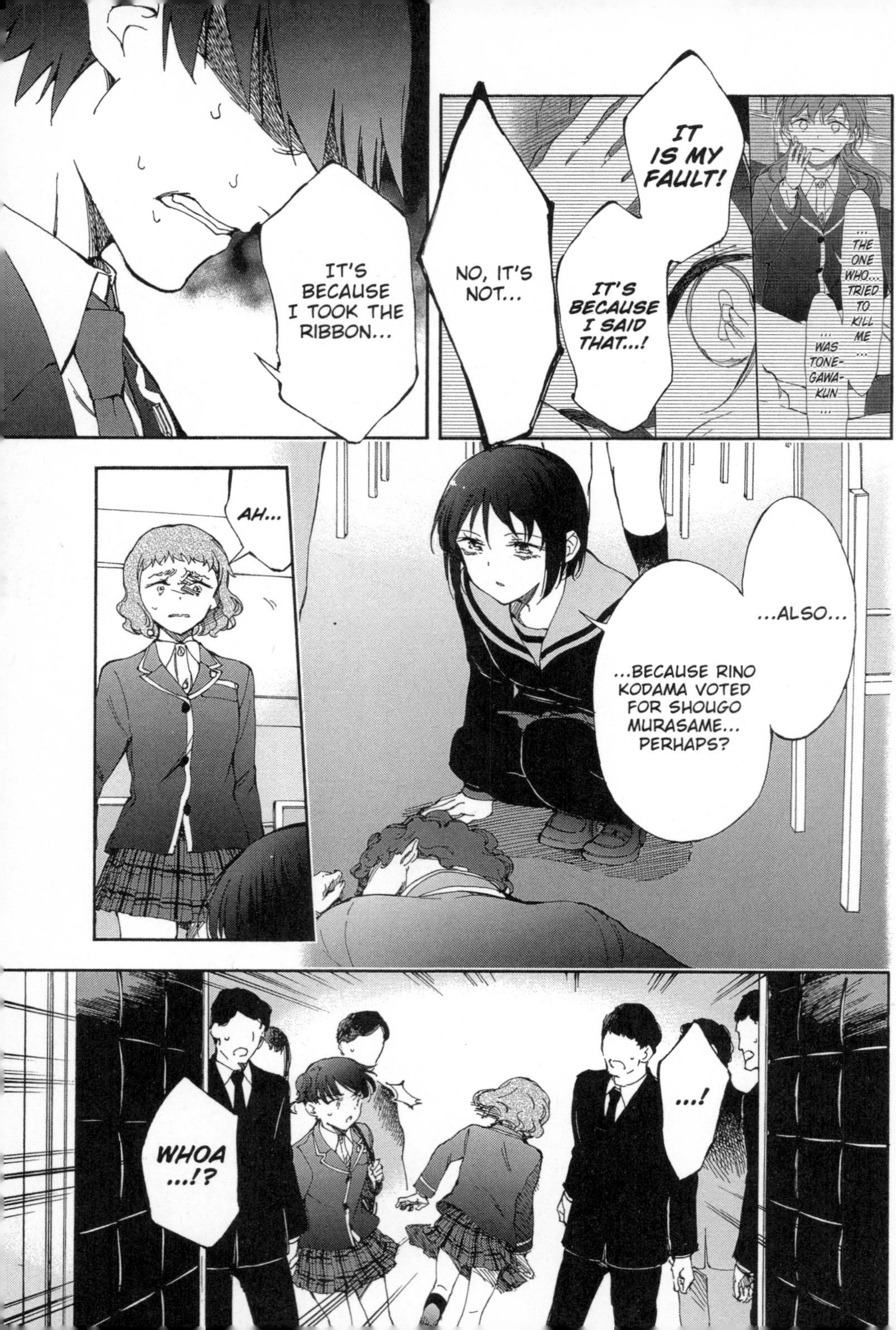
...THE ONE WHO... TRIED TO KILL ME...
...WAS TONE-GAWA-KUN...
IT IS MY FAULT!
IT'S BECAUSE I SAID THAT...!
NO, IT'S NOT...
IT'S BECAUSE I TOOK THE RIBBON...
...ALSO...
...BECAUSE RINO KODAMA VOTED FOR SHOUGO MURASAME... PERHAPS?
AH...
...!
WHOA ...!?

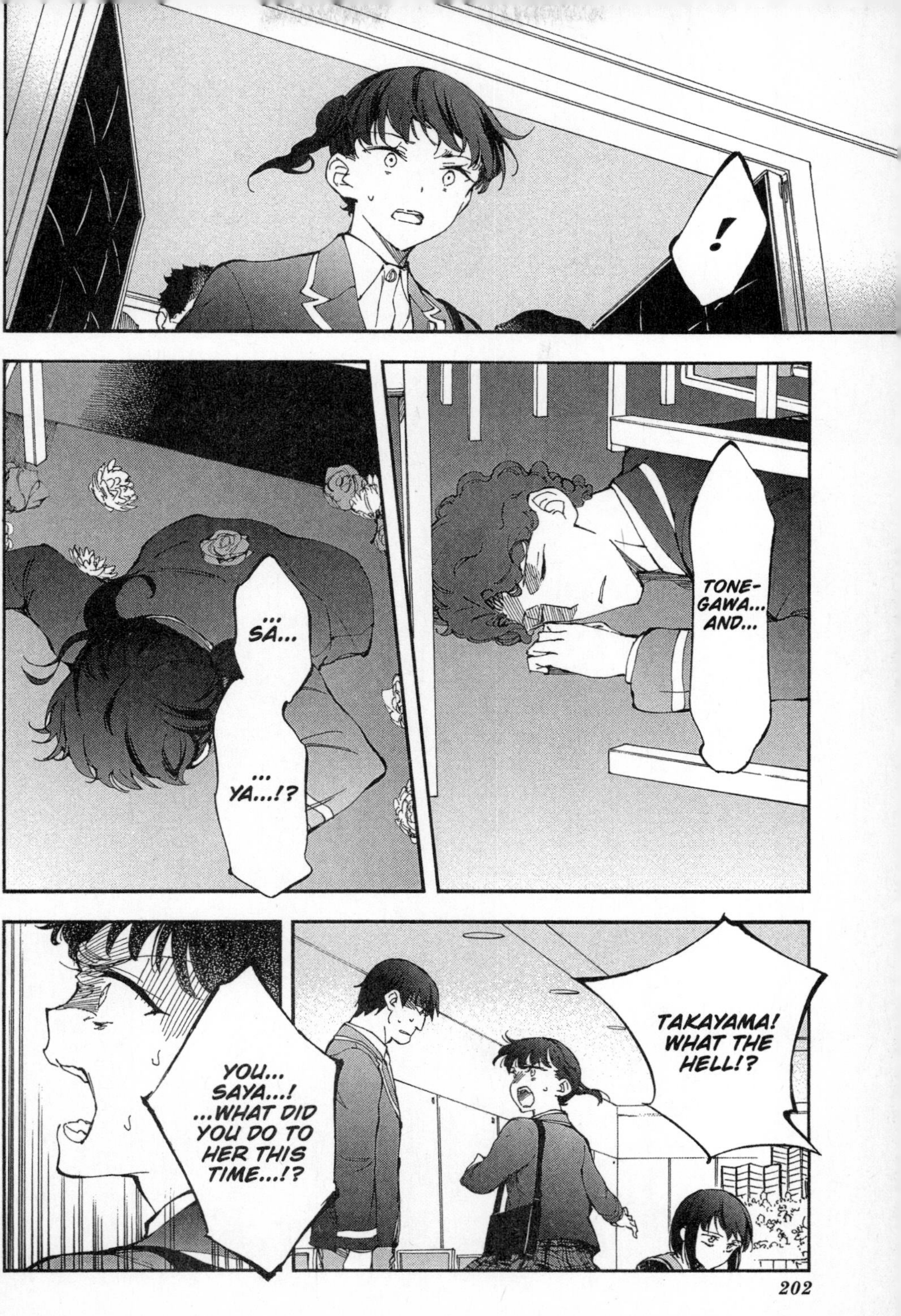
!
TONE-GAWA... AND...
... SA...
... YA...!?
TAKAYAMA! WHAT THE HELL!?
YOU... SAYA...! ...WHAT DID YOU DO TO HER THIS TIME...!?

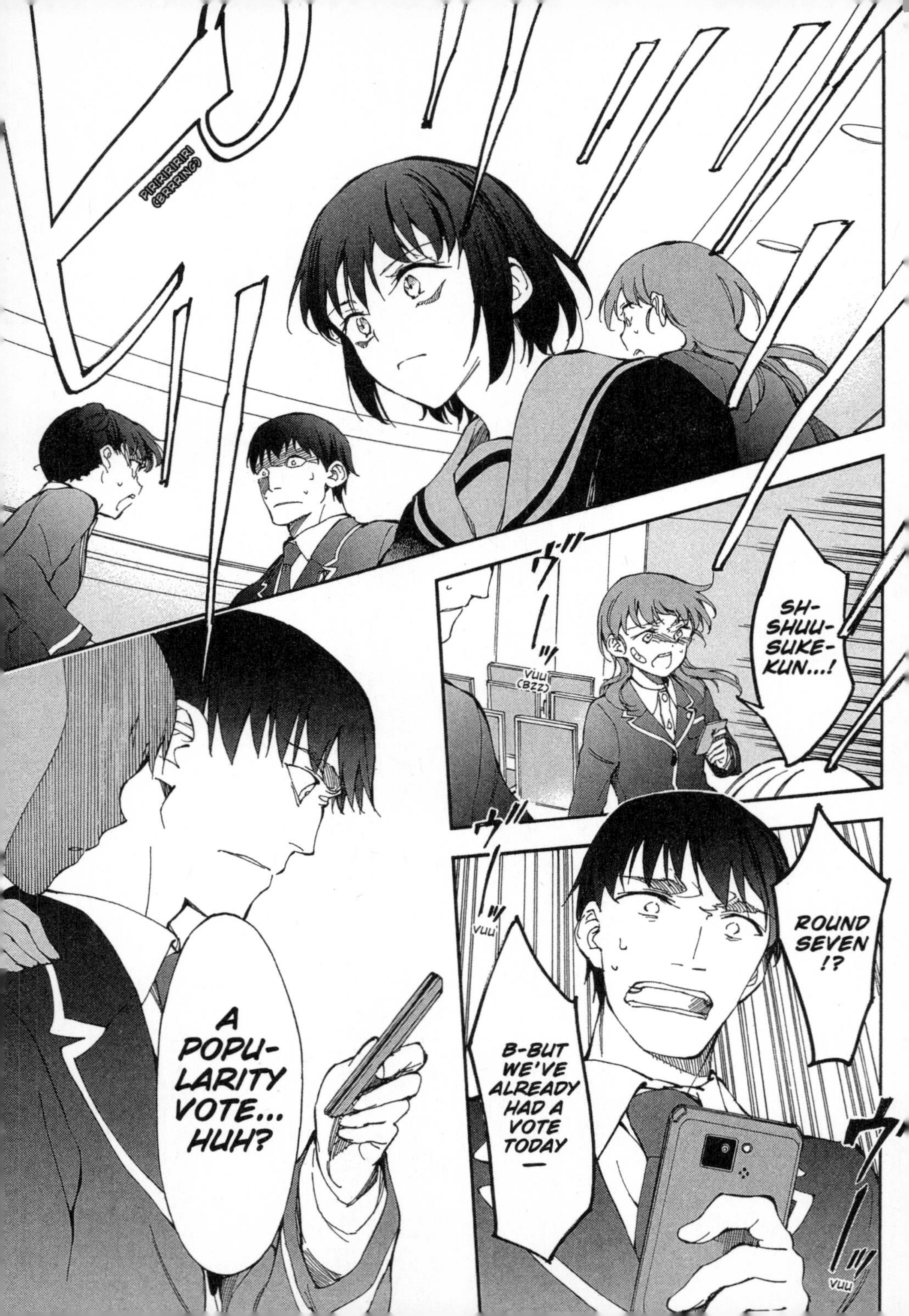
PIRIRIRIRIRI
(BRRRING)
VUU
(BZZ)
SH-SHUU-SUKE-KUN...!
ROUND SEVEN!?
B-BUT WE'VE ALREADY HAD A VOTE TODAY—
VUU
VUU
A POPU-LARITY VOTE... HUH?

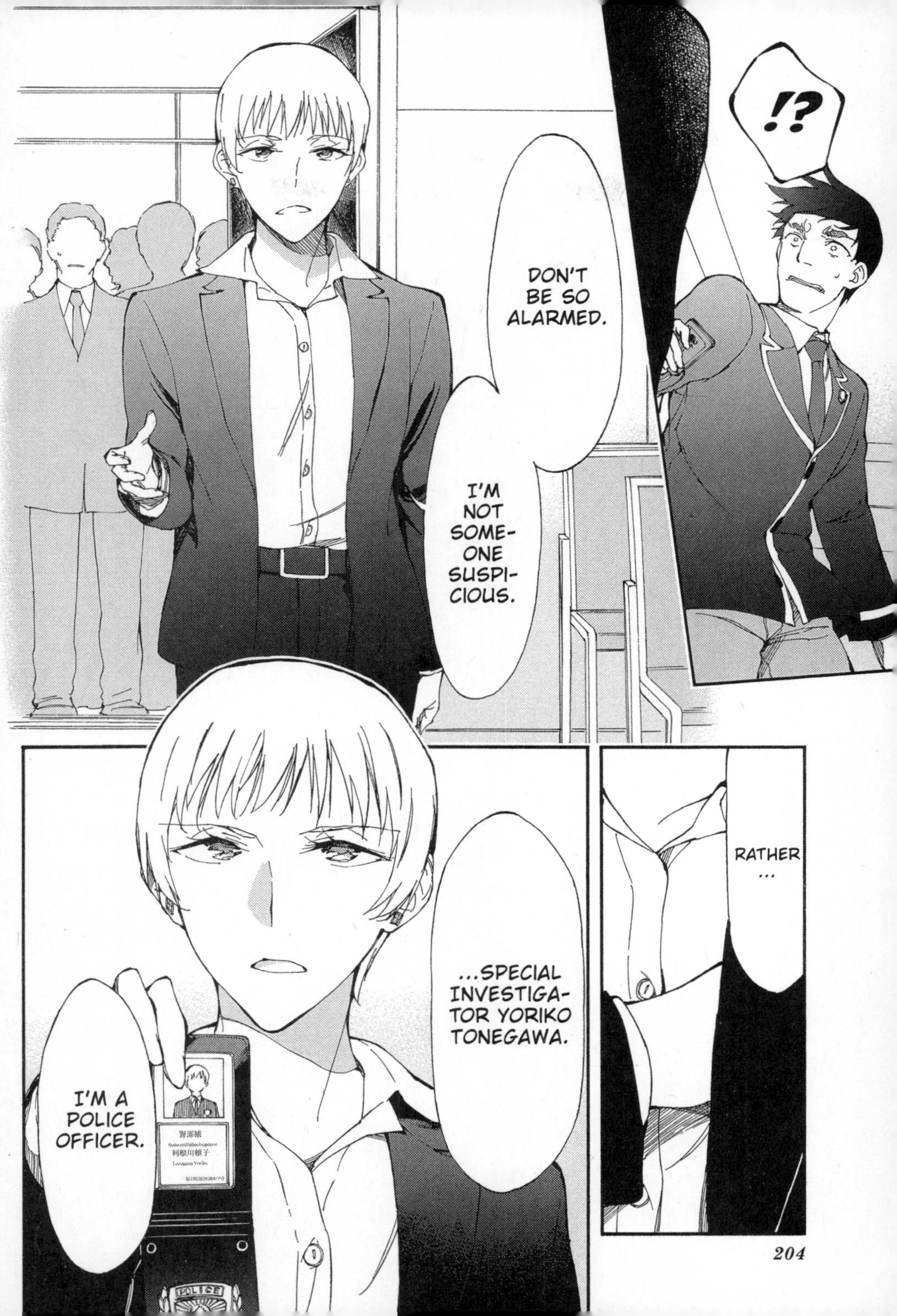
!?
DON'T BE SO ALARMED.
I'M NOT SOME-ONE SUSPICIOUS.
RATHER...
...SPECIAL INVESTIGA-TOR YORIKO TONEGAWA.
I'M A POLICE OFFICER.
POLICE

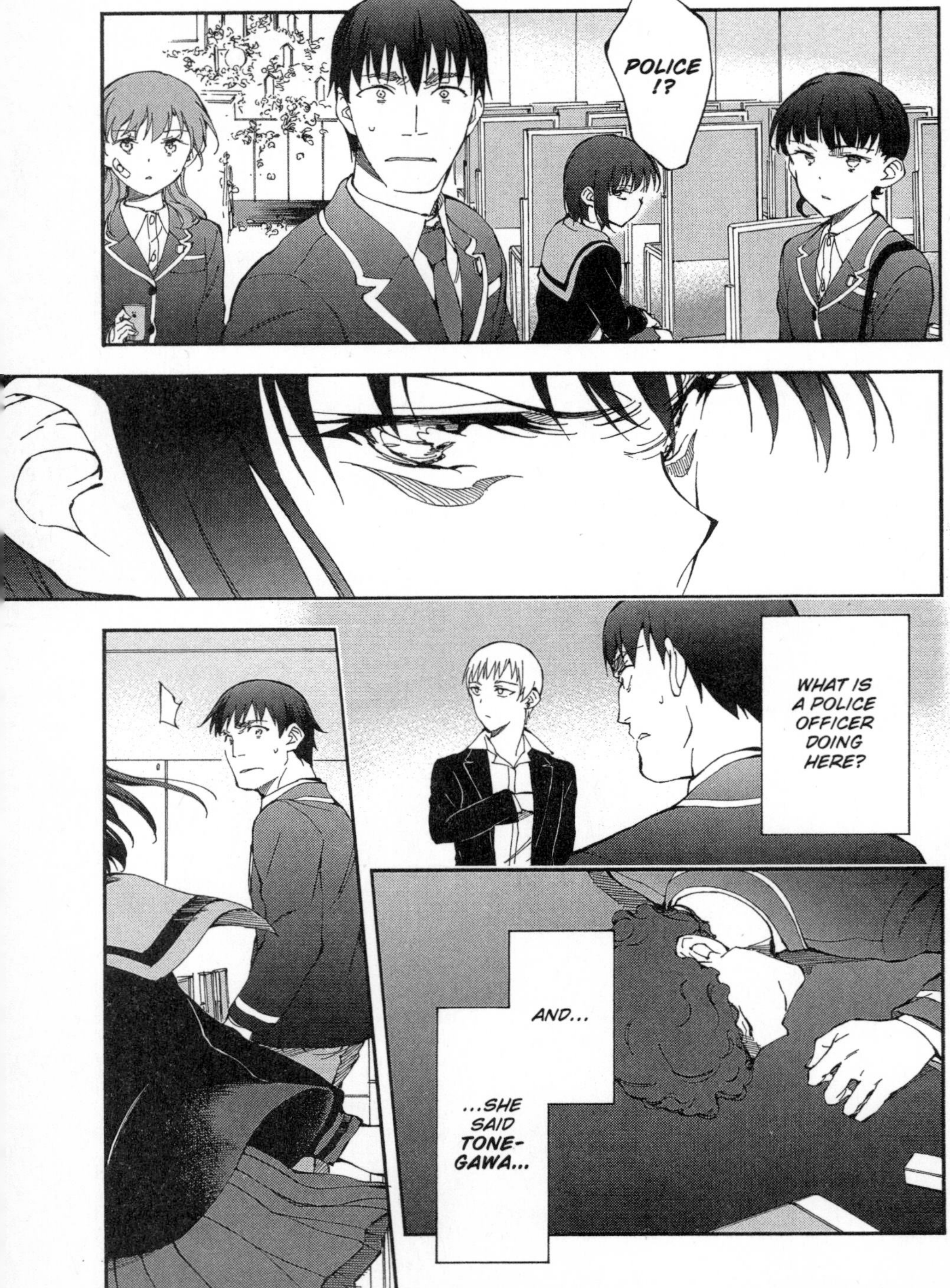
POLICE !?
WHAT IS A POLICE OFFICER DOING HERE?
AND...
...SHE SAID TONE-GAWA...

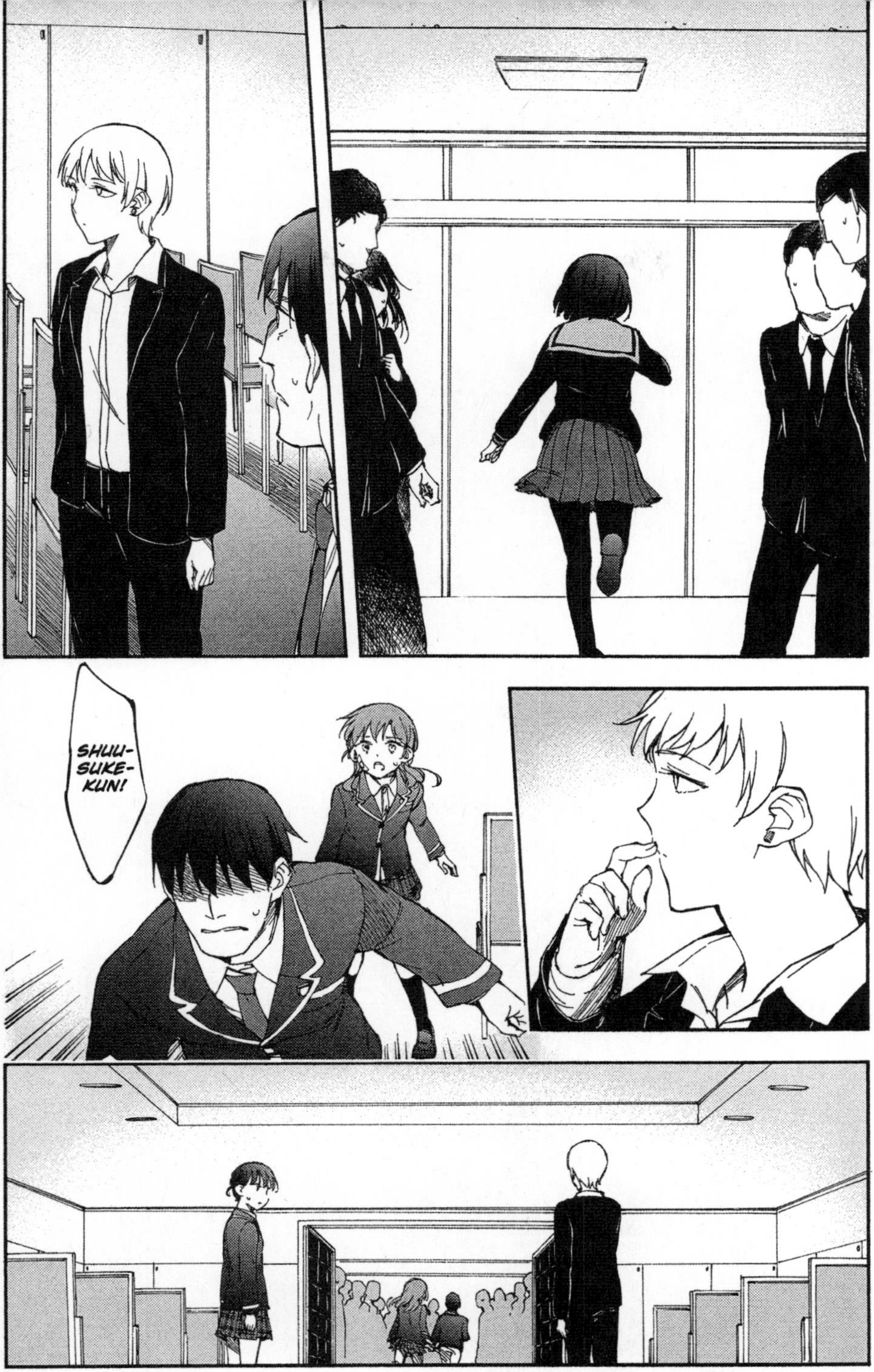
SHUU-
SUKE-
KUN!

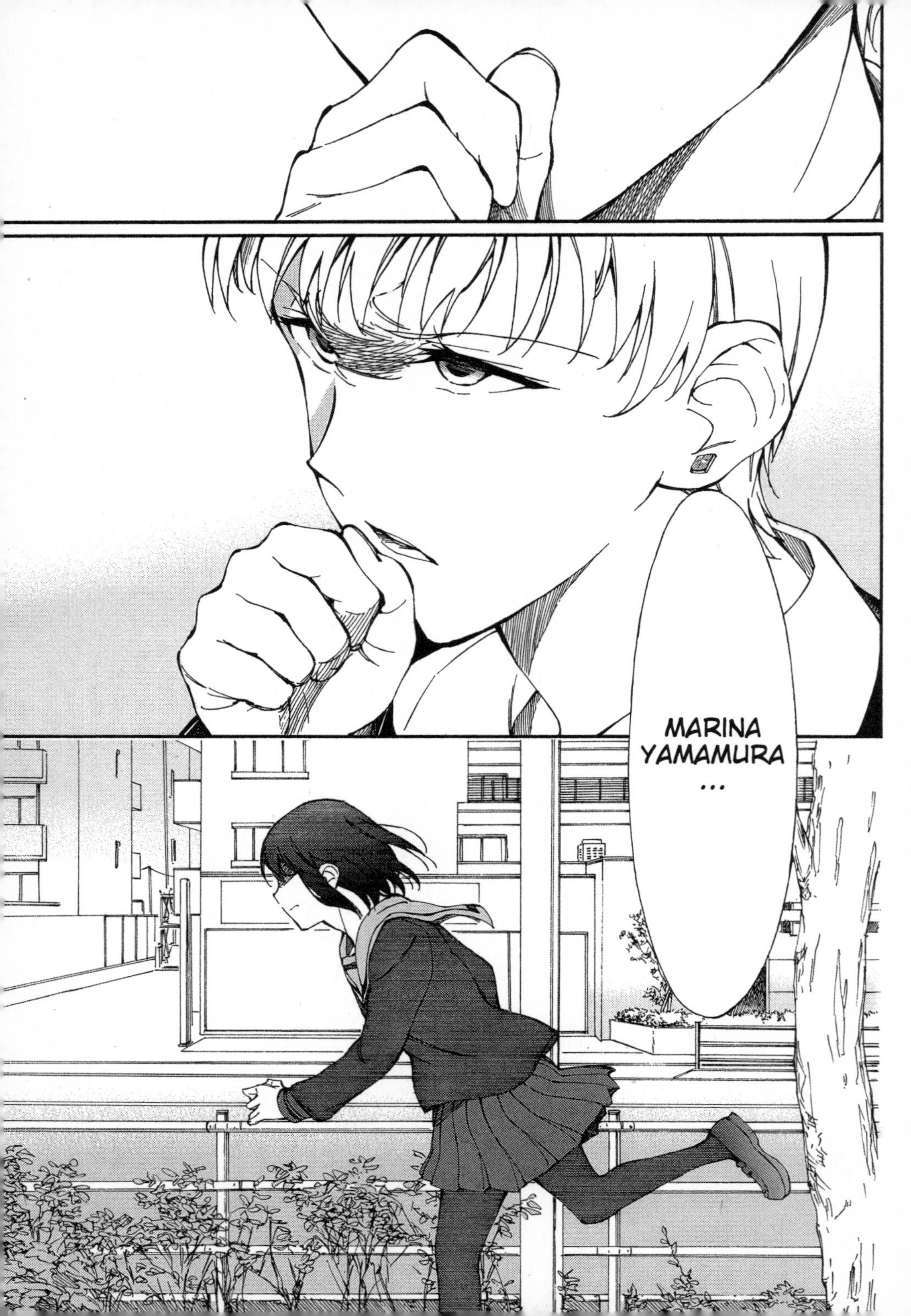
MARINA YAMAMURA
...

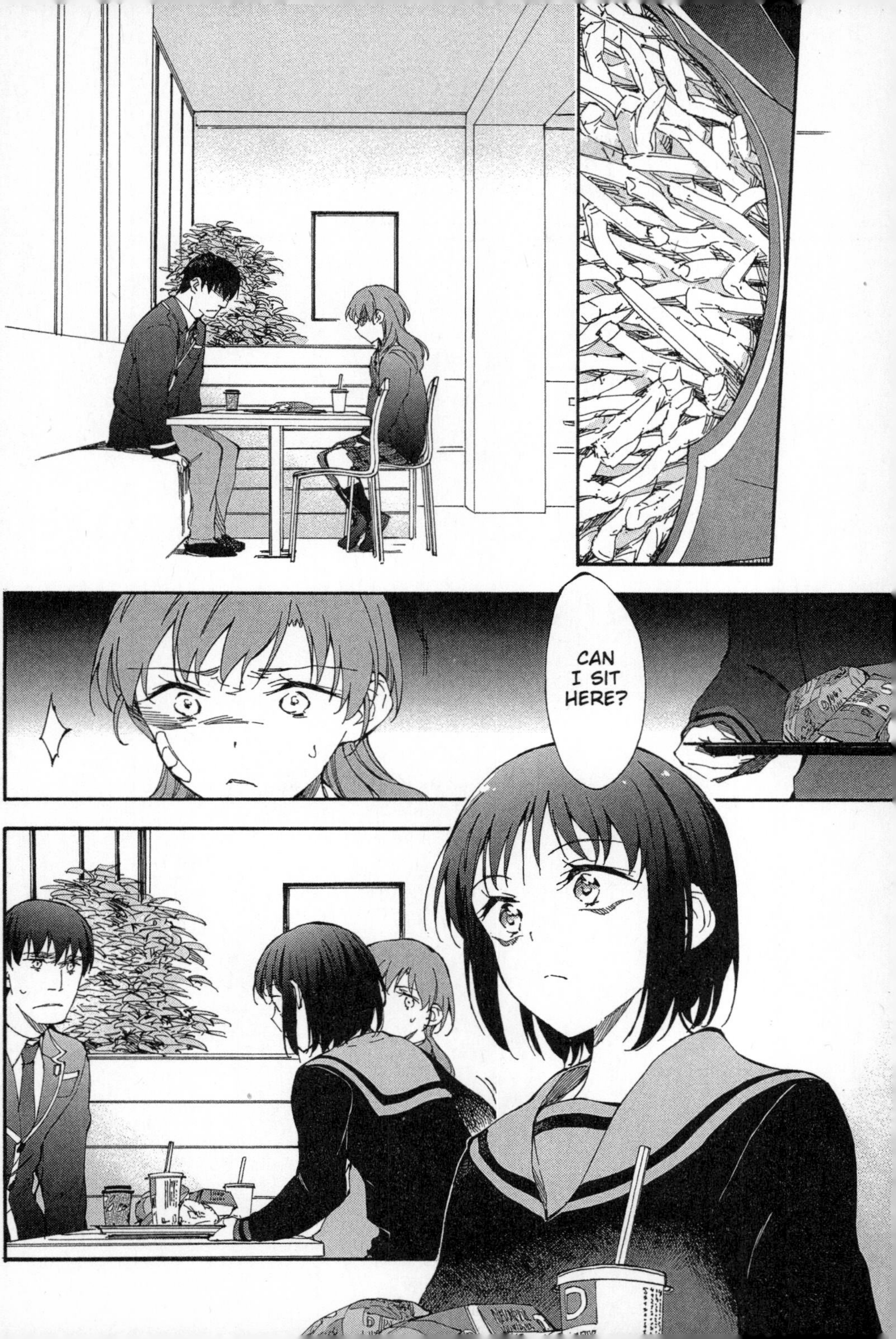
CAN I SIT HERE?

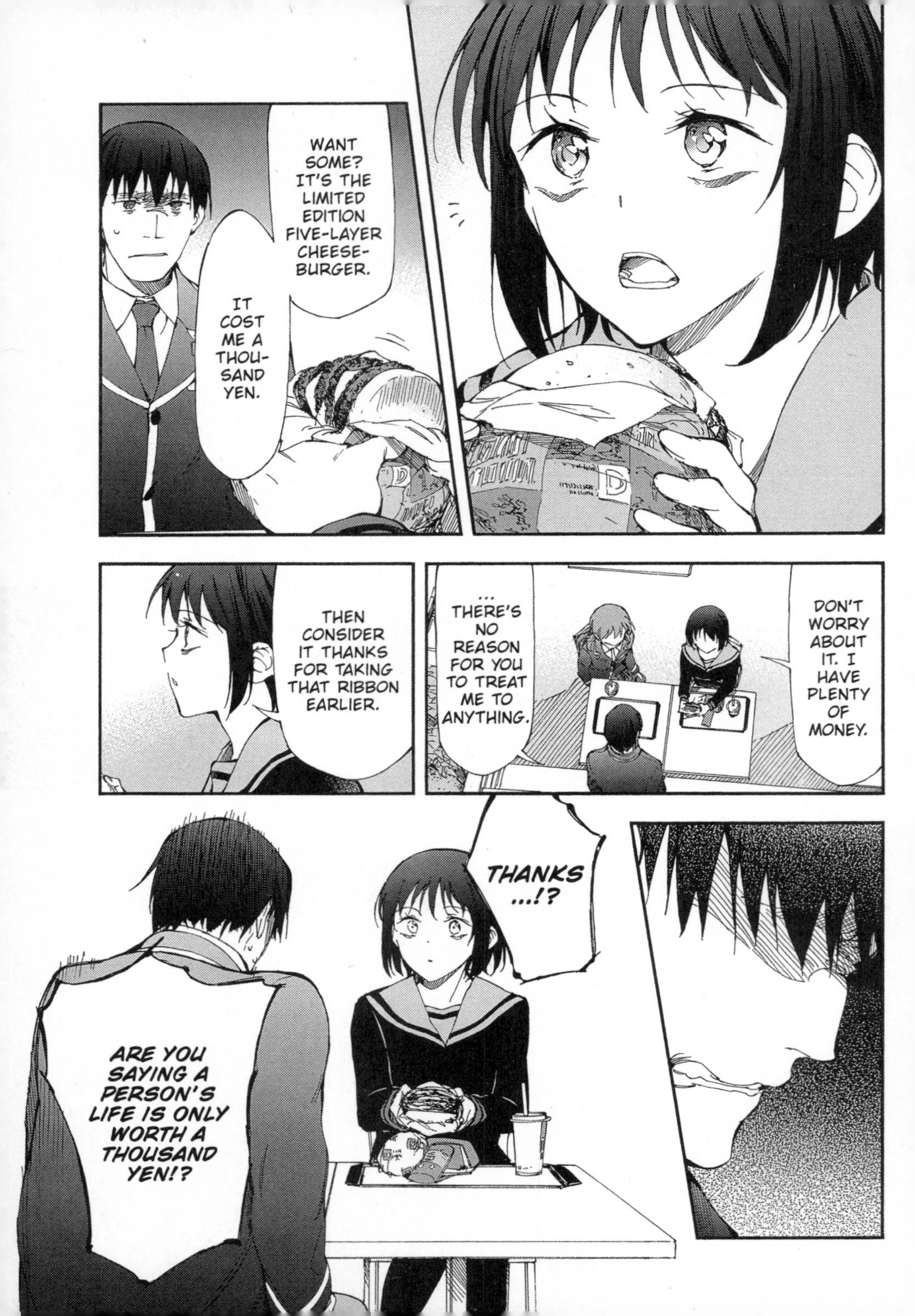
WANT SOME? IT'S THE LIMITED EDITION FIVE-LAYER CHEESE-BURGER.
IT COST ME A THOU-SAND YEN.
DON'T WORRY ABOUT IT. I HAVE PLENTY OF MONEY.
... THERE'S NO REASON FOR YOU TO TREAT ME TO ANYTHING.
THEN CONSIDER IT THANKS FOR TAKING THAT RIBBON EARLIER.
THANKS ...!?
ARE YOU SAYING A PERSON'S LIFE IS ONLY WORTH A THOUSAND YEN!?

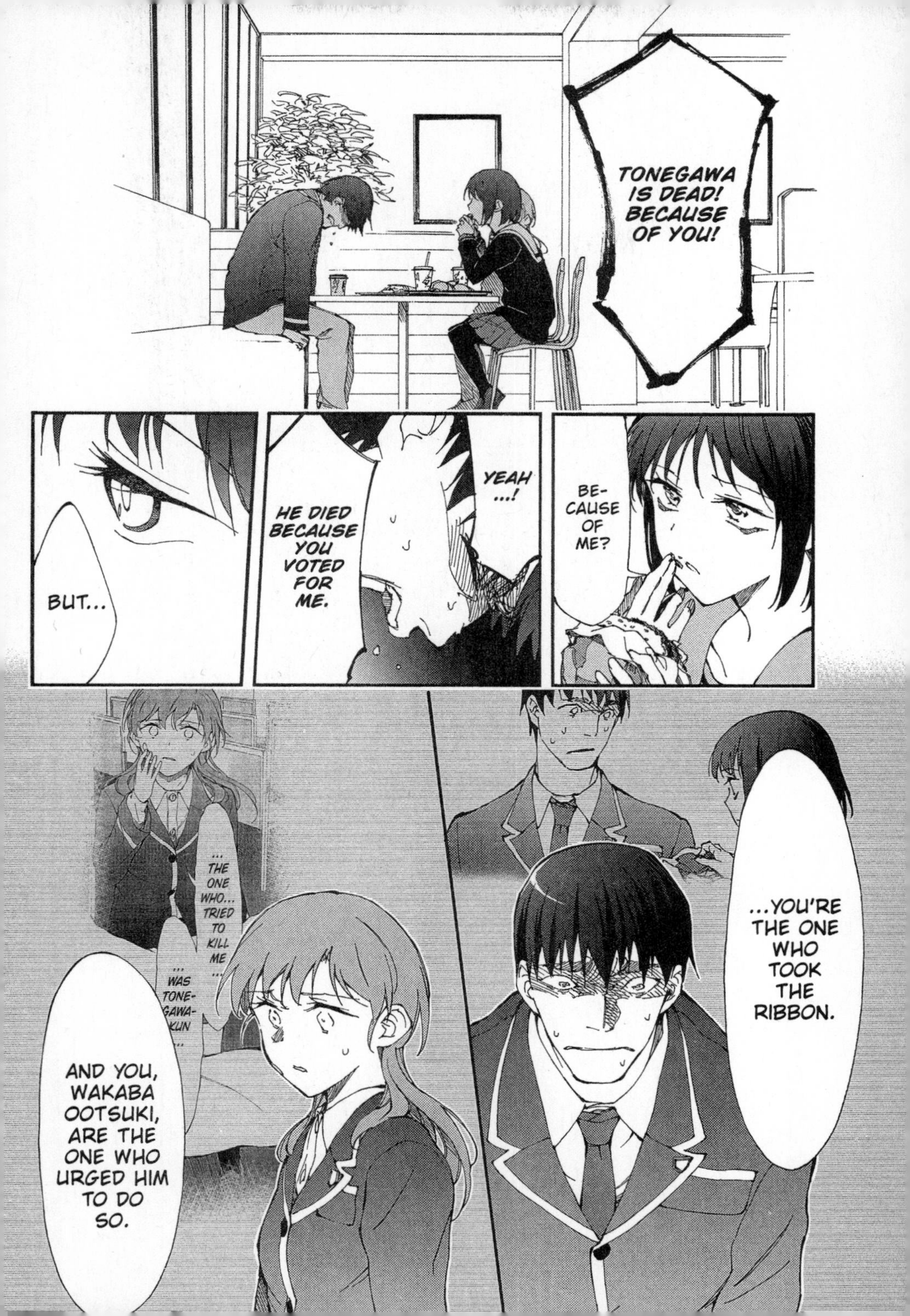
TONEGAWA IS DEAD! BECAUSE OF YOU!
BE-CAUSE OF ME?
YEAH...!
HE DIED BECAUSE YOU VOTED FOR ME.
BUT...
...YOU'RE THE ONE WHO TOOK THE RIBBON.
...THE ONE WHO... TRIED TO KILL ME...
...WAS TONE-GAWA-KUN...
AND YOU, WAKABA OOTSUKI, ARE THE ONE WHO URGED HIM TO DO SO.

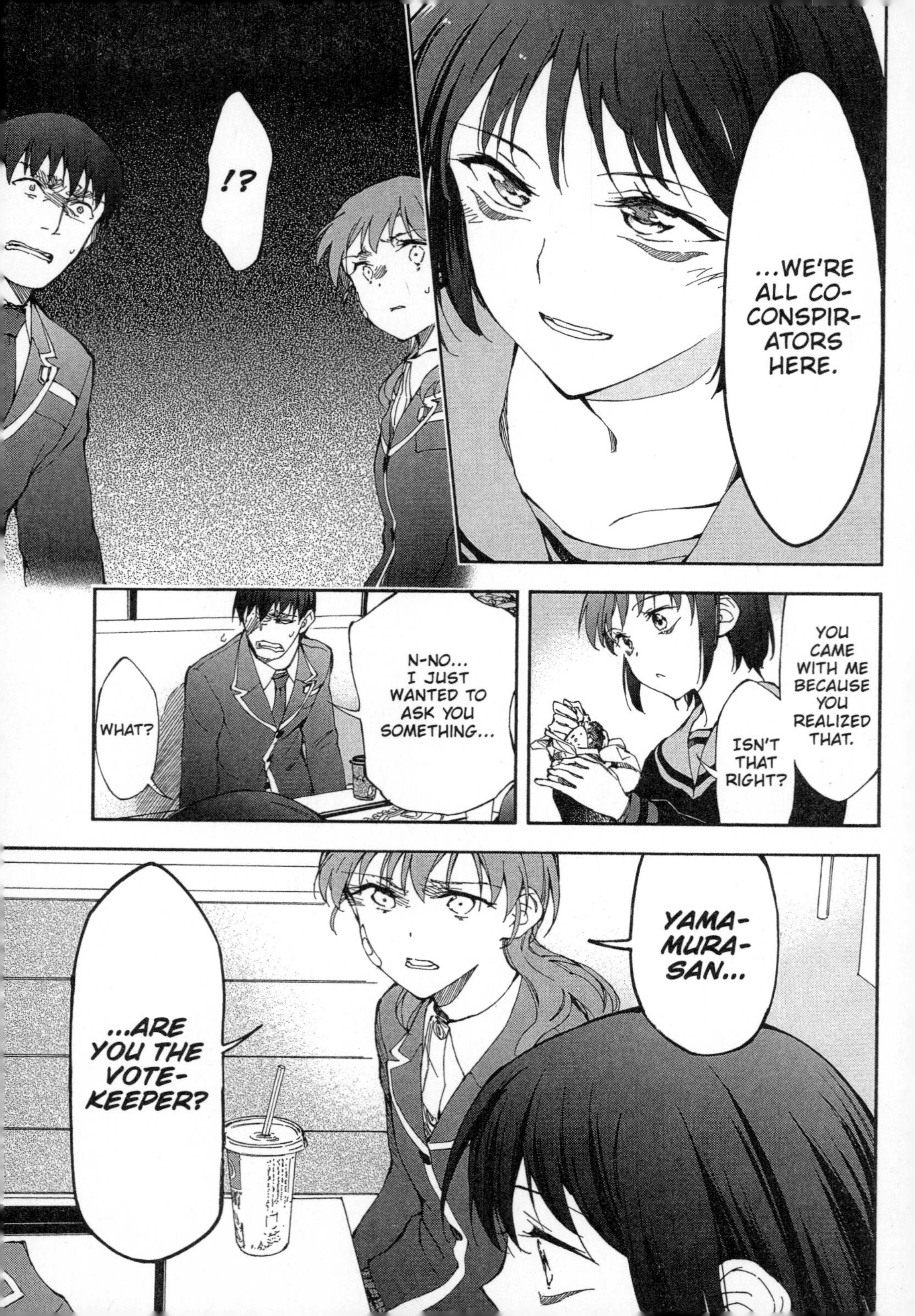
...WE'RE ALL CO-CONSPIRATORS HERE.
!?
YOU CAME WITH ME BECAUSE YOU REALIZED THAT.
ISN'T THAT RIGHT?
N-NO... I JUST WANTED TO ASK YOU SOMETHING...
WHAT?
YAMAMURA-SAN...
...ARE YOU THE VOTE-KEEPER?

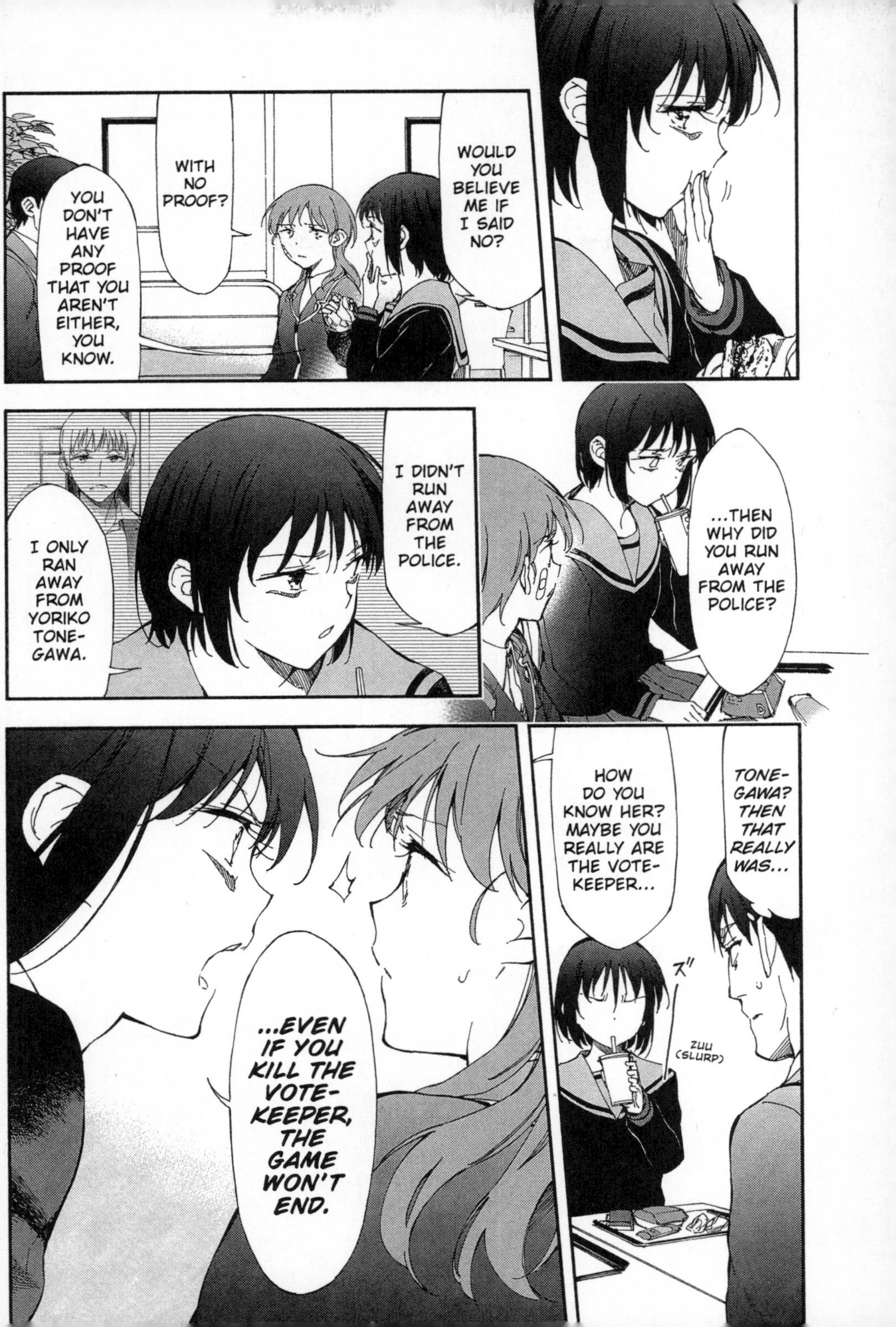
WOULD YOU BELIEVE ME IF I SAID NO?
WITH NO PROOF?
YOU DON'T HAVE ANY PROOF THAT YOU AREN'T EITHER, YOU KNOW.
...THEN WHY DID YOU RUN AWAY FROM THE POLICE?
I DIDN'T RUN AWAY FROM THE POLICE.
I ONLY RAN AWAY FROM YORIKO TONE-GAWA.
TONE-GAWA? THEN THAT REALLY WAS...
HOW DO YOU KNOW HER? MAYBE YOU REALLY ARE THE VOTE-KEEPER...
ズ
ZUU (SLURP)
...EVEN IF YOU KILL THE VOTE-KEEPER, THE GAME WON'T END.

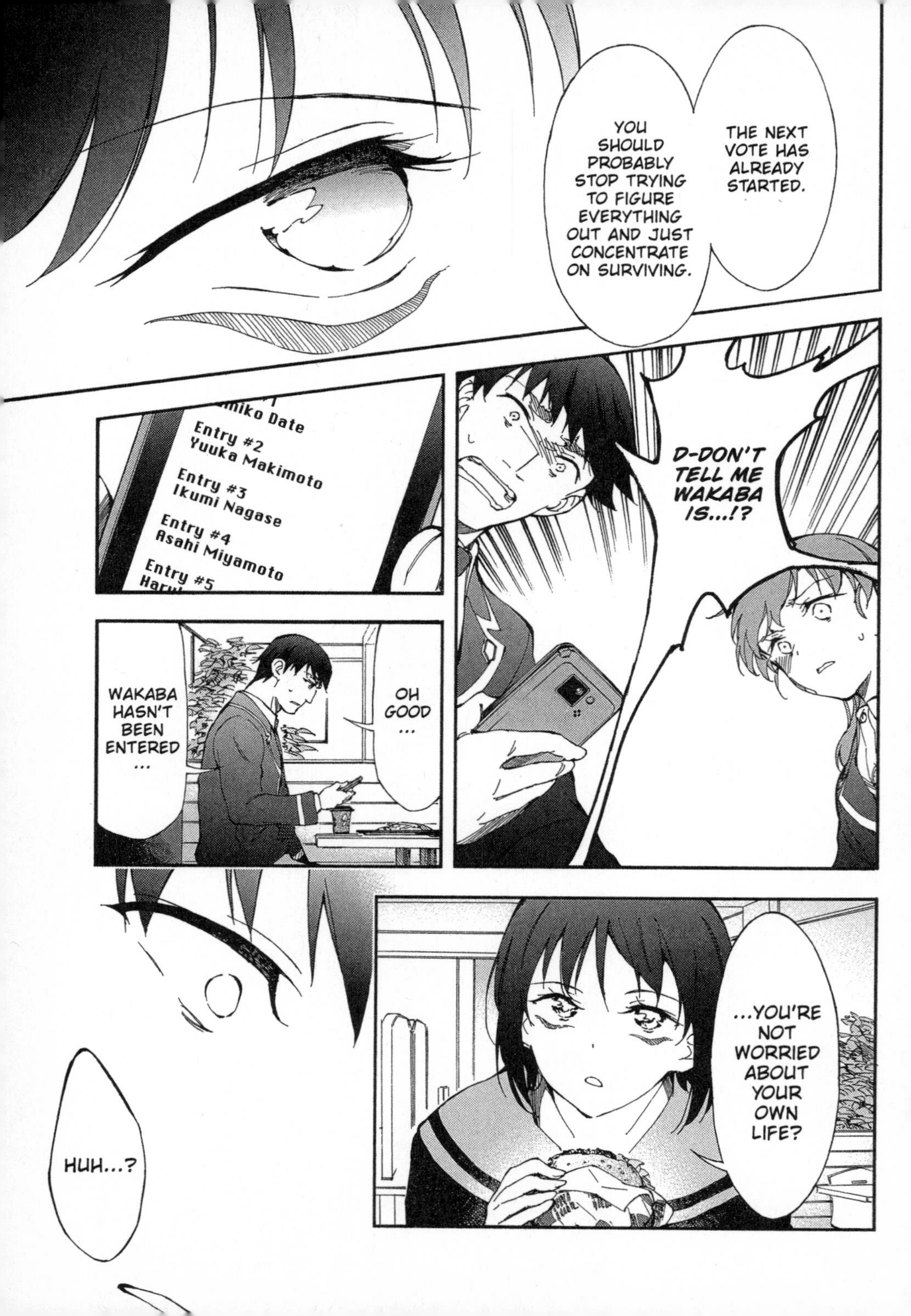
THE NEXT VOTE HAS ALREADY STARTED.
YOU SHOULD PROBABLY STOP TRYING TO FIGURE EVERYTHING OUT AND JUST CONCENTRATE ON SURVIVING.
D-DON'T TELL ME WAKABA IS...!?
Entry #2
Yuuka Makimoto
Entry #3
Ikumi Nagase
Entry #4
Asahi Miyamoto
Entry #5
OH GOOD ...
WAKABA HASN'T BEEN ENTERED ...
...YOU'RE NOT WORRIED ABOUT YOUR OWN LIFE?
HUH...?

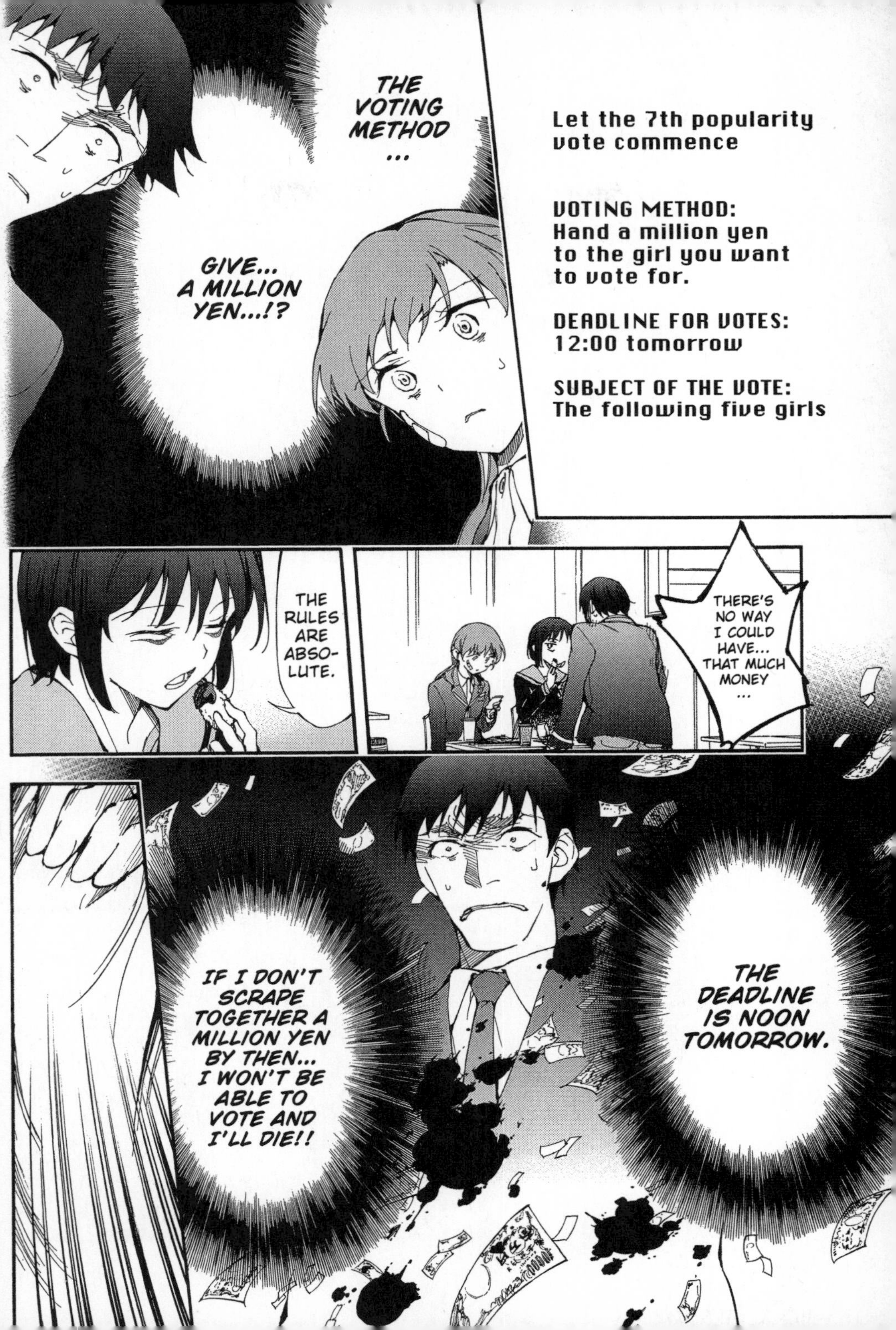
Let the 7th popularity vote commence
VOTING METHOD: Hand a million yen to the girl you want to vote for.
DEADLINE FOR VOTES: 12:00 tomorrow
SUBJECT OF THE VOTE: The following five girls
THE VOTING METHOD ...
GIVE... A MILLION YEN...!?
THERE'S NO WAY I COULD HAVE... THAT MUCH MONEY ...
THE RULES ARE ABSOLUTE.
THE DEADLINE IS NOON TOMORROW.
IF I DON'T SCRAPE TOGETHER A MILLION YEN BY THEN... I WON'T BE ABLE TO VOTE AND I'LL DIE!!

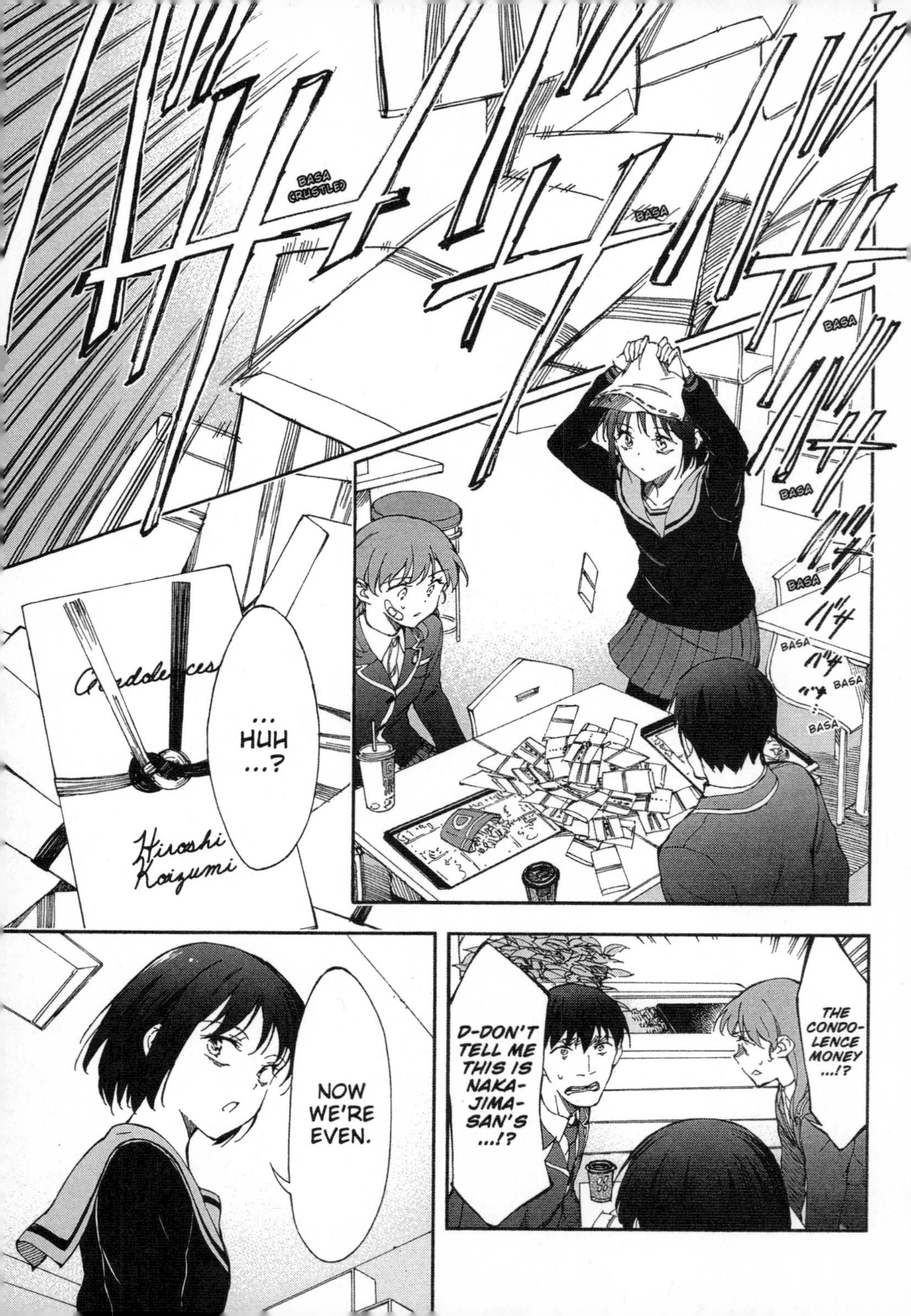
BASA (RUSTLED)
BASA
BASA
BASA
BASA
BASA
BASA
BASA
Condolences
Hiroshi Koizumi
...HUH...?
THE CONDOLENCE MONEY...!?
D-DON'T TELL ME THIS IS NAKAJIMA-SAN'S...!?
NOW WE'RE EVEN.

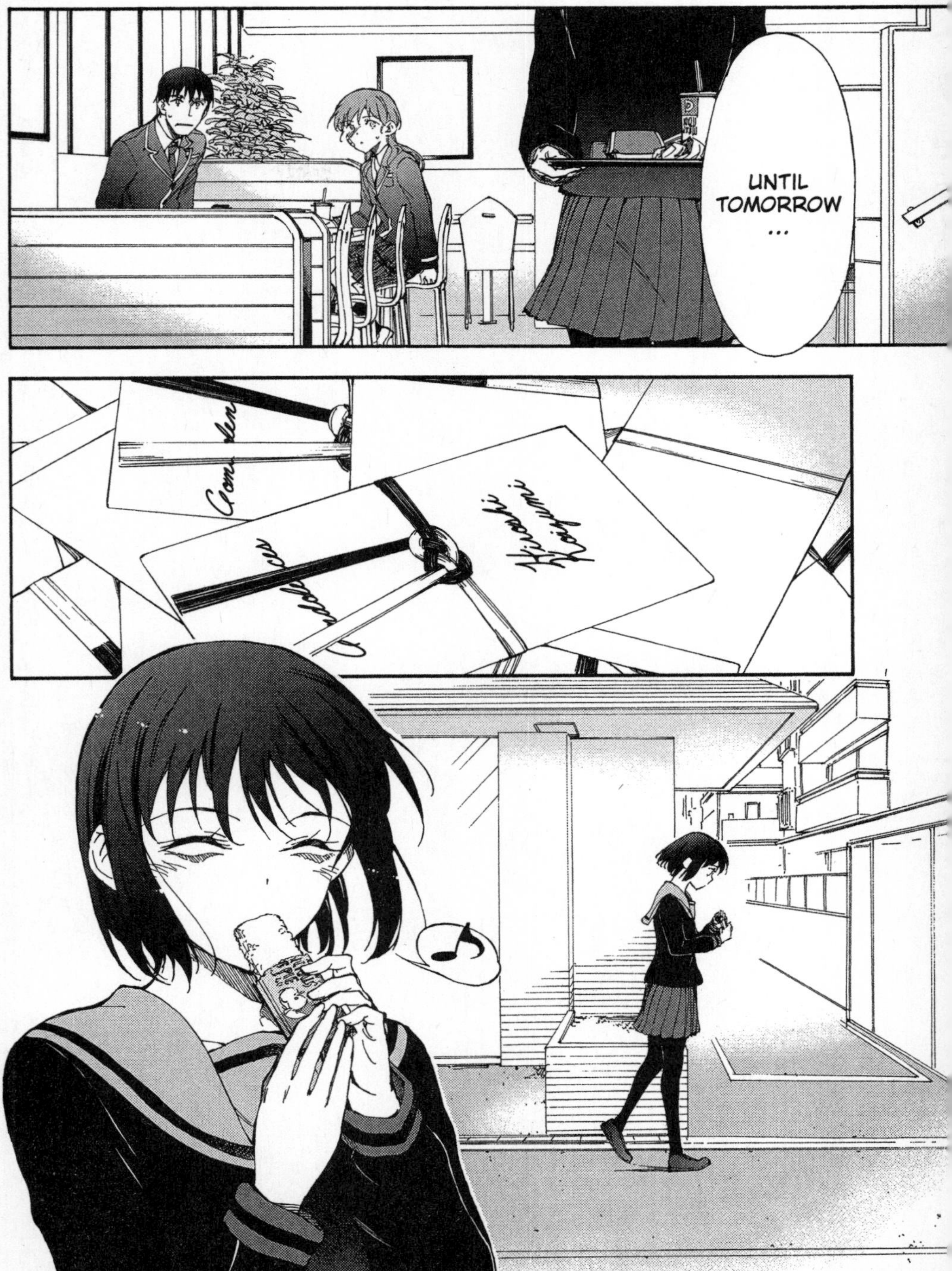
UNTIL TOMORROW ...

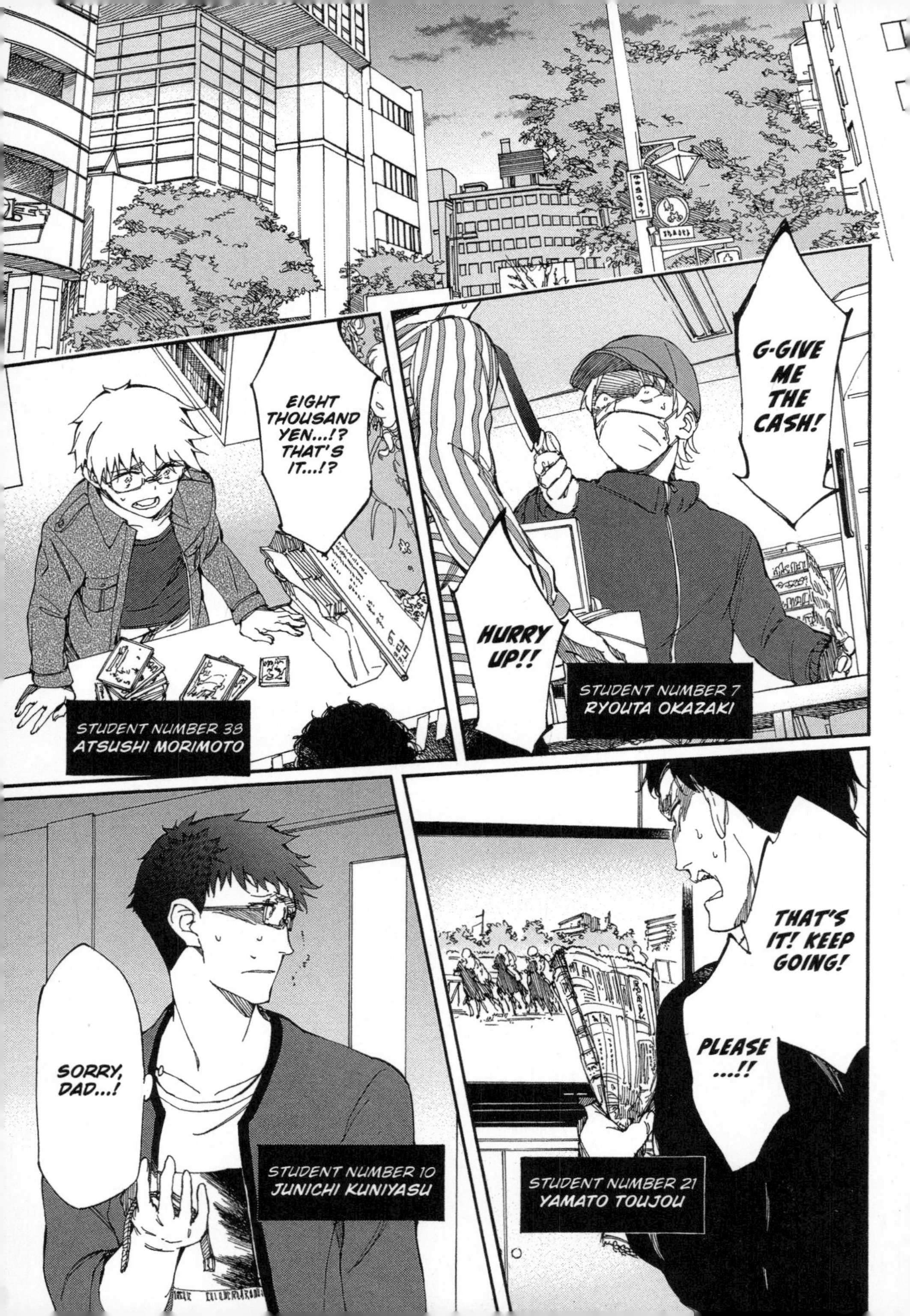
G-GIVE ME THE CASH!
HURRY UP!!
STUDENT NUMBER 7
RYOUTA OKAZAKI
EIGHT THOUSAND YEN...!? THAT'S IT...!?
STUDENT NUMBER 38
ATSUSHI MORIMOTO
THAT'S IT! KEEP GOING!
PLEASE ...!!
STUDENT NUMBER 21
YAMATO TOUJOU
SORRY, DAD...!
STUDENT NUMBER 10
JUNICHI KUNIYASU

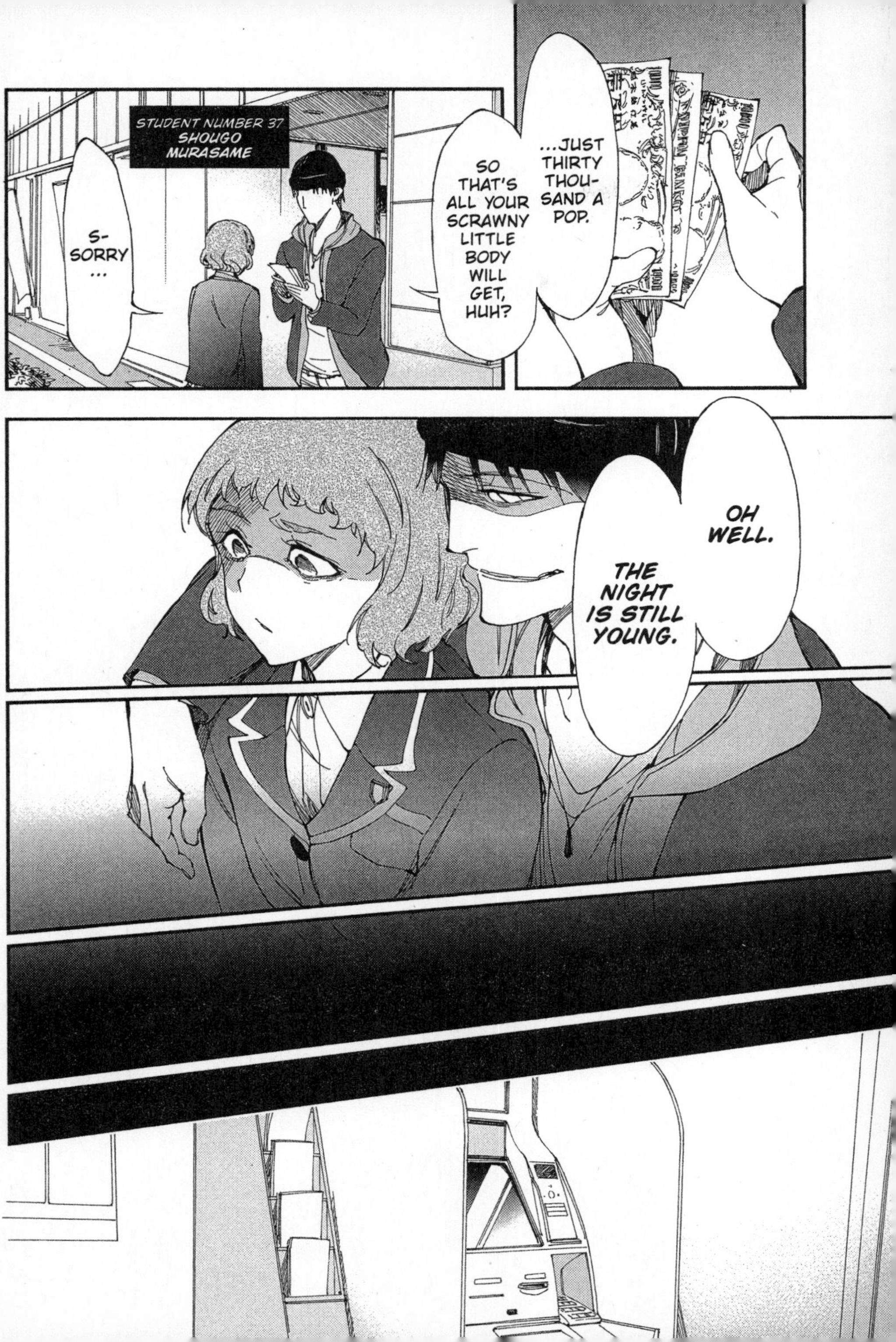
...JUST THIRTY THOU-SAND A POP.
SO THAT'S ALL YOUR SCRAWNY LITTLE BODY WILL GET, HUH?
STUDENT NUMBER 37 SHOUGO MURASAME
S-SORRY ...
OH WELL.
THE NIGHT IS STILL YOUNG.

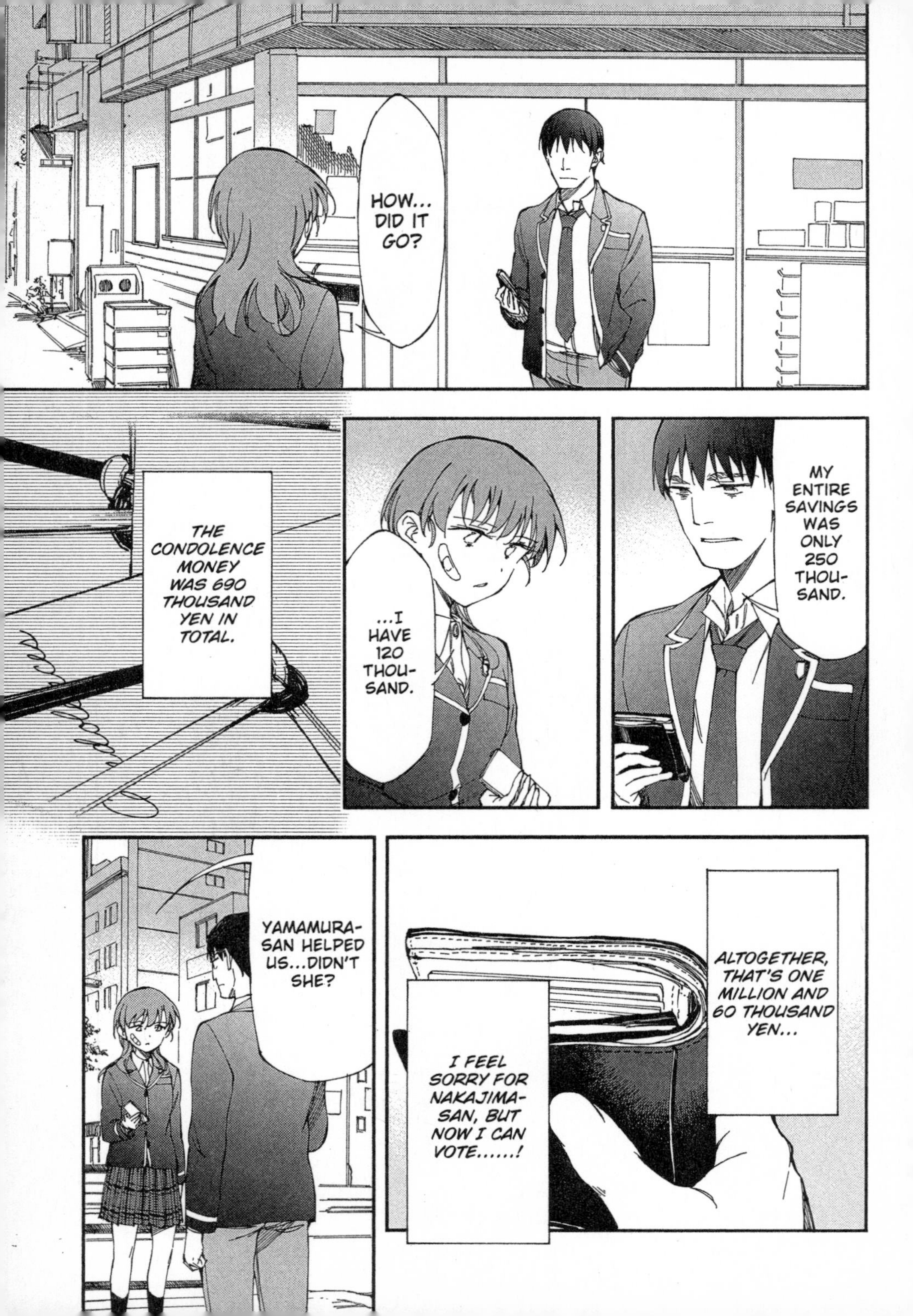
HOW... DID IT GO?
MY ENTIRE SAVINGS WAS ONLY 250 THOUSAND.
...I HAVE 120 THOUSAND.
THE CONDOLENCE MONEY WAS 690 THOUSAND YEN IN TOTAL.
ALTOGETHER, THAT'S ONE MILLION AND 60 THOUSAND YEN...
I FEEL SORRY FOR NAKAJIMA-SAN, BUT NOW I CAN VOTE......!
YAMAMURA-SAN HELPED US...DIDN'T SHE?

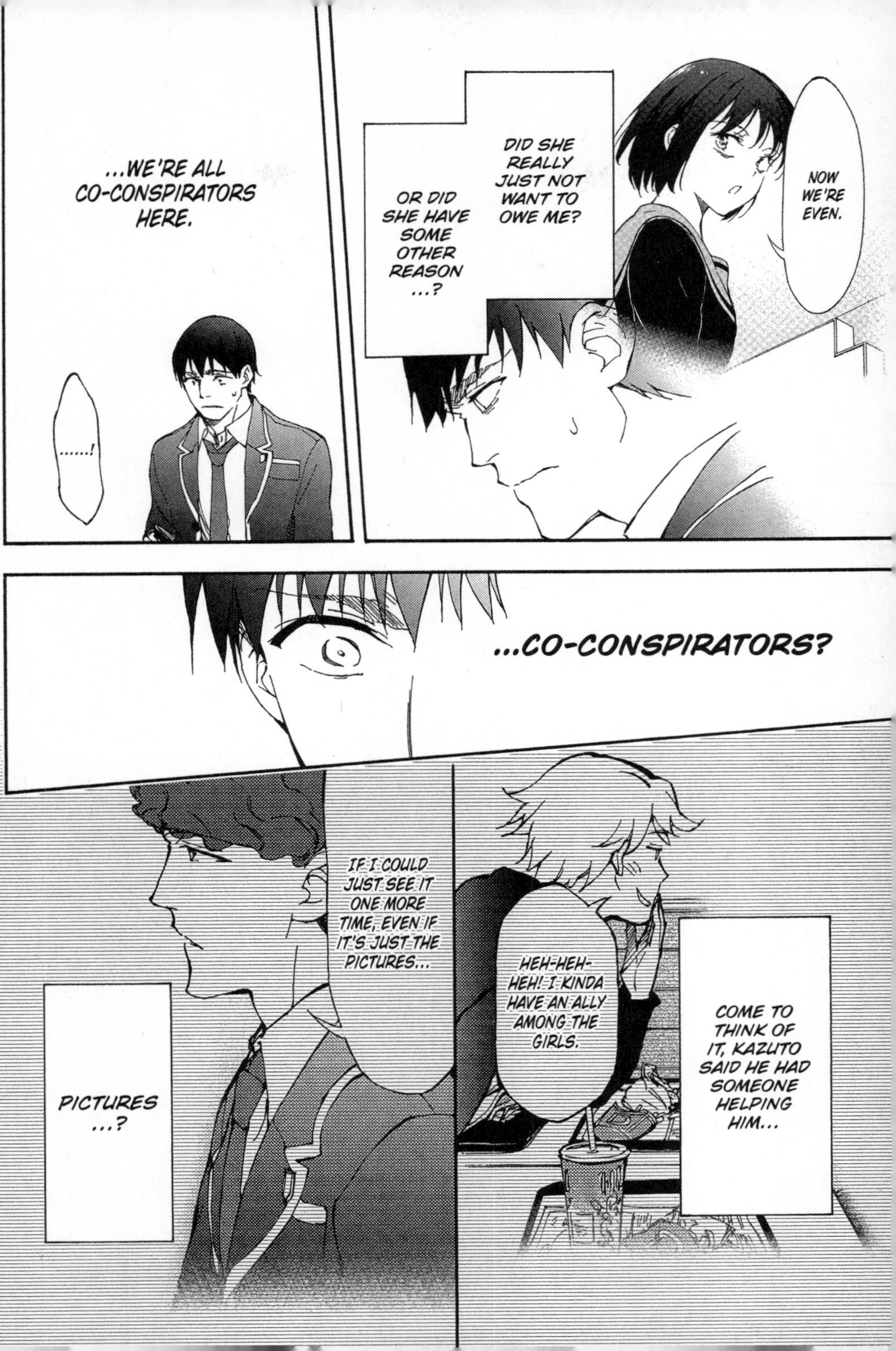
NOW WE'RE EVEN.
DID SHE REALLY JUST NOT WANT TO OWE ME?
OR DID SHE HAVE SOME OTHER REASON ...?
...WE'RE ALL CO-CONSPIRATORS HERE.
......!
...CO-CONSPIRATORS?
COME TO THINK OF IT, KAZUTO SAID HE HAD SOMEONE HELPING HIM...
HEH-HEH-HEH! I KINDA HAVE AN ALLY AMONG THE GIRLS.
IF I COULD JUST SEE IT ONE MORE TIME, EVEN IF IT'S JUST THE PICTURES...
PICTURES ...?

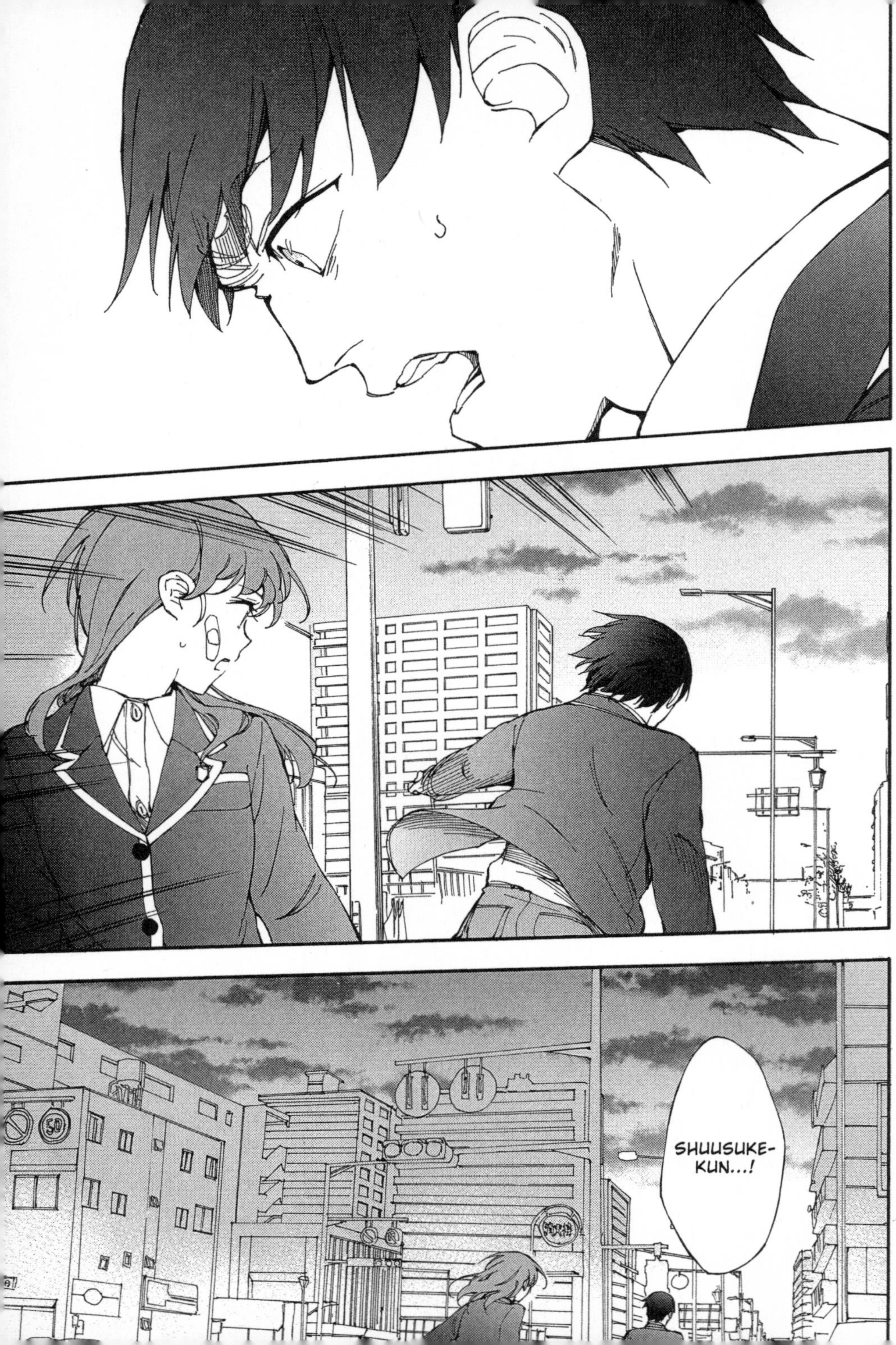
SHUUSUKE-
KUN...!

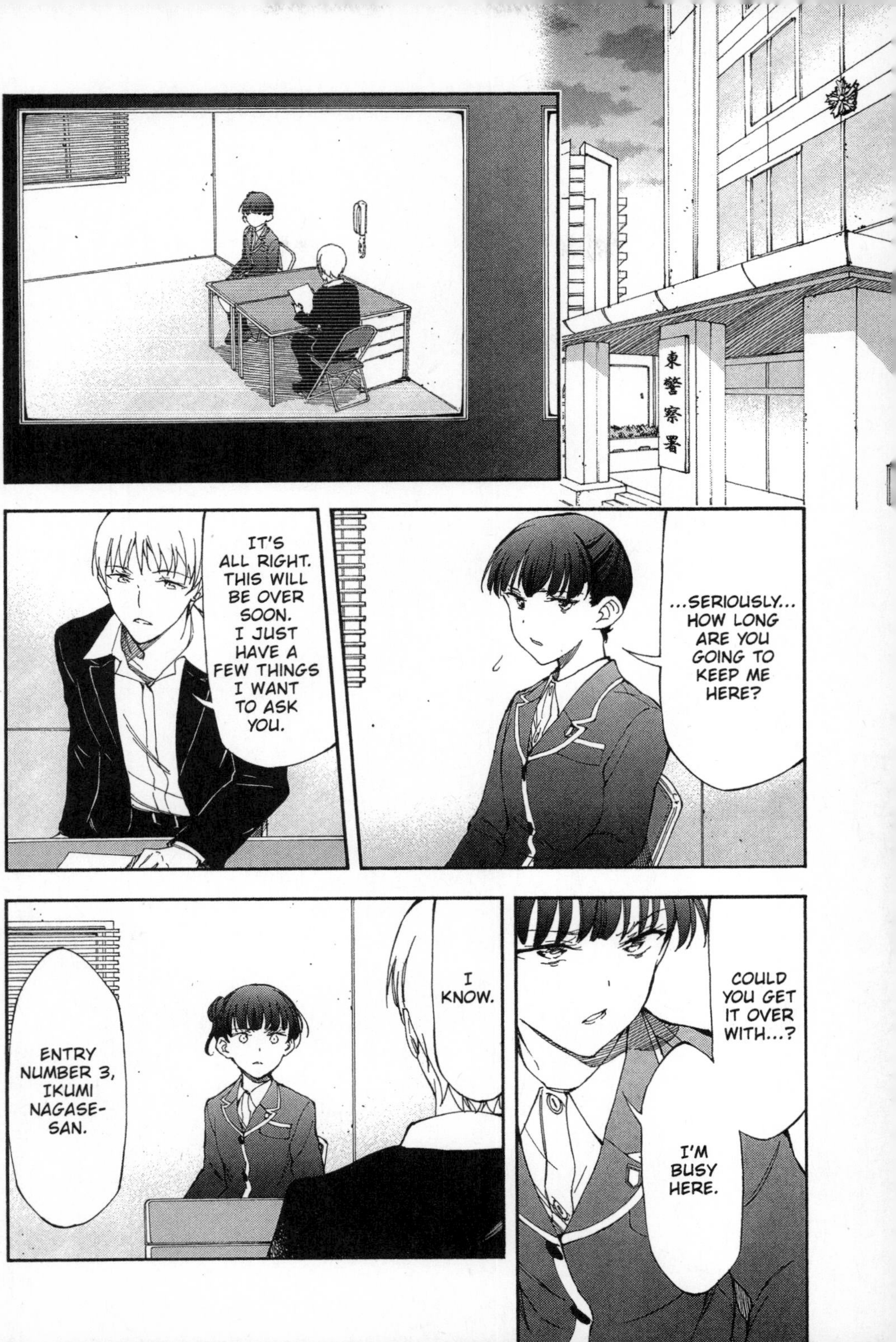
東警察署
...SERIOUSLY... HOW LONG ARE YOU GOING TO KEEP ME HERE?
IT'S ALL RIGHT. THIS WILL BE OVER SOON. I JUST HAVE A FEW THINGS I WANT TO ASK YOU.
COULD YOU GET IT OVER WITH...?
I'M BUSY HERE.
I KNOW.
ENTRY NUMBER 3, IKUMI NAGASE-SAN.

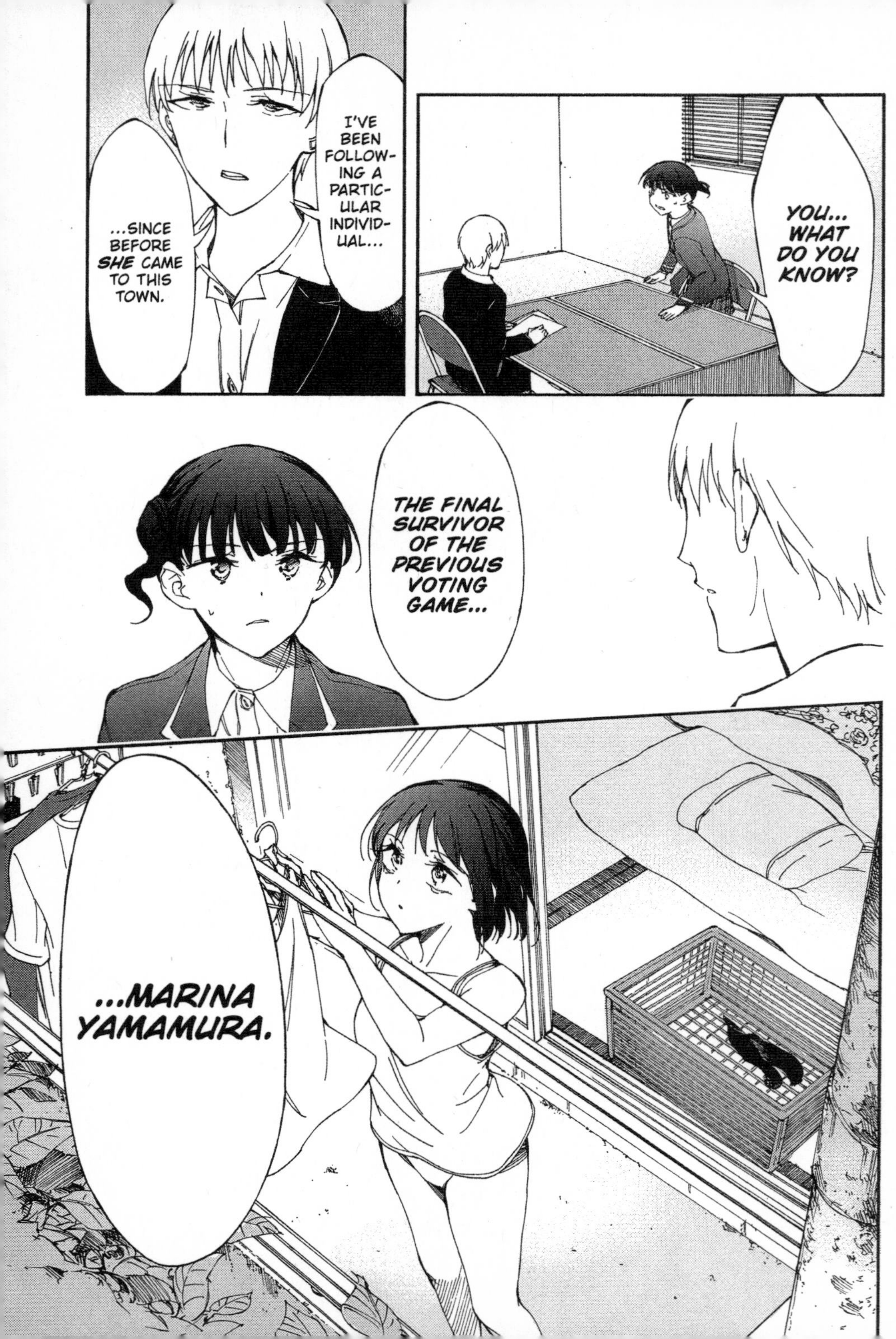
YOU... WHAT DO YOU KNOW?
I'VE BEEN FOLLOWING A PARTICULAR INDIVIDUAL...
...SINCE BEFORE SHE CAME TO THIS TOWN.
THE FINAL SURVIVOR OF THE PREVIOUS VOTING GAME...
...MARINA YAMAMURA.

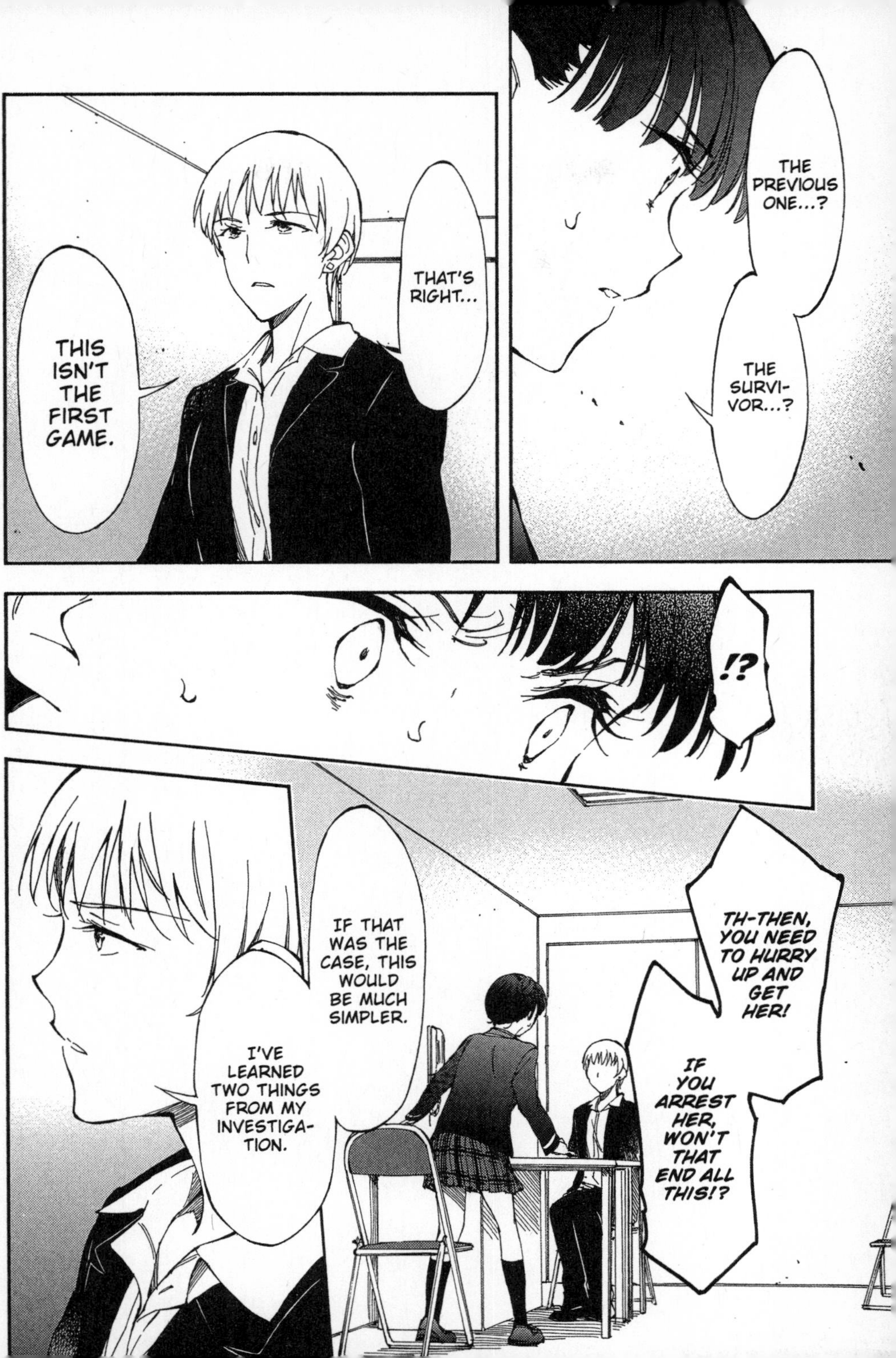
THE PREVIOUS ONE...?
THE SURVIVOR...?
THAT'S RIGHT...
THIS ISN'T THE FIRST GAME.
!?
TH-THEN, YOU NEED TO HURRY UP AND GET HER!
IF YOU ARREST HER, WON'T THAT END ALL THIS!?
IF THAT WAS THE CASE, THIS WOULD BE MUCH SIMPLER.
I'VE LEARNED TWO THINGS FROM MY INVESTIGATION.

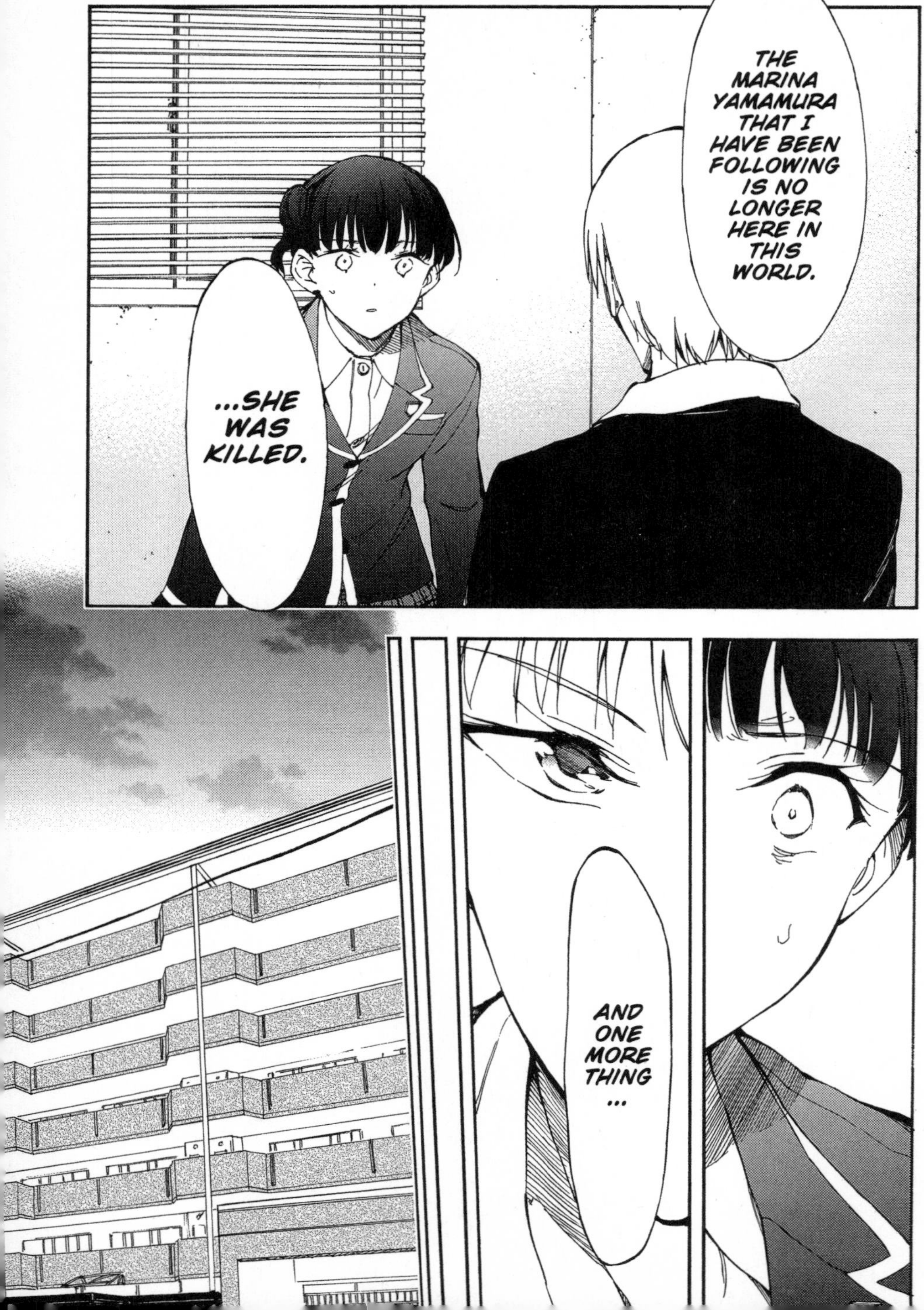
THE MARINA YAMAMURA THAT I HAVE BEEN FOLLOWING IS NO LONGER HERE IN THIS WORLD.
...SHE WAS KILLED.
AND ONE MORE THING ...

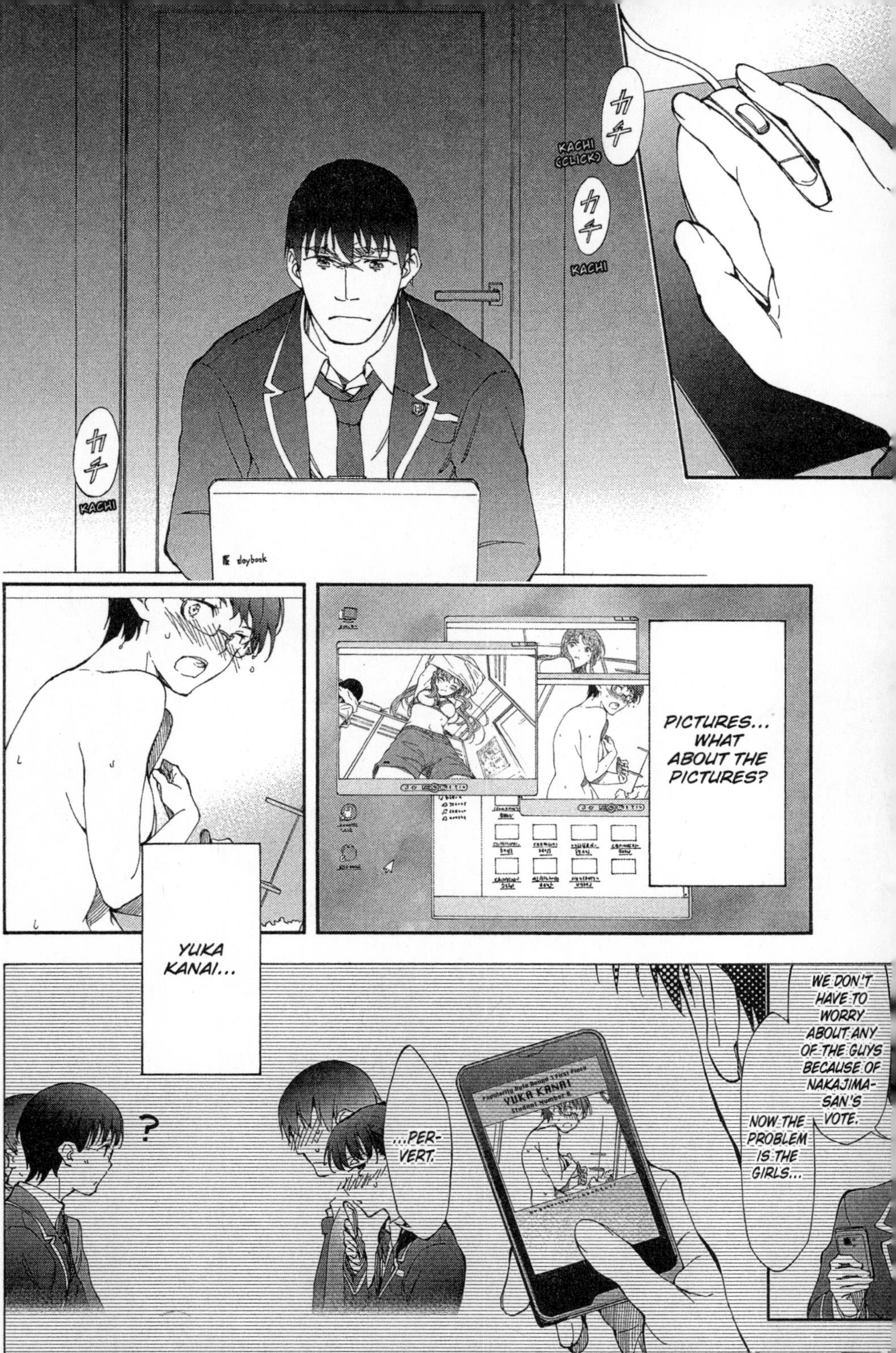
カチ
KACHI (CLICK)
カチ
KACHI
カチ
KACHI
PICTURES... WHAT ABOUT THE PICTURES?
YUKA KANAI...
WE DON'T HAVE TO WORRY ABOUT ANY OF THE GUYS BECAUSE OF NAKAJIMA-SAN'S VOTE.
NOW THE PROBLEM IS THE GIRLS...
YUKA KANAI
...PER-VERT.
?

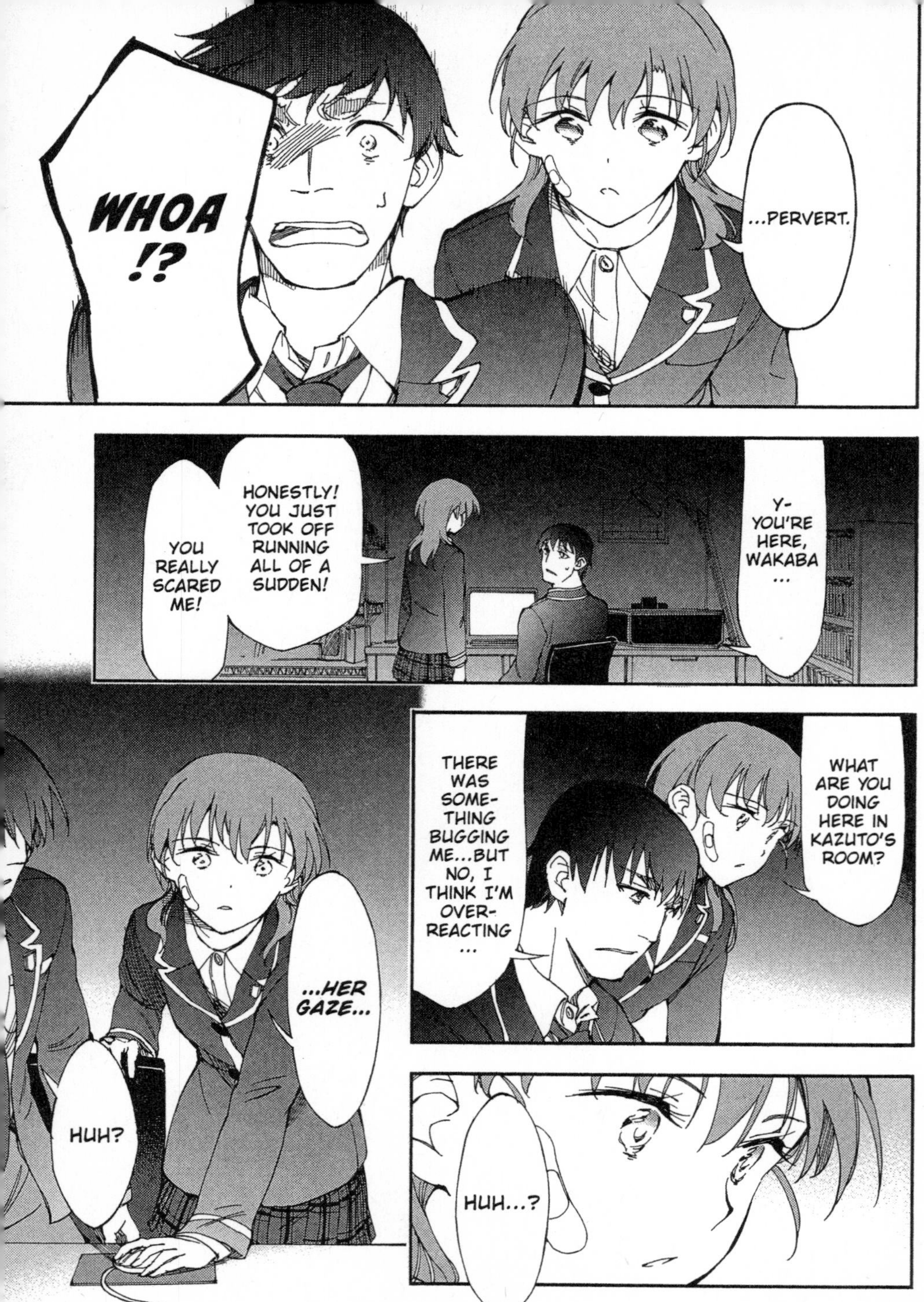
...PERVERT.
WHOA!?
Y- YOU'RE HERE, WAKABA...
HONESTLY! YOU JUST TOOK OFF RUNNING ALL OF A SUDDEN!
YOU REALLY SCARED ME!
WHAT ARE YOU DOING HERE IN KAZUTO'S ROOM?
THERE WAS SOME-THING BUGGING ME...BUT NO, I THINK I'M OVER-REACTING...
HUH...?
...HER GAZE...
HUH?

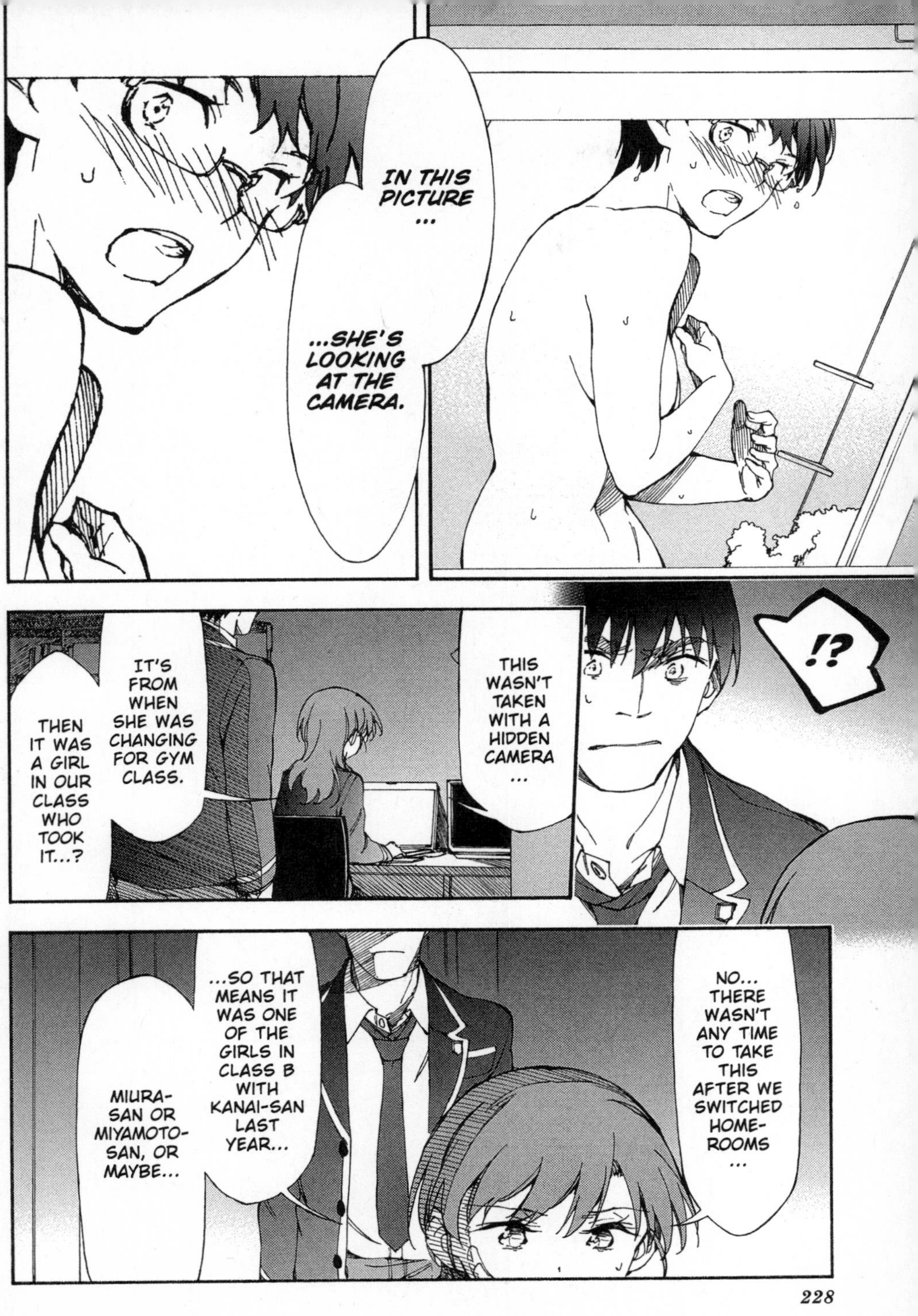
IN THIS PICTURE ...
...SHE'S LOOKING AT THE CAMERA.
!?
THIS WASN'T TAKEN WITH A HIDDEN CAMERA ...
IT'S FROM WHEN SHE WAS CHANGING FOR GYM CLASS.
THEN IT WAS A GIRL IN OUR CLASS WHO TOOK IT...?
NO... THERE WASN'T ANY TIME TO TAKE THIS AFTER WE SWITCHED HOME-ROOMS ...
...SO THAT MEANS IT WAS ONE OF THE GIRLS IN CLASS B WITH KANAI-SAN LAST YEAR...
MIURA-SAN OR MIYAMOTO-SAN, OR MAYBE...

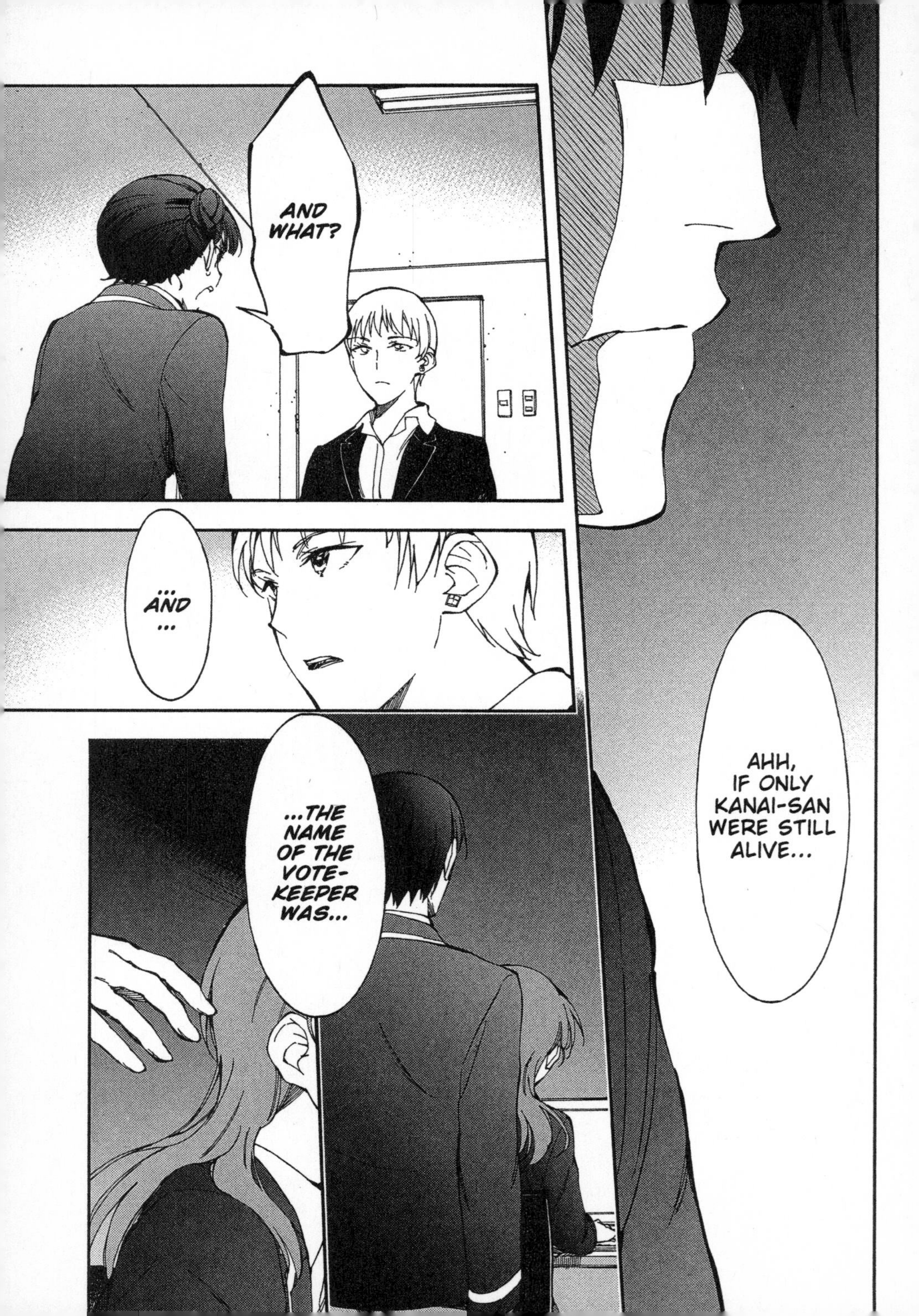
AHH, IF ONLY KANAI-SAN WERE STILL ALIVE...
AND WHAT?
...AND...
...THE NAME OF THE VOTE-KEEPER WAS...

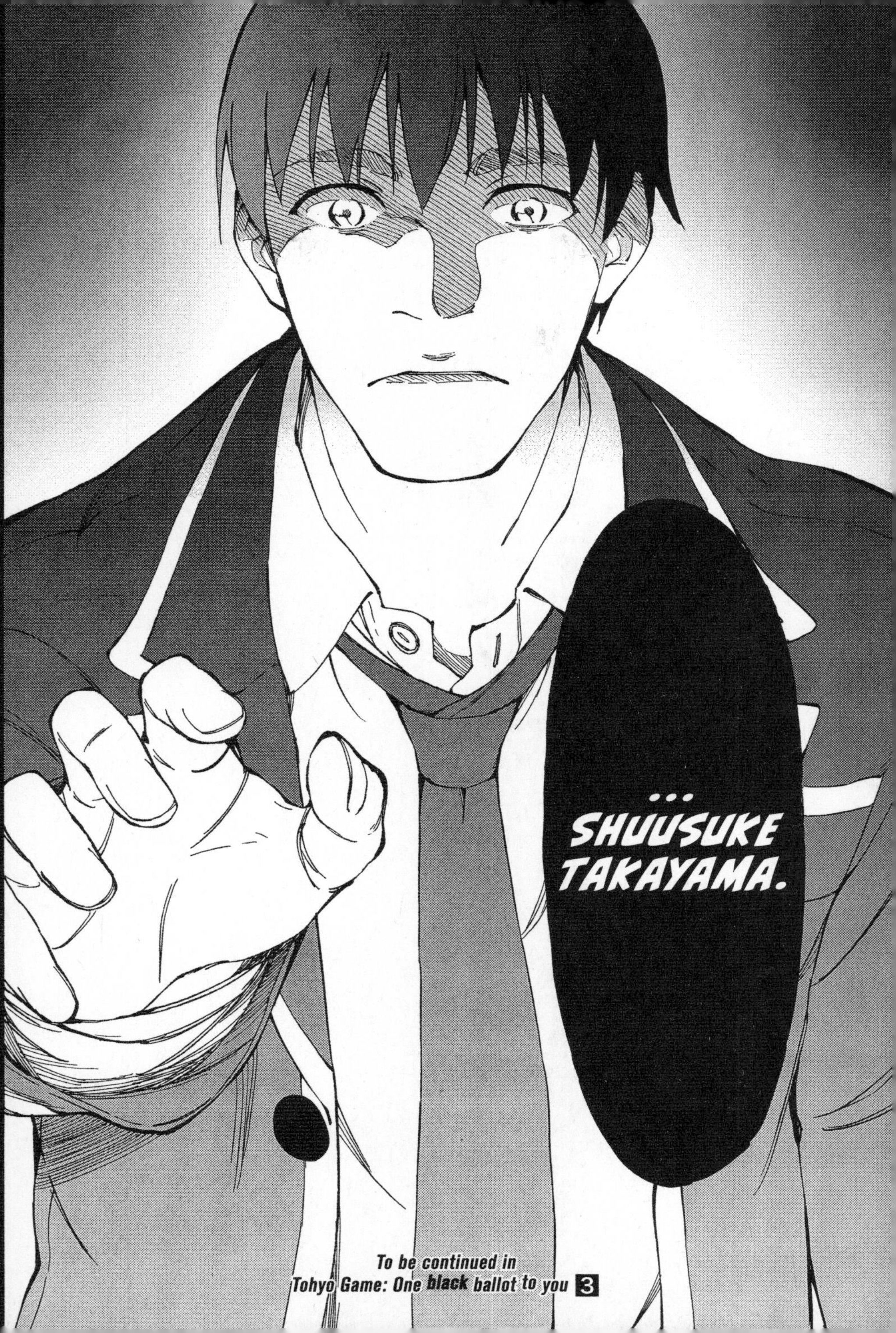
... SHUUSUKE TAKAYAMA.

To be continued in
Tohyo Game: One **black** ballot to you 3

TOHYO GAME
One **black** ballot ^{to} you

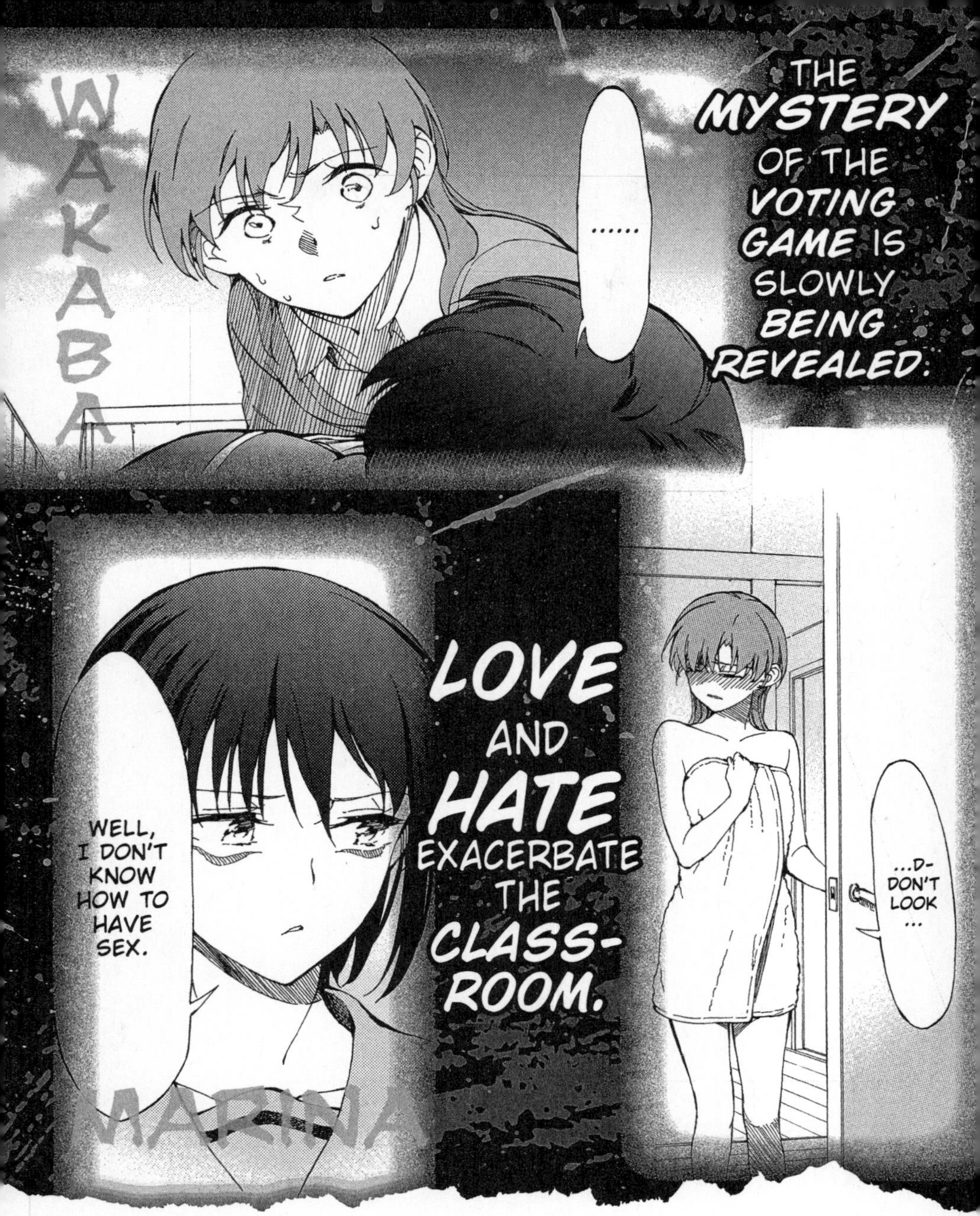
THE MYSTERY OF THE VOTING GAME IS SLOWLY BEING REVEALED.
......
WAKABA
...D-DON'T LOOK...
LOVE AND HATE EXACERBATE THE CLASSROOM.
WELL, I DON'T KNOW HOW TO HAVE SEX.
MARINA

ORIGINAL STORY: G.O. /ADAPTATION: CHIHIRO/ART: Tatsuhiko

VOLUME 3 ON SALE APRIL 2017!

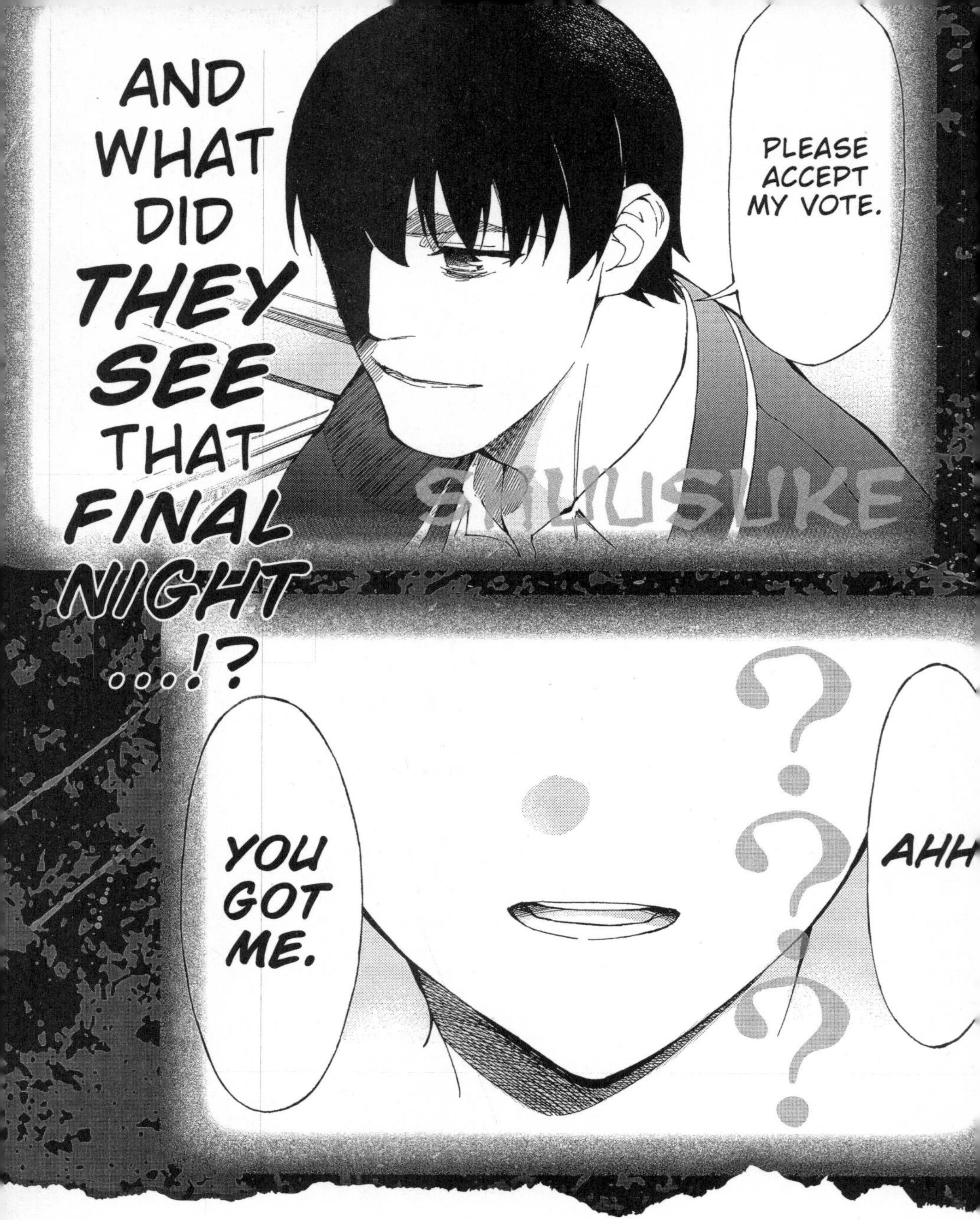
PLEASE ACCEPT MY VOTE.
SHUUSUKE
AHH
YOU GOT ME.
AND WHAT DID THEY SEE THAT FINAL NIGHT...!?
???

TOHYO GAME

One **black** ballot to you

> GO

STUDENT NO.06

Wakaba Ootsuki

STUDENT NO.07

Ryouta Okazaki

STUDENT NO.08

Yuka Kanai

STUDENT NO.09

Tomoaki Kayama

STUDENT NO.10

Junichi Kuniyasu

STUDENT NO.16

Yui Shimakawa

STUDENT NO.17

Chiharu Suzuki

STUDENT NO.18

Shuusuke Takayama

STUDENT NO.19

Rumiko Date

STUDENT NO.20

Nobuki Tamura

STUDENT NO.26

Ikumi Nagase

STUDENT NO.27

Tadanori Nakamura

STUDENT NO.28

Nana Nishino

STUDENT NO.29

Hazuki Negishi

STUDENT NO.30

Himari Nomura

STUDENT NO.36

Asahi Miyamoto

STUDENT NO.37

Shougo Murasame

STUDENT NO.38

Atsushi Morimoto

STUDENT NO.39

Marina Yamamura

*There were mistakes in some student names and numbers in Volume 1. The names and student numbers on this page are the official ones. We apologize for this oversight.

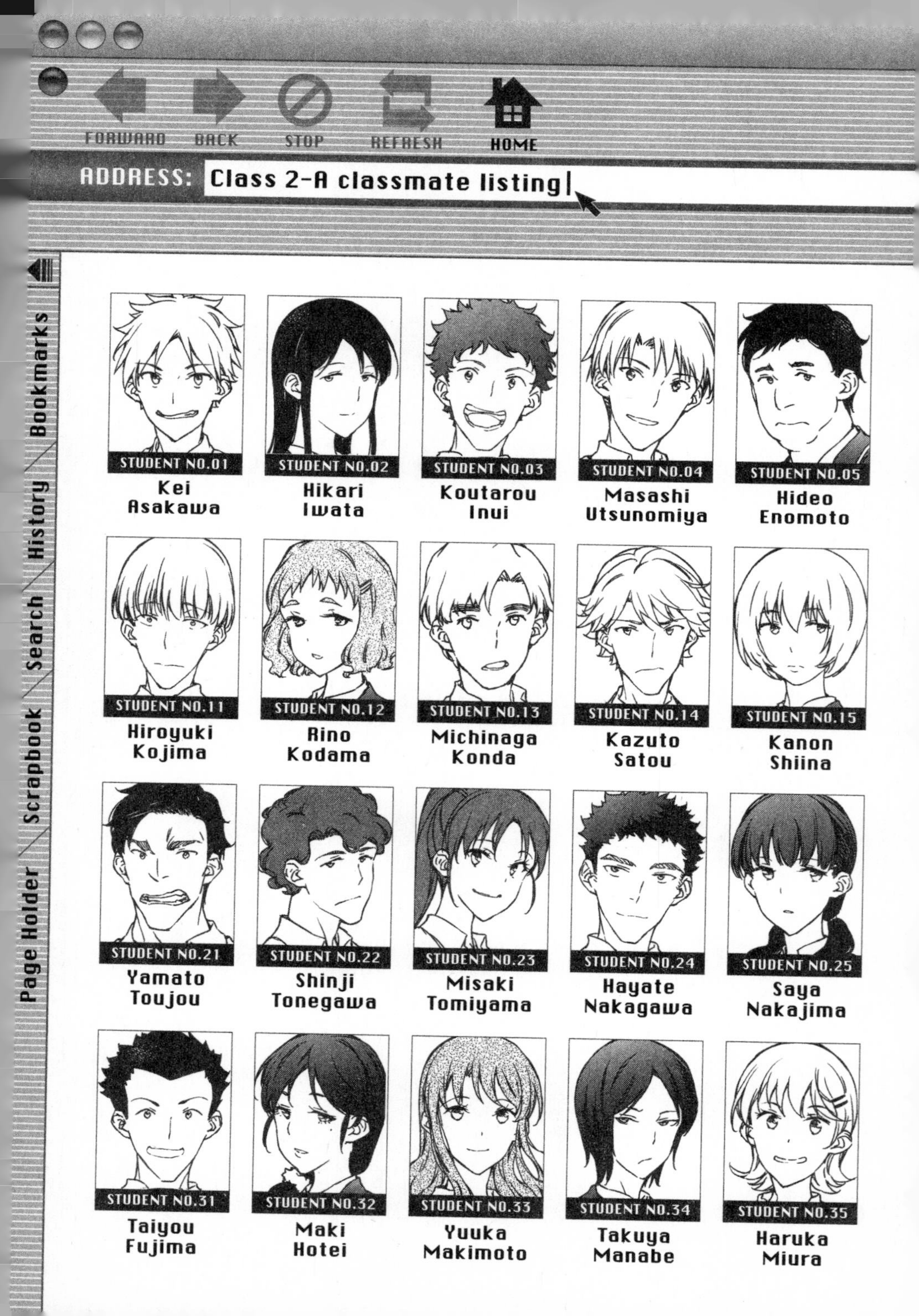
FORWARD
BACK
STOP
REFRESH
HOME
ADDRESS: Class 2-A classmate listing
Bookmarks
History
Search
Scrapbook
Page Holder
STUDENT NO.01 Kei Asakawa
STUDENT NO.02 Hikari Iwata
STUDENT NO.03 Koutarou Inui
STUDENT NO.04 Masashi Utsunomiya
STUDENT NO.05 Hideo Enomoto
STUDENT NO.11 Hiroyuki Kojima
STUDENT NO.12 Rino Kodama
STUDENT NO.13 Michinaga Konda
STUDENT NO.14 Kazuto Satou
STUDENT NO.15 Kanon Shiina
STUDENT NO.21 Yamato Toujou
STUDENT NO.22 Shinji Tonegawa
STUDENT NO.23 Misaki Tomiyama
STUDENT NO.24 Hayate Nakagawa
STUDENT NO.25 Saya Nakajima
STUDENT NO.31 Taiyou Fujima
STUDENT NO.32 Maki Hotei
STUDENT NO.33 Yuuka Makimoto
STUDENT NO.34 Takuya Manabe
STUDENT NO.35 Haruka Miura

END-OF-VOLUME EXTRA STORY BY CHIHIRO

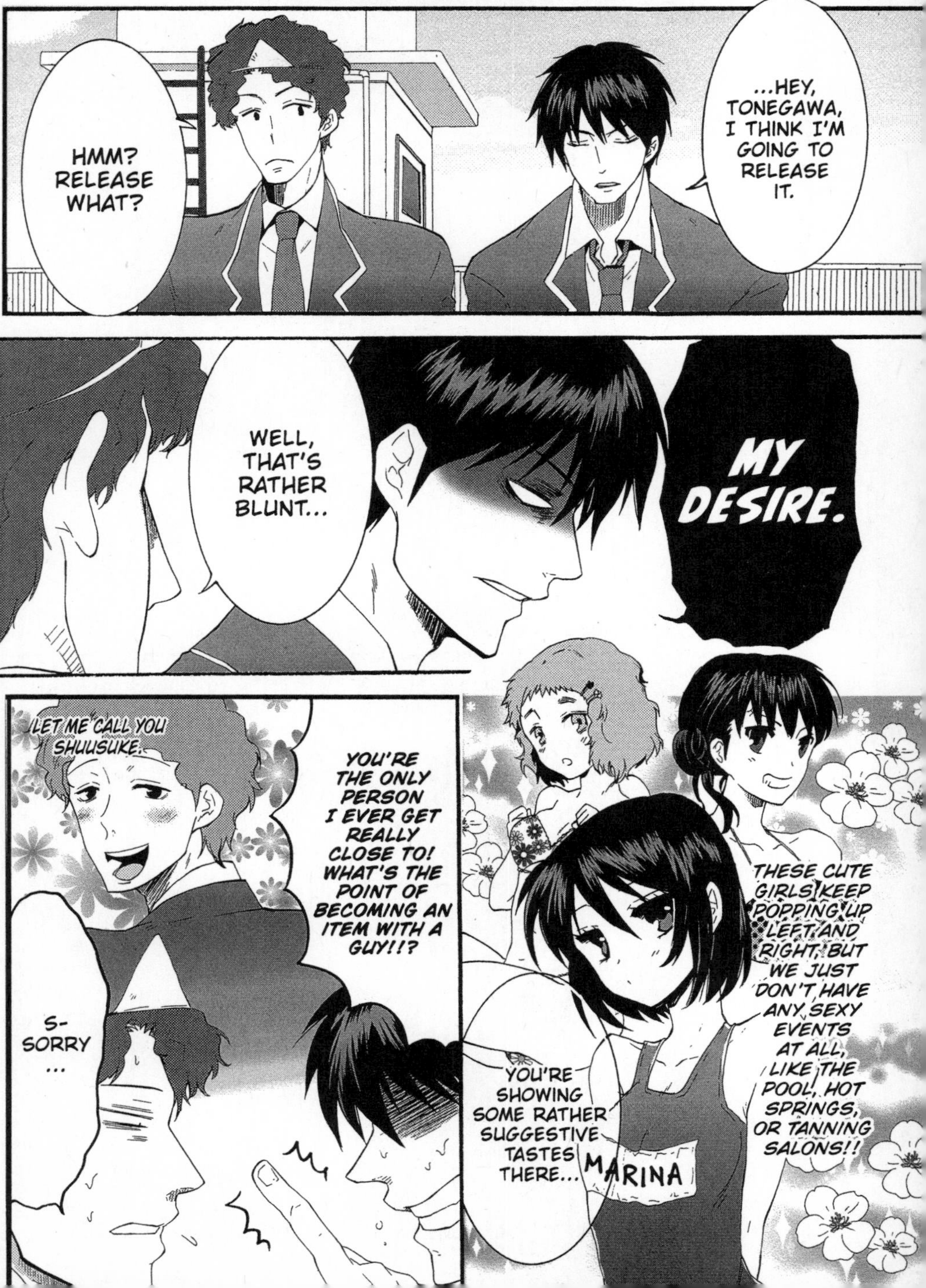
...HEY, TONEGAWA, I THINK I'M GOING TO RELEASE IT.
HMM? RELEASE WHAT?
MY DESIRE.
WELL, THAT'S RATHER BLUNT...
THESE CUTE GIRLS KEEP POPPING UP LEFT AND RIGHT, BUT WE JUST DON'T HAVE ANY SEXY EVENTS AT ALL, LIKE THE POOL, HOT SPRINGS, OR TANNING SALONS!!
MARINA
YOU'RE SHOWING SOME RATHER SUGGESTIVE TASTES THERE...
YOU'RE THE ONLY PERSON I EVER GET REALLY CLOSE TO! WHAT'S THE POINT OF BECOMING AN ITEM WITH A GUY!!?
LET ME CALL YOU SHUUSUKE.
S-SORRY...

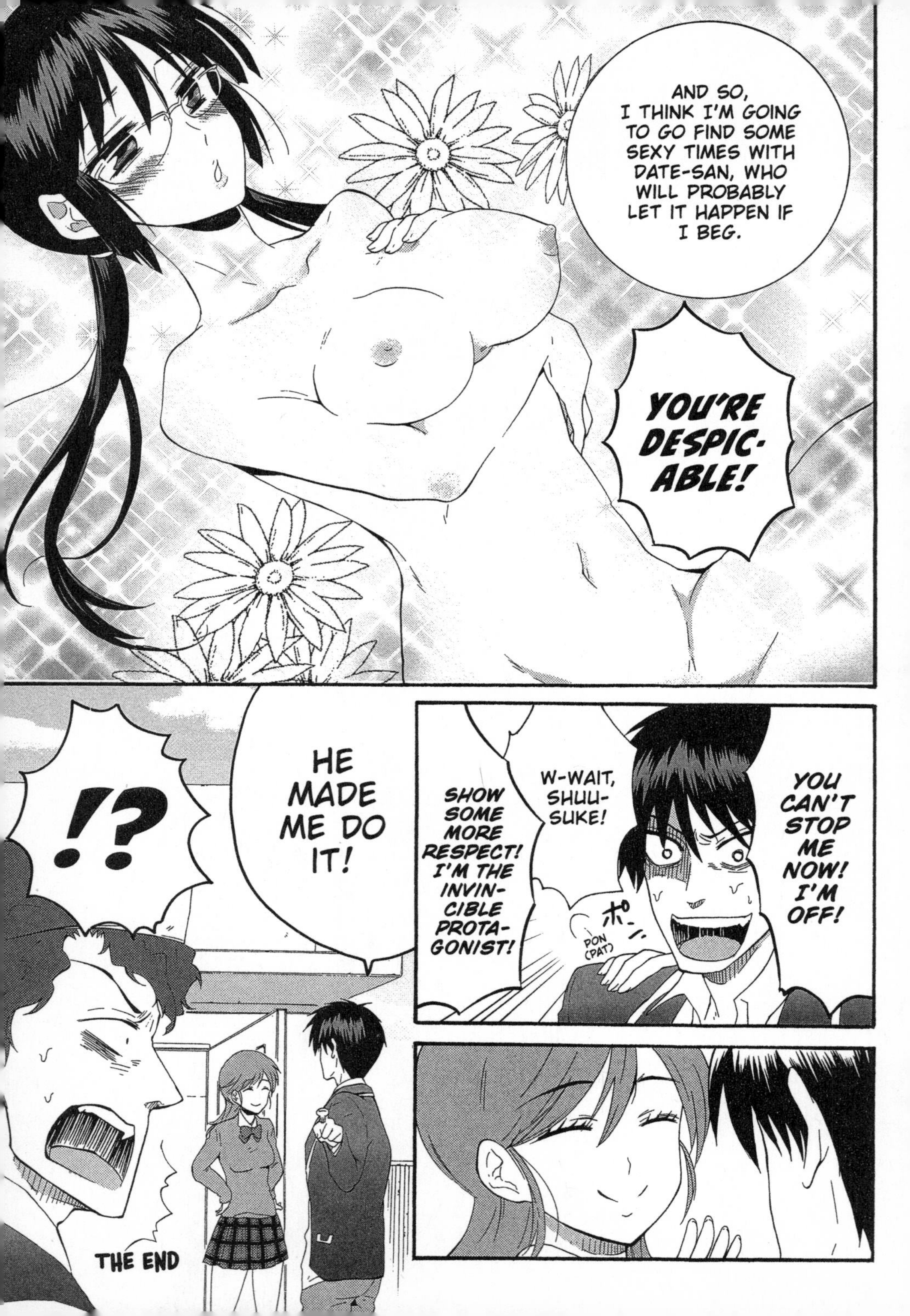
AND SO, I THINK I'M GOING TO GO FIND SOME SEXY TIMES WITH DATE-SAN, WHO WILL PROBABLY LET IT HAPPEN IF I BEG.
YOU'RE DESPICABLE!
YOU CAN'T STOP ME NOW! I'M OFF!
W-WAIT, SHUUSUKE!
SHOW SOME MORE RESPECT! I'M THE INVINCIBLE PROTAGONIST!
PON (PAT)
HE MADE ME DO IT!
!?
THE END

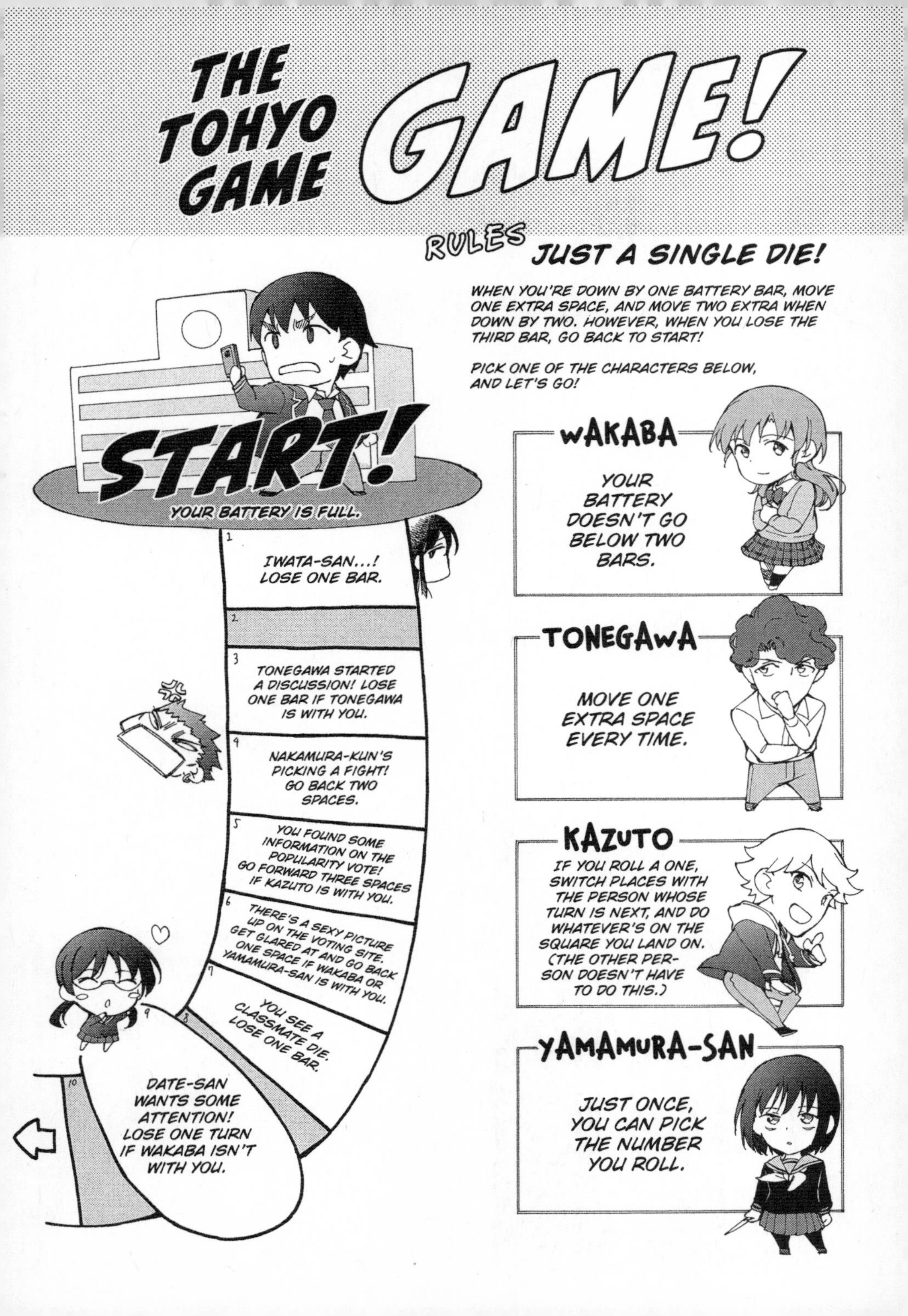
THE TOHYO GAME
GAME!
RULES
JUST A SINGLE DIE!
WHEN YOU'RE DOWN BY ONE BATTERY BAR, MOVE ONE EXTRA SPACE, AND MOVE TWO EXTRA WHEN DOWN BY TWO. HOWEVER, WHEN YOU LOSE THE THIRD BAR, GO BACK TO START!
PICK ONE OF THE CHARACTERS BELOW, AND LET'S GO!
START!
YOUR BATTERY IS FULL.
1 IWATA-SAN...! LOSE ONE BAR.
2
3 TONEGAWA STARTED A DISCUSSION! LOSE ONE BAR IF TONEGAWA IS WITH YOU.
4 NAKAMURA-KUN'S PICKING A FIGHT! GO BACK TWO SPACES.
5 YOU FOUND SOME INFORMATION ON THE POPULARITY VOTE! GO FORWARD THREE SPACES IF KAZUTO IS WITH YOU.
6 THERE'S A SEXY PICTURE UP ON THE VOTING SITE. GET GLARED AT AND GO BACK ONE SPACE IF WAKABA OR YAMAMURA-SAN IS WITH YOU.
7 YOU SEE A CLASSMATE DIE. LOSE ONE BAR.
8
9
10
DATE-SAN WANTS SOME ATTENTION! LOSE ONE TURN IF WAKABA ISN'T WITH YOU.
WAKABA
YOUR BATTERY DOESN'T GO BELOW TWO BARS.
TONEGAWA
MOVE ONE EXTRA SPACE EVERY TIME.
KAZUTO
IF YOU ROLL A ONE, SWITCH PLACES WITH THE PERSON WHOSE TURN IS NEXT, AND DO WHATEVER'S ON THE SQUARE YOU LAND ON. (THE OTHER PERSON DOESN'T HAVE TO DO THIS.)
YAMAMURA-SAN
JUST ONCE, YOU CAN PICK THE NUMBER YOU ROLL.

*THE SQUARES WITH THINGS LIKE "IF TONEGAWA IS WITH YOU" OR "IF YAMAMURA-SAN IS WITH YOU" HAVE BEEN LEFT OUT. JUST TRY TO IMAGINE THEM THERE.

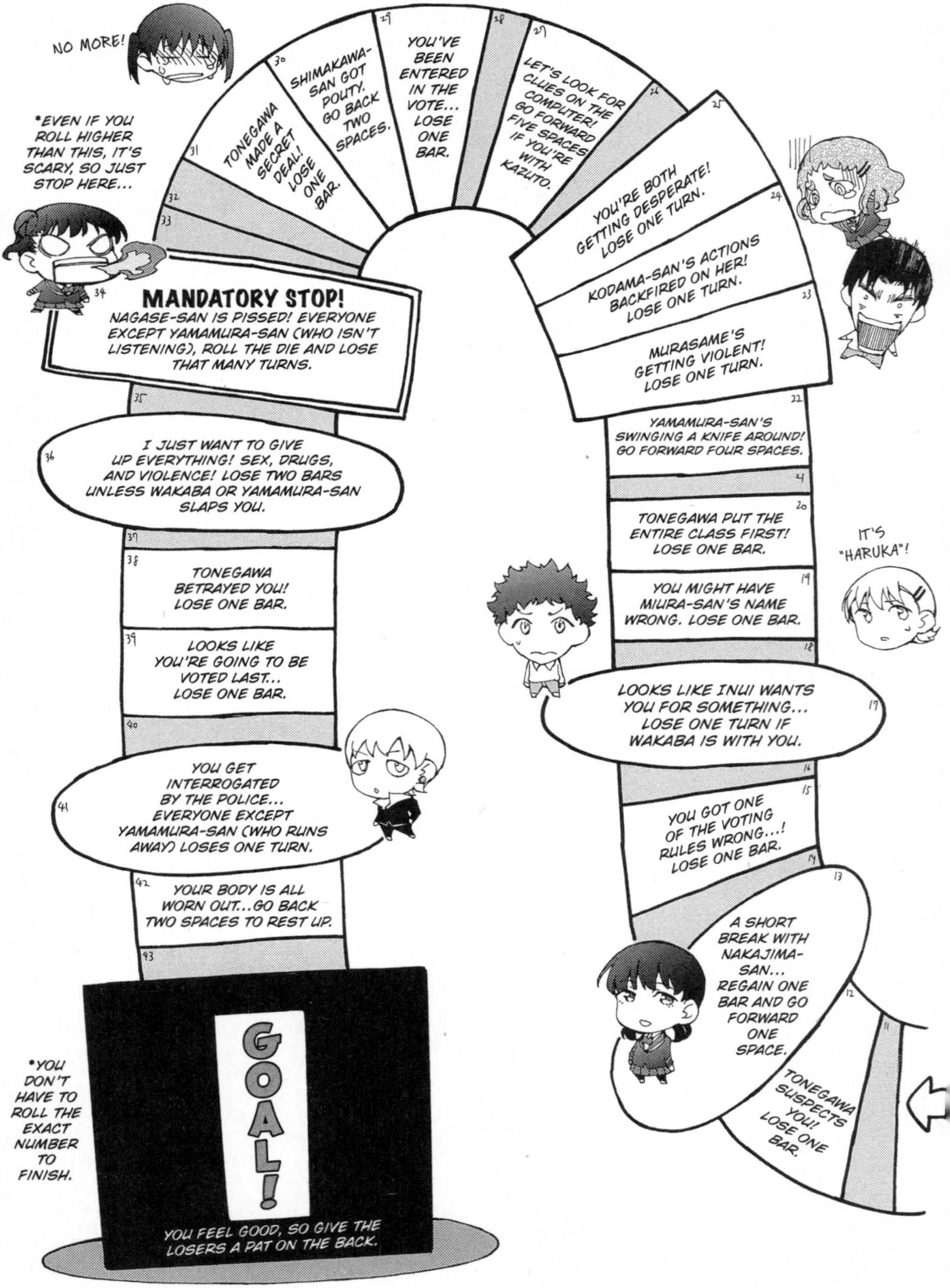
11 TONEGAWA SUSPECTS YOU! LOSE ONE BAR.
12
13 A SHORT BREAK WITH NAKAJIMA-SAN... REGAIN ONE BAR AND GO FORWARD ONE SPACE.
14
15 YOU GOT ONE OF THE VOTING RULES WRONG...! LOSE ONE BAR.
16
17 LOOKS LIKE INUI WANTS YOU FOR SOMETHING... LOSE ONE TURN IF WAKABA IS WITH YOU.
18
19 YOU MIGHT HAVE MIURA-SAN'S NAME WRONG. LOSE ONE BAR.
IT'S "HARUKA"!
20 TONEGAWA PUT THE ENTIRE CLASS FIRST! LOSE ONE BAR.
21
22 YAMAMURA-SAN'S SWINGING A KNIFE AROUND! GO FORWARD FOUR SPACES.
23 MURASAME'S GETTING VIOLENT! LOSE ONE TURN.
24 KODAMA-SAN'S ACTIONS BACKFIRED ON HER! LOSE ONE TURN.
25 YOU'RE BOTH GETTING DESPERATE! LOSE ONE TURN.
26
27 LET'S LOOK FOR CLUES ON THE COMPUTER! GO FORWARD FIVE SPACES IF YOU'RE WITH KAZUTO.
28
29 YOU'VE BEEN ENTERED IN THE VOTE... LOSE ONE BAR.
30 SHIMAKAWA-SAN GOT POUTY. GO BACK TWO SPACES.
31 TONEGAWA MADE A SECRET DEAL! LOSE ONE BAR.
NO MORE!
*EVEN IF YOU ROLL HIGHER THAN THIS, IT'S SCARY, SO JUST STOP HERE...
32
33
34 MANDATORY STOP!
NAGASE-SAN IS PISSED! EVERYONE EXCEPT YAMAMURA-SAN (WHO ISN'T LISTENING), ROLL THE DIE AND LOSE THAT MANY TURNS.
35
36 I JUST WANT TO GIVE UP EVERYTHING! SEX, DRUGS, AND VIOLENCE! LOSE TWO BARS UNLESS WAKABA OR YAMAMURA-SAN SLAPS YOU.
37
38 TONEGAWA BETRAYED YOU! LOSE ONE BAR.
39 LOOKS LIKE YOU'RE GOING TO BE VOTED LAST... LOSE ONE BAR.
40
41 YOU GET INTERROGATED BY THE POLICE... EVERYONE EXCEPT YAMAMURA-SAN (WHO RUNS AWAY) LOSES ONE TURN.
42 YOUR BODY IS ALL WORN OUT...GO BACK TWO SPACES TO REST UP.
43
GOAL!
YOU FEEL GOOD, SO GIVE THE LOSERS A PAT ON THE BACK.
*YOU DON'T HAVE TO ROLL THE EXACT NUMBER TO FINISH.

TRANSLATION NOTES

COMMON HONORIFICS

no honorific: Indicates familiarity or closeness; if used without permission or reason, addressing someone in this manner would constitute an insult.

-san: The Japanese equivalent of Mr./Mrs./Miss. If a situation calls for politeness, this is the fail-safe honorific.

-sama: Conveys great respect; may also indicate that the social status of the speaker is lower than that of the addressee.

-kun: Used most often when referring to boys, this indicates affection or familiarity. Occasionally used by older men among their peers, but it may also be used by anyone referring to a person of lower standing.

-chan: An affectionate honorific indicating familiarity used mostly in reference to girls; also used in reference to cute persons or animals of either gender.

-sensei: A respectful term for teachers, artists, or high-level professionals.

-onii-chan, **nii-san**, **aniki**: A term of endearment meaning "big brother" that may be more widely used to address a young man who is like a brother, regardless of whether he is related or not.

-onee-chan, **nee-san**, **aneki**: A term meaning "big sister," the female counterpart of the above.

Tohyo Game: The title directly translates as "voting game."

Page 84

"My name is spelled with a 'K,' not a 'C.'" In the Japanese edition, Inui has used a simpler, more common character for Haruka's name instead of the correct one, which is rarer but similar in appearance. For a corresponding translation, this edition has him misspelling Haruka's name with a *C*.

Page 122

"No...Shuusuke." Tonegawa suddenly switches to using Shuusuke's first name after previously calling him by his last name, Takayama. Tonegawa is trying to indicate that they've made the transition from just classmates to the more familiar first-name basis of friends in an effort to get Shuusuke's help.

Page 214

The exchange rate for the US dollar to the Japanese yen usually comes out as roughly $1 = ¥100. So, **one million yen** is about ten thousand dollars.

Page 215

Condolence money is a tradition at funerals in which the family of the deceased is given monetary gifts in special black, white, and silver envelopes. The amount enclosed depends on the relationship of the guest to the deceased.

TOHYO GAME

One **black** ballot to you

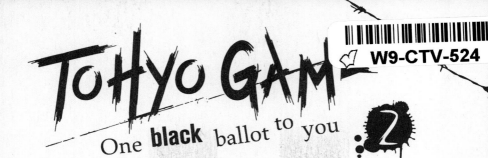

TOHYO GAME
One **black** ballot to you
2

Original Story	Adaptation	Art
G.O.	CHIHIRO	Tatsuhiko

Translation: **Leighann Harvey**   Lettering: **Rochelle Gancio**

TOHYO GAME ANATANI KUROKI IPPYO WO vol. 2 © 2015 G.O., CHIHIRO, Tatsuhiko / SQUARE ENIX CO., LTD.
First published in Japan in 2015 by SQUARE ENIX CO., LTD. English translation rights arranged with SQUARE ENIX CO., LTD. and Yen Press, LLC through Tuttle-Mori Agency, Inc.

English translation © 2017 by SQUARE ENIX CO., LTD.

Yen Press
1290 Avenue of the Americas
New York, NY 10104

Visit us at yenpress.com
facebook.com/yenpress
twitter.com/yenpress
yenpress.tumblr.com
instagram.com/yenpress

First Yen Press Edition: January 2017

Yen Press is an imprint of Yen Press, LLC.
The Yen Press name and logo are trademarks of Yen Press, LLC.

The publisher is not responsible for websites (or their content) that are not owned by the publisher.

Library of Congress Control Number: 2016946116

ISBNs: 978-0-316-46375-1 (paperback)
978-0-316-50860-5 (ebook)

10 9 8 7 6 5 4 3 2 1

BVG

Printed in the United States of America